WIPERS

A Soldier's Tale From The Great War

BY JEFF SIMMONS

1

Dedicated to my family for their undying support
2009

PROLOGUE

It seemed as if it had been raining for a week without even the slightest glimmer of sunshine anywhere to be found. It wasn't one of those misty, refreshing rains that one usually anticipated during the English summer; these raindrops were the size of marbles and icy cold.

"My, what a gorgeous day," Richard Gardener said to himself as he wiped the fog off of a windowpane and peered outside. The rainwater streaked down the glass, blurring his view of the garden behind his flat. He reached down and scratched the ears of the aged gray mutt sitting next to his chair.

"I guess we won't be going to the park today, Henry," he said. "We'd catch a cold. That's what she'd tell us, Henry. We'd catch our death going out on a day like this. That is certain."

He turned on the cooker to make some tea. He was out of whiskey, and tea was the next best thing on a damp, chilly day. He looked at the clock. While he waited for the kettle to whistle, he rubbed the fog from another pane.

"Peter will be coming by soon, Henry," he said. "You know he always brings you a bone from the butcher."

The dog perked up at the mention of Peter's name. Richard perked up a bit himself. He always looked forward to seeing his son. He was so proud of him. Tall and broad-shouldered, Peter was as handsome as he was smart. Like himself, Peter was a veteran of war; he'd served honorably as a fighter pilot during the Battle of Britain and flew scores of missions against the German Luftwaffe, eventually shooting down eight enemy planes. He and a handful of others prevented Hitler from ever trying to invade the British Isles. A father could not ask more from a son.

Richard also looked forward to Peter's visits because he usually brought something wonderful baked by his wife, as well as a bottle of whiskey and cigarettes. He was about out of those, too.

He reached for a cup on the shelf and his back creaked. His arthritis was acting up, probably because of the weather. His hands didn't feel too good, either. He pulled down an extra cup, anticipating that Peter would arrive soon. It was a strain.

"I guess that is what it's like to be sixty-two, Henry," he said. The dog looked up and nudged his hand, looking for another scratch. "But I guess being old is better than the alternative, right Henry?"

He heard a door close and footsteps coming up the wooden floor in the hallway, followed by muffled cursing and a rap on the door. The dog barked and ran to the door, wagging his brushy tail. It was Peter.

"It's open," Richard called. The teapot was whistling. He turned off the burner and poured two cups. The door opened and the dog jumped up and down. Peter could barely get inside.

"Henry!" Peter shouted. "Henry! How's my favorite mongrel? You know Dad, if this dog were any uglier, you'd likely have to pay a special tax or something."

He gave Henry a pat nonetheless, and reached into the paper sack he was carrying. The dog sat alert, whining slightly under its breath. He shifted back and forth on his haunches, his tail beating the floor. Peter pulled out a ham hock wrapped in newsprint. The dog barked and Peter taunted him briefly before turning over the goods.

"That ugly dog is going to chew your arm off one of these days," Richard said. "There never was a more vicious beast. Isn't that right, Henry?"

Henry didn't pay any attention. Peter shook off his coat and hat and hung them on a hook on the back of the door. He sat the bag on the table and pulled out a seat. Richard was staring at the bag, nearly salivating.

"Go ahead, Dad," Peter said. "The rest is for you. Happy birthday."

There were a half-dozen authentic Bakewell tarts wrapped in waxed paper on top. Peter's wife actually grew up in Bakewell and knew how to make them right. There was also a newspaper, the usual carton of cigarettes and a bottle of American bourbon whiskey. That was odd, Richard thought, and the look on his face betrayed his surprise.

"You told me once that you had some of that during the war," Peter said. "The man at the spirit store got some of this in last week and had it on discount. You said it was good, right?"

"Yes," Richard said. "If I remember correctly, it's a treat."

"Well, then, pour us some," he said, taking two small glasses out of the cabinet. "I've been looking forward to it since I bought the bottle this afternoon."

Richard uncorked the bottle, put it to his nose and took a smell.

"That brings back some memories," he said. "Blurry memories, but memories nonetheless."

As he was pouring drinks, Peter reached for the newspaper and unfolded it to the third page. There was an article circled in blue ink.

"I saw this yesterday morning, and thought you'd be interested," Peter said. "Have a look."

The headline read, "Belgian Village Shaken By Explosion." He pulled it closer to his nearsighted eyes and read the small print:

*YPRES, Belgium – A cache of explosives buried during the
First World War near the village of Messines exploded with
violent force yesterday, leaving a crater 100 feet deep and
rattling windows miles away.*

*Local authorities said the blast occurred when lightening
struck a steel utility pole, which had been unknowingly erected
above the charge years after the war. It is estimated that the
charge weighed as much as 1,000 pounds.*

*Military historian Bennett Wallace, who has written
several books on the battles fought in the vicinity of Ypres, said
the charge was most likely that of an unexploded offensive
mine laid beneath the German lines in preparation for the
Battle of Messines in 1917.*

*Twenty-one mines were laid for that offensive, but only 19
were detonated, Wallace said.*

*Unexploded artillery shells and aerial bombs are
commonly found by farmers around Ypres, the scene of some
of the heaviest fighting of the First World War...*

Richard put the paper down, lit a cigarette and took a long
drag. He knocked back his glass of whiskey in one gulp and stared
out the window.

"Are you all right?" Peter said. "You've turned pale."

"I'm fine," he said. "Just fine."

He put his cigarette up to his lips and his hand was shaking a
bit.

"I didn't know that would upset you so," Peter said. "I know
you don't like to talk about the war. But I knew you'd served
some time in Belgium, and thought maybe you'd want to read
about this."

There was tense silence. Peter poured two more glasses of
bourbon.

"I always wanted to ask you about it," he said. "You've heard
all of my stories over the past few years. But Mother said when I
was a child that I should never question you about anything to do
with your military service. I know you were wounded, but that's
all."

"That's all that matters."

"No, it's not. You heeded the call when the king needed you
the most. Your service is a big part of our family's history. And if
the wife and I ever produce a grandson for you, I'd like for him to
know what his grandfather did in the war. I would like to know."

Richard sipped out of his glass and took the last drag on his
cigarette before stamping it out. He cracked his knuckles and
rubbed his eyes.

"You don't want to know," Richard said. "There's no glory. There's no heroism. It's not what you read in the books. And I could sit here all afternoon and tell you what I remember, but you'd never know what it was really like. That was so many years ago. Things were different then. You wouldn't understand."

"Dad, I do know what it's like to be under fire. I would at least like to have the chance to try and understand what you went through."

Richard lit another cigarette. Maybe it was all right to talk about it now. He'd been silent about his military service for more than three decades, but the memories were as vivid as if the events had taken place the day before.

"It's a long story," he said. "I don't want to bore you or waste your time dredging up the remnants of the past."

"It's my time, and I'll waste it however I want."

"All right," Richard said. "All right. Where do you want me to start?"

"Start at the beginning."

"It was all so long ago. Sometimes it seems like a lifetime, and other times it seems like I'm still there…"

CHAPTER 1

"The Yorkshire coal fields were home to me from the day I was born in 1888 to the time I joined the Army to fight the Germans in the Great War. I was raised in a small village twenty miles or so from Sheffield, although I never ventured that far until 1914 when I enlisted. Until then, I hadn't found it necessary to do so. I lived a simple life there, and was content in it.

Our village had a four-room school, two churches -- one Catholic and one Church of England -- a pub called the Beehive, a butcher shop, a bakery and a grocer that also sold general merchandise. Those who did not work in one of these establishments worked in the coal mine about a half-mile up the valley. My father labored there five or six days a week for more than twenty years.

We lived in a stone house with a thatched roof and a large living room with a brass and iron stove for heating and cooking. I'll never forget that stove. It was an elaborate, ancient affair that my father had scavenged from a derelict farmhouse. He told me that it wasn't really stealing since no one had used it for years, and if not cared for, it would have rusted to pieces anyway.

There were two small bedrooms, which was plenty of room for Dad and I. We had been on our own since I was five, when Mum died giving birth to my sister. Not wanting to raise a daughter alone, he sent baby Rose off to live with his sister in Manchester. She seemed to like living in the city, and with my aunt's guidance, Rose became a proper little lady. Over the years, her visits with Dad and I became less frequent. By the time I left home myself, an occasional letter was all the contact we had.

School didn't come easy for me. I liked to read, especially the newspapers my father brought home, but I didn't care for many of the books I had to digest for my classes. I especially hated mathematics, but I struggled along, doing the best that I could, because it was important to my father. He wanted me to do better in life than he did. I was his only son, and he worked like a slave to keep me fed and clothed. He wanted me to excel, and I did my best to live up to his expectations. I felt I owed him at least that much.

I think his greatest fear was that someday, I would be working alongside him in the mine. He said it was an awful way to make a living, and no son of his would ever step foot in a cold, damp mine. He would get extremely agitated when I complained about my schoolwork.

9

"Do you want this?" Dad would ask, pointing to a large, black scar over his right eye where he was hit by falling rock in a cave-in. "I almost lost that eye, and I was one of the lucky ones that day!"

My Dad's good fortune ran out on a cold winter day in 1903. I was sitting in class, learning about the Magna Carta, when I heard a loud thud that rattled the windows. Everyone ran to look. There was an ominous billow of black smoke rising up the valley. I knew then that there had been an explosion of some sort in the mine, and I knew that Dad was at work. I immediately said a prayer for him.

There was a warning siren blowing. Since nearly all of the students had family employed in the mine, school was dismissed within a few minutes of the blast. I didn't even bother to pick up my books. I ran down the slick marble stairs and out into the street, and didn't stop running until I reached the entrance to the mine. Many wives and children had already gathered there, and most were either wailing or praying. Some stood silent, peering into the darkness, hoping to catch a glimpse of a loved one coming up the shaft.

Dense smoke poured out of the hillside. The first load of injured men came to the surface, but Dad was not with them. Minutes passed like days as a stream of coughing men, many burned or injured in some way, made their way to safety. My chest got tight and tears filled my eyes. I pushed my way through the crowd until I found Simon Keaffe, who lived with his parents next door to Dad and I. Simon was my age, but he had already been working in the mine for over a year. He, too, was looking for his father.

"What happened?" I asked him, trying to keep my voice from cracking.

"I don't know," he said. "I was working near the entrance to the shaft when the ground shook, enough to knock me down. There was dense smoke, so I made my way out as fast as I could. I don't know where our fathers were when it blew."

Soon, Simon's father came walking out with one arm in a sling and there was blood running down his black face from a gash in his scalp. Simon ran to him. He saw me waiting and stumbled over with one arm around his son.

"Richard," he said, "I'm so sorry to have to tell you…"

I didn't really pay much attention to what he said after that. It didn't matter what happened, I guess, because any way around it, he was dead. But I stayed at the mine until late that night, with a persistent hope that Simon's father was wrong. They brought out more and more mangled, burned bodies as the hours passed.

Many weren't even recognizable. I was able to identify Dad by the small watch he always carried in his pocket. In all, 32 men died.

I stayed there most of the night; I don't know why. Tired and cold, I made my way back to the empty house. I sat by the stove and tried to eat something but I could not. I realized that I was on my own, and that the accident had changed my life forever. Eating seemed trivial by comparison.

I went to the cupboard in the kitchen and pulled out a tin cup and Dad's bottle of whiskey. I had never tasted liquor before, but I felt that since I was the man of the house now, I could drink if I wanted to. I poured some in the cup and took a big swallow. My whole body shuddered, but it gave me a warm feeling inside. I poured some more in the cup and had another swallow. I liked the feeling it gave me. After my third cup, I had to lie down, and I went to sleep in my clothes.

Caskets lined the main street through the village for about three days, until all of the bodies were recovered and buried. The coal company paid for a large burial plot just down from the mine because there wasn't enough room for all of them in the church cemeteries. They also bought a small headstone for each man.

I never did make it back to school. I knew that I had to work to take care of myself, so I started looking for a job in a shop or on one of the sheep farms that dotted the valley. But after three weeks, I was down to the last few potatoes from a package brought to me by the vicar, and it became clear to me that I was going to end up in the mine after all. The thought alone chilled me to the marrow.

I had a drink and went next door to talk to Simon and his father. His mother invited me to stay for tea, and I sat down at the kitchen table with the Keaffe men. Simon's mother was a grand cook, and I was truly looking forward to a terrific meal. I was not disappointed; she made roast beef and Yorkshire pudding, as well as potatoes and carrots and a loaf of home-baked bread. I ate a whole plateful without stopping, so she loaded my plate again.

"How are you getting along, Richard?" she asked. "Are you going to finish school this year?"

"No, I don't think so," I said. "It's more important for me to get a job."

"Your father would be upset if he knew that," his father said.

"Well, I can't go on forever taking food from the church or from my good neighbors," I said. "Besides, I'm 15 years old now. I'm old enough to work for a living."

"Have you had any luck finding a job?" he asked.

11

"No," I said, "and that's what I wanted to talk to you about. Do they need anybody up at the mine?"

You could have heard a mouse hiccup. Simon's father put down his tea and stared me in the eye.

"You don't want to do that," he said. "It's not the place for you."

"It's the only place I haven't looked for work yet," I said.

"We could use another strong man down there, what with all of those who won't be coming back again," Simon said. "He's fit and smart. If he wants to work in the mine, then I say let him."

"It can be a scary place," his father said. "It's darker than the darkest night, damp as a swamp and dangerous as can be."

"I can do it," I said, almost believing myself. "I need to do it."

"Give it some thought first," he said. "Sleep on it. And if you still want to give it a try, meet us in the morning. We leave at 5:30."

We sat and talked while we finished our tea, and I stayed a little later than I should have because I had been so lonely without Dad. I found it difficult to pull myself away from the company. Simon's father used the opportunity to relate to me all kinds of horrible stories about mines and mining accidents. I have to admit I was scared, but not deterred.

I awoke before dawn the next morning, and I put on my boots and dungarees and waited for the Keaffes to come out. I stood outside with my hands in my pockets and my collar turned up, trying not to look nervous. At 5:30, they came out and headed up the valley. When we got there, they introduced me to a man named Smithers who was in charge of hiring. He looked me up and down and nodded to Simon's father. The Keaffes went down the shaft.

"Do you know anything about mining?" Smithers asked.

"Not a thing," I said. "But I can learn, and I'm sturdy."

"I can see that," he said. "You must be nearly six feet tall. You look a lot like your father. Harold was a fine worker. If you are anything like him, then you've got a job."

I didn't start out actually working in the mine. My first job was to pick slate out of the coal that had been dug. The first day I tore off two of my fingernails and my hands were bloody. After a few months Smithers put me to work taking care of the mules they used to haul out the coal cars. I liked animals, so that I enjoyed. I stayed on that for about a year before I finally went into the mines for my first shift below ground.

At first, all I did was shovel coal all day long. The more advanced work – drilling and laying charges, for instance– was done by more experienced miners. But I paid close attention to

12

how they did their work, so that within a couple of years I was handling drills and using dynamite. Smithers said I was a natural, and eventually he made me a supervisor.

That doesn't mean I enjoyed mining much. It was especially hard when the days got shorter in the winter, and we'd go down into the mine before the sun came up and come back to the surface when the sun had already set. So for about three months in the winter, you don't see much daylight at all. I also had to deal with my fear of being trapped, which lessened with the years below ground but never completely disappeared.

So I started using my time off to get outdoors where I could see the sun. I would get up before the break of day and go hiking and fishing. I would go from one village to the next on paths that had crisscrossed England since the time of the Romans, finding streams and shady spots to take naps. Some days, I'd cover as much as 15 miles on foot. I'd come dragging back to the village, sometimes after dark, carrying my pole and a stringer of fish to share with the Keaffes.

My simple life started to change in June of 1914. It was a beautiful summer by many accounts, but things were brewing on the continent that didn't bode well. A Bosnian Serb shot and killed the archduke of Austria-Hungary and his wife, and when I read the newspaper account, I didn't understand the gravity of the event. Tragic, yes; earth shattering, no, I thought.

But things started spinning out of control rapidly. Austria-Hungary decided to declare war on Serbia in retaliation for the assassination. The Russians were committed to help the Serbs and the Germans stepped in to back up Austria-Hungary. Germany knew the French would attack them to help their ally, Russia, so Germany decided on a preemptive strike against France. In doing so, they invaded Belgium. Great Britain had signed a pact ensuring the sovereignty of Belgium, so we declared war on Germany and company soon afterward. Somewhere along the line, an assortment of other countries, including the Bulgarians, the Italians and the Turks, got pulled into the mess. By fall, Europe was aflame.

Many people thought for sure that the war would be over and done with by the end of autumn, by Christmas at the latest. If only that had turned out to be true…well, I guess I wouldn't be telling you this story then, would I?

Simon and I were walking home one night in September when we saw a man putting up a poster of Lord Kitchener, the war secretary, his finger pointing out, asking for new recruits for the army. I didn't pay much attention, but Simon was intrigued.

"Maybe we should sign up," Simon said.

"Why in creation would you want to do that?"

"It seems like a good thing to do. For king and country, I say. You must admit that it would be good to get out of the mine for a while, even if it means marching to Germany. I think it sounds like a great adventure."

"I don't know, Simon. I don't know what kind of soldier either of us would make."

"Look at us," he said. "We're physically strong and used to harsh conditions. I don't see how being a soldier could be any tougher than being a coal miner. Do you see yourself being a miner the rest of your life?"

"I don't know. I guess so. It's not necessarily what I want in life, but it's what I've got."

"We can change what we've got. How long did it take you to become a foreman? They might even make you an officer for all you know."

"I rather doubt that…"

"But you don't know! If we sign up, you might not have to ever walk down a cold, dark mine again. You might even win a medal or something. Then maybe you could get a better job when we come back home."

"Do you think so?"

"I'm certain. I think your father would want you to do it, too."

We talked about it all the way home. Mrs. Keaffe was outside working in the small flower garden she had kept since I could remember. She invited me in for tea, which she had done several times a week since Dad died. I accepted, as always. She had made steak and kidney pie, which was probably my favorite dish of hers. Over the meal, Simon was stupid enough to mention his notion that he and I should join the army. His father, an ardent socialist, exploded.

"This war is a rich man's fight," he said. "The kings and dukes and so forth started this mess. There's no benefit to victory for the working class. It's just a way for the powerful to retain their power by spilling the blood of the common man. It would be stupid to volunteer and die for a cause that is not your own."

"Well, someone's got to stop the Germans," Simon said. "What if they decide to invade England once France and Russia are finished?"

"That's not going to happen," his father said. "If it does, I'll worry about it then."

"I say they need to be stopped now, not tomorrow or next year. Look what they did to Louvain! They burned it! And the Huns rape women and stab babies to death with bayonets. They're

14

vicious, the Huns are. Those beasts would probably kill their own mothers if the Kaiser said to do so. Bunch of Hun bastards."

"Simon, watch your tongue!" his mother blurted. "We'll have no cursing at the table. And I agree with your father. You don't need to join the army. You are my only son, and I don't want to lose you anytime soon."

"Besides," his father said, "the military needs the coal we dig. We can't keep our navy afloat without coal for the boilers. We contribute to the war effort every day we go to work. You can do your part by staying right here at home."

"I'm twenty-six years old, Mum," Simon said. "I've never been out of this valley in my life. Sometimes I wonder what's out there. I think it's time I moved on."

His mother started to protest, then began crying.

"Don't do this, Simon," she said through her tears. "Don't go. I just know something bad will happen if you leave."

I was done eating and I was getting a bit uncomfortable. There was a palpable tension. I took the last swallow of my tea and excused myself.

"Don't let him give you any bad ideas," Simon's father said. "This isn't our fight."

I was inclined to believe him. I went home, had a drink of whiskey and lay on the bed. Simon was right; I didn't want to be a miner forever, and this sounded like an exciting opportunity. But his father was right, too; what did I stand to gain from the war? Probably not much. My mind was racing, but I soon fell asleep.

I awoke from a nightmare at around two o'clock, soaked in sweat and my heart pounding. I had dreamed that I was in the mine with my father the day it blew up. There were flames and smoke and dust and screaming men being burned alive. It was so real that it took me a minute after awakening to figure out where I was.

Now I don't know if the dream was a prophecy, but the next day at the mine, I came close to losing my life. I was working at the face with Simon, Jack Jamison, John Baker, and Pick Pickens. Pick's real name was Percival, but Pick suited him better. He could swing one like Thor. You pretty much stayed out of his way when he was working, and he rarely slowed down. We were about halfway through the shift, trying to put in some ceiling supports at the end of the gallery. We muscled the beams in place and took a break. We sat down on the stack of beams and passed around a jug of water. Except John. He was standing near the face, looking up at the ceiling.

"Hey fellows," he said. "This doesn't look too solid to me. I think we're going to have to shore this up better."

15

He took his pick in his right hand and banged the top of it against the ceiling.

"Sounds hollow…"

Right then, before he'd finished his sentence, an enormous chunk of rock and probably a ton of smaller stuff fell on top of him. We dug and screamed for help. The big piece pinned down his head and torso, and I knew as we lifted it, there was no way he was alive.

"Damn it!" Jack said. "Damn it to hell!"

"That could have killed us all," Pick said, his voice cracking a bit as he wiped the sweat from his brow. "That was a near miss for certain."

Two men showed up with a stretcher to take John to the surface. They rolled him over on his back and lifted. His eyes were still open, but he wasn't breathing. Simon walked over and put his hand on my shoulder.

"See? You wouldn't have to worry about stuff like this in the army. How is this a better way of life? Do you want to die like John? Or like your father? What does it take to convince you?"

Simon, amazingly, was beginning to sound like the voice of reason. At the moment, all I wanted to do was leave the mine and never come back. The army would be a way for me to do that. And apparently, I wasn't the only one following that particular line of reasoning.

"Maybe that's not such a bad idea you have," Pick said. "If you want to join up, I'll join up with you. What about you, Jack? Are you in?"

"I've got a wife and two children."

"All the more reason to get out of the mine. You know you'll die here. At least fighting the Germans, you've got a decent chance."

"You're right," Jack said. "I don't want to die here. Where do you stand on this, Richard?"

"Yesterday, I was against it. Today, I don't know."

"Come on, Richard!" Simon said. "They let you sign up with your pals and you get to serve with your pals. We'll be together through it all, and we'll come home with some amazing stories. And I've heard the girls in France are, uh, frisky."

"France? How do you know we'd end up in France?" I asked. "We could end up fighting Germans in Africa as far as you know. Or in the desert or something."

"Now you're just being ridiculous," Simon retorted. "I don't care what you say, anyway. I'm going."

"I'm going, too," Pick said. "It can't be any worse than this."

We argued for a few more minutes before Jack capitulated.

16

"Oh, well, I guess you can count me in, too, Simon," he said. "I don't want to be the only one that doesn't do his bit in this war."

That left me as the final objector, and I didn't hold out long. By the time the shift was over, I had decided that it was going to be my last day in the mine.

And it was.

CHAPTER 2

We took that evening to wrap up loose ends at home. I had a jar full of coins, probably five or six pounds worth, and I gave it to Mr. Keaffe so that he would have some money if something needed to be done to the house while I was gone. I had tea with Simon and his parents that night, but there was no conversation. They were very upset with our decision.

The next morning we walked to the train station, where we met Jack and Pick. Jack's wife and children were there to see him off. His wife started crying, and soon both his son and daughter were in tears. I could tell it was hard for him to pull himself away.

"I'll be home soon, dear," he told his daughter. "The king needs me now, but the war won't last long. I'll bring you and your brother some presents when I come home."

His consolation wasn't effective. They were still wailing when we pulled out of the station.

It was early when we rolled into Sheffield. It was the farthest I'd ever been from home. There was a recruiting depot in the station, and there was a long line of steel workers, miners and other working sorts who were heeding Kitchener's call.

There was this one fellow, though, that stood out like a black sheep in a white flock. He was wearing an expensive-looking bowler and a green wool suit that had clearly been slept in, and carrying a sort of doctor's bag that looked as worn as he did. He sat on a bench by himself, scratching his unshaven chin and looking at the clock on the wall, almost staring as the minutes passed before the train came into the station.

The four of us from the mine queued up for the train, and the man in the suit got in line behind us. He went back to looking at the clock and fidgeting. He tapped his feet and paced in a little circle.

"Hey," Pick said to him, "you're not from 'round here, are you?"

It was more of an accusation than a question. He looked over at Pick and extended his hand. Pick didn't take it.

"No, I'm not," he said. "I'm from Hull originally, but most recently from London."

"I'm Richard Gardener," I said, shaking his hand. "That's Pick, Jack and Simon. We work in the same mine."

"I'm Francis Thomas," he said. "I'm glad to meet all of you."

The conductor blew his whistle and we climbed aboard a long silver and black passenger car. I hadn't ridden on a train that fancy before, and my eyes were wide, like a child experiencing a rare treat. It was bigger inside than I expected. We sat in opposing bench seats, and Thomas, now knowing us better than anyone else on the train, took an adjacent seat across the aisle. He held his bag on his lap and fiddled with the latch. He finally relaxed when we got a few miles out of the station.

I, on the other hand, got increasingly anxious as the miles passed beneath me. We were going to a training camp somewhere near London. Then to the front, most likely in France. This made me nervous to say the least. Now I was the one fidgeting.

I wondered what the people in France were like. I had never met a Frenchman before and what I'd heard about them wasn't too flattering. But I decided to reserve judgment until I got to know a few of them myself. We were fighting a common enemy, after all.

I stared out the window. The land was getting flatter, with the black ridges of the mountains in the north smoothing into slow-rolling hills, cattle farms and barren winter fields.

"There's not much to look at," Thomas said to me. "I've ridden this line many times before."

"How far is it to London?" I asked.

"We've probably got about four more hours to Victoria Station. We could be stopping there or changing trains."

"You seem to know your way around," Pick said.

"I've been around a bit," Thomas said. "I travel a lot for work."

"What do you do?" Simon asked.

"I'm a magician," he said. Simon and Pick looked unimpressed. He pointed to his case, which was now under his seat. "That's my traveling gear."

He pulled the bag from underneath and took out a big, silver coin – an ancient magical coin given to him personally by the King of Siam or some such thing, he claimed – and began rolling it back and forth across his knuckles, doing little hand acrobatics. He had the patter of a carnival barker. His routine soon drew the attention of men to the front and rear of the car and they gathered around him to watch.

After making the coin disappear and reappear several times, once in Pick's shirt pocket, he made it multiply into five coins. Then he clasped his hands together, one atop the other, and slowly pulled them apart vertically. The coins ascended through thin air from the bottom hand to the top.

A burst of laughter followed by applause came from both ends of the car. Simon and I were clapping and Pick went from his usual state of irritation to being dumfounded. The coin was just an appetizer, however. He got out a deck of cards and straddled the back of his seat so everyone could see. He must have done twenty tricks, each one more incredible than the one before. We watched him in amazement.

His status as an outsider disappeared like a vapor. His confidence and charisma immediately won us over. From that day on, he was known to most of the men he served with simply as "the magician." As for me, I would call him Frank.

It would have been impossible for me to know at the time how much this chance meeting would change my world. I still often think how different my life would have been had Frank not been sitting there in the station that morning. He had a bigger impact on my destiny than anyone I had ever met before, or for that matter, anyone I have met since.

CHAPTER 3

We arrived at a training camp outside of London that night. It was a non-descript sort of affair that appeared to have been erected quite hastily. Our barracks smelled of fresh-cut lumber. I learned there were many camps just like it. The British Army had entered this fight with less than a million trained men. That was hardly enough to stave off five million Huns. A lot of men were needed, and they were needed sooner rather than later.

We were issued uniforms and boots and so forth that night. It was the best suit of clothes I had ever owned. The boots fit well and seemed comfortable. I thought I looked rather dashing in my gear. Frank spent the better part of the evening trying to find the funniest way to wear his. Eventually, he got everything on backwards and his pack on upside down on the front.

I was looking forward to firing a rifle for the first time. I had a 28-gauge single-shot back home that I'd had since I was 13, and my father had taught me to shoot game birds on the moors. We didn't get to hunt very often, but I became a pretty good shot. Sometimes Dad would let me use his 12-gauge shotgun, and I had always planned to buy one of my own when I got older. The few times that I did go hunting after his death I always carried that gun. Sometimes that was all I'd do. I just carried it around the moors on my shoulder, not even shooting when I had the chance. Just being out there reminded me of the great times I'd shared with Dad. The cool fall breezes, a bit of a chill, the smell of gun oil, the long shadows at the end of the day. Somehow, I guess, the idea of being given a rifle to carry romanticized the whole notion of being in the army.

But it was a while before I ever got to lay my hands on one. All they did for the first week or so were scream at us and make us march about the parade ground with broomsticks for weapons. We called it "square bashing." This whole routine started before daybreak and often our work details lasted into the evening. There wasn't much time to relax or get bored for that matter.

We succeeded as soldiers in varying degrees. Frank was obviously not born to wear a uniform. He patronized the higher ranks with thinly veiled sarcasm. A couple of times, he was assigned extra duties in the kitchen or wherever because he laughed at attention or some such nonsense. After that, the NCOs singled him out for all kinds of abuse. He got every foul job there was, and then some that they just made up especially for him. I seriously expected Frank to end up in front of a firing squad before we even got to France.

Pick was a little awkward at the drilling aspect, and instructors were constantly howling at him. He was a big fellow, and he wasn't used to being treated that way. He also had a hot temper, but somehow he kept it all in check. I think he tried hard because he truly wanted to be a good soldier. I personally had a great deal of faith in him, probably more than he had in himself. He was the strongest man in our barracks, and his wits had been sharpened from spending nearly two decades working underground. He had survived the blast that killed my father, and in my mind, I figured he could survive anything.

Simon was almost sent home because of his bad teeth. He had to go through a couple of rounds with a dentist while we were there, but they decided to keep him. He was also a bit slovenly, having lived his entire life with his mother to do his washing and so on. One time he was assigned to scrub the barracks' loo and didn't get it very clean. The sergeant made him strip down to his long underwear and crawl around on the floor, wiping up mildew and other nastiness with his clothes. Simon never made that mistake again. But he habitually complained about everything when the sergeant wasn't within earshot. They say every unit has its core complainers. Simon was our first.

Jack Jamison turned out to be the most natural soldier among us. He was agile and quick, having played a good bit of football when he was younger. He excelled at bomb – or grenade -- throwing and boot-polishing. He was a snappy driller, kept his gear in pristine condition, and followed orders to the letter. He was well liked by everybody, including our sergeant. He emerged as a natural leader, and I expected him to get promoted soon after we got to France. He was good.

Surprisingly, I found myself adapting quickly to army life as well, although I was not the athlete that Jack was. My father was meticulous about everything, and while I found it mildly annoying when I was growing up, it did teach me to pay attention to detail. It was a good skill to have in the army.

I was taller than everyone else in the barracks, and I was strong but a bit gangly, even uncoordinated at some things. Bayonet practice gave me fits. I could never get my timing right. The whole idea of using a bayonet in combat sort of spooked me, anyway. It seemed so barbaric a weapon, very personal and up-close. I hoped I wouldn't have to resort to its use.

And out of the lot of us, I was the best shot. We got these wonderful rifles. Lee Enfield .303-caliber bolt-action repeaters. They were easier to handle than the 12-gauge, and a lot more accurate at a much greater distance. The first time I fired my rifle, I drew the attention of the instructor by putting my entire magazine inside the bull's eye. Granted, that first target was only about 50 yards away, but it still impressed him. Soon I was nailing targets 100 yards or more away, with precision accuracy.

"Where did you learn to shoot?" our sergeant asked me.

"Hunting birds on the moors, sergeant," I said.

"Well, hunting Huns shouldn't be any harder than that," he said. "You've got some real talent."

"Thank you, sergeant," I said, and went back to shooting. I loved my new rifle, and I was sure it would save my life one day. In fact, I got a bit cocky, thinking momentarily that no German could touch me.

For a while, I remained arrogant about my shooting abilities, but when our training ended, and it came time to get on the boat across the channel, I felt like I was totally unprepared for what awaited me. When I watched the white Dover cliffs disappear into the distance, I was hit with that same feeling I had when I left our village. The enemy was out there, and he wanted to kill me.

I said a prayer. My life was in God's hands. There was little else protection I could hope for.

The engines fought against the heavy sea. The vibrating deck plates and the pitching made me a bit ill, although I didn't get sick like a lot of the other boys. Frank stood at the bow of the ship, not even flinching when the saltwater splashed in his face. He stood there for the entire trip.

About two hours later, I stepped on French soil for the first time. I got a doomed feeling when I walked down the gangplank. I realized that I might not make it back across the channel alive. I realized that none of us might make it. I was scared.

CHAPTER 4

We went briefly to another training camp in France, where we learned more advanced trench-fighting techniques. There was a lot of grousing about this, particularly by Simon, who felt that he was more than prepared to whip the Huns all on his own. I, on the other hand, was grateful for the additional instruction. I was plagued with anxiety about the prospect of going into combat; I hoped that feeling would go away soon, but it just seemed to get worse.

The first week of March we got word that we were going to the front. This time we didn't get the luxury of passenger cars. They packed us into freight cars with just enough room left for our equipment. There were only four small windows in the upper corners, hardly enough for proper ventilation. It reeked of mildew, cigarettes and sweat. Once they shut us inside, we were forbidden to open the door until given orders to do so.

That was our condition for the better part of two days. Although it wasn't particularly warm outside, the inside of the car got stuffy and hot in the afternoon sun. We all tried to get some sleep, but had little success. The train kept stopping and starting again. Every time the brakes started squealing, the men would get up and hoist on their gear, only to be sorely disappointed when the train started rolling again.

The only person who didn't seem to get annoyed by all of this was Frank. He sat in the corner, his legs outstretched and his cap pulled down low with the bill on his nose. It was like he didn't pay any mind to any of it. Then about dawn the second day the train started braking for another stop. Frank got to his feet, put on his pack and shouldered up his rifle. He stepped over to the door and waited.

"What is this?" Pick said. "He's losing his mind."

Everyone laughed until the train came to a complete stop and the door slid open. A burly staff sergeant ordered us to get out and form ranks on the station platform. Frank jumped out without saying a word. The rest of us were briefly stupefied.

I leapt out of the door without a thought as to how far down the platform was or that I had fifty pounds of gear on. I hit the concrete hard, and it jarred me to the spine. I was regaining my balance when the staff sergeant started bellowing at me.

"Get your arse out of the way or I'll kick it out of the way!" he yelled, and there was no need for him to repeat himself. I fell in with the others. I could smell something cooking nearby. We hadn't had a decent meal in a couple of days, and I was hoping that what I smelled would be breakfast. My belly growled like an angry bear.

The staff sergeant called us to attention. An officer came out of the station, walked to the front and exchanged salutes with him. The officer, obviously quite young, was narrow at the shoulders, with sandy blonde hair and deep-set eyes. He carried a leather map case on a strap over his shoulder, and a chunky Webley .455-caliber pistol on his hip. His slightly loose uniform was a bit faded from being in the sun.

"Good morning, gentlemen," he said. "I am First Lt. Rampkin, and this is Staff Sgt. Hendershot. You'll be with us now that you're going up to where the war is. We've got a little show planned for the Germans, and I'm sure you'll all teach Fritz a thing or two.

"The sergeant and I have been in more than a few scuffles since last summer. We were at Mons together. We know how to fight and survive. Listen to us and your odds of making it out of here in one piece are far greater.

"Now then, there are field kitchens behind the station where you can get a meal. You have thirty minutes to eat, and then reassemble at the north end of the station. Dismiss the men, sergeant."

Staff Sgt. Hendershot barked the order, and we all ran to try to be first in line for food. There were baked beans, bacon and hunks of bread with butter. We sat on the ground, our backs against the wall of the station, and devoured our food. I couldn't remember the last time anything tasted so good. Jack grunted his approval and let out a ferocious belch. We finished and walked over to the assembly area. There was a second train pulling in, its cars stretching in the distance farther than I could see.

"There must be a whole division in those cars," Pick said.

"Probably more," said Simon.

"If we're all headed the same way, there must be one serious fight coming up," Frank said. "Where do you think we are, anyway?"

Everyone shrugged. Frank walked back around the station and came back about two minutes later with a disgusted look on his face.

"You won't believe this," he said. "We've gone less than forty miles in the last two days. We could have walked here faster than that train!"

"I would have preferred the walk," I said, stretching my back. "I figure we'll be going on foot from here on. I sure don't want to get back on a train."

The lieutenant and Hendershot came out of the station, and we put on our packs and rifles. We lined up six abreast, and the sergeant gave us the order to move out. The sky was a little cloudy, pierced occasionally by warm rays of sunlight. The pack was heavy, but it fit pretty well after everything shook down a bit.

"Good day for a hike, wouldn't you say?" Frank said as he strode beside me.

"It is a fine day at that," I said. "I just wish I knew where we were headed."

"Probably won't know until we get there," Simon said with a sigh.

The rhythm of the march took over and everyone quieted down. The pace picked up, and I figured the column was covering about two and a half miles per hour by late morning. It was musical; the clinking of metal on metal and the percussion of boots on the road made a lively cadence.

Around noon we joined in the back end of a much larger column of troops who I figured were heading for the same fight. Another company caught up to our back end, and soon the line of marching soldiers stretched from horizon to horizon. More soldiers fell into the line the farther we went.

A column of lorries and horse-drawn wagons came up from the rear. When they got closer the sergeant told us to get into single file on one side of the road. The pace slowed to a crawl. They were carrying all variety of gear for an attack: artillery pieces of every size, coils of barbed wire, crates of rations and ammunition. The road got jammed up and we stopped, giving us a much-needed break.

I tried to keep count of how many wagons and motorized vehicles passed us, but I stopped at around 200. It took about four hours for the entire line to pass. The last few were carrying telltale oblong boxes.

"Those are for all the Huns I'm going to kill," Simon said, and we laughed nervously. We were so naïve.

We remounted the road and covered another six or seven miles before the sun started getting low. My pack was cutting into my shoulders and I was ready for a hot meal and some rest. We were approaching a wood when I spotted kitchens set up just inside the tree line. The air was getting cold, and billows of steam floated up through the trees.

Much to my disappointment, we passed the kitchens and went into the wood. We were told to pitch our tents beneath the high branches of firs and hardwoods.

"Looks like this is it for the day," Frank said.

26

"I bloody well hope so," I said. "My shoulders are killing me."

"Get situated, then get yourself some food," the lieutenant said. "We'll be leaving in the morning. I'll let you know exactly when as soon as I know myself."

We peeled off our gear and I felt like I was almost floating. We hastily erected our shelters and ran for the kitchens. There were fried potatoes, sausages, cheese, bread, and tins of butter and plum jam. We all took good healthy portions and plopped down on a bed of needles under a pine tree. Nobody said anything for a while. The only sound was Simon chewing with his mouth open. Then Frank broke wind loudly, and everyone laughed.

"So where do you think we are?" Frank said, leaning up against a tree and pulling off his boots. He unbuttoned his tunic and sat cross-legged on the ground.

"I figure we came about fifteen miles today, heading basically north," I said.

"More northwest, but fifteen miles at least," Pick said. I trusted his judgment and orientation better than my own. Hundreds of feet below ground in a mine, Pick could always sense depth changes and general directions. His opinion was valid.

"All I know is that it was a bloody long way," Simon moaned. He took off his boots and socks, revealing blisters on both feet. "I don't think I'll be able to get these boots back on."

The longer we sat, the more fatigue kicked in. I took off my tunic and found that the straps had rubbed raw spots on my shoulders. My back and neck were stiff. I didn't have any blisters on my feet like Simon, but when I stood to gather some firewood, they ached badly. Not far across the road we found an abundance of dead branches and boughs on the forest floor. We all took an armload back to our tents. I used my spade to dig a little pit, and then gathered some dry leaves, pine needles and tiny twigs and put them in the bottom. It only took one match to get it started, clearly impressing Frank, and he wasn't impressed by much. I broke up some branches and carefully placed them on the flaming kindling. Soon, we had a nice little fire going.

"Don't you think we need to put on some more wood?" Frank asked. "It's getting cold out here."

"Pile on the wood and you'll use up your supply before morning," I said. "Plus it gets too hot and you have to sit way back. Build a small fire, and then you can sit real close, get warm, and have plenty of wood to get you through."

We stretched our blankets out around the fire and lied down. Frank had some Woodbine cigarettes and he passed them around. I had never smoked before, but I took one anyway. It burned my throat and eyes, but I didn't let on; I liked the feeling I was getting from the nicotine. When Frank offered me another one, I took it. That was when I started smoking. I was rarely without cigarettes from that day on. Frank always seemed to have some stashed away "for emergencies." He sort of had a knack for "finding things," he said.

After sunset, the air got colder still and the wind picked up. We threw some wood on the fire and wrapped ourselves in our blankets. I could see the soldiers on the nearby road warming their hands over a brazier. Frank shuddered.

"Is it me, or is everyone else freezing?" he groaned through clenched teeth. "It's cold enough to freeze the balls off of a brass monkey."

Everyone chuckled.

"Well, I don't see none of them around here," Pick said.

Frank then got up and started rifling through his pack. After he'd pulled out a whole bunch of non-military items, he came up with a silver flask.

"How about a little nipper to take the chill off?" he asked, then took a swallow.

"What is it?" Jack asked.

"Who cares what it is," Simon interjected as he reached for the flask. He tipped it up and gulped. His eyes got wide and he started coughing.

"It's gin," Frank said, snatching back the flask. "And despite that nonsense there, it's pretty good gin."

"I hate gin," Jack mumbled. "Give me the bottle."

He took a sip.

"You're right," he said. "For gin, that's not too bad."

I agreed. That taste of alcohol was good after the day we'd had. Soon we were all feeling tired, and we crawled off to our tents. I fell asleep almost immediately.

Frank's snoring woke me up sometime in the middle of the night. I was trying to get back to sleep when I heard raindrops hitting the tent fly. Then, in the distance, I could faintly hear the unmistakable thud of exploding shells. The wind and rain started coming harder and the sounds of battle were drowned out. I prayed the rain would stop by morning and tried to go back to sleep.

I awakened again just at dawn. I stuck my arm out of the tent and didn't feel any rainfall. I took that as a good sign, and I thanked the Lord for answering my plea. I got into a habit of praying a lot after that.

I pulled on my boots and crawled outside. The fire was completely cold because of the rain, of course, so I looked around for something dry to start a new one. Not finding anything, I resorted to burning some of the loo paper I had stashed in my coat pocket. To my own amazement, I got a nice fire going by the time the others woke up. I thought about telling the lads about hearing the guns in the night, but I decided not to. We smoked cigarettes without talking and warmed ourselves as best we could.

The sky was getting lighter, but there was no sunshine. Dark gray winter clouds hung low in the sky. The air was heavy and visibility was poor. I did not like the looks of it.

"What a gorgeous day!" Frank said flamboyantly. He got this stupid grin on his face and then laughed at his own joke.

"Looks like it might snow," I said, putting some more branches on the fire. "Wouldn't that be lovely?"

"Cold enough to freeze the balls off a brass monkey," Frank said.

"What the hell is that supposed to mean, anyway?" Pick said.

"Well, see," Frank said, "back in the old days, they used to carry cannon balls on a ship on a brass rack called a monkey. And I say it's cold enough to freeze the balls off a brass monkey."

"I don't think it's going to snow," Simon said. "I can smell snow, and I'm not smelling it now."

"You can't smell snow," Pick said. "Who ever heard of smelling snow? You must be a bit daft."

"Sod off," Simon countered, revealing his limited wit.

"You sod off, you bugger," Pick shot back.

"I think both you buggers ought to sod off," I said. Frank and Jack were laughing at them. They went at it for a minute or so until we caught the smell of food in the breeze. We stoked up the fire and headed quickly to the kitchens. We had boiled eggs and sausages and beans that I think were left over from the previous night. The tea was strong, and just what I needed. There was even a fellow at the end of the food line passing out tins of Woodbines.

We carried our food back to the fire and ate sitting in a circle around it. It didn't take us long to polish it off, either. It tasted quite good. Then a corporal and a couple of privates came around carrying a jug.

"You want your rations?" the corporal asked.

"Rations of what?" Frank asked.

"Rum. Do you want your rum ration?"

We all looked at each other.

"Yes," I said, holding out my empty cup. "Absolutely."

The others did the same. When we all got our share, we clinked our cups together.

"Here's to killing Huns," Simon said. We were all a bit shocked, but we drank anyway. The rum tasted like the tin cup it was served in, but I came to look forward to that particular ritual every day.

"I wonder when we're going to move out," Pick said.

"I don't know, but I think we're going to find out," Frank said, pointing behind us. "Here comes the lieutenant."

Lt. Rampkin was walking up the line of tents, stopping to talk to the individual groups of men encamped there. He walked over toward our fire, and we started to stand and salute, but he motioned for us to stay seated.

"Sir," Pick said. "When do we go?"

"That's what I'm going to find out now," he said. "Just be ready to move out."

Traffic on the road started picking up, and the more time went by, the more anxious Pick got.

"What are we supposed to do?" he said impatiently. "Just sit here?"

"I don't mind sitting here," Simon said. "My feet still hurt from yesterday."

"You whimper like a little girl," Pick said. The two of them went at it again, swearing at each other like avowed enemies. Pick was a master of cursing. Simon just said things that made no sense. It was actually pretty amusing.

The morning came and went like that. We hadn't seen the lieutenant or Hendershot for quite a while. I checked and rechecked my gear and generally fidgeted my time away. There was a lot of nervous talk about where we were going and when we would fight. Everyone was on edge except for Frank. He was leaning against his pack under a tree, his ankles and arms crossed and his hat pulled down in his now-usual fashion.

We waited. Then it started drizzling again, so we covered up in our waterproof sheets. Those were some of the most useful items included in Tommy's kit, I'll tell you. I smoked a couple of cigarettes and tried to relax. I succeeded, and was actually nodding off when Pick slapped me on the back.

"Here comes the lieutenant," he said. I rubbed my face and uncovered my head. Lt. Rampkin was rousing men up and pointing to the road. It was time to go. We all took turns pissing on the fire before leaving.

"Smells like your house, Pick," Jack said with a grin as steam rolled off the embers.

"What did I do to you?" Pick said sarcastically. "Smells more like your wife's perfume. That's what it smells like."

For some reason, it occurred to me right then that they were being a bit flippant for men who might never see another morning.

30

I next realized *I* might not see another morning. I looked at the sky. There was snow mingling with the raindrops.

We headed through the wood. We passed a number of other camps, each one empty. We came out into open country, and then halted at a crossroads. There were several vehicles parked there, as well as a couple of motorcycles. There were four officers looking at a map that was spread out on the bonnet of a staff car. The lieutenant walked over and saluted, then had a look for himself. They talked for a few minutes with the lieutenant paying close attention and nodding a lot. They gave us a disheveled corporal as a guide and sent us off down a smaller farm road. We were going to be at the front soon, and I was "getting the wind up," as they said then. The road had been shelled in a couple of places, and knowing that I was now in range of the enemy's guns made it worse. My mouth was dry and my chest felt tight.

I heard a buzzing in the distance, an odd sound that I didn't recognize. I wiped the rain out of my eyes and looked around. There were three airplanes approaching from the north, flying high and unchallenged. It was one of the first times I'd ever seen a plane, and I'd never seen three flying together before, so I pointed them out to the others.

"Are those ours or theirs?" Jack wondered aloud.

"I can't tell," I said. "The visibility is terrible."

The planes were headed in our direction and soon passed overhead. I still couldn't tell anything about them, but Frank decided they were German.

"They're having a good look at us," Frank said. "They're wondering what we're up to. I don't like the looks of this."

They circled and headed back the way they came. A couple of minutes later there was a roaring, screaming sound.

"Get off of the road!" the lieutenant yelled just as a shell exploded behind us. "Take cover!"

A second shell came tearing through the sky and hit the road up ahead. Men went flying in all directions. I spotted a ditch and jumped in, landing in the mud. Frank was right behind me. The shells were dead on. One landed just across the road from our hiding place and shook the ground below us. We were immediately showered in dirt and rocks.

"What a gorgeous day!" Frank shouted, covering his head with his hands as the shelling continued. It lasted only a couple of minutes, but it seemed much, much longer.

We got up and surveyed the damage. There were at least a dozen dead boys lying on the road, and a like number injured. I didn't see anyone among the casualties that I recognized. I looked around for the boys and found them all. Everyone was all right

31

except Pick, who had apparently dumped in his pants in all of the excitement. He had them pulled down and he was trying to clean himself. Simon was laughing hysterically.

"Sod off, Simon," Pick swore. He was red in the face and his hands were shaking.

I didn't say anything and neither did Frank, though Simon's twisted sense of humor was disturbing. I think he had a complete absence of compassion; he would soon demonstrate that in combat. I, on the other hand, was embarrassed for Pick. It had nearly scared it out of me as well. I couldn't find anything funny about that at all.

We helped get the casualties straightened out, and ambulances began arriving to take them away. A round of morphine stopped their screams and cries. The rain washed their blood from the road.

CHAPTER 5

We continued, fewer in number, and a couple of miles on we entered a village in name only. It had been hit hard at some point, and nearly all of the buildings were damaged or burnt. A hot meal and a rum ration were provided, and we found a roof to get under for a while. We were told not to start fires, as it would tip off German artillery spotters. I chain-smoked cigarettes until darkness fell and we moved on. Then we were told not to smoke, because snipers liked to shoot at flickering matches. We were that close to the enemy.

"Mind the 'ole," someone would whisper in the darkness, hoping those in the rear would hear in time. They usually didn't, and a crash and vehement cursing usually followed the warning.

There was a faint light up ahead, almost undetectable. As we got closer, I could see a kerosene lantern sitting next to a fieldstone fence that ran alongside the road. There were braziers sitting amidst the shattered remains of a large farmhouse, and soldiers were milling about, trying to get warm. We joined them.

The guide led the lieutenant over to a cellar door at the back of the house. He opened it, and light pierced the darkness for a brief moment until the door closed. He emerged a few minutes later with orders.

"Command says we stay here for a few hours while a carrying party moves up ahead of us. Get some rest; be ready to move at 0400."

The night was still and I drifted off for a while. I awoke around two to hear sporadic rifle and machine gun fire. It sounded very close. I sat up, and found that I was the last one awakened by this. The others were debating as to how far away the shooting was.

"It sounds like it's about a half-mile to the north," Jack speculated.

"Definitely north," Pick said, "but I'd say even closer than that."

I decided to go outside and find out. I stared into the darkness and couldn't see a thing. There was no moon and it was getting foggy. I was about to go in when I saw a fellow with a torch walking across the yard. He was leading the carrying party that was supposed to go up before us. They were laden with ammunition, bombs and jugs of rum, the things they deemed necessary to wage war. The line of men crossed the yard and disappeared just on the other side of the farmhouse. A star shell burst in the sky about 500 yards away, and for a moment, through the mist, I could make out trenches stretching from our position toward the horizon, and men lined up to go in. There were artillery batteries in a line not 50 yards from the house, with piles of shells at the ready. It looked like it was going to be one major firestorm. I went back inside.

"We're right on top of the trenches," I said. "That carrying party we were waiting on just passed. We'll be going soon."

Everyone got excited, except for Frank, of course; he had fallen back asleep by then.

"What time do you think it is?" Simon wondered aloud.

Jack pulled a watch out of his pocket.

"It's about midnight," he said.

"I didn't know you had a watch," I said. "Looks like a nice one."

He handed it to me for inspection. It was very simple in design, with a smooth front and back. I pushed on the release and opened the cover. There was a picture of his wife on the inside.

"I always thought Gillian was quite a catch," I said, handing back the timepiece.

"That was taken on our tenth wedding anniversary," he said.

"Has it been ten years already?" Pick said.

"It's been twelve."

"It seems like your wedding was yesterday. Remember how drunk we got the night before?"

"I don't remember much of anything from that night," Jack said, and we all had a good laugh.

I knew it was going to be a long day ahead, and I wanted to get some rest. They continued talking for a while and I, too, fell back asleep. I don't know how; I was incredibly nervous by then.

The lieutenant roused us just before four. He had rounded up everyone in our unit and brought them into the house. We sat on the floor and he briefed us on our mission.

"The idea," he said, standing with his hands clasped behind him, "is to take the village of Neuve Chapelle in the morning. There are hedgerows and enemy trenches between here and there. It will be your duty to take these trench lines and eventually the village itself. If all goes well, we'll push on past the village and take the Aubers Ridge. It's so flat here that you can see for miles from that position, so it would be best if we had it. Once there, we will regroup and make a final push toward Lille.

"We will be in the first wave of the attack, and that is an enormous responsibility. Luckily, we'll have a bit of help. There are more than a thousand artillery pieces out there, lined up nearly wheel-to-wheel, and ready to pour it on the Huns. They'll start the show at daybreak. It will be low and up close: direct fire, mostly.

You need to stay down and keep your heads covered until the guns shift to deeper targets.

"The German front line is about 400 yards from where we sit. There's a lot of barbed wire between here and there, but the artillery should take care of most of it before we go over. Behind that first line is a hedgerow, and that may be a bit tricky to penetrate. Once through, we should be able to take the village and move on."

A group of soldiers came inside carrying crates that appeared to be quite heavy. One little fellow was really straining. He was so small I wondered how he got into the army.

"Set them down right there," the lieutenant said. "Thank you."

He bent over and opened one of the crates. He pulled out a pair of wire cutters and a leather lanyard.

"Just in case the artillery doesn't destroy the wire, these are very important," he said. "I'm sorry to say that we've only got enough for a third of you, but if we are careful, that will be enough. If you take a pair, attach the lanyard, keep them secure, and make sure you are at the front of the attack. If a man carrying a pair is wounded, another man is expected to take them before moving on. This is imperative.

"I also have your ammunition here," he said. "You should each get 20 clips if supply did the mathematics correctly. Get yours and be ready to move out in five minutes."

In the shelter of the house, I checked and re-checked my rifle and smoked two cigarettes, leaving my mouth parched. It started raining again.

"What a gorgeous day!" Frank said, holding his hand out to feel the raindrops. I was beginning to think that he was either half-simple or half-loony. Maybe both at the same time.

Hendershot told us to get into battle order, which meant leaving behind our packs and carrying only what was necessary for the attack: our rifles, bayonets and trenching tools; a haversack containing our iron rations, which were a one-pound can of corned – or "bully" -- beef, 12 ounces of biscuits, 5/8 ounce of tea, two ounces of sugar, ½-ounce of salt, two broth cubes, three ounces of cheese and a brew kit for boiling water; our webbing-belt and ammunition pouches; and two canteens of water.

We followed a guide into the trenches. They started out shallow, getting deeper and narrower as we moved forward. We passed several communications trenches that were packed full of men awaiting the attack. We kept moving ahead. For some reason, I recall the smell more clearly than anything. It was a putrid combination of sewage, sulfur and rotten meat. That was where the rear ended and the war started.

"Keep your heads down, lads," Hendershot said in a half-whisper as we arrived at our jumping-off point, a shallow breastwork trench in front of the village. There was a nest of barbed wire over parapets of earth and sandbags. A star shell burst in the sky, and despite the sergeant's warning, I decided to take a peek. I rose up and got a glimpse of the hedgerow about 100 yards away. Hendershot grabbed me by the collar of my greatcoat and pulled me down to the bottom of the trench.

"I told you to stay down!" he yelled. "Now stay down, you stupid fool!"

I got up off the ground and sat on the fire step. I didn't try any more reconnaissance. The hedgerow weighed on my mind; crossing it without being shot at would probably be a great venture in itself, I thought. I hoped the artillery would clear the way. I hoped the Huns on the other side would already be dead.

My anxiety crested as dawn approached. My hands were sweaty on my rifle and my heart was pounding so loud that I was sure the others could hear it. I wanted another cigarette but we weren't allowed. I licked the rain off my lips.

About seven o'clock by Jack's watch, some fellows came by with cotton wool for plugging our ears during the barrage. We also got a double rum ration. I took it all in one massive gulp. Frank and the others did the same. Nobody said anything, and there for a moment, the battlefield seemed to go quiet. As the sun edged up on the horizon, we were told to put in the cotton. The only thing I could hear was my own heartbeat.

That silence was shattered at 7:30 when an 18-pounder just behind us awoke with a mighty roar. I couldn't imagine what it must have sounded like without the earplugs. The shell went screaming just over our heads, and before it could explode, a half-dozen more guns fired. The ground began to tremble as hundreds and hundreds joined in. The enemy was surely taking a beating; even the walls of our own trench began to shake and crumble as the shock waves pierced the earth. The cannonade began to sound like a mighty drum roll, and flying debris rained down on our heads. I hunkered down, closed my eyes and held onto my hat with both hands. Something dropped out of the air and bounced around at my feet. I kept my eyes shut.

Frank started beating me on the shoulder, trying to tell me something. He was screaming something in my ear, but I couldn't hear him. I finally opened my eyes to see what he was so excited about. He was pointing toward my feet. I looked down, and there was a bloody German *pickelhaube* with bits of hair and scalp inside. The sight disgusted me, but for a moment I could not avert my eyes. I could hear my heart again, only louder.

36

I felt another slap on my shoulder. I turned around expecting to see Frank, but this time it was Staff Sgt. Hendershot. He pointed to the bayonet fixed on the end of his rifle, then motioned for me to do the same. He held up a brass whistle around his neck, and then pointed over the top of the trench. We all understood. The battle was at hand.

Jack, who was issued a pair of the cutters, crawled up on the parapet and waited to charge out ahead. Other men with the same dubious distinction prepared to jump off to our left and right. There were red distress flares shooting into the air all along the enemy line. The sun was up but obscured by clouds and fog, and the drizzle had stopped, although it was hard to tell with all of the other stuff dropping in on us.

The next minute or two passed like years. The cannonade was one steady roar. I started to choke from the acrid smoke that hung in the air, and it got worse as the gunfire reached yet a new crescendo. I was getting quite edgy and I didn't think I could stand still anymore. I tried to take a few deep breaths, and coughing, I got in behind Jack. Simon stepped in behind me, slapped me on the shoulder and gave me the thumbs-up sign.

I didn't have to wait much longer. A second later the guns abruptly stopped. The sergeant blew his whistle. A barbaric cry rose from along our trench. The lieutenant climbed atop the parapet, his revolver drawn.

"Over the top, boys!" he shouted, waving us along with his pistol. Jack jumped up and I followed him into No Man's Land. Hundreds of men advanced in unison toward the wire, bayonets pointed forward.

Thinking back, I don't know how I did it. My legs were shaking the whole time, but they kept going forward. I went into a jog, trying not to slip in the mud or fall into shell holes which became increasingly difficult to avoid. I looked up and saw what was left of the enemy's breastwork defenses. It was blown to pieces, at least in our sector. The hedge was another forty yards or so beyond that. I could hear Simon's massive boots pounding the mud behind me. I ran faster. The horizon was bouncing to the left and right. Shrapnel shells were bursting in the air, and high-explosive rounds were crashing into targets I could not yet see. Jack reached the wire. He didn't even have to stop; the guns had apparently cut it. I thanked the Lord and followed him into Hun territory. My heart was pounding hard and fast and my sinuses burned. I screamed and jumped over the breastworks and down into the trench.

There was nobody there. At least no one alive, anyway. There were bodies and pieces of bodies, busted weapons and other

37

remnants of the unit that had held the trench. I didn't have much time to get a good look. The lieutenant was up above, waving his pistol and yelling at us to keep advancing. I could hear some rifle fire and a machine gun in the distance. I climbed up the back of the trench, got to my feet and headed for a gap that had been blown in the hedge. Beyond the hedge I could see the village. It was taking a good beating. Smoke and flames rose from the battered buildings. Through the haze I could see a tall, gaunt crucifix standing amid the destruction. I took it as a good sign.

I guess it was. We reached a decimated second line of defense and took it without a fight. A few Germans who had survived quickly threw down their rifles and threw up their hands, yelling "*kamerad*!" It was beginning to look quite easy. For the moment.

Jack was out ahead, even ahead of the lieutenant. We were advancing into the village, right behind the artillery barrage. I passed the lieutenant and tried to catch up to Jack when he suddenly fell to the ground face-first. I ran to check on him, and another man to my left fell. I dove to the ground next to Jack and rolled him on his back. He was stone dead, shot through the neck. He had this startled look on his face that I'll never forget. Someone landed in the mud beside me. It was the lieutenant.

"There's a sniper up there!" he shouted at me. "Bloody hell!"

He was going on about something but I wasn't listening. I was in shock. My mind was confused. I thought about Jack's family. I thought about a lot of things in that few seconds. My sadness quickly turned into raging vengeance.

A bullet ricocheted off of a shattered tree stump just in front of me, and that brought me back to the situation at hand. I closed Jack's eyes and tried to get his wedding ring off, but it wouldn't budge. I took his watch out of his pocket and put it in my coat. I would mail it to his wife as soon as I got the chance.

"He's gone!" the lieutenant yelled. "Get his cutters and move on!"

I untied his lanyard and the lieutenant continued cursing. The sniper had the whole advance pinned down. I had to find him. I had to kill him.

I crawled on my belly until I got behind the tree stump. I eased over to the side, and rested my rifle on an exposed root. I got down behind it and surveyed the scene in front of me. I studied it. I could see about a dozen dead Germans, a couple of dead horses, the crucifix, a number of burning buildings and a whole lot of places for a sniper to hide. I decided to narrow it down by looking only at the buildings that weren't burning; I doubted the sniper would stay in a building that was on fire. Then I looked for places that he could have taken the shot that killed Jack. That eliminated all but a couple of possible locations. I stared at them, waiting for the killer to show his face.

Then in a doorway about 75 yards away, I saw him peeking out to find another target. He was partially protected by the door, which was dangling crossways, seemingly from one hinge. He had his rifle resting in the notch that used to house the lock mechanism. He rose and took a shot. I instinctively covered my head, but he didn't seem to be aiming at me. I hoped it was because he didn't see me. The thought made me a bit braver. I opened my eyes and peered down the end of my rifle. I put his head in my sights and pulled the trigger.

I didn't even hear the rifle go off, but I saw his head snap back and his rifle drop over the front of the door. I had just killed my first German, with the very first shot I had fired in France. I got a rush of adrenalin, and my blood lust swelled. I had never felt anything like it. I stood and let out a mighty yell, shaking my fist at the sky.

"I got him! I got the sod!"

"No time for celebrations," the lieutenant said as he stood and wiped his revolver on his trouser leg. "We've got a long way to go to Lille. Let's keep moving!"

The advance resumed, and I decided that I needed to take a look at the fellow I shot. I walked over quite casually to the doorway. His Mauser, fitted with a telescopic sight, lay on the ground where he dropped it. I could see the bottom of one of his boots. I looked inside; he was lying on his back behind the door. I could see his pale, white face, with a moustache and a bloody wound over his left eye. There was blood pooling under his head, and his helmet was halfway across the room. I stared for a moment, and considered taking something from him as a souvenir. But I decided I would not, and turning around, ran to catch up to the lieutenant.

We made our way into the village as the artillery again shifted to targets on the other side. I felt around in my pocket and found Jack's watch. It was a little after nine. We passed the crucifix, and on closer examination I saw that an unexploded artillery shell was sticking in the upright, about halfway up from the bottom. The church behind it was in utter ruins. It was the most peculiar thing I'd ever seen. One lad just stood there gawking. And I remember that shell was still there when I passed back that way some time later.

We passed the church and its cemetery, where the coffins and cadavers had been unearthed by shellfire, and now lay strewn about the wreckage. It was grotesque, but not unusual by front-line standards; a number of other soldiers who fought in a variety of places told me after the war that they'd seen the same thing somewhere along the line. Every town worth taking had a cemetery, I guess.

The destruction of the village had been complete. There wasn't a wall standing, or a window intact. Here and there among the wreckage lay dead Germans, one holding a leash with a dead dog on the other end. The smoke hung low to the ground and, between that and the fog, one could hardly see a hundred yards. It was drizzling again.

As we approached the other side of Neuve Chapelle, I was startled from my daze by the terrifying rattle of a machine gun. Our crews hadn't had time to move up yet, so I knew it was a German gun that was firing. That was frightening; just one of their Maxim machine guns could lay down 600 rounds of 7.9 mm ammunition per minute, making it equal in firepower to about 40 men with rifles. One gun could stop the advance of hundreds or even thousands of men. I knew it had to be disabled, and that men would die in the process.

I looked around and saw everyone was clearing the road, hugging the partial walls on either side. I ran to my left, just as a hail of bullets danced across my path. I looked sideways as I sprinted and I could make out a breastwork trench through the mist. It appeared to run in a jagged fashion roughly parallel to their first line of defense. There was another machine gun burst, and that time, I saw the muzzle flash. I could see the nest straight ahead, and still riding the rush from shooting my sniper, I arrogantly believed I was the only man who *could* see it. I ran along the line of men hugging the left side of the street until I came to the lieutenant, squatting with his back to a broken wall, reloading his revolver. I got in behind him and crouched down. The machine gun was very close now.

"What should we do, lieutenant?" I said. "Machine gun's got us blocked."

"All right," he said, "what's your name, private?"

"Gardener, sir."

"Well, Gardener, we need to get some bombers up here. They can work their way down this wall. Then there are a couple of shell holes farther on. Maybe they can make it to one of them. If we keep moving at this rate, we could be in Lille by morning."

He inched his back up the wall and looked down the road.

"I don't see the sergeant or my corporals anywhere, so I guess you'll have to do, Gardener. I need two bombers and another three rifleman in addition to you. We should be able to knock that gun out of action."

40

I saluted and ran back down the side of the street. I was pleased to see Frank, Simon and Pick hunkered down together not thirty yards back. I stopped.

"You fellows see any bombers around here?" I hollered. The boys all shrugged their shoulders, but a fellow kneeling behind them pointed out a couple of grenadiers farther back. I gave him a "cheers" and made my way down to the men carrying haversacks of bombs.

"Lt. Rampkin wants you two up front," I said. "There's a machine gun up there that needs to be dealt with."

"You don't say," one of them said. "I thought we were just taking a break here in this lovely little spot. I know there's no place I'd rather be right now…"

He went on like that for a while, but he and the other bomber got up and followed me forward. I still needed three others, so I got the boys on the way back.

"Come on," I said, "The lieutenant needs us."

There was a bit of grousing from Simon, of course, but they followed me up to the front of the line anyway.

By the time I got back, a telephone line had been brought up and the lieutenant was trying to raise a cavalry unit. He apparently wasn't having much luck. He handed the phone back to Hendershot, who had miraculously appeared from somewhere.

"Keep trying, sergeant," he said. "And if you can't get that thing working, find me a couple of runners. It's wide open, but it won't stay that way for long."

Hendershot got busy cranking the box and yelling into the handset. The lieutenant took a drink out of his canteen and wiped his eyes. He shook his head a couple of times and looked over at us.

"I see you found some volunteers," he said. "Have I got a job for you. We've got a machine gun up here, and the whole party is shut down. You need to move in as close as you can; I don't want you wasting your entire supply of bombs on this nest. I understand we're a bit short on them today.

"You two," he said, pointing at Simon and Pick, "carry their haversacks. Gardener, you and…what's your name?"

"Thomas, sir."

"Gardener, you and Thomas give cover fire. If the grenadiers get clicked, you take their places. Is everybody set?"

We nodded.

"Well then," the lieutenant said, "over the top with the best of luck."

The grenadiers took the lead, and we followed closely, up to the end of the wall. We stopped and took a closer look to see what

41

kind of cover was available. About 20 yards away, there was a nice, deep shell crater with a high lip. Another 20 or so yards beyond that was another good crater, and the nest was about 15 yards from there, at the end of a breastwork sap with barbed wire on both sides. To rush it, we would have to take it straight on. There was a crew of three in the nest, all of whom would have to be eliminated. That was the bad news. The good news, though, was that there didn't appear to be much fire, if any, coming from the adjoining trench, which ran about 20 feet or so behind the wire. It was still a gamble, however, as to whether we could outrun the gun.

The complaining grenadier became a bit more curious than the rest of us, and stuck his head way out to get a better look. He was greeted with a hail of bullets. He pulled back quickly.

"Damn it!" he gasped. "Those Huns know what we're up to. They're waiting for us to show ourselves!"

The grenadiers reached in their haversacks and took out two Mark I bombs each. In those early days we were still using the Mark I. It had a percussion fuse and wasn't particularly reliable. They looked kind of like a mace, with an explosive head and a cane handle, with these linen strips attached that helped ensure that it would land top end down and hit on the striker. While they did tend to land on the right end, sometimes they just didn't go off. We got the Mills bomb later. It had a timed fuse and was a lot more reliable. But at that time, we were stuck with the Mark I.

"Here's how we're going to play this little game," the complainer said. "Me and Smitty here will go for that big hole first, while you two pour it on. We'll try to hit them from there, and then run to a closer position. While they're ducking our bombs, you blokes make for that first hole. We'll leap-frog right up on them."

He took another look.

"Go on my word," he said.

"Look what you've gotten us into," Frank said under his breath. "I don't like…"

He didn't have the chance to finish his objection.

"Go!" the complainer yelled. They bolted ahead and we opened fire on the nest, trying to keep the Maxim gun quiet. I managed to shoot the gunner, but he was quickly replaced. We had done our job, nonetheless, and the grenadiers made it to cover.

"Good shooting, Richard," Frank said. "That's two for you, right?"

I found his question a bit chilling, but I didn't have time to ponder it much or offer a reply. The grenadiers popped up for a moment and hurled two bombs at the nest. As they sailed through the air, Frank and I dashed forward. The grenadiers ran for the next hole.

One of the bombs fell short, and blew up against the front of the sandbag revetment protecting the gun position. The other one exploded off to the right, amid the barbed wire entanglements. Frank and I dove into the hole just as bullets swept across the forward lip. They must have fired for about a minute solid. We were so close that I could hear the shell casings clinking after being ejected from the magazine.

When the gun finally stopped, I could hear rifle fire from our rear. I peeked over the lip. I saw two more bombs sail through the air, and again, neither one of them hit the nest square on. I was cursing when I heard Simon and Pick come crashing in behind us. They, too, were chased by the Maxim gun.

"The sods!" Simon yelled. "Dirty Hun sods!"

"Are you going to curse them to death, Simon?" Pick said, gritting his teeth.

"To hell with you," Simon said, "you fat bastard."

"Now isn't the best time for this lads," I said. The machine gun had stopped again, so I took a peek. Two German bombs came hurling over the revetment; one was lobbed at the complainer and Smitty, the other one at us. I ducked down into the hole on my back.

I heard one blast in front, followed by a much closer one that showered us in dirt. I looked over the top and saw smoke coming from the hole occupied by the grenadiers. The complainer was lying backward over the lip, apparently killed by the blast. I made the assumption that Smitty had met a similar fate.

"Now what are we going to do?" Simon said. "We're stuck out here!"

"Hold on a minute, Simon," I said. "Don't start panicking yet."

"What the hell are we going to do?"

"We've got two whole bags of these bombs. How many are in there?"

Simon and Pick looked in and poked around.

"We've got at least a dozen between us."

"I got one of them when he was firing the gun before. Maybe we can get them to show themselves, and I'll try and get another one."

I rolled over and inched up the lip of the crater. I parted the loose dirt with my hands and made a notch for my rifle. The gun crew saw me and let me have a good dose. I ducked down until they stopped firing. When I heard that last shell casing hit the ground, I popped up and looked down my rifle. I could see a helmet, then an entire head. I pulled the trigger and the German's head twisted around, an arc of red haze spurting from his face. I slipped back down into the hole.

"Got another one," I said.

"There's one more," Frank said.

There were a few more shots fired about the lip. We all got down a bit lower.

"So what do we do now?" Simon whined.

"If you ask that question again, I'll shoot you myself," Pick said. It was amazing. Even under fire, those two found time to badger each other.

"Shut up," I said. "Let's use some of these bombs."

"From here?" Simon complained. "Can you throw that good? I can't."

"Well, we're going to try," I said. He was beginning to annoy me.

"How do you work these things?" Frank asked. "Didn't we get some training on this?"

"We only had dummies," Pick said. "This is rather inconvenient, isn't it?"

While I wished I had asked the grenadiers about it before we got separated, I pulled one out and took a look, and for some highly unlikely reason, my instruction on this weapon back in England came to me with crystal clarity.

"All you've got to do is pull this safety pin on top and give it a hurl," I said. "I think if you hit anywhere close, even if the bomb doesn't explode, it will get him to try and fire his gun. I can peg him."

"As long as it doesn't involve me charging him with a bayonet, I'm in," Frank said, quite seriously.

"All right," I said. "All of you blokes start tossing bombs until one of us hits him."

The machine gunner was getting nervous. He fired about our hiding place while I wasn't looking. Then he ducked back down.

"Sounds like a good plan," Pick said. "You've got my vote."

"I'll get ready, then give you the go."

I inched back up the lip. There was nothing to draw a bead on; he was staying below the sandbags. I hoped the bombs would draw him out. I laid my rifle in the notch.

"Go!" I shouted, and the boys started pulling pins and throwing. A couple of them hit pretty close, and soon the remaining German decided it would be a good time to throw something back. He quickly popped up – not where I was expecting -- and raised his arm back to throw.

It was one of those mostly instinctive shots normally reserved for when a game bird unexpectedly flies up out of cover. This

44

method of shooting usually requires simultaneous swearing, as you are as startled as your quarry. The boys later claimed I shot him from the hip, but I think that was a bit of an exaggeration. Whatever the case, the German fell backward and dropped the bomb on himself. It exploded a second later, and the smoke rising from the nest let us know it was safe to pass.

I stood and hailed the lieutenant. He walked out in the road, and waved the waiting troops forward.

I went over to the crater where the grenadiers lay. They were both unidentifiable. The German bomb had blown them to pieces. I walked on to the enemy revetment. I stood looking over the sandbags at the three men that I had just shot. They were all young men, younger than me, probably. There wasn't the exhilaration I'd felt earlier. There was a pang of guilt and remorse, and I guess it showed on my face. Frank walked over and put his hand on my shoulder.

"We're not going to keep count anymore," he said.

We climbed into the nest and down into the adjoining trench. There was a lot of abandoned equipment, but no one manning it.

"Gardener!" the lieutenant called from my rear. I turned about. He was standing on the parapet with his map in one hand and his Webley in the other. He tucked the map under his arm, holstered the pistol, and jumped down into the trench.

"You've earned your pay today, Gardener," he said. "I want you and you're pal Thomas to stay with me for the rest of the way. I heard Corporal Harris and Corporal Dunning clicked it back there. I need to know I have someone to get things done. Where is Hendershot?"

"Don't know, sir," I said.

"Well, go find him. And get him and that telephone line up here. Move! Move!"

I saluted and started back down the road to where I'd last seen the sergeant. I found him there crouched in the dirt with a fellow who had just arrived with a new spool of wire for the buzzer.

"Sgt. Hendershot," I said, a bit out of breath, "the lieutenant says he needs you to move up with the telephone."

"What the hell does he think I'm trying to do? Tell that public-school bastard that I'll get there as soon as it is properly wired, or else it won't work worth a damn."

Speechless, I saluted and ran back to the captured trench, where I found Lt. Rampkin.

"He says he's on his way, sir," I said as I saluted.

"I'm sure that's not exactly what he said, but thank you. And quit saluting me out here. If a sniper sees us and you salute me, he'll know I'm an officer and shoot me rather than you. Don't stack the cards against me, Gardener."

The trench was filling with advancing men. We were apparently holding at that line, awaiting artillery support. It was better than waiting in the open. The lieutenant climbed up the back of the trench and took a look.

"That's the River des Layes up there. See that bridge up the road?"

I had a look myself, figuring if it were safe enough for him, it was safe enough for me. The bridge was about 100 yards away, and there were machine guns behind redoubts on either side.

"Yes sir, I see it. It looks pretty tough."

"Well, that's our next objective. And don't expect the big guns to take out those machine guns. They would run the risk of blowing up the bridge."

It was a long way. I felt sick.

He looked at a watch strapped to his wrist. It was the first time I'd seen such a device; a military invention, they were issued to officers as standard equipment and soon became coveted items. He rubbed the crystal.

"It's ten," he said.

I climbed up on the fire step and looked back into the village.

"I think I see the sergeant coming, sir."

He had a look.

"Yes, I do believe you're right. I've got to get through to command. We're moving ahead of the clock."

The sergeant came carrying the telephone in one hand and the spool of wire in the other, letting it roll off as he moved ahead. The engineer who had brought the wire trailed close behind. Hendershot lowered down the equipment and slid down the parapet and onto the fire step.

"Should be working now, sir," he said.

The lieutenant started cranking the box, and eventually raised command. He had a bit of trouble being understood.

"Yes! That's what I said! It's wide open. No. No, they seem to be fleeing. There's a lot of gear left lying around up here. Where? I'd imagine they are going into the Bois du Biez. The Bois du Biez! That bit of wood just beyond the village. Yes, it's on the map. To whom am I speaking again?"

The lieutenant gave the phone the "V" sign and rolled his eyes. The sergeant laughed.

"Now who is this?" the lieutenant said, apparently talking with someone else. "Yes, sir. Glad to reach you, sir. Yes, the advance is doing quite well, sir. Well, we could use some help, sir. Yes, I know we're ahead of schedule. We need artillery support against the wood. That's where we think the enemy is hiding. Other than that, there seems to be a pretty good gap in the line, sir. Aerial reconnaissance would be good, and the cavalry could go 'round the wood and break through into open country."

The lieutenant started shaking his head.

"Too foggy, sir?" he said. "I understand it might be a bit foggy for the airplanes, but for the cavalry as well? Sir?"

He shook his head.

"Yes. We'll wait for the artillery. Sir. Thank you."

He put down the telephone.

"Damn it," he said, looking at the ground. "What are we supposed to do? Just sit tight, that's what. I think every twit and village idiot in England became a commanding officer. I haven't met a single one that was worth his salt."

He looked up at us.

"They say we'll be here until the guns give the wood a good pounding, but there's no aerial observation to see what we should hit. There's no cavalry to exploit the breakthrough. Essentially no way of exactly knowing the right course of action. Typical army operation."

I was a bit surprised at the lieutenant's comments. His sarcasm was unexpected, and didn't seem to fit his demeanor. But it was easy to sympathize with him. We were here, capable of pushing forward, yet not given what we needed to do the job. The infantry was out front; the others seemed far, far behind, both in distance and thinking.

"Have either of you got a fag?" the lieutenant said, looking at Frank and me. "I know the sergeant doesn't have any."

"Those things will kill you, lieutenant," he said.

"So will wine, women and bullets, but I can't seem to do without those, either," he said. "So, do you have one?"

"*Voila*," Frank said, pulling a tin out of his pocket. He opened it up and offered it to Lt. Rampkin.

"Thanks, Thomas." He pulled out a box of matches and lit it. "I'll give you the ones I get in rations next time."

"You don't smoke regular, sir?" I asked.

"He doesn't want his mother to know," Hendershot said wryly.

"Sergeant, if you weren't such a good chess opponent, I'd knock you down to private," the lieutenant said, grinning just slightly.

I climbed up and looked out ahead. I could see very little beyond the bridge. Smoke and fog hung low to the ground. It seemed to be getting colder. I had worked up a sweat before, and now I had a chill. I wished I had a steaming cup of tea, but I was certain it would be a long time before I would.

I was surprised when I heard the buzz of an airplane coming up from our rear. Apparently someone had decided that the need to know where the enemy was outweighed the safety of the pilots. I looked into the sky and saw a biplane with two more trailing it. They were flying low to the ground, practically hopping over the hedges. I could hear them gunning their engines as they flew in near the treetops of the Bois du Biez.

The pilots must have confirmed the enemy's presence in the wood. I soon heard cannon fire to my rear, followed by explosions off beyond the tree line. It was sporadic for a few moments, and then trailed off entirely. There was an eerie stillness, and then I could hear some rifle fire and a machine gun tattering away in the distance. I heard the cranking of the telephone. The lieutenant was trying to raise command again.

"Yes, this is Lt. Rampkin again. Lt. Rampkin. Yes. I wanted to know when we're supposed to advance, sir. No, I can't get a good look at it from here, but there seems to be a machine gun at the bridge and at least a few riflemen at the tree line. Yes, sir, I can hear them, but it doesn't appear to be particularly organized. No, sir, I don't know where my flanks are. They're not advancing as quickly? How about the Indian units? I see."

The lieutenant didn't look too pleased.

"Yes, we'll hold here until the rest of the line is ready to advance. Do you have any idea of when that might be, sir? I understand. We'll wait on your word."

He handed the receiver back to the sergeant.

"Looks like we might be here for a minute more, lads," he said. "In the mean time, we're supposed to consolidate and hold. Have everyone find a firing position on the back of this trench in case of a counter-attack. They've never taken too long to regroup."

"Yes sir," the sergeant said, and turned to us. "Get up there and keep your eyes open. Shoot at anything that moves."

We followed his orders, and crawled up over the parados. There was a big, splintered beam lying there, and I inched in behind it. I had a good view of the bridge and wood from there. For now, the men operating the guns at the bridge weren't to be seen. That didn't mean they weren't there. They were probably hiding down below the sandbags, awaiting our approach. I had no respect for machine gunners. A dirty lot, they were.

I laid my rifle over the top and stared at the horizon. The attack could come now. It could come an hour from now. But I knew it would come eventually. We'd taken a big piece of land that they surely wanted back.

Yet afternoon came and there was still no attack, nor any word from command. I found it odd that men miles from our position were making decisions as to what we could or could not do. I saw a few more reconnaissance planes pass over. There were no signs of German planes.

For the time being, we were going nowhere, so the lieutenant told every other man to take a much-needed break. He said to go ahead and eat our iron rations. I was tired and hungry, and it tasted good. A warm meal would have been better, but under the conditions, I was grateful for what I had. Little did I realize that it was the first of probably a million cans of bully I would eat in the next two years. I grew to hate it.

It wasn't until nearly five o'clock that we got orders to move forward. I had been hoping quietly those orders wouldn't come, and I had become more and more hopeful as the day passed. Now, we faced an enemy that had been given five hours to get their defenses organized. I did not underestimate their abilities at this. Germans have a knack for getting things organized.

And if something wasn't done about the machine guns at the bridge, there would be a massacre. There was nothing but flat, open ground between them and us. It was a long way to go without any cover. It seemed an impossible demand. I wondered if we would take it or if our attempt would be in vain, and how many men would die either way.

CHAPTER 6

The telephone buzzed and the lieutenant answered. He listened for a moment.

"Understood, sir," he said, and hung up the receiver.

"The attack is at hand," he said. "The guns are ready to go. We'll wait for them, then take the bridge and push on toward the wood."

The lieutenant told me to find fellows with wire cutters, and rounding up a few, I took them back to him.

"You fellows will go right behind the grenadiers. We'll give you cover, but you must clear the way or we can't take that bridge."

There was some activity behind me and I turned to see that the sergeant had found his "volunteers" for the bombing aspect of our attack. They crowded in among us, staying low but ready. I decided not to follow them too closely on the way over. I was beginning to get the feeling that I shouldn't press my luck any further than I already had.

Nothing seemed right. The sunlight was waning and the air seemed to be getting colder. I was damp from rain on the outside and sweat on the inside. A steady, chilling breeze came in from the west. I was tired.

The trench began to get crowded as the rest of the advancing troops and carrying parties and engineers and stretcher-bearers and so on caught up to us. I was glad they had arrived, but it made me feel a bit entrapped. I didn't see any officers in the crowd, other than Lt. Rampkin. He was busy on the buzzer again.

A heavenly blessing came as we awaited the imminent barrage. There, coming up the trench, was a steaming, steel cauldron of tea. I could not believe my eyes. We held out our cups and inhaled the vapor.

"Glad to see you boys," Frank said.

"We had to move up," one of them said. "We're supposed to bring you a hot meal when you dig in for the night."

That gave me hope. If we could take the bridge, and establish a line at the wood, we would get hot food. Bread. Beans. Bacon. I didn't care what. It sounded like a good deal any way around it.

A cannon fired behind us, not as close as that morning but likely from somewhere in the village. The shell whizzed through the air, sounding like a toy whistle. It hit with a mighty bang in the field in front of the wood, sending up a column of dirt and black smoke. There was a pause, and then another fired. Then nothing.

"What's going on, lieutenant?" I asked.

"Those artillery blokes are trying to sight their guns," he said. "They take a few practice shots, and a spotter calls back with adjustments. They'll do this for a bit before really opening up."

I could hear them in the distance and then near. It was half past five, and the waiting agitated me further. But somehow, they managed to get through the lines with rum. It was doled out amply, and in what was becoming my usual style, I tossed it back in one gulp.

"No reason to fool around," Frank said, and did the same. "Ah, I think I feel the ice falling off my balls."

"That's hair growing," the sergeant said.

We all laughed at that one. I believe it was some sort of nervous response. I know I was scared to death, and I felt strange with a grin across my face. The thought crossed my mind right then that it might be the last time I would laugh. I got that doomed feeling again, and tried to shake off a shiver.

At about twenty to six the guns began their assault. It was neither as heavy nor as close-up as the morning's barrage. It seemed merciful by comparison. I could barely see beyond the bridge. But little beyond the bridge interested me. The hundred yards or so between where we were and the bridge and the machine guns on the other side. Those were my concerns. Nothing mattered beyond that.

There was a shriek overhead and a shell burst near the bridge redoubt. It was the first time I distinguished between a shrapnel-type shell and a high explosive shell. The shrapnel shell went off with a unique, piercing bang, almost a popping sound. They were trying to soften up the stronghold without destroying the bridge in the process. The high explosive shells, thunderous and mighty, were hitting farther away on targets I could not see.

The sergeant and the lieutenant were getting the ranks organized into single-file lines, with the wire-cutter men and grenadiers at the front. They crawled out of the trench, and we got in line behind them. My heart began pounding harder as the guns peaked.

A tap on my shoulder startled me, and I turned about. It was the lieutenant. He cupped his hand next to my ear.

"Get in the back of the line," he said. "I might need you if this doesn't work according to plan."

He pulled Frank, Simon and Pick out of line as well. They all looked a bit relieved, as I am sure I must have. We went to the back of the line with a shared sense of guarded optimism.

Naturally, that didn't last long. The German artillery, having been given plenty of time to get situated for our inevitable drive, began hitting us with counter fire. It wasn't heavy, but it was very accurate. One shell hit close enough that it knocked me off my feet. I landed on my ass in the mud next to Pick. I was still shaking my head when our guns fell silent. I stood and picked up my rifle.

"That's it?" I wondered.

"I guess it is," the lieutenant said.

A whistle blew farther down the line. The lieutenant joined in.

"Let's go, boys!" he shouted.

The first wave went over the top. The lieutenant scurried up the wall of the trench and found a vantage point. I heard a machine gun kick in, followed by another. A couple of bombs went off, and some of the men fired at the nests. The machine guns stopped and I could hear wailing.

The lieutenant cursed under his breath, and then blew his whistle again. Another group of men charged forward. There were more bombs and more machine gun fire. Then more wailing.

"Gardener!" the lieutenant shouted. "Get up here!"

I crawled up the back of the trench and lay on the ground next to the lieutenant. I looked out into the field beyond. It was dotted with bodies.

"Do you think you can hit them from here?" he asked.

"I don't know, sir," I said. "That's a long way off."

"Well, you're a better shot than anyone I know," he said. "When they show themselves again, I want you to give it a go. And don't shoot any of our boys in the back."

"I'll do my best, sir."

The lieutenant blew his whistle, and another line of men advanced onto the field. The machine guns swept across them, and the men who weren't hit outright went scurrying for the little cover to be offered. I got off two shots, but I couldn't be sure that I hit anything.

I could see a group of three grenadiers making their way across the field. The machine gunners saw them, too, and let them have it. That time, I managed to clip a man feeding one of the guns. It stopped long enough for the grenadiers to move even closer, and from there, they began their assault.

These blokes were much better than Smitty and the complainer. They hit the nests dead on, one bomb after another. When the smoke cleared, the guns were silent. The able men on the field advanced toward the bridge with ease.

The lieutenant slapped me on the shoulder, grinned, and stood up. He blew his whistle again, and waved us on. I stood and walked out into the field. There were dozens of dead soldiers, some who were hit within a few yards of the trench. There were a like number wounded, and stretcher-bearers came in behind us and began picking them up.

Frank, Pick and Simon caught up to me and we crossed the bridge together. I couldn't help wondering what kind of fish I might catch in that brook. I figured there were probably some pretty nice trout in there, and I wished I were there under different circumstances.

We moved on toward the wood without artillery support. The sun was getting low, and we started meeting heavy resistance from the tree line. It seemed unlikely that we would move much further before nightfall.

We got orders to dig in at our present position and prepare for a morning assault on the wood. We took our spades and dug into the ground about 18 inches before we hit water.

"Now what are we supposed to do?" Simon whined.

"Would you shut your mouth?" Pick replied.

A carrying party came by with the solution: a load of sandbags waiting to be filled. My arms and back ached as I shoveled. It must have been the cold. Frank was looking particularly miserable, and could barely lift the full bags by the time we were done.

When tea arrived, we had a three-foot breastwork built. While we ate a fine meal of roast beef and potatoes, engineers came by and strung two thin lines of barbed wire in front of our new trench.

"That isn't much of a defense," Frank said, talking with his mouth full.

"Maybe they'll get more by morning," I said. "I don't think they want us holding this line anyway. They want us to keep moving."

After dark we got hot tea and more ammunition. The lieutenant told us to divide into watches.

"I expect those of you not presently on watch to get some rest," he said. "We've got a long day ahead of us tomorrow. You'll feel a lot better if you sleep for a few hours."

Frank and I took the first watch while Simon and Pick rested. I don't think Pick got much sleep, if any. Simon, on the other hand, was snoring in ten minutes.

"You think we'll get to Lille tomorrow?" I asked Frank. I couldn't see his facial expression in the dark, but I could almost *hear* him smirk.

"What do you think?" he asked. "After what we've seen today? I'd say that's a fantasy. That's got to be 20 miles from here. We advanced maybe a half-mile since this morning. And that was with the advantage of surprise. But figuring we could move a half-mile a day, Lille is a month and a half away, old man."

I learned not to ask Frank questions like that. He wasn't one that constantly groused about everything like Simon, but he had a knack for predicting the absolute worst in any situation. The problem was that he was often right.

Like this time.

CHAPTER 7

The night became almost still. I'd hardly slept in two days, and yet I was wound tightly, every nerve aware. I could hear Jack's watch ticking in my breast pocket. I could hear voices in the darkness, and some of them weren't English. There were sounds of work accented by the occasional crack of a rifle.

A star shell popped overhead, and as my eyes had adjusted to the darkness, it nearly blinded me. I sat up and rubbed my eyes. I looked over at Frank. He had his cheek rested against his rifle, apparently focused on the tree line. The shell drifted down and went out. It was dark again.

"I'm going to piss," I said, slapping him on the shoulder. He didn't move. I slapped him again. He still didn't move.

"Frank, wake up." I shook him and he bolted upright. He looked around. He shook his head a few times and rubbed his eyes.

"I didn't know where I was for a second there," he said. "Crap. Still here."

"Keep your eyes open," I said, and went about my business. When I turned back, he was asleep again. I decided that I would wake him only if there was an attack, and stood watch alone until sometime after midnight, when I roused Simon and Pick for their turn. I sat with my back up against the sandbags and smoked a couple of cigarettes before fatigue set in and I drifted off.

I, too, dreamed that I was somewhere else, although I don't know where. Wherever I was, I was trying to get home and I couldn't find the train station. I walked until my legs wouldn't carry me. The dream left me uneasy when I awoke about an hour before dawn.

The lieutenant told us to expect a barrage at daybreak, after which we were to advance toward the Bois de Biez. Just as the sun began to show itself through the fog and mist, our guns started laying it down on the edge of the wood.

A lot of times in war, even with the best intelligence and so forth, it is that crucial bit of information you don't know that dooms you. What we didn't know at this point was that the Germans, in preparation for our attack, had moved out of the Bois de Biez and had established a new trench line about halfway between our line and the wood. They were always prepared, and usually wasted no time trying to find a more advantageous position from which to kill us. And since we didn't know this new line existed, neither did the artillery batteries behind us. The result was that our shells went sailing right over top of them, and hit where they weren't

The barrage lasted a mere fifteen minutes, and when we went over the top, we were greeted with a hail of bullets. In the dim light I could see hundreds of muzzle flashes up and down the field. We made it just a few yards before becoming hopelessly pinned down in the mud alongside men that died there the day before.

That was where we stayed for the rest of the day, lying there in the filth of battle, barely able to raise our heads without getting shot. The Germans had reinforced the line with the much-dreaded *minenwerfer*, a large-caliber mortar that fired shells at a high arc. They pounded us brutally. The only good side of this was that the shells left good craters for cover. But we were stuck there.

Reinforcements came up to the trench behind us and tried to make a breakthrough, but it never happened. The more we pushed, the more they laid on us. When the day came to an end, we'd taken just a few yards of ground, and about a third of the boys in our platoon were dead or wounded. We tried our best to get the ones we could move back to the trench, but the Huns cut down our stretcher men.

By nightfall, orders came up to fall back to our line and consolidate. Thus we gave up what yardage we'd taken, leaving behind a blood-soaked patch of ground that we'd paid so highly for. I cursed the Germans, and vowed that I would make them pay, too.

The situation got worse after sunset. The Huns knew we'd try and hit them again in the morning, so until after midnight, they hammered our line and the village behind us. The supply chain was broken, and we didn't get any hot food or tea or anything else. It was another meal of bully and biscuits, and predictably, Simon started grousing.

"I hate this shit," he said, setting down his tin. "I'm freezing and I need a warm meal. I'd eat just about anything right now. Anything other than this if it was hot."

"Would you eat a steaming dog turd off of a stick?" Frank asked him.

"What's that supposed to mean? What are you getting at?"

"Well, you said you'd eat anything right now that was warm, and I asked you if you'd eat a steaming dog turd off of a stick. That simple."

"Oh yeah?" he retorted, stammering for the right words. "And I suppose you would, wouldn't you?"

"Of course not."

Simon started cursing, then cut himself short. He got out his cigarettes and lit one, and stared at the ground. I could tell he was thinking hard. A few drags later an idea hit him. You could see it in his face.

"Well, would you eat the willy off a dead goat?" he said to Frank. There was a moment of silence, and then Frank busted up laughing.

"You're timing is a little off," he said, still chuckling, "but you're catching on. Pretty good one, old man."

Simon grinned big and basked in the moment, but his smile didn't last long.

"A hot meal would be really great, though," he said.

After tea we had a long night of digging, filling more sandbags, and ducking for cover. Our guns scarcely answered the German challenge. They seemed to have been better prepared for our surprise attack than we were.

Things got relatively quiet around two o'clock. The lieutenant came by, walking hunched over behind the protection of the sandbag revetment we'd built. In the sputtering light of a star shell I could see a bloody tear on his left shoulder.

"What happened lieutenant?" I asked.

"Just a scratch," he said. "I think I got clipped."

"Did you see a medic?"

"Medics are for men who are really hurt."

"A few more inches to the right and you'd be clicked," I observed.

"You can't think about that sort of thing. A few inches here, a few seconds there. It'll drive you insane, Gardener."

He asked me for a cigarette and a light, and crouched low behind the sandbags.

"I suspect they'll be probing our line now," he told me. "They'll be patrolling, looking for a weak spot. We're going to send out a couple of patrols along our wire just to make sure the Germans don't get too familiar. They'll be close in, but if you're not sure who's there, challenge them. They'll give you the password 'Piccadilly.' If you see anything out there that doesn't identify itself – a German, a dog, I don't care what – you shoot it, understood?"

"Understood, sir," I said.

"Split up into watches again," he said. "Try to get a little rest. I have a feeling tomorrow is going to be one long day. Again."

"Yes, sir."

Simon, of course, was already asleep.

CHAPTER 8

The much-awaited German counter attack began before dawn on the third day. I had my eyes on the wood, as they had been all night because I couldn't sleep. Pick was beside me, fidgeting and cursing for most of that night. We saw a flash of light behind the trees, followed closely by the sound of a cannon belching to life. There was a scream overhead, but before that first shell could hit, there were several more flashes and what sounded like rolling thunder.

"Get down!" the lieutenant yelled, and we covered our heads. Simon and Frank awoke when the first shell hit about fifty feet away. Pick started screaming and practically buried himself in the mud. I thought maybe he'd been hit with a piece of shrapnel, but he hadn't been. He was just scared out of his wits, the poor man.

"I think he's going to crap in his trousers again!" Simon yelled above the din of battle.

Having previously occupied the ground we now held, the Germans must have had excellent maps, because they hit us dead on despite the fog and the darkness. They weren't wasting any shells, of which they seemed to have plenty. Huge shells, too. I figured they must have spent the last two days bringing up the big guns just for this moment.

Our guns replied with a comparative whimper. There was very little outbound fire, just inbound. Where at first it all seemed the same to me, I began to distinguish between the two.

"What a gorgeous day!" Frank yelled into my ear as the cannonade reached a frightening new level. He was definitely loony.

The sun rose, but was masked behind the haze. As it inched up, several German Fokkers flew overhead, circled, and headed back toward Hun territory unchallenged. There was no sign of our planes.

The aerial observers must have called in a favorable report via wireless, and the German guns fell silent almost in unison. The lieutenant blew his whistle.

"They'll be coming across now!" he shouted. "Stand to! Stand to!"

I wiped the mud off my face, turned and laid my rifle upon the sandbag wall. Simon was on my left and Frank was on my right. Pick was still lying in the mud with his head covered. The lieutenant saw this and came running over with his head down. He slapped Pick on the back of the head and knocked his cap off.

"I said stand to!" he shouted, drawing his Webley. "That means you!"

Pick rolled over. There were tears running over his muddy face. The lieutenant grabbed Pick's rifle and dropped it on his lap.

"Now fight or I'll shoot you myself!"

He took his rifle and crawled in beside Frank. Simon started saying something to him, but I paid it no attention, for at that moment, I saw a whole line of roaring, gray-clad men rising from the trench halfway across the field. Our machine guns kicked in. The fight was on.

I looked through my sights. Our machine gunners cut down many of the attackers, but about half of them continued their charge on our line. I picked one and drew a bead on his chest. The rifle kicked against my shoulder and my Hun fell. I shot several more before the Germans were pinned down in the mud. I had emptied my magazine and rolled over to put in a new clip. Frank was doing the same.

"I shot two of those buggers," he said, wiping his brow.

"I got a couple of them, too," I said. I pushed the clip down through the receiver, worked the bolt and rolled over again to look at the field. Another wave of Germans hopped up from their trench and headed across. This time they got much closer than before, and started bombing our machine gun emplacements. They must have been pretty good, because in a matter of minutes our machine guns stopped, and a third wave made for our line. It looked like an entire regiment was headed straight for us.

"Fix bayonets!" Hendershot yelled.

"Bloody sods!" Simon yelled as he attached his sticker on the end of his rifle. "I'll kill all of you!"

We couldn't hold them this time, despite our best efforts. They got closer, close enough that I could make out their faces. The next thing I knew, they were on top of us. Red distress flares shot up to my left and right. They crossed our thin line of wire and poured into our trench. From there, it was total chaos, with each man fighting his own battle.

A Hun leapt over the revetment in front of me, and I jabbed him with my bayonet on his way across. He hit the ground and I pulled it out. I pointed my gun at his head and pulled the trigger, but nothing happened. I had run out of ammo in all of the excitement and didn't even know it. So I ran him through again.

I looked up and there were Germans everywhere. Pick and Frank were stabbing with their bayonets, and Simon had lost his in one, so he commenced to swing his rifle like a club. I guess I was paying too much attention to everyone else, because I was blind-sided and knocked to the ground. I dropped my rifle. I looked up

59

and a German was about to stab me. I instinctively picked up a spade that was lying on the ground and swung it at my enemy. I got him sideways on his knee and he was down. I rolled over and hit him in the face with my spade. It split his head wide open.

I managed to get up and I saw another German coming at me across the sandbags. He leapt over, and I knocked his rifle aside with the spade. Then I kicked him right in the balls with all my might. I clubbed him again when he hit the ground. I realized I was yelling at the top of my lungs. I turned and hit another German in the neck with the edge of the spade. I nearly took his head clean off. Blood squirted across my face.

This melee went on for about a minute, probably not even that long, but it seemed like hours. I heard a machine gun firing again. There were dead and wounded Germans all up and down the line. The ones that were left standing started hollering at each other. I turned and looked out at the field, and saw the enemy was falling back. They were abandoning the assault. I threw down my spade and picked up my rifle. I slammed in a new clip and shot three of them in the back as they tried to get home.

Everything stopped for a moment and I could hear Simon cursing unintelligibly. He had one last German on the ground and he wasn't going to let him get away. Simon was kicking him with everything he had, and beating him about the head with his rifle butt.

"*Bitte*," the German was crying. "*Nein!*"

Simon kept beating him anyway. Frank was watching with a look of horror on his face.

"I don't think he's a threat now, Simon," Frank said. "That's enough."

Simon kept beating the man. Frank stepped over and put his hand on Simon's shoulder. He jumped and spun around. There was a cut across his cheek and blood splattered on his face. He had a wild look in his eyes. He let out a mighty war cry.

"That sod tried to kill me!" Simon screamed.

"Well, he's done for now," Frank said. "We'll take him prisoner."

"Bugger off, Frank," Simon said. "This Boche is on his way to the devil!"

He put a new clip in his rifle, worked the action and put it to the German's head.

"*Nein! Nein! Bitte!*" he pleaded.

Simon paid no attention and pulled the trigger. His head practically exploded. Simon cocked the bolt again and put it to the man's chest.

"It's over, Simon," I said. "It's all right. He's done for."

Simon looked up and wiped his face. He looked at the blood on his hands and slid down the back of the revetment onto the ground. He wiped his forehead and rubbed his eyes. When he looked up at me, I could see tears streaking through the filth on his cheeks. I sat down beside him and put my arm around his shoulders. He started sobbing.

I looked up and down the line. There were bodies everywhere. The ground and the sandbags were awash in blood. It was raining again, and the puddles were crimson.

"Stand to!" the lieutenant was calling. "They'll probably try again! Stand to!"

I picked my rifle up out of the mud. There was a lot of fog and smoke, and I could barely make out the enemy line. There were a few shots fired here and there, but nothing was moving out front.

That didn't last long, however. The Germans gave us some more punishment with artillery and mortars, and about thirty minutes after the initial drive, made another attempt to take our line. We stopped them, and then they repeated the process again. And again.

Somehow, the four of us survived that day, and when dusk came, the Germans gave up. I started counting bodies that I could see in between the lines, but I stopped at a hundred. I had lost count of the number that were mine. I just didn't want to think about it anymore.

That night, we got a hot meal, a double rum ration, tea and more ammunition. Reinforcements came up with the carrying parties, and we spent the night sleeping in shifts and improving our defenses.

The fight that would become known as the Battle of Neuve Chapelle was over after three days. In all, we had pushed the Germans back 1,200 yards on a two-mile front. For that piece of territory, we paid a horrible price; I found out later that there were about 30,000 British boys killed or wounded.

We were nowhere close to Lille or even the Aubers Ridge, as had been the plan. Those objectives were still miles away. And how far beyond was Berlin? I didn't know, and I didn't want to know.

If there were any glory in war, I certainly hadn't seen any, and I wasn't in any hurry to try and find it. I was tired. I wanted a hot bath and a warm place to sleep. I wanted to go home.

CHAPTER 9

We stayed at our position outside of Neuve Chapelle for more than a fortnight, rotating between the front line and the reserve line behind the brook. We dug new trenches and strung barbed wire by the mile. On the days we were supposed to rest, Staff Sgt. Hendershot would round us up for some kind of work detail, usually carrying supplies from the nearest railhead to the front.

There was a monumental amount of supplies that had to be brought in each day. A single soldier's daily rations were: 1-1/4 pounds of fresh or frozen meat, or one pound of bully; 1-1/4 pounds of bread, or one pound of biscuits or flour; four ounces of bacon; three ounces of cheese; 5/8-ounce of tea; four ounces of jam; three ounces of sugar; ½ ounce of salt; 1/36 ounce of pepper; 1/20 ounce of mustard; a half-pound of fresh vegetables or a pound of dried vegetables; 1/10 gill of lime juice if vegetables were not available, to prevent scurvy; ½ pint of rum; and two ounces of tobacco per week. In addition, that one soldier would use about 40 pounds of other supplies daily. That amounts to nearly 30 rail cars filled with supplies for every division of 17,000 men, and there were several of these holding the line in our sector. There were few vehicles in use by the army at that time, so the need for carrying parties never ceased.

The good side of it was that it left us little time to get restless or bored. When we did have a few moments of peace, Frank always pulled out a deck of cards to show us some tricks. He must have known about a million of them, all sleight of hand without using any special trick decks. It was amazing.

There were a lot of new words we learned from the old-timers at the front, what few of them were left. A lot of this slang was based on foreign words: "buckshee," meaning "free," came from the Indian troops, as did "barndook," which meant "rifle." "Lousy" referred to infestation with lice, but could be used to convey that there was a lot of something bad, as in, "That ridge is lousy with snipers." But probably the most widely used words in the trench-slang vocabulary were those that had to do with death. The most common was "napoo," which meant "dead" or "finished." It came from the French phrase, "*il n'y en a plus*," or "there is no more." To "get clicked" or "go west" also meant, "to die."

We fell into a fairly standard routine. When we were in the front line -- the "fire trench" -- the day revolved around sunrise and sunset, the two most likely times for an attack. In the morning we would have stand-to, when every available man would stand

and await dawn with his rifle pointed at Fritz. When the sun came up, we would give him the "mad minute," with each man firing 15 rounds in rapid succession. I always tried to aim at something specific, but a lot of the fellows just slammed the bolt and fired wildly in the general direction.

Once we woke up Fritz, we would settle in for roll call and breakfast, which usually meant bully and biscuits, hot tea, and a rum ration. It wasn't very appetizing first thing in the morning, and on many days, we'd have the same thing for lunch and dinner. It was enough to break your heart.

After breakfast came sentry duty or a work detail. We added new communication trenches, machine gun nests, steel sniping loupes in the sandbag walls and drainage ditches in the bottom of the trenches, with planks called duckboards covering them over. These duckboards were better than standing in the mud, but they got really slippery if wet. We fixed this by nailing chicken wire across them when it was available.

We also excavated dugouts below the back of the trenches, in which we could hide if we came under artillery fire. We lined them with wood, installed benches and bunks, and covered them over with corrugated steel and a double-layer of sandbags. The lieutenant said they would withstand anything aside from a direct hit from a siege howitzer, but I didn't want to find out if he was right or not.

The Germans apparently had their own routines to follow. They generally let us eat breakfast in peace, probably because that was when they ate as well. It was sort of understood by both sides that nobody tried anything during that time, unless there were Prussians across the way. Their harassment never ended. You could always tell when they were there. But Prussian or not, they would hit us with artillery and mortar fire at about 10 o'clock. Some days it was a couple of shells, and some days it was a hundred, but it always happened every day. So just before ten, we'd head into the dugout and wait for it to start.

I had already learned the difference in the sound of an inbound shell versus that of one flying toward the Germans, which meant I only had to duck about half of the time. Then I began to distinguish which ones were coming in close, and what type of shell it was. The most common one we called a whiz-bang, because it came through the air with a whizzing sound, followed by a sharp bang. Others sounded like gurgling water, slide whistles or steam whistles. My own philosophy on shells in general helped me get through all of this; I believed that if I got hit with a shell, I probably wouldn't know it anyway, so there was no point in worrying about it.

63

We all caught on to this pretty fast, except for Pick, who dove for cover no matter what, and was always the last one to come out of the dugout when it was over. His nerves just didn't have the strength that the rest of ours did, and we all realized he was suffering because of it. Even Simon quit picking on him after a while.

After our daily shelling we would come out of our holes and figure out what we needed to repair. Keeping the telephones working was a never-ending nightmare. There were miles and miles of cables and the shells always cut them in several places. And trench walls always needed to be shored up, sandbags replaced, and so forth. So we spent most every morning working on these kinds of things.

About noon, we would break for lunch, and like at breakfast time, we had a general understanding with the Germans that no one would attack during that time. On a good day, we'd get fresh bread, cheese, or maybe some stew. But a lot of days, there was only bully and biscuits.

After lunch, we'd have what was known as a "shirt hunt." That was when we sat around and picked lice out of our clothes. Millions of them. We'd snap them between our fingernails or flick them onto a burner made out of an empty bully tin and a candle. Then we would take the candle and run the flame along the seams of our clothes to kill the eggs. This usually took about an hour every day, but you'd find just as many the next day and the day after that.

In the afternoon, we'd continue on work detail until tea. It was usually a more substantial meal than the others. Carrying parties would come up with steaming dixies full of soup or stew and either coffee or tea. Sometimes we got potatoes, steaks, roast beef, sausages, and maybe even some Yorkshire pudding. But then sometimes we had to make due with bully and biscuits. I haven't eaten bully since I got out of the army, and I probably never will.

At sundown we'd have a second stand-to, but without the mad minute. Sentries were posted for the night, while those that worked during the day got a chance to sleep. Others got assigned work details that could only be completed at night, like stringing wire. That was a terrible job. You had to go out into No Man's Land, and pound in steel pickets and unroll wire. You had to be dead quiet, so we would use empty sandbags to muffle the sound of our mallets. If the Germans knew you were out there, they'd cut down on you with a machine gun, and you could be stuck on your belly for hours. And you always prayed that the boys in your own trench knew you were out there, because they might shoot you otherwise.

There were also nighttime patrols. Fritz liked to work at night too, so we had to go out in front of the wire to be sure he stayed on his side of the field. So naturally, he sent out patrols as well. Occasionally the patrols would come into contact and commence firing at one another. Then it was a struggle to get back behind the wire before dawn, lest you be stuck out there in broad daylight.

I'll never forget the first time I had to go out on patrol. Frank and I, along with two other riflemen and two bombers I didn't know, were assigned to go with Sgt. Ellenwood, a lanky fellow from Bristol. He was a capable leader and I was glad to be with him. There wasn't any moon, which was good, but I could barely see my hand in front of my face. We crawled out a sap that went under the wire. At the end of the sap there was a wooden frame with wire laced across it, designed to keep the entrance safe from raiders. We lifted it like a cellar door and emerged into the killing zone.

Never in my life have I felt more naked and unprotected than when I stood up and looked into the darkness, not knowing what could be hiding within, and definitely knowing there was nothing between us and the Germans but open space. I could hear the usual work noises, along with hushed voices, some in English and some not. Ellenwood tapped me on the shoulder and motioned for me to fall in behind him. I had to stay close or risk getting lost in the night. And No Man's Land was no place for that.

We stumbled along, trying to avoid shell holes and other obstacles. My eyes adjusted well enough that by starlight, I could see twenty feet or so in any direction. There was a cold trickle of sweat running down my temple. If we had actually stumbled across the enemy, I don't know what I would have done. We did have a bit of a scare, though, when the Germans fired a star shell into the air. We dove into the nearest crater just as machine gun bullets came ripping across the ground. They weren't shooting at random; they knew we were there, and were determined to get us. They fired more star shells and machine gun rounds, and we were stuck there for the better part of an hour or maybe longer before they lost interest. We moved on.

About two we turned and made our return sweep. I had gotten confident for some reason, assured in my mind that danger had passed us by for the night. I wasn't paying real close attention to where I was walking, and I tripped over something lying on the ground. My foot got stuck. I squinted my eyes and looked down to find that I had stepped on a rotting corpse, and my boot was lodged in the rib cage. I tried to shake it loose, which agitated it and made the smell worse. I couldn't get my boot out.

"Gardener," Ellenwood hissed as he passed me. "Quit mucking about and get moving!"

I stabbed the corpse with my bayonet and finally wrangled my foot free. I jogged to catch up to Frank and the others.

We found our sap somehow and after Ellenwood gave the password, they let us back inside. I went down the trench to our dugout. There was a faint light coming from behind the canvas tarp we were using for a door, and I could smell coffee brewing. I pushed back the curtain and stepped inside the bunker. Simon and Pick were playing a hand of nap at a makeshift table fashioned out of bully crates. Simon turned around.

"You'll never believe what happened to me," I said, and Simon cut me off.

"What on earth is that smell?" he asked. "What's that muck on your leg?"

I looked down, and in the dim light of the kerosene lantern I saw them: maggots by the dozen, big and fat from feasting on rotting human flesh. I was glad my puttees kept them from crawling up my trouser leg.

I stared in disbelief, and then went back outside. My skin was crawling. I took a deep breath to calm the onset of nausea, but I just got a better whiff of the goo. I took my bayonet off of my rifle and used it to scrape what I could off of my leg. I held my guts down, but it was a close one.

The first week of April we got word that we were going to rest billets in the rear, but I refused to believe it until we were actually on the move. It was a Sunday morning and the chaplain had been by for a bit. We followed our normal routine, and I was cleaning my canteen cup after breakfast when our replacements arrived. There was a short briefing between the lieutenants, and we were off.

New trenches ran from our position all the way back through the village. We passed the cross with the shell imbedded in the side. It was still standing, yet the buildings that had been standing when we came through before were now reduced to piles of rubble. The trenches got wider and straighter as we moved back, and were deeper than the breastwork defenses that we'd held for more than two weeks. Our boys were now using the captured German lines as a defensive position. They had improved them greatly, using timbers and bricks from the wreckage to shore up the sides and construct proper parapets. We crossed what used to be No Man's Land, past the place where Jack had been killed. It reminded me to post his watch back home, which I would do later that day, with a short note detailing his bravery under fire.

About a mile past Neuve Chapelle we found our billet. It was an old barn with rows of triple bunks built inside. Our unit designation was written on the door in chalk. Frank found a piece of chalk lying there, and wrote beneath our number, "What's left of us."

We picked bunks back away from the door, near a wood-burning stove, and dumped our gear. A delousing station had been set up in a nearby building, and we wasted no time getting into the queue, which stretched out the door. We stripped down to our underwear and left our crusty, stained uniforms lying in a pile outside. Inside, a corporal took our underwear, and we waited, shivering and naked, for our turn. They had a large vat of warm water with delousing compound mixed in. There were three steps up, and we went in one at a time and scrubbed off, paying particular attention to our hair and privates. Then we climbed into a second vat of soapy water and washed again. We didn't get much time to get clean, as everyone was yelling for us to hurry up.

I got out of the water and dried off with a towel that was too small and too thin. A fellow with a can of cootie powder doused us down, front and back, and handed us fresh, clean underwear. It felt wonderful against my skin.

Outside was a row of spigots, tubs and washboards for cleaning our uniforms. I beat my tunic and pants against the wall, knocking off as much dirt and dust as possible. I scrubbed until my hands cramped, then rinsed and wrung everything. We went back to the barn in our boots and underwear, carrying our wet clothes. We hung them on the rafters to dry.

We got a mail delivery when we returned to our billet. Everyone was happy to get letters from home, especially Frank. There were five letters for him, all from the same woman. Simon got two from his parents. I got one from Rose, who seemed to be quite worried about me and the other boys. She promised to say a prayer for me every morning and every night until I got to go home. It made me feel better, and I hoped it would make her feel better, too.

That afternoon I found a stack of yellowed newspapers left under one of the bunks by the previous occupants. We hadn't seen any papers in a while, so we sat there smoking cigarettes, catching up on what had happened in England in our absence. We read and enjoyed the silence.

"My word," Frank said after a few minutes. "Look at this."

He handed me a London paper from March 14. The headline declared, "British Smash Germans at Neuve Chapelle." The story said we took all of our objectives with "only light casualties." The German casualty figures weren't given for comparison, but still it concluded that we had "dealt a decisive blow" against the Boche. Some general I had never heard of was quoted as saying that the Germans would soon be defeated entirely.

"I had no idea it went so jolly good for us," I said. "I wonder what the general would consider to be heavy casualties."

"It makes it sound like a walk in the park," Frank said. "They couldn't be talking about the same battle. It doesn't say anything in here about Fritz's counterattack. This is tripe. To hell with it."

The story was inflated, but it didn't upset me as much as it did Frank. I was just happy that I had survived and had something to read, and a warm, dry place to read it. I sat there the rest of that afternoon reading, and it made me feel closer to home, something that I hadn't felt in a while. I read until the light got too dim. It was time for tea, so I roused Frank. I grabbed the paper about our battle and took it with me to show the others over dinner. Some of the men beamed with pride after reading it, while many others sided with Frank. Some laughed out loud.

"The folks back home think we're heroes," Pick said, grinning broadly.

"Well," Simon said, "some of us are heroes and some of us aren't."

"What's that supposed to mean?" Pick retorted.

"You did a pretty good job of filling your trousers…" Simon said, but Frank cut him off before he could finish.

"I think anyone who survived that mess is a hero," he said. "A hero to himself, to his wife and family, to his brothers and sisters and to his friends. I'm just glad I'm here now, eating this sorry excuse for food and reading these lying newspapers. I'm alive, and that's all that matters to me. It should be all that matters to you, too."

The next morning at roll call, we got a visit by a colonel from headquarters. He returned the lieutenant's salute and gave us a quick inspection, nodding his head in approval. Then I got a surprise.

"Private Gardener, front and center," the lieutenant said. I got a knot in my stomach and my mouth dried up. I stepped out of line and walked to the front, squaring my turns like a smart soldier and standing as tall as I could. What did I do wrong? I stopped in front of the lieutenant and colonel and turned left to face them. We exchanged salutes.

"Private Gardener," the colonel said, "for your instrumental role in clearing our way through Neuve Chapelle, and your excellent marksmanship, I present you with the Distinguished Conduct Medal."

He pinned it to my chest above my breast pocket, then extended his hand. I shook it, and we all exchanged salutes again. I turned and as I walked back to my place in line, I could see the boys grinning broadly. I stood in my spot quietly. I hadn't planned on winning a medal, and I knew they would tease me about it. When we were dismissed, a few of the boys came by to chuck me on the shoulder and offer their "attaboys." Pick pumped my hand vigorously.

"I just met my first certified hero of the war," he said with a toothy smile. "The fellows back at the mine will be excited to hear about this. I wish your dad were still with us. He'd be proud of you, Richard."

I laughed and tried not to let it go to my head. I was proud, but I didn't think the medal made me anything more than I was when I came to France. And I wasn't in a hurry to win any more of them.

As we disbursed, I got my second surprise of the day.

"Gardener and Thomas, stick around," the lieutenant said. "I need to talk with both of you."

"What have you gotten us into?" Frank muttered. "You and your senseless valor."

"I don't know. I don't have any idea."

"I hope it's not latrine duty. I can't take that today."

"I promise it's not latrine duty," the lieutenant said as he walked over. He must have ears like a beagle, I thought.

"Here's the situation," he said. "As you are aware, I'm sure, we lost a lot of men up the line: a lot of good ones, especially among our NCOs. A number of corporals and sergeants didn't make it back. Some of those lads had been with me as long as Hendershot."

"My point is this," he continued. "We have to install some new NCOs because we have replacements coming up in the next two weeks. They'll be green, fresh out of school or younger. They'll need help settling in, learning how to survive. They'll need direction. I thought you two could handle the responsibility."

We looked at each other, and then looked at the lieutenant. We didn't say anything.

"So," he said, reaching into his pocket, "here are your stripes. You've both been promoted to lance corporal. Congratulations. I know I can count on you."

We exchanged salutes and shook hands and so on, and the lieutenant left with the colonel. Frank and I just stood there for a second, looking at our new insignias. I didn't know what to say. We walked back to the barn.

"Well," Frank finally said, "this ought to be good for a lot of headaches. That and a few extra pence a month."

I still didn't have anything to say. Frank's pessimism dampened my enthusiasm, but I walked a bit taller nonetheless. My father *would* have been proud. Still, I knew that Frank's sour predictions usually came to pass. I cursed under my breath.

I took the medal off of my tunic and had a good look at it. It had the king on the front, and the words, "For Distinguished Conduct in the Field" on the back. It was attached to a ribbon a little over an inch wide, with a silver bar at the top. I rubbed it with my thumb and put it in my pocket.

Despite his negative perception of the situation at hand, Frank must have written ten letters home about our adventures so far. He wrote one to his girl in London, Lizzy, that was so long he had a hard time fitting it into the envelope.

"She'll never believe this," he said. "I told her about your medal. She'll be excited to know my best friend is a war hero."

Best friend. No one had ever called me that, not even Simon, who I'd known since I was a kid. But I figured if I were to have a best friend in France, Frank was a better one than most.

"So how does it feel, Lance Corporal Gardener?" he prodded. "The newspapers want to know!"

"It feels bloody lovely," I said, struggling to sew my stripes on. "Leave out the 'bloody' part if you're writing to a lady."

I didn't know anything about sewing, but they looked pretty good once I was done.

"I'll give you a tin of fags to do mine," Frank said.

"No thank you. My fingers feel like pin cushions."

"How about two tins of fags?"

"Where are you going to come up with two tins of fags?"

"I don't think that's the issue."

"Forget it," I said with a laugh. "Sew your own."

"All right. I'll do it myself. If you want to use my pad and pencil to write home, help yourself."

"That's all right."

"Mother? Father?"

"No, they're not around anymore. But maybe I'll write to my sister."

"What about a girl? A fellow as handsome as you must have a girl."

"No, there's no girl."

"Well, we'll do something about that when we get back to Blighty. I'll introduce you to some of London's finest, I promise."

"Sounds like a great time to me."

"We'll get blind, stinking pissed, and chase girls all over town."

He did his sewing, and I wrote a short note to Rose, telling her I was alive and doing fine. I told her that I would like to see her upon my return, and that I loved her. I also decided to write a letter to Jack's wife. I told her he died bravely, and that I was sorry I couldn't do anything to save him. I enclosed his watch and the letter in an envelope, then folded it and put inside a second envelope so that the watch would be protected. When I was done writing, I polished my boots. They were already showing signs of wear, but they were comfortable. I was lucky. Most of the men could barely stand theirs.

Frank and I talked late into the evening about what we wanted to do when we got back home. All I could think of was getting back to South Yorkshire and finding a job that didn't involve digging anything. I'd already had enough of that. Maybe I'd work in a steel mill in Sheffield. Frank had much bigger plans that involved traveling the globe and opening his own theater in London's West End. Live magic four nights a week, he said.

"That sounds fantastic," I said.

"It's dreaming is what it is. I think I'll just be happy to get back in one piece. Living through this might be enough adventure for a lifetime."

Our replacements arrived the second week of April. Although I'd only been in France a matter of weeks myself, they seemed so young and naïve, most of them around 18 or 19 years old. We were already old-timers. We would teach them how to stay alive. That was the only comfort we could offer.

They piled into the barn until it was full, and the rest moved on somewhere else. Two of the boys gave Frank and I the once-over before taking the bunks next to us. One was tall with fair hair, and the other was about average size, ruddy-faced with messy brown curls. They dumped their packs, took their boots off and gingerly examined their blisters. One offered the other a cigarette and they both lit up.

"Hey, mate," Frank said, pointing at the tall one. "Aren't you going to share? We always share up here."

He looked at Frank half puzzled, half scared. He held out his Woodbines, and Frank took one for me and one for himself. Then he took a third one and put it behind his ear for later. He was one bold fellow.

"I'm Lance Corporal Thomas," he said, emphasizing his new rank. "And this is Lance Corporal Gardener."

Frank blew a perfect smoke ring. It impressed both the replacements and me. He took another drag.

"Who are you?" Frank asked, with smoke coming out of his mouth.

"I'm Andreson, and this is Potts," the tall one said. "We just got to France a week ago. We've been marching ever since."

"No joking," Frank said. "So how are things in Blighty?"

"Splendid."

"What are people saying about the war these days?"

"Most people say it will be over by summer," Potts said. "We decided to join while there was still time."

"Did you hear that Richard? We're going to go home soon!"

"You don't say," I replied. "I'm glad to hear that. It sure makes a fellow feel better."

It took the boys a minute to catch on to our sarcasm, and then they smiled meekly. Potts looked kind of sick.

"Have you two been in since the beginning?" Andreson asked.

"No," I said, "and there aren't too many left who were, other than the lieutenant and Staff Sgt. Hendershot. We got here just in time for the last round, being the lucky sods we are."

"Where did you fight?" Potts asked eagerly.

"Just up the line," I said. "In Neuve Chapelle."

They both looked excited.

"I heard that was a tremendous victory," Potts said.

"Yes, that's what we heard, too," Frank said. He blew another ring into the air. There was a nervous pause.

"That must have been magnificent, teaching those Germans a lesson."

"Well, it wasn't," I said. "We lost a lot of good men up there."

"How many is a lot?" Andreson asked.

"Count the number you came up here with," Frank said. "That's about how many."

"I can't wait to have a crack at the Boche," Andreson said. I theorized that he was the one that talked Potts into joining up.

"You'll get your chance," Frank said. "Sooner rather than later now that the weather is warm. And it won't be a walk in the park, either. I couldn't care less if I never saw another Hun. Ever. How about you, Richard?"

"As far as I'm concerned, they can stay on their side of the line and I can stay on mine. I'd be a lot happier that way."

"That from the mouth of a war hero," Frank said, but I wished he hadn't, as this excited the boys even more. "He's even got a medal to prove it."

"What did you win? What did you do?" Andreson asked. He could hardly contain himself. A few more of the new boys had drifted over to listen. I suddenly felt as if I were on stage.

"I didn't do anything more than I was supposed to do," I said. "I just happened to do it in front of the lieutenant."

"Well, there's got to be more to it than that," Andreson said.

"Go on Richard," Frank said with a grin. "Tell all."

I told them about the sniper in the village, and tried to explain how I spotted him. I figured there might be something in there that these boys might use later. Then I told them about taking the

72

machine gun nest. The crowd grew and I passed my medal around.

"I'm going to get a whole box full of these," one boy said. "I'm going to send them all back to my girl, and we're going to have a baby for each one when I get home."

The replacements wanted to know all kinds of things about life in the line. We felt obliged to answer their questions, as no one had told us anything before we went up there.

"How's the food?" one boy asked.

"It's excellent," Frank said, "if you like cold bully beef and biscuits. That's about all you get in the line. The food back here is better. There's more of it, and it's always hot. You'll learn to eat anything if it's hot, even look forward to it."

There was some joking about the food and I could see the boys were starting to relax a little. They followed us over to the field kitchens in a single-file line, like ducklings following their mother. We ate our dinner, then laid back on the ground under a tree, staring at the sky. There was a breeze blowing from the north and the sun was low but shining. Frank got out his deck of cards and did a few tricks for the new boys, who were sitting there with us. They watched him, stupefied, until a squad of Fokkers flew overhead unchallenged, and that gave us a new topic to discuss.

"What do you think they're doing up there?" Potts wondered.

"Having a good look at you, I'd imagine," Frank said. "They want to know if we've got anything brewing back here. Like new replacements."

Potts got that sick look again.

"I hadn't thought of that," he said.

It was almost dark and we were heading back to the barn when a staff car came careening up the road at full throttle. It slid to a halt in the middle of the compound. A sergeant leaped out of the door.

"Where's headquarters?" he yelled at Andreson.

"I don't know," he said. "I just got…"

"Where the hell is headquarters?" he yelled again.

"You'll find everyone in the chateau a quarter of a mile up the road," I said.

"I'm glad at least someone knows what's going on," he said, and jumped back into the car. It spit gravel tearing away in the direction I'd given.

"What was that about?" Potts said with a dumb look on his face. It was a good look for him, I decided.

"God only knows," I said. "God only knows."

We went back to the barn and I sat down on my bunk. Frank was agitated. He sat next to me for maybe a minute, sucking down a cigarette. Then he stamped it out and started getting his pack together.

"What's going on?" I asked.

"I've got a bad feeling about this," he said. "Get your gear ready."

"What are you talking about? What are you doing?"

"Just get your kit organized and..."

Hendershot came crashing through the door and cut him off.

"Pack up lads!" he shouted. "We're moving out in ten minutes!"

"What's going on?" I asked.

"German devils," he said. "They pulled a stunt and a half up north of here on a bunch of Canadians and Frenchmen. Hit them with some kind of gas. All hell's breaking loose. There's a hole in the line, and we have to go plug it up."

"Where…"

"You'll find out soon enough. Now get ready! You've got seven minutes!"

We assembled outside with our packs and rifles. Officers were trying to find their NCOs, and the NCOs were trying to find their men. And in the middle of this were the poor replacements! They had been walking for days and needed a rest, but they would not get any.

We marched in close order, heading north by northwest by Pick's reckoning. At first, the road was good, but the farther we went the worse it got. It had been shelled all to pieces and wasn't worth spit to walk on, especially in the dark. Several long columns of lorries, ambulances, and other assorted vehicles passed us in the night, dodging the holes and giving us a little light to see by.

We covered about 10 miles before midnight, I figured, with Simon griping the entire time. We arrived at a railhead where there was complete chaos. The station platform was strewn with dead and wounded and there were red rivulets running over the concrete. There were men with horrible wounds and some with missing limbs, some lucky to be comatose from the pain, some struggling in wide-eyed horror. A couple of the new boys lost their dinner right there. Potts stayed cool until one of the mangled men grabbed his leg.

"Help me!" he begged. "Help me, please." His eyes were bandaged and he had a tremendous chest wound. He grabbed Potts tighter.

"I can't help you," he said. "I'm sorry."

He tried to pry the man's hand off of his leg. I could see tears forming in his eyes.

74

"The doctor said he'll be over to you next," I said, helping Potts break free. "Hold on for a few more minutes."

"It will be all right?" the wounded man asked.

"Yes," I said, my voice cracking. "It will be just fine."

"I've got to get home…"

He trailed off and shut his eyes. Potts wiped the tears from his cheeks.

"Come on," I said. "He'll be fine. Let's go."

Potts walked behind me to the end of the platform. He didn't say anything more about the wounded man, and neither did I. I've tried to forget about him for more than 30 years, but I haven't been able to yet. I sometimes wonder if he made it, but I'm pretty sure he didn't.

The lieutenant was waiting beside the tracks with instructions.

"Gardener," he said, "you and Thomas take your men down the track to an empty car. Stay in the car until I give you orders to do otherwise. I'm counting on you."

About twenty of the new boys followed us in the darkness for about 100 yards until we found one. We piled in, and sat on our packs with our rifles between our knees. There were pools of blood all over the floor, and it smelled like horses had been in there. We sat there for about two hours before the train pulled out. I slid the door shut. The only light inside was from glowing cigarettes. We picked up speed. Everyone was silent. The only sound was the steel wheels rolling on the tracks.

I was a nervous wreck, so I could only imagine how the new boys felt. Frank wasn't his cool self, either. He sat next to me, smoking one cigarette after another. It was odd for him to be so edgy.

I could see the dim dawn light coming through a small window in the upper corner of the car, and I was getting to where I had to piss very badly when the train came to a stop. Frank stood up, hoisted his pack and slung his rifle. We all did the same. The door slid open, and the lieutenant was standing there to meet us as we climbed down.

The scene at this station was worse than the last. Dead men and pieces of men were in a great heap at one end. There were dead and wounded men laying atop each other all over the platform, and blood covered the ground, the walls, everything. These men were the ones that were too bad off to make the trip down the tracks. I could smell blood, sewage and death.

"Welcome to Wipers," a corpsman said to me as he hoisted a stretcher case. "Welcome to bloody hell."

75

CHAPTER 10

There were quiet sectors -- *bonne* sectors we called them – and there were hot sectors where there always seemed to be trouble. Then there was Wipers. It was a uniquely horrible place to be.

Wipers was what Tommy called the section of line around the Belgian town of Ypres along the Yprelee River. In the Middle Ages, Ypres was known across Europe for its excellent hand-woven cloth, and the English besieged it unsuccessfully during the Hundred Years' War. But like me, most of the Englishmen who arrived there had never heard of it, and were equally unfamiliar with the proper pronunciation of its name. So they called it Wipers.

Ypres was surrounded by ramparts and defensive works designed by the French military architect Vauban. There were remnants of its medieval past; the old infantry barracks was on the south side, and the prison, water tower and reservoir were on the north side. The tallest buildings were the Cloth Hall, a vestige of the cloth industry built in 1214, and the Cathedral of St. Martin across the street, also built in the 13th Century. Both of the buildings could be seen from miles away because the land was so flat. Looking west from the towers of either one on a clear day, you could see all the way to the English Channel.

Ypres sat in the midst of fields of grain, hops and beets. The farms were once unusable bogs, but farmers who developed an intricate system of canals and dikes reclaimed them over the years. The watercourses ran in random directions, the grade of the land being so slight that normal drainage patterns didn't seem to apply. Still yet, the plains would usually flood during the heavy rains in the late summer and early fall.

Roads and rail lines radiated out from the town like spokes of a wheel. On the east perimeter of Ypres was the Menin Gate, which arched over the road to the city of the same name. On the north side was the Dixmude Gate, opening to roads going to the nearby towns of Poelcappelle and St. Julien. Passing on the west side was the canal running from the Belgian coast in the north to Comines on the French border to the south. Heavy-gauge rail lines ran northeast to Roulers and southeast to Comines.

Now what made Wipers such a nightmare was the topography I've described. You could stand on a molehill and see for miles. The single dominant feature in the vicinity of the town was a chain of low ridges that formed an elongated semicircle running from north to south just east and southeast of the town. The ridges weren't very impressive to anyone who'd actually seen a real mountain chain. They averaged about 150 feet above sea level. One of the highest of these hills was man-made; it was a heap of spoil left behind from a cut made for the Ypres-Comines railway. The British military dubbed it Hill 60 because it was 60 meters in elevation. I would spend the better part of two years trying to wrestle it from the Germans, but I'll get on to that later.

As you can imagine, Hill 60 and these other ridges provided a great view of Ypres below and the fields leading up to the slopes. It was as if Ypres sat on a stage, with the ridges creating a natural amphitheater. This being the case, it isn't hard to understand why the ridges took on great significance when war came to Flanders in 1914. In repeated efforts to outflank each other, the German and Allied lines extended across France to the Belgian coast, with the French loosely straddling this high ground. The lines bulged to form a salient, about nine miles wide and four miles deep, with Ypres in the center. By the end of 1914, the Germans had taken Hill 60 and the ridges to the south, but the Allies held stubbornly and prevented the capture of the town.

The salient turned into a killing ground like no other. There were Germans on the north, east, and south, and they could watch all military operations below. German observers could call down a rain of steel to disrupt anything from troop buildups to trench construction. Snipers provided endless harassment.

The wisdom of holding the salient versus backing off to a position west of Ypres was debated in the chambers of generals miles away from the battleground. It would have shortened the line, making it possible for fewer men to hold it, and it would have created a better defensive position. But the final decision was made to hold Ypres and the plains below the ridges at all costs.

By the time we arrived, Ypres had been nearly flattened. The inhabitants were virtually gone altogether. It was a ghost town in the daytime; troops stayed below ground in nearly a thousand interconnected dugouts and cellars, only venturing out under the cover of darkness. Even at night, it was still dangerous. The flicker of a lantern or candle was enough to trigger a bombardment.

The real misery was out in the salient beyond the Menin Gate. It meant certain death to peek above the parapets in the daytime because of the snipers up on the ridges. Shelling could come from the front, or it could come from the sides or even the rear of your position. The only protection was to dig in deeper.

The situation at Wipers became critical in the hours before we arrived. Fritz had decided to take a crack at flattening the salient by attacking the northeast side of the bulge. It started with the usual hellfire bombardment, right about dinnertime. But this time

77

Fritz had a new weapon. He had set up a system of tubes and pumps all along the front, and when the wind started blowing in the desired way, he turned them on and blew out a monstrous, greenish-yellow cloud. It swirled toward our boys, and they had no idea what was coming.

It turned out to be chlorine gas. Nasty stuff. One good whiff and napoo. Our generals had believed that even the Huns wouldn't stoop to that barbaric level, so our boys didn't have gas masks or any idea of how to deal with it. So when the mist reached our line, men started falling by the score. The section held by Algerians broke first. The horrified Africans nearly bolted en masse. The French broke next, and suddenly there was a four-mile-wide gap in the line.

The Germans could have done some serious damage at that point, but there were a few factors working against them. First, the Germans could only advance as quickly as the gas moved. And for the time being, the cloud was moving slowly. Second, the German commanders had been hesitant to commit troops to the fight because they didn't think the gas would work. They just didn't have enough manpower to exploit the advantage.

But the toughest obstacle, by far, were the Canadians. Their flank was fully exposed when the French collapsed, yet they refused to yield. They covered their mouths and noses with wet handkerchiefs and stubbornly fought on, stopping wave after wave, coughing and gagging and dying by the dozen. They were some tough lads.

We arrived at Wipers at about four the next morning and the battle was still hot. Hendershot told me that we were going to go up and fill the gap left by the French. We followed our guide out of the station and took a road into town. It was lined with scrapped lorries and dead soldiers, many of them Algerians. There were dead horses by the dozen. The road was pocked with shell holes, and the vehicle traffic had churned it into mud. It was slick and I had a lot of trouble staying on my feet.

"Snap it up!" Hendershot barked. "We want to get up there before sunrise!"

We did the best we could. It got worse, though, when we were pushed off of the road by a column of lorries and ambulances running with their headlamps off. The guide led us up another route: one narrow line of duckboards leading across a muddy field and off into the distance. We passed four burial grounds. I could see rows of crosses in the predawn light.

Ypres came into sight through the darkness and smoke, backlit by the flashes of artillery pieces at work. The towers of the Cloth Hall and cathedral were silhouetted against the deep blue sky. I

78

couldn't tell whose guns were firing, but we were getting closer and they were getting louder.

We entered the gates of the town and were soon under fire. Frank and me ended up hunkered down behind a broken wall. The shells started dropping everywhere. It was one of the first times I can remember being convinced, positively, that I was going to die.

"What a gorgeous day!" Frank screamed above the bursting shells. There was definitely something wrong with him.

After a few horrifying moments that seemed to last a lifetime, the barrage lifted; we remounted the road and moved on through the desolate streets. I didn't see a single building intact. Piles of brick and burned timbers lined the road. The place smelled vile. A skinny dog barked at us as we pushed on.

We headed out the Menin Gate into the salient, past a junction identified by a hand-painted sign as Hellfire Corner. We went northeast toward the sound of the guns. I could see them firing behind the ridges in front of me, off to the left and to the rear. I felt as if we were walking into the very jaws of the enemy. I got a cold chill and a nervous knot in my stomach. Frank slapped me on the shoulder from behind.

"We'll stick together, right?" he asked.

"We will," I said, clearing my throat.

"Now you watch my back, and I'll watch yours."

"That's right."

"Then quit worrying, I say."

"Yes, we'll quit worrying."

"A cigarette would be really good right about now, wouldn't it?"

The lieutenant hushed us. I hadn't realized he was right behind us.

"This isn't the time for idle conversation, lads," he said. "Keep moving."

The guide directed us along a dike and into what used to be a wood. Splintered stumps were all that remained of the trees, with not a one passed over. The fallen trunks and treetops were difficult to traverse, but I figured it would make for a good defensive position if worse came to worse.

We eventually entered a trench, in name only. It was a string of connected shell holes, knee-deep in mud and water, and the sides and tops were littered with the boys who had made a stand at the wood the day before. We waded through the mess slowly, and came to the end of the trench on the far side of the wood. There was a man there calling for us to help. He had somehow gotten himself sunk from the waist down in a muddy shell hole.

"I'm going to die here if you don't help me," he begged. "I keep sinking deeper."

Pick and I set down our rifles and grabbed the man's arms. We pulled but he barely budged. I heard his shoulder pop.

"Try again," he said, wincing. "I think I'm coming loose."

Simon and Frank came over to help. Between the four of us we got him pulled free, but he'd lost his boots in the process.

"I guess you'll be going back barefoot," Frank said.

"I'll get me a pair of boots off of one of those fellows," he said, pointing at a pile of bodies. "That one over there looks about my size. Cheers."

The four of us, along with four others, went with Hendershot up to the edge of the wood, where we met up with the rear guard of a Canadian unit holding the line there. There were still more bodies, freshly dead, with pale, white faces and wide eyes. It was disturbing.

"Keep low, boys," one of the Canadians said. "They've got a few dozen snipers over there that would be all too happy to click you."

We crouched with them in their shell hole.

"The Germans are just over that little rise out front," he said. "We aren't more than 100 feet from them right here."

"Closer than that," their sergeant said. "I'd say 75 feet at the most. Too close either way. Lousy with snipers. Sun's coming up. You'd better get under cover."

We took up positions in a string of shell holes off to the left. Frank and I got down in one of these, behind a couple of tree trunks. I found a log on which I could rest my rifle and still have a wide field of fire. One of the Canadians came hopping over into our hole.

"Hey fellers," he said with an odd drawl, "if they turn on the gas again, wet down your handkerchief and cover your nose and mouth. It's better than nothin.' "

"You don't sound Canadian," Frank observed. "Not even slightly."

"You got that right, brother," he said. "Name's Mullins. I'm from Pikeville, Kentucky. That's in America."

"I know where Kentucky is," Frank said sarcastically. "But what I don't know is why on earth are you here. America's not in this fight, the last time I checked."

"Well, ya see, when this here shootin' started, I jumped a train up to Dee-troit, went over the river and hitched up. Volunteered. That's what I did."

"That was a serious error," Frank said. "Now look where you are."

"It sounded better than workin' in a coal mine," Mullins said, "and I didn't wanna miss any of the action, know what I mean? This sorta thang don't happen every day, don't ya know."

I looked at him in disbelief. My expression betrayed my thoughts.

"Yer thinkin' I'm a dern fool, ain't ya, slim?"

"Maybe," I said, "but then again, I volunteered to get out of the mines, too."

He laughed and shook my hand.

"So you's a miner? Shoot far! And what about him? He sure as heck ain't no miner. I can tell. No, sir."

"I'm not," Frank said. "I'm a magician."

He laughed again, this time a little louder.

"Well, I reckon I don't know what your excuse is, pardner."

"I reckon I don't, either," Frank said, imitating his twang.

There was a shot, and a bullet ricocheted over our heads. Mullins rose up and peered over the tree trunk. There was another shot, and he ducked back down into the hole.

"Y'all wouldn't happen to have any chewin' to-backy, would ya?" Mullins asked. "I'd give a week's pay for a good chaw right now. Yes, I would."

"No, fresh out," Frank said. Mullins looked disappointed.

"But I do have some Woodbines I'll share with you," Frank said, reaching into his breast pocket. He took out a few and handed them to Mullins. He smiled broadly, showing brown teeth that looked almost as bad as Simon's.

"Thanky very much, slim," he said. "They ain't Lucky Strikes, but they'll do right nice."

"'Lucky Strikes?'" Frank asked.

"You ain't never heard of no Luckies?" Mullins said in disbelief. "They's only the best damn cigarettes in the whole wide world, yes sir. Everybody back home smokes 'em."

He looked across the field.

"Now you fellers keep your eyes peeled," he said. "These Huns is up to somethin,' I believe. And I bet I could spit on 'em from right here. Cain't let 'em get any closer, no sir. Now y'all keep low, and holler if ya need anything."

"We'll 'holler,' " Frank said mockingly. Mullins just smiled and crawled back to his position.

"Odd sort of fellow, wasn't he?" Frank said. I didn't answer. I "had my eyes peeled" as Mullins had suggested, and suddenly I could see a German through my sights. He was much closer than I'd expected. I popped him in the head and kicked out the shell.

"You don't waste any time, do you?" Frank said.

"I don't have any to waste," I said.

Mullins jumped back over to our hole.

"Damn, slim!" he said. "Where'n tarnation did you larn to shoot like that? I believe you could shoot the eyeballs off a horse fly!"

"My dad taught me," I said. "We used to hunt together."

"Really? What did y'all hunt?"

"Grouse, mostly. And rabbits now and then."

"I'll be damn! You and me, we got lots in common, slim. Ain't nothin' better than huntin' is there?"

"I enjoy it, but I don't go as much as I used to. What do you hunt in Kentucky?"

"We got rabbits and grouse, like y'all do. And we got deer, and turkeys, and wild boar and so forth. Whatever walks, crawls or flies is fair game to me."

"What about bear?" Frank asked. "Do you hunt those?"

"Well, we got 'em, but they ain't no good for eatin' purposes. Meat's too tough. Good fer makin' rugs, but I don't need none of them. If I see a bar...well, I just let him go about his business. Figger it's his mountain, not mine."

"If I ran into a bear in the woods, I'd probably die of a heart attack," Frank said. "I hear those things are vicious."

"Yeah, they's pretty dag-gone mean. Ya don't wanna make 'em mad, that's for sure."

"I read somewhere that a bear can run as fast as a horse," I said. "Is that true?"

"Yep. For the first hunnerd yards or so they can."

"So what if one chases you? You can't outrun it."

"Well sir, ya don't hafta run faster'n that ol' bar to git away."

"No?"

"Nope. Ya jest hafta run faster'n the feller yer with, that's all."

Frank and I looked at each other with raised eyebrows. Mullins laughed so hard I thought he was going to split his gut.

"You English boys is funny," he said with a chuckle. "Ol' Mullins is jest pullin' yer leg, now!"

We laughed with him for a moment, but our merriment was cut short by incoming mortar fire, heavy and accurate.

"Here we go again, boys!" Mullins shouted. "Git ready!"

Not thirty seconds later, a war cry rose from the line in front of us, and before the last shell could burst, they charged. We took most of them out with machine gun and rifle fire. One poor lad came tumbling in on top of me and I knocked him across the teeth with my rifle butt. He hit the ground and started to get up, but I shot him through the chest. We threw his body back over the lip of the hole when the assault stopped.

That was how the morning went: mortar fire, frantic rifle and machine gun fire and attempts to overrun our line. We held them off well. Only a few reached our hole, and we killed them in quick order. However, somewhere in the fray, Mullins got ran through with a bayonet. Blood gurgled out of his mouth as he gasped for breath. Then he stopped.

"Hell," Frank cursed. "I guess he'll never see Kentucky again."

I didn't want to think about it, but I did anyway. I wished that I could have given him the chewing tobacco he wanted. At least then he would have died satisfied. Now he was just napoo, thousands of miles from home. All I could do was take the blanket from his pack and cover him up.

About noon, some boys came up the line with more iron rations and a jug of rum. I knocked back my ration and ravenously ate my bully and biscuits. I hadn't realized how hungry I was. I hadn't eaten since the night before, and the bully tasted quite appetizing for once.

We stayed at high alert all afternoon. We ascertained that the Germans were running out of steam. They were holding their new gains, but they weren't sticking their necks out to get any any more land.

Nightfall came and another group of reinforcements arrived with a hot meal, more ammunition, several Lewis machine guns and a couple dozen crates of bombs. I felt a lot more confident with fresh troops and plenty of supplies. We'd be able to hold off another wave if it came. And if it did, it probably wouldn't happen until dawn.

The four of us sat in the bottom of a hole, trying to get some rest. We took out cigarettes, and Frank struck a match. It was amazing how much light it put off. He lit his cigarette, then Simon's, and then mine. A bullet ricocheted off of the log in front of our hole. Then several more.

"Sod it," Frank cursed and dropped the match.

"What the devil?" Simon blurted.

"It was the match," Frank said. "You could probably see us a mile away."

"So what are we supposed to do?" Simon said. "Quit smoking after dark? That's rotten!"

"You just don't keep the match lit long enough for someone to get a bead on you," Frank said. "Three lights on one match are too many. It's bad luck."

We didn't say much the rest of the night. Flares, either theirs or ours, almost constantly lit the sky. There was some artillery fire here and there, but not a lot. I got the impression that, for all intents and purposes, the Germans had exhausted themselves. At least for the night.

Sometime after midnight, a work party passed in front of us stringing wire. I remember thinking that took a lot of fortitude, with the Huns being so close by. They continued working through the night, and by the morning we had a good band of wire about ten yards deep. It was a major improvement.

Dawn brought a renewed attack, with the usual shelling and waves of screaming Germans. With the added machine guns and more riflemen, we stopped them cold. Somewhere in the process, however, both Andreson and Potts were killed. So were many others whom I didn't know.

In between all of this, we found time to dig in a bit more, and by the second night we had connected our holes with a trench about four feet deep. Little by little, our new front line emerged. I finally managed to get a few hours of sleep that night.

The fighting continued, day after day, and we stayed in that front line for a little more than a week. We got replacements, and then rotated back to the reserve line to the rear of the wood. It was marginally more comfortable. The trenches were a good six feet deep, with high parapets and dugouts. It was still muddy and wet, but the trench was lined with duckboards and you didn't have to worry so much about sticking your head over the top to have a look around. Supplies and rations came more regularly. We were also issued the first, primitive versions of gas masks, which were basically gauze patches you could moisten, then tie around behind your head and neck. They looked like surgical masks.

We stayed in the reserve trench for about ten or twelve days, and it rained the last three. Then we moved back up to the front line for another ten days. The battle was still hot, with a constant artillery duel coupled with the occasional trench raid by the Huns. We held on tight, not yielding another inch. No Man's Land was littered with their dead, many of whom were bloated and rotting out in the open. Huge rats feasted on the bounty of human flesh, and came into the trenches looking for more. It was horrible.

Late one night there was an unexpected lull in the seemingly endless cannonade. Frank and I relaxed and sat down on the fire step for a smoke. It was a clear night and the stars were bright. There were so many in the sky that they almost appeared to be touching one another.

"This place might be nice," Frank said, "if it weren't for the shells and bullets and so forth."

"And the rats and lice," I said.

"And the food. And the mud."

"And the rain."

"And the pay."

We had a bit of a laugh, and then sat quietly, finishing our cigarettes.

"That's funny," I said, stamping out my butt. "I don't think there's any way things could possibly be worse."

"You could be German," he said.

"What do you mean?"

"For the last three weeks or so, they've been trying to take our trench. And we cut them down every time. They've got to be losing more men than we are. And if you were some miserable Hun bugger you'd have to wait, knowing that your orders to attack were coming. Just a matter of time."

"Do you think they'll give up?"

"Well," he said, "someone's going to have to."

I looked up at the stars again. There they were, twinkling just as they had been for eternity. And I knew they wouldn't change, or come tumbling down, no matter who held this trench tomorrow or the day after that. But somewhere in the darkness, I could hear someone faintly sobbing.

CHAPTER 11

It neared dawn. What hadn't occurred to me was that such a clear night would be an excellent opportunity for a trench raid. It had been weeks, and the Germans were still unwilling to give up on flattening the salient. To be honest, they caught us off guard.

Frank and Simon were still sleeping when the first mortar shells came flying over No Man's Land. The shells split the night, and they were immediately awakened, as were our mortar crews, which began firing back. Our machine gunners started "finding the wire," swiveling their guns on their tripods until they saw the telltale blue sparks of bullets hitting the enemy entanglements. That was where the German defenses stopped, and it was where they would be the most vulnerable if they tried to come across.

The machine gun to our left was soon taken out with a direct hit from a well-aimed *minenwerfer*. The machine gun on our right was next. While the starlight had given us a bit of visibility, the smoke from the shells soon cancelled that advantage. Then it was just us riflemen and mortar crews left to defend the line. We didn't know what was going on.

Someone on our side decided to illuminate the situation with a volley of star shells. When they burst overhead, I could see a whole line of Germans running toward us. I fired a few rounds, but they kept advancing. When I realized we weren't going to hold them off, I pulled the bayonet from the end of my rifle and waited for them to come pouring into the trench.

A German came right in on top of me and knocked me to the ground. He pointed his rifle at my chest, but I pushed it aside with my left hand just as he fired, then stabbed him in the gut with my right. The look on his face was horrifying. He was a young boy, maybe 17. He fell limp as I shoved my bayonet in up to the hilt, all the way into his heart. His sticky blood ran over my hand. I pulled it out and looked for another one to kill.

A Hun to my left tried to get me with his bayonet, but I dodged it and pulled his rifle out of his hands. I hit him in the head with the butt of his own rifle, knocking his helmet off. Then I swung it like a club, as I'd seen Simon do, hitting him again across the jaw. Blood spurted from his mouth and he fell to the ground. I dropped to my knees and raised my bayonet above his chest.

"Please don't kill me!" he shouted in English, but with an accent. "Please don't! I surrender!"

I looked around to see if anyone else had heard him. There were no more Germans left standing. The raid was over seconds after it began, and one of the machine guns nearby was up and working away. Men were throwing bombs into the darkness. We had held them off again. There was just this one under my bayonet. I paused, stood above the man, and decided to take him prisoner.

"Finish him off!" Simon shouted at me. He was covered in blood.

"No!" the German shouted. "I beg of you, no!"

I dropped my bayonet to my side. I stepped back and leaned against the side of the trench, wiping the sweat from my brow. I could smell the sweet blood on my hand.

"You sound like an American," Frank said, pointing at the man with his rifle.

"I am an American," he said. "My name's Kurt Schumman. I'm from Milwaukee."

"Never heard of it!" Simon shouted. "You're lying!"

"No," he said. "It's in Wisconsin. In the States."

"Do you know where Kentucky is?" Frank asked.

"Of course," Schumman said.

"Well, you fellows just killed a man from there the other day," Frank said. "He was with the Canadians. What in creation are you doing in the German Army?"

"My parents are from Lubeck," he said. "I was born there. Dad was in the Imperial Army. Then we immigrated to America. Settled in Milwaukee when I was a child. Dad got a job in a machine shop there. When the war started, he wanted me to go help the Kaiser, so I did. What a mistake that turned out to be."

"You're lucky this man didn't run you through with his sticker," Simon said. "We don't make a habit of taking prisoners, you see."

"Well, I thank you for the exception," Schumman said. "I'm glad you took me prisoner. It's over. I'd rather spend the rest of the war in prison than up here in this muddy mess. That's for sure."

We weren't sure what to do with Schumman so we sat him on the fire step and kept him under guard. We lit cigarettes, waiting for the lieutenant or Hendershot or someone to come along and tell us what to do.

"I'd die for one of those," Schumman said. "Can you spare one?"

I hesitated, and then gave him a fag and a light. Simon cursed at me. Schumman took a long, deep drag and exhaled through his nose.

"Ah, that's it," he said. "I haven't had a cigarette in three days."

He'd just about finished it when the lieutenant came walking up the trench.

"Making sure the prisoner's comfortable, are we, Gardener?" he asked. Frank and I stood but didn't say anything.

"What's the story here, lads?"

"He surrendered, sir," I said.

The lieutenant said something to him in German. He sounded authentic and I was impressed.

"He speaks English, sir," Frank said. "He's an American."

"An American?"

"That's right, lieutenant," Schumman said.

"What are you doing here?"

"Serving the Fatherland, but not doing a very good job of it," he said, stubbing out his cigarette. "I don't want to fight anymore. This is where it ends for old Kurt."

"With men like you, Germany will never win this war," the lieutenant said. "Do your *kammerades* feel the same way?"

"Only the smart ones," he said.

"Gardener," the lieutenant said to me, "you and Thomas escort this man back to HQ. Follow the stretcher men back to the aid station and you'll find it. They'll want to question him before sending him to a camp. And don't cut him any slack because he's a Yank. Treat him like you would any other German sod. Tie his hands in back and guard him carefully."

I saluted and tied Schumman's hands with a leather thong. I could see a little better in the dark than Frank, so I took the lead. We followed the stretchers like the lieutenant said, beyond the wood and past the reserve line.

I figured we were close to Hellfire Corner before we found headquarters. We saw a sentry there who pointed out the entrance to a dugout. We went down ten steps and pushed back a tarp to reveal a small room warmly lit with a kerosene lantern. I was surprised they didn't have electricity this far back.

"What can I help you boys with?" a sergeant asked us. "Do we have a guest this evening? A jolly little Hun bugger for Intelligence?"

"He can understand you," Frank said. "He's a jolly little American Hun bugger."

"Is that so?" the sergeant said sarcastically. "Well how about that."

A lieutenant and a captain came down the stairs. The sergeant turned and saluted.

"Sir," he said, "we have a prisoner for interrogation. And you won't need Loechler to translate because he's a Yank."

The two officers looked a bit surprised.

88

"So how is it than an American ends up in the Kaiser's army?" the captain asked. "That's awfully strange."

"It's a strange war," Schumman said.

"Should I call Cranson and Baxter to escort him back to the holding area?" the sergeant asked.

"Yes, please," the captain said. "You fellows can go now. Thank you."

Frank and I saluted, walked up the steps and headed out into the night. We moved a lot faster without the prisoner. We were nearing the reserve line when we came to a sap that I hadn't noticed on the way out.

"Stop here for a second," Frank said, lighting a cigarette. "I want to take a look at something."

I followed him into the sap and found some rations that had been stashed there by a carrying party. There were crates and crates of bully and biscuits, as well as ammunition and bombs. Then we found a half-dozen jugs of rum, sitting there as pretty as could be.

"Care for a nip?" Frank said, lifting one of the jugs. He motioned me over to the end of the sap and we sat down. There wasn't anyone around, so we uncorked it. Frank had a gulp, and then passed it over to me. I tipped it up and took two big gulps.

"Wow," Frank said, "you must be thirsty."

"No, just tired," I said. "Tired of this wretched place. We've been here more than a month and the fighting hasn't stopped yet. These Boches are determined."

"We've just got to wait them out," he said, then tipped the jug up for another drink and passed it back to me. "They'll get tired after a while. They're probably worn as thin as we are right about now."

"The last time we whipped them in a couple of days," I said, wiping rum off of my chin.

"And we were plenty lucky, too," he said.

We sat there for about an hour. Frank produced a new tin of cigarettes, from where I don't know, and we chain-smoked and drank rum until we were a good bit pissed. About half of the jug was left, and we decided we should share it with Simon and Pick and the other boys. We stumbled out of the sap and went back up past the reserve line to our position. The first person we ran into was Hendershot.

"What are you doing with that jug?" he asked. "Looks to me like you've had a good healthy ration."

"A fellow in a carrying party asked me where I was going," Frank said. "I said I was headed for the front line and he asked me to deliver it."

"Is that right, Gardener?" Hendershot asked.

"Absolutely," I said, slurring it a bit.

Hendershot just eyeballed us real good for a minute, not saying anything. Then he motioned for Frank to hand him the jug. He took a swallow, then another, then passed it back to Frank.

"Thanks for the drink," he said. "Be sure to share it with the rest of the lads. No need to be stingy."

We found our position just up the line a ways. Simon and Pick were waiting there, and they took triple rations each. Frank and I took another drink each, and then passed it on down the line. I was drunk, and it felt good. I sat down and stared at the stars some more. I fell asleep in the arms of Bacchus, without a care in the world.

CHAPTER 12

The skirmishing at Wipers continued back and forth with no one making any progress. It got to be routine until the last week of May. Just after midnight one evening, they started hitting us with every gun they could muster. The hurricane bombardment intensified even further as dawn approached.

"My, what a gorgeous day!" Frank yelled into my ear. He was insane, for certain.

Getting shelled was bad, but what made things worse that particular morning was that we had been waiting on supplies when the barrage started. We were low on everything: ammunition, bombs, food, but especially water. And there wasn't any way for us to get re-supplied given the immediate situation. I'd finished off my canteen with dinner the night before, and was dying for a drink.

The shortage of water wouldn't have been that much of a problem except that Fritz decided to turn on the gas just after daybreak. We dug through our packs to find our gas masks. We were instructed to dampen them, but as I said, we were out of water, aside from what was needed to cool our machine guns. The yellow-green cloud came swirling toward us, and I was beginning to think about running. My eyes and nose started burning.

Frank, being the quick thinker, unfastened his trousers and urinated on his mask. Cursing, he put it on his face. By that point, I'd gotten a good whiff of the gas and it made me cough violently. I decided to piss on my mask, too, and Simon and Pick did the same. Others couldn't stomach putting piss on their faces, and attached the masks without wetting them. They started dropping one after another, coughing up their lungs as they writhed on the ground in agony. Hendershot came stumbling down the trench, tripping over the dead and dying.

"Stand to!" he shouted. "They'll be coming close behind!"

He must have had a sixth sense, because the bombardment ended a minute or two later. The four of us climbed up on the fire step and waited for the onslaught. I put my rifle to my shoulder. My eyes were burning and I could barely see through the mist.

The machine guns were already running wide-open when the Germans came into view, crossing No Man's Land at a walking pace, wearing ghoulish masks that made them look like pig-monsters. It was a horrifying sight. Trembling, I wiped the sweat off of my right palm, gripped my rifle, and put my finger on the trigger.

"Open fire!" Hendershot barked.

91

I took aim at one of the men and shot him down. Another Boche tried to help him, so I shot him, too. After that, I lost track, burning one clip after another. More were advancing and more were falling. The field was dotted with dead Huns. I couldn't count them all.

After a few very long minutes, I realized there was nothing left to shoot at. I rubbed my eyes in disbelief and looked again. They had stopped coming. Our machine guns stopped, and Hendershot told us to hold our fire. Their attack had been in vain, without even one German reaching our trench. I guess you could say we'd won that round at least. But the price we paid was tremendous; about half of the boys around me were dead or dying from the gas. Men with stretchers came up and started hauling away the wounded, leaving the dead where they lay.

"What do you think they'll do now, sergeant?" I asked.

"Why are you asking me?" he snapped. "Do I look like the bleedin' Kaiser here? Just stay alert and don't take your eyes off the field!"

I did what he told me to do, and watched for more Huns. About that time, I noticed that the wind changed directions, blowing the gas back over the enemy lines. That was some good luck, but it didn't hold them up very long. After about ten minutes, a larger second wave came out of the haze, running with their bayonets pointed right at us.

"I am so tired of this shit!" Frank yelled, shooting into the approaching formation. "When are they going to give up?"

I didn't pay much attention to him. I'd already emptied one clip and I was putting in another. I noticed that I only had three or four left. It gave me the feeling that we were in deep trouble this time around. There were too many, and the action on my rifle was getting sticky. The machine guns were firing almost parallel to our line, trying to stop them at the last possible moment.

"Fall back!" the lieutenant yelled as he came running up the line, his pistol in one hand and his other holding a mask over his face. "Fall back to the reserve line! We can't hold them here!"

He didn't have to tell us twice. We ran down to the communication trench and went zigzagging back to the second line. The trench was clogged with gas victims, and it was hard going.

The Germans were hot on our trail. Despite the machine gunners and bombers, they took the front trench entirely. Our left flank was in danger of being turned. A couple of men with a Lewis gun ran past us in the opposite direction. They set up the tripod in the communications trench for the impending wave.

We got to the reserve line and doubled up on the fire step with the men already there. The wire in front of this line was still pretty much intact, and there were four machine guns in fortified pits, two on either side of us. I heard the Lewis kick in, and I knew that the Germans were trying to come up the communications trench. Then I heard some bombs go off, and it fell silent. But the guns on our left and right went into full-throttle. Maybe they would hold them off for a while, I prayed.

The fact was that we had withdrawn faster than the Germans could advance, plus their artillery was not adjusting quickly. It gave us time to tie our flank in with the reserve line, and when they got close, we cut them to ribbons. A few unfortunate souls actually made it to the wire, but no further. We had won that round, too.

And the Huns didn't try again. They had run out of steam, fortunately before we did. We'd fought them off for six weeks, most of which we were in the firing line. I knew we'd lost a lot of men; later, I heard that we'd taken 70,000 casualties altogether. The whole episode would come to be known as the Second Battle of Ypres, and it was now history.

The night was quiet. We got a good hot meal, cigarettes, hot tea and extra rum rations. Frank and I sat on the fire step and looked up at the stars in the clear, deep blue sky. He pointed out constellations his father had shown him, and told me how they moved and what they were used for. It was a pleasant break from what we'd been through.

Eventually, though, we started speculating as to when and where the next great battle would be fought. Would we be sent there, and would we survive? The one thing we agreed upon was that it was pointless to try and reason that out, as logic doesn't apply to the illogical.

"But we have been lucky so far," I said. "Maybe it will hold out for us, Frank."

I don't know whether I was trying to convince him or myself. If it was myself, I didn't do a very good job of it. I'd seen too much by then to hold out much hope for tomorrow.

CHAPTER 13

We moved back to our new reserve trench after things cooled down a bit, relatively speaking. The fighting never seemed to stop altogether: gas attacks in the middle of the night, constant and deadly harassment by snipers, trench raids that seemed to come at the most inopportune times. I adjusted rather well, and I found myself relaxing from time to time when we weren't in the firing line. I often daydreamed about getting a hot bath, however. I hadn't washed, nor had I cleaned my uniform, in nearly two months. My clothes were full of lice and I reeked. You know it's bad when you notice your own odor.

The days were getting warmer, and that was good, but the late spring also mean lots of rain in Flanders. It rained at least a bit each day it seemed, but about three days a week it would pour buckets. Everything turned to slick, gooey mud. Our trenches were knee-deep in water about half of the time, or collapsed altogether. The deluge always flushed out the makeshift privies and waste dumps, filling the streams, canals and ponds with the sewage and refuse of thousands of men on both sides. The ditches and shell holes brimmed with black, greasy water. There was no efficient way to drain it; you stood in slime nearly up to your hips and baled until you couldn't lift your arms any more, then someone else would take over. It was an eternal venture, much like that fellow in Greek mythology who had to roll a stone up a hill over and over again. I can't remember his name, but I sure sympathized with him.

The worst thing at the front, though, was the corpses. There were decaying bodies by the thousands lying in between the pinched lines, with no one willing to risk their life to drag them out of No Man's Land and back to a burial ground. Then there were thousands more who had died in the front trenches and were simply buried in the walls and parapets. Digging new trenches, or shoring up old ones, inevitably meant disinterring dead soldiers.

I remember the first time I dug into a dead body. We started construction on a new reserve line that ran right through a burial ground out in the salient. I was swinging a pick when I hit a dead Frenchman. I could tell because of his uniform. He'd been there for a while, and when I hit him, his head just popped off and rolled over to my feet. The rest of his rotting, oozing body came out in pieces. We just tossed it all up over the top and kept digging.

The bodies out in No Man's Land went through several distinct stages of decay. First, the skin turned white, then pale gray. Next it turned a greenish color and the body bloated with methane until the clothes wouldn't stretch any further. Eventually, a bullet or a hungry rat would puncture the flesh, releasing the most horrible smell you could imagine. If one of those things popped nearby, it was enough to make you wretch up your lunch. Sometimes, when the wind was blowing toward Fritz, we would snipe bloated, dead bodies near their trench, unleashing the smell upon them. Then we'd all have a good laugh. I guess that's kind of sick, but it's the kind of thing that happens in war.

After they ruptured, the bodies turned brownish, then black, and the skin started falling off, leaving a slimy pile of bones and organs. The remains would then be devoured by rats, which got enormous from the bounty of food. I saw rats the size of dogs, and I'm not lying. Sometimes, there were so many rats eating away inside the uniform that the body seemed to come back to life. I once saw a dead man roll completely over as the rats fought to expose new, juicy flesh on his backside.

Naturally, the rats would come looking for more food in the trenches. They would run across your boots, or across your bunk when you were trying to sleep. The only good side of this was that killing rats provided endless recreation. No amount of killing seemed to diminish their numbers or their tenacity. We would bait them sometimes, then beat them with spades or clubs fashioned from pick handles. Then we'd take the dead ones by the tails and hurl them across at the Germans. We made a little game of it.

What the rats didn't eat got eaten by flies and maggots. They came in swarms, and on bad days, you couldn't keep them off of you. They would bite your exposed flesh, leaving terrible welts. You couldn't keep them out of your food, either. One day, I was making soup on a little cooker Frank had fashioned from a bully tin and cotton wadding, and by the time it was hot, there were at least a dozen flies floating on top. I just strained them out and ate it anyway.

We did attempt, when possible, to abate some of the corpse problem, but that was equally gruesome if not more so. We'd go out and pick up bodies and parts of bodies and pile them on a limber, which we then took back to the rear to more permanent burial grounds. You couldn't do that if you were close enough for the snipers to get you, so this wonderful detail was at least fairly safe. Only the big guns could reach you, and logically, the Germans weren't really interested in shelling corpses.

Nonetheless, no one ever volunteered for burial detail, but you always got stuck with it from time to time. We tied handkerchiefs over our faces and tried not to get sick as we gathered up the remains. We did our best to identify each corpse by the identity tag around its wrist, but sometimes the wrist wasn't there. Some soldiers took to wearing a second disc around their necks, but sometimes the head was gone, too. So they went listed as "unknown."

Most of the time, the bodies were piled into a mass grave with a dusting of lime on top. Deep shell craters made excellent repositories. We'd heap them in until there was no more room, and then cover them over with a foot or two of dirt. Later, there would be crosses erected nearby in straight rows, with the names of the boys in the pit on them, to at least give the illusion that each man had gotten a proper gravesite.

One particular day, the boys and me went out on burial detail. We had several limbers, with bodies piled four or five high on all of them. Most of them were from a recent trench raid gone awry, so they weren't too bad. But some of them had been there for a while and were in the latter stages of decay. Simon and I went to pick one up, with him grabbing the arms and me with the legs. When we lifted, the body broke in two at the waist, and a pack of rats came running out. I dropped the bottom half in disbelief.

Simon nearly laughed his balls off.

CHAPTER 14

It was the middle of June before we finally got a few days of rest. We went back out of the salient to our billets just beyond Wipers. Frank and I were promoted to corporal the first morning we were there, and we sewed a second stripe on our uniforms. This sort of irritated Simon and Pick, who were still privates. But baths and good, hot meals assuaged their feelings of jealousy, I guess. We remained a tight-knit crew.

We were given five days of leave, but the only place to go within walking distance was the town of Poperhinghe, a few miles down the road from Wipers. We called it Pop. We had heard that there was everything a soldier might want in Pop: wine, food, and women. We had saved up a few weeks' pay, and were looking to blow it. So we headed out one afternoon following dinner. We hitched a ride on a beat-up Ford lorry that was headed in that direction. It was better than going on foot, as we were tired beyond belief.

We got into Pop just about dark. It seemed that every other home had been turned into a pub of some sort. Others were converted to makeshift cafes called *estaminets*, with hand-painted signs advertising their fare. You could get a plateful of chips, fried eggs and sausages for virtually nothing. We stopped in one of these and filled ourselves until we were all good and bloated. Simon himself ate nine eggs, a dozen sausages and probably a pound of chips. He was a world-class eater. As we walked out the door, he let a monstrous fart.

"Damn, Simon," Pick said. "I'm glad you're so relaxed."

"At least I didn't fill my trousers," he said. "That's your job."

They went at it for a minute or two as we walked down the street. We saw brothels by the dozen; the ones with red lights were for enlisted men, and the ones with blue lights were for officers. Some of these had lines of men out the door. We passed them by, looking for a good place to load up on wine, because we'd heard the Belgian beer wasn't worth drinking. We found one soon enough, and walked inside.

It was a dimly lit room, with a long improvised bar made of bully crates with two-by-tens nailed across the top. Down at the end of the bar sat Staff Sgt. Hendershot, looking like he'd had plenty already. I thought it was quite a coincidence. Besides him, the place was pretty much empty. We walked over and sat down next to him.

"Corporal Gardener, Corporal Thomas, good to see you," he said, slurring his words a bit. "But those two privates have to leave. This *estaminet* is for NCOs only."

We all looked at each other, a bit puzzled. Then Frank spoke up.

"Do you think maybe we could give them a field promotion?" he asked Hendershot. "Just for tonight? They need a drink as much as we do."

Hendershot gave Simon and Pick the once-over. He stamped out the cigar he was smoking and spit on the floor.

"Well, yeah, I guess we could make them lance corporals for the night. Besides, I don't think anyone's going to make a fuss here. Go ahead and stay."

A moment later a barmaid came down and said something to us that I didn't understand.

"Red or white, boys?" Hendershot asked. "What do you want?"

"How's the red?" Frank asked.

"It'll get you good and pissed, if that's what you want to know."

"That's fine," I said. "We'll take the red."

"*Vin rouge, si vous plait*," Hendershot said, motioning to the lot of us. She poured us good healthy glasses and Hendershot laid some money on the bar. She smiled and put it in her apron. We guzzled our glasses and ordered more. This time I paid.

"Here's to peace," Frank said, lifting his glass. We all did the same except Hendershot. He looked irritated.

"What's the matter, sergeant?" Frank asked. "Don't you want this to be over?"

"I want it to be over," he said, "but I don't think it will be. Not any time too soon."

"You're a pessimist," Frank said boldly. "Surely, we'll all be home soon. It's in all of the papers."

"Don't believe what you read in them," he replied. "They lie."

"Then what's the truth?" Simon asked.

"I've been in this army since '05, since I was old enough to serve. I know that the way the military operates, we could be here until I'm ready to retire."

That shut us up. We drank our wine and ordered more. Frank paid and offered Hendershot a cigarette.

"No thanks," he said. " I can't stand the taste of a cigarette. Maybe if you had a cigar on you, but that's all."

"In the army how long, and you don't smoke fags?" Frank persisted. "I guess we don't know you that well."

98

"What is there to know about a soldier?" he asked. "You're either a good soldier or a bad one. One is a rare commodity, and the other is useless. And much more common."

"Did you always want to be a soldier?" I asked. "I never thought about it when I was growing up, yet here I am."

"I didn't have a lot of choices," he said. "My family was dirt poor in Birmingham, hardly a potato in the pot or a shilling in my pocket. I figured the army would at least give me a warm place to sleep at night, three hot meals a day, free clothes and reliable pay. What more could you ask?"

"You've certainly made the best of it," Frank said, "rising through the enlisted ranks."

"I earned every bit of it, too," he said. "It's a lot harder to become an NCO when people aren't dying around you every day. You got to be a corporal how long after you got here? It took me a year or more to get that stripe."

Clearly, Hendershot resented us for our ranks, but then I felt I earned my stripes, too. I knocked back my glass and ordered another as I stamped out my fag in the ashtray.

"Did you ever do any service overseas, aside from here?" Pick asked.

"I did two years in India," he said. "Bloody hot place. Some days it would get up to a hundred in the shade."

"How could you stand it?" I asked.

"Well, the good things about India are the beer is cheap and pretty fair, and the local food is excellent: spicy as a Saturday night in a whorehouse. Once we were done for the day, we'd go out, get some food, and get pissed like there was no tomorrow.

"The bad things about India would take too long to list, though," he said. "The poverty is absolutely unbelievable. In places like Bombay or Calcutta, one out of ten men might be doing all right, maybe a job and a small house. But the rest live in squalor. The slums go on forever. The women are so desperate to feed their families that they sell themselves to anyone who has a few pence. A lot of the fellows I served with enjoyed such sordid pleasures. I did not."

We were running out of wine, and the waitress was sitting at the other end of the bar, fighting off the advances of five burly Australians that had wandered in off the street. They were boisterous and plainly drunk. I interrupted their conversation to ask for more wine, which seemed to annoy them quite a bit. The waitress was able to get away, and she seemed relieved. She went behind the bar and got out two more bottles of red.

"These are free," she said with a thick accent. I tried to pay her anyway, but she motioned me to go back to my table. There were a couple of teeth missing from her smile.

"How about some free wine for me, *mademoiselle*?" the most extroverted of the Australians asked. He said something under his breath to the other four and they burst into raucous laughter.

When I got back, Frank pulled out his deck of cards.

"Anyone up for a game?" he asked. "How about a hand of nap?"

"Know why they call that game 'nap'?" Hendershot said. "It's because it's so boring that it will put you to sleep. And besides, I know better than to play cards with you, Thomas."

We laughed. Frank was grinning from one ear to the other, his cigarette pasted to his lower lip.

"Well," Frank said, "we'll have to find something better to do with these."

He fanned them out with grace and started into one of his routines.

"Staff Sgt. Hendershot, take a card," he said. Hendershot looked annoyed.

"Go ahead, take a card," he said.

"I'll take a card," the loud Australian said, staggering over to our table. Hendershot leaned in close to me.

"This could get real ugly," he warned. Frank didn't hear him and offered a card to the Aussie.

"Now memorize the card," Frank said, "and slide it into the deck."

The man did as instructed, and Frank shuffled the cards thoroughly. He laid the deck face down on the table and tapped the top card with his finger.

"Turn it over," he told the Australian. It was the card he'd chosen. We all laughed, but the Australian looked perturbed.

"Show me another one," he said, as the others made their way over. Frank obliged them with a trick even more stupefying than the first. The loud one scratched his head.

"So how do you do it?" the Australian asked.

"Can't tell you," Frank said. "Magician's code."

"Oh, come on, now," he said. "We're all on the same side here, mate. You can tell me how you did that."

"Sorry, lads, I can't," Frank said.

The Australian got in Frank's face.

"You know, mate," he said, "you are being very rude, and you don't want to make us angry. Show us the trick."

Hendershot scooted out his chair and stood. He was a good six inches taller than the Australian, and he looked down his nose at him.

"If my corporal says he doesn't want to show you the trick, then he's not going to show you the trick. You, my Kiwi friend, are the one being rude. Why don't you go back to your table and get pissed some more?"

The Australian moved in close to the sergeant.

"Why don't you make me, Englishman?" he said, and poked Hendershot in the chest. Hendershot pushed him back.

"Maybe I will..."

We all jumped up, and the next thing I knew, fists were flying. Hendershot and the loud one went crashing across the bar, kicking and punching each other all the way down to the floor. The waitress was screaming at the top of her lungs, batting at them with the business end of her broom.

One of the Aussies grabbed me from behind, but I put an elbow into his gut. I broke free and reeled around. He took a swing and I dodged it, then I hit him across the face as hard as I could. Blood spurted from his lip. It knocked him back on his heels, but soon he came back at me again and gave me a good one in my left eye. I got him by the shirt and put my knee into his privates. That dropped him.

I looked over to see Frank and one of the Aussies trying to choke each other. Frank was losing until he butted his opponent in the forehead. He went falling backward, pulling Frank with him. They rolled across the floor, knocking over chairs and bottles as they went. Frank ended up on top, and he beat the man's head against the floor until he stopped moving.

As for Pick, he was in rare form. He punched his opponent in the gut, and then doubled him over backwards with an uppercut to the face. The man went falling to the floor without even landing one punch. Simon, on the other hand, had taken quite a beating and was bleeding from his nose and mouth. But he picked up a chair and broke it over the other man's head. He fell, groaning and holding his napper. It was a tremendous fight, and we left them all bleeding on the floor.

Frank stood and straightened his tunic. He ran his fingers through his hair and put his cap on.

"You boys all right?" Hendershot said from behind the bar. He had a good welt under his right eye.

"We're fine, sergeant," I said. "How about you?"

He nodded and spat blood on the floor. The waitress was screaming at us and herding us to the door with her broom.

"And now for my next trick," Frank said, "we will all disappear. Rapidly."

We stumbled out into the night and headed down the street.

"Well," Simon said, "I hope the next place is friendlier than that one."

Frank started laughing, and pretty soon, we all joined him.

"What a night," Hendershot said. "What a bloody night. I haven't been in a fight like that since I was in Hong Kong."

I gingerly touched the welt on my face. It was stinging like fire.

"That'll look real good by morning," Hendershot said. "Keaffe, you're going to look like a train hit you."

"Yeah," I said. "An Australian train."

We went on out to the edge of Pop where we figured the Australians wouldn't come looking for us. We found another place to drink, and the wine there was much better. We stayed there until well after midnight, and then set out for Wipers. We staggered down the road, trying to hitch a ride, but all of the lorries and train cars were loaded going into the salient. They were only empty on the way back out. So we ended up walking the whole distance. We were dead tired when we arrived back at our billets. I crawled into my bunk and was soon asleep.

Daybreak came early it seemed, and when I sat up, I still felt a bit drunk. Frank, Simon and I looked like we'd just come out of a rough trench fight, although there wasn't a mark on Pick. One of Simon's eyes was almost swelled shut. I had a terrible headache.

We lined up for roll call, trying to get into the back of the formation so maybe the lieutenant wouldn't see our "battle scars." But he spotted us nonetheless, and called us over after dismissal.

"Gardener, Keaffe, Thomas, Hendershot," the lieutenant said, shaking his head. "You all have been brawling. That is something I frown upon. Don't you get enough fighting up the line? Or do you have to go out and look for more on your time off?"

"It was a bunch of drunk Australians, sir," Hendershot said meekly. "They jumped us. We were just minding our own business."

"And you did nothing to provoke this?" he asked. "I find that hard to believe."

He stared at the ground for a moment, in his usual fashion when he was thinking.

"Thomas, I bet you had something to do with this, didn't you?"

"No, sir," he said. "It was just as Staff Sgt. Hendershot told it."

"I don't care for an explanation, or an excuse for that matter," the lieutenant said. "You are not going to go about fighting. The next time I suspect that you've been up to such foolishness again, it's going to be Field Punishment #1. I'll chain you to a limber wheel for a week if that's what it takes. But no more fighting. Is that understood?"

"Yes sir," we said.

"You're dismissed, damn it." He started to walk off, then stopped and turned around.

"Hendershot, are we still on for a game of chess tonight after tea?" the lieutenant asked.

"Absolutely, sir," Hendershot said.

"Good. Because I'm going to give you another good beating."

"Only if your luck changes, sir."

The lieutenant went on his way looking down at the ground, his hands clasped behind his back.

"I think that went rather well," Frank said. "What do you think, sergeant?"

"He's definitely serious," Hendershot said. "He'll have us all chained up next time. He might even knock off a stripe or two. I suggest you all lay low for a while. As for me, I'm going back to bed. You should do the same."

He walked off toward his billet. We stood there for a minute without saying anything.

"Well, what do you fellows want to do today?" Frank finally said.

"I could use some more chips and eggs," Simon said.

"Yes," Frank said, "and I could use a drink. What do you say we go back to Pop this morning?"

"Didn't you hear what Hendershot just said?" I asked him. "There can't be any more trouble."

"There won't be," Frank said. "We'll just avoid drunk Australians."

We started down the road just after nine. We were good and pissed by noon.

CHAPTER 15

We took the lieutenant's advice and stayed out of trouble, at least for the time being, despite the fact that we were drunk pretty much every day. There was little else to do. We ran out of money, but Frank won a good bit playing cards with some Scottish lads he'd met, and he shared the wealth. His winnings kept us in wine and cigarettes until the time came to rotate back up to the firing line.

In August there was a great deluge that lasted for most of four days. Naturally, we were in the fire trenches that week, so we got the worst of it all. We toughed it out, as always, slopping about in the gooey mud. There was no use trying to stay clean or dry or otherwise.

I thanked God aloud on the morning of the fifth day, when I finally saw the sun rising in a clear sky. After stand-to, a carrying party came up with more duckboards for the line. It was an unusual luxury.

"It would have been better if they'd arrived a few days ago," Simon whined. We all guessed as to what this might be about, and the consensus was that there was going to be a trench raid staged from our position. That night.

The lieutenant came by and explained the mystery, and I was relieved to find out there would be no raid.

"Fellows," he said, "there will be a certain Colonel Tilton from headquarters coming up for an inspection at 10 o'clock. He's a tough old soldier, so make sure you are manning your positions when he shows. And try to look sharp."

I had never seen anyone with a rank higher than a captain up where we were, so a visit from a colonel would be something to write home about. And there we were, unshaven and filthy, our boots and uniforms crusty and covered with mud. I hadn't been out of mine in weeks. We got a gasoline tin full of water and used it to wash off our rifles and faces, but little else. I spread out my waterproof sheet on a stable section of the fire step and sat down. I got my bayonet out and used it to scrape all of the excess mud off of my worn boots. I took off my puttees and scraped them as well. I tried to comb my matted, dirty hair with my fingers, but ended up hiding it under my cap and combing only what was left showing.

Some men with hot tea and a rum ration came around, and we were enjoying it, sitting there on the fire step, when we were abruptly ordered to attention. I dropped my cup and stood up.

It was the colonel, more than two hours before he was expected. No one was at his firing position, and a lot of the men were hunting lice in their shirts. I could hear him cursing as he made his way down the line of disheveled men. He stopped in front of Pick and shouted in his face.

"Where's your lieutenant?" he screamed.

"Don't know, sir," Pick replied. It was the truth, but it wasn't what the colonel wanted to hear.

"You're probably the smartest man here, you idiot," he replied through his clenched teeth. "Does anyone know where Lt. Rampkin is? Anyone?"

The lieutenant suddenly appeared from the communications trench, accompanied by men carrying long-awaited rations and supplies. He was visibly startled.

"Sir," he said. "Lt. Rampkin reporting, sir."

"You're running one ragged unit here, lieutenant," the colonel said. "What if the Germans attacked at this very moment?"

"Not likely, sir…" the lieutenant said.

"I don't want your opinion," he said. "Look at your men! My grandmother could do a better job of manning this trench! And I don't think I've ever seen a dirtier lot than this!"

The colonel ranted on, striding up and down the trench waving his arms, then stepped in front of the lieutenant and stared him in the eyes.

"You are just like your father," he said. "Coddling your troops like they're on holiday. What do you have to say for yourself, Rampkin?"

"Sir," he stammered, "the men were having breakfast…"

"I can see that, lieutenant!"

"Well, let me finish, if you will…"

"Spit it out!"

"Sir, it has been raining for four days straight, and this is the first dry meal they've had in a while."

"This isn't a bloody nursery," the colonel said, "it's a war!"

The lieutenant gave up. There was no point to it, and we all knew it, too.

"By Jove, I'll make sure everyone knows about this. I'm going to write up a full report on this wretched excuse for a platoon and make sure that you get all of the credit for its unworthiness."

"Yes, sir," the lieutenant said in a low voice.

The colonel went on about a few more of his pet peeves and gave us all a good yelling. There wasn't one among us that didn't want to give him a healthy clobbering. How dare he come up from his cushy confines, up to where the real war was? He didn't know a thing about what it was like trying to live and maintain your sanity while knee-deep in mud and filth. He and his entourage finally left after a couple of sniper shots whistled by.

"Don't lose any sleep over it, fellows," the lieutenant said to us. "It might be a smudge on my record, but to be honest with you, I don't really care."

We rotated back to rest billets two days later. The first night we were back, Frank disappeared after sundown and came slinking back well after midnight. It was odd, because he rarely spent time by himself. He always wanted to be in the middle of a crowd, just like the performer he was.

"Where have you been, old man?" I said as he climbed into his bunk.

"Well, I sure wasn't out chasing the ladies, now was I?" he said, and that was all.

The next night, he did the same thing, slipping off by himself and coming in late. And he did it the night after that. By breakfast the next morning, he was ready to share his secret. He sat down with me and Simon and Pick and leaned over the table.

"Boys," he said, "I think we've got a special mission tonight."

"What do you mean?" Simon asked. "We don't go back up the line until next week."

"This is a personal mission of mine, and I'd like you three to assist me," Frank said. "See, I've been watching Colonel Tilton…"

I knew right then that he was out for vengeance. And I knew it was going to be good.

"Here's how it is," he said, leaning over the table a bit more. "Every night at 2300 hours, almost on the dot, our Colonel Tilton comes out of his billet to take a crap in his very own privy. He never carries a torch, either."

"So?" Pick said, a bit too loud for Frank. "I couldn't care less about his toilet habits."

"Hold on a minute," Frank said. "See, I got a good look at this privy, and found out that it's not really anchored to the ground that well…"

"You want to steal his privy?" Pick said, cutting him off.

"No!" Simon said eagerly. "You want to tip it over with him inside!"

"No, lads, I've got one better than that. But you have to come with me tonight to set it up. And you've got to keep your mouths shut. That's the only way to smell clean coming out of this."

We all vowed silence and with a great deal of excitement we awaited sundown. We set out at about 9:30 and went off toward the colonel's billet, a run-down chateau a couple of miles away. About halfway there we got off of the main road and went overland in a roundabout fashion for secrecy. Pick's uncanny sense of direction came in handy.

It was good and dark when we approached the chateau from the rear. I could see rather well in the faint light of a waning moon. We inched closer and stopped at a hedgerow right behind the chateau.

"The privy is on the other side of this hedge," Frank said.

"Yeah," I said. "I can smell it."

"Now the idea," Frank said in a whisper, "is that we pick up the privy and move it back three feet."

There was silence. It was clear to Frank that we didn't get the joke.

"See, by moving it back three feet, the mouth of the dung pit below will be right inside the door, not under the seat like it should be."

"So he'll splash in like a great sewer rat!" I said a little too loud.

"Shhh..." Frank said. "It's almost 2300 now. Show time."

We crept through the hedge in silence. We teamed up on opposite sides and inched it back. The smell would have knocked a buzzard off of a shit wagon, and I thought how nasty it would be for the colonel. I curled my lip in a twisted smile.

Frank motioned for us to stop, then opened the door and checked inside. He took a look and waved us back into the hedge to wait. Frank shut the door and came back in last.

"The key now is silence," Frank whispered. "Don't make any noise while the colonel is within earshot. And remember, no one says a word about this to anyone, period. Not even in letters home. Are we square?"

We all nodded and peered through the hedge. Sure enough, at the appointed time, the colonel opened the back door of the chateau and came outside. I nearly burst out laughing as he crossed the yard in his white nightshirt, clearly visible in the moonlight. Then he opened the door and stepped inside. There was a tremendous splash, and the colonel started screaming.

"Oh, bloody hell!" he yelled. "Someone get me out of here! I'm in up to my armpits!"

He splashed about for a few seconds, and no one showed up to help. We were trembling with fear but deeply gratified at the same time. No one flinched though personally I had the urge to get out of there, and quickly.

The colonel finally pulled himself out of the hole, and he came crawling out the door. He was black with sewage from the neck down, and had some smeared across his head and face. Then he started throwing up, quite violently.

Frank hit us on our backs and motioned for us to go, and none too soon for my taste. We ran in silence for about a half-mile without slowing down. I had never seen Pick move that fast, not even during a shelling. We stopped when we got to a road, and Frank pulled out a flask of scotch he had in his back pocket.

"Thought a drink would be in order right about now," he said, and we all took a slug. We lit cigarettes and caught our breath. We were stunned quiet, until Simon snorted, trying to suppress a giggle. That got the rest of us started and I laughed until my side hurt. I even cried a bit. That poor sod got what was coming to him.

"Well," Frank said, wiping his mouth after a second drink, "now he knows what it's like to live in a trench."

We hit the flask again and headed down the road, which Pick was certain would take us home. We tried to walk quickly without being conspicuous. I settled down some after we passed a few crossroads. An alibi, at that point, became more believable.

It was a bit after midnight that we ran into the lieutenant. I was quite surprised, when out of the darkness, he gave us a big "hello." I don't know what he was doing out there by himself on that road, but he smelled like he'd been drinking and his gait had a bit of a swagger.

"How are you this fine evening?" the lieutenant asked.

"Good, sir," Pick said nervously.

"So what brings you out here in the middle of the night?" he asked.

No one said anything.

"Well?" the lieutenant prodded.

"Well, we couldn't sleep," Frank said.

"All four of you?"

"Yes sir," Frank continued, and we were glad to let him weave the story, as it surely would be a dandy. "It is a bit too quiet to sleep back here out of the line."

"That's exactly what it is," Simon chimed in, trying to be supportive.

"You don't say," the lieutenant said, rocking on his feet and slurring a bit. "It helps you sleep if you go out and take a walk?"

"Well, sir, it does help you relax, especially if you take along a bit of medication," Frank said, pulling out the flask. He offered it to the lieutenant, who surprised us all by taking a couple of big gulps, draining it to the bottom. The only officers I knew of that drank with their subordinates were the Australians, and their men called them by their first names. The lieutenant coughed.

"That's some really awful scotch you've got there, corporal," he said. "They should pay you boys enough to buy some of the good stuff."

The lieutenant rubbed his eyes and yawned.

"You know," he said, "you don't have to go off and hide to have a drink. It's part of the business of soldiering. I think this whole situation would be better if everybody had more to drink."

He rambled on for a minute or two about the value of spirits, and then told us to get on home. He sauntered off into the night.

"Do you think he suspected anything?" Pick asked.

"No, stupid ass," Simon said. "He didn't suspect anything because he was drunk, and because he doesn't know a thing about the colonel's little accident."

"Shut up," Frank said. "I said not to talk any more about this. Anyone could hear you. And if they get us for this, we'll surely be shot at dawn, and I am not joking here. Now I suggest we make knots back home and never mention it again. Never."

It was close to one o'clock when we crawled into our bunks. I had a couple of fags to calm down. I didn't fall asleep for at least a couple of hours, and then it was time to get up again.

That morning, we said nothing as we prepared for roll call. It all seemed to have a bit more gravity in the daylight. We stood in the warm morning sunlight coming over the horizon. I felt a bit cocky, even, until roll call was over.

"Thomas, Gardener, Keaffe, Pickens," the lieutenant shouted. "I need to talk with you."

The hair on my neck stood up and my gut dropped. If it had been possible to sweat blood, I surely would have done so at that moment. We stood together and tried to look innocent.

"Gentlemen," he said, "how are you this morning?"

"Everything's *bonne*, sir," Frank said. "It's a gorgeous day, wouldn't you say, lieutenant?"

The lieutenant didn't answer. He looked us over, up and down, and scratched the back of his head. Then he pointed at Frank.

"Corporal, do you know of anything, say, out of the ordinary, that may have happened last night? Somewhere around headquarters, let's say?"

"No, sir," Frank replied. "I wouldn't know of anything like that at all, sir. I don't even know where headquarters is. What about you, Corporal Gardener?"

"No, I don't know of anything, lieutenant," I said. My mouth was parched and it was hard to speak. The lieutenant rubbed his eyes and pointed at Simon.

"Private Keaffe, where were you going last night when we met up on the road?"

"Out for a walk, sir," Simon said. "A walk and a drink. Couldn't sleep, sir."

"How about you?" the lieutenant said to Pick. "Out for a stroll?"

"Yes, sir," Pick said. "Absolutely. Awful scotch, remember, sir?"

The lieutenant stared at the ground and shuffled back and forth a few times, kicking little stones with his boot.

"Well," he said, still looking down, "just make sure nothing happens anywhere near there again. Don't even look in that direction. Understood?"

We all nodded and he turned and walked away, his hands clutched behind him. We stood there silent for a moment.

"Let's go get some breakfast," Frank said. There was no discussion as we waited in line for our food. We sat at a table away from the others and started eating in silence.

Then I noticed that Simon was trying to stifle a smile, putting a hand over his mouth. Pick turned and slapped him on the back of the head, knocking off his cap. In that moment, Frank blew tea out of his nose, trying not to laugh. Then we all broke into laughter, pointing at each other and grinning.

"All right," Frank said, motioning for us to quiet down, "everybody get it wired together and quit acting like school girls."

There were a few more chuckles, but we never mentioned our stunt again. And we never saw the colonel around our stretch of the line again, either.

CHAPTER 16

The days began getting shorter as we approached the fall. The weather was fair and the sun was warm. It was raining less, and that was a blessing. We rotated back up to the reserve lines out in the salient for a week, then on into the firing line for ten days. It was a long ten days. There was constant harassment from the Huns perched above us on Hill 60, which they had retaken in May after a brief British occupation of the position. They let us have it about every night with shells or gas or both. We didn't get much sleep.

I felt a great deal of relief that last morning in the line, as I knew replacements would be coming up at dusk. It was a Sunday, so after stand-to and breakfast, the vicar came around to say a few encouraging words and to pray with those who wanted to do so. I always prayed with the vicar. I figured it certainly couldn't hurt, and it always gave me a good dose of confidence. It made me worry less about dying.

I had been out on patrol most of the previous night, and I was exhausted. We hadn't run into any trouble, but it was strenuous nonetheless. I decided I would get some sleep, so I went down into the dugout to lie down. It smelled awful in there: a nasty combination of sweat, mold and cigarettes. So I decided to lie on my waterproof sheet out on the fire step. I stared at the gray sky above and hoped it wouldn't rain. After shifting and adjusting a few times, I dozed off, only to be awakened about an hour later by shellfire from the hill. I tried to ignore it and go back to sleep, but I couldn't. I sat up and lit a cigarette and cursed the Germans up there.

Staff Sgt. Hendershot came along the line and rounded up a half-dozen of us to help rebuild a trench that had collapsed in the most recent rain. We worked for hours, in mud halfway up to our knees, shoveling and filling sandbags. The work continued after a brief lunch of bully and biscuits, and by the end of the day, I could barely walk or stand up straight. I hobbled back to our trench to await relief.

The new platoon arrived just as the sun was disappearing. A few of the lads, mainly the NCOs, looked old enough to be there. The rest were as green as the grass in Scotland. It was a miserable sight.

"Welcome to Wipers, boys," Frank said, slapping one of the younger lads on the back. "Keep your heads low, now. This stretch is lousy with snipers."

We shouldered our rifles and hoisted our packs and filed out through a zigzagging communications trench, which got straighter and wider as we moved farther back. We reached the Menin Road and passed Hellfire Corner without incident. We went through the Menin Gate and into the remains of Ypres, which looked worse than when we'd last passed that way over a fortnight before. Soldiers were starting to come out of their subterranean hideouts for the evening. Everything was blacked out until we got to the other side of town and on the road to Pop.

We walked about a mile down the road and arrived at our billet at about 10 p.m. It was the basement of a farmhouse, and as far as accommodations went, these were first class. It had a clean stone floor and a couple of high windows that even had the glass intact. There was an oblong wood burning stove at the end of the room, good for cooking and plenty enough for heat. We settled in without saying much. Frank and I smoked a couple of cigarettes and collapsed on our bunks.

I awoke before dawn and for a moment I did not know where I was. I sat up startled and put my feet on the floor. The stone was cold on my feet and I got a shiver. I decided to stoke up the stove and make some tea. Frank awoke and sat up, ran his fingers through his hair and lit a fag. We were sitting by the stove in silence, waiting for the tea, when two military policemen came through the door at the far end of the room. They walked over to the stove quietly, showing respect for the men still sleeping.

"Could either of you tell me which one is Francis Thomas?" the older of the two policemen asked.

I looked at Frank and he turned white as a ghost. I didn't answer and neither did he. We just stared at each other.

"Are you simple?" the policeman asked. "I need to know which one of you is Corporal Francis Thomas."

"He, it seems, would be me," Frank replied slowly. He reached for his trousers and pulled them on as he stood up.

"Would you also be known as the Fantastic Franklin?" the younger policemen asked.

"What do you want?" Frank stammered. "I haven't done anything. Just ask him. I've been up on the line for the last two weeks…"

"Save your excuses," the older one said. "You are wanted in connection with a theft of art from the estate of Sir Arthur Hanrahan."

"Hanra-who? I don't know any sir anybody. There must be some kind of mistake here, fellows. You've obviously got the wrong man!"

"I'm afraid not," the older one said. "You are going to the brig at Etaples, where you'll be held until you stand trial."

Frank continued to protest, but to no avail.

"Get dressed," the younger one demanded, and Frank complied. They put him in wrist irons and led him out the door. Everyone was awake now, shaking their heads and shrugging their shoulders at one another. The only one that really knew what was going on was Frank, and he wasn't giving up any secrets. I followed them out to the road, where they put Frank in the back of a car.

"I'll mind your gear!" I shouted as the car pulled away, spitting gravel in my general direction. I had no idea what had happened, but I believed Frank when he said he was innocent. I'd seen him pinch fags and little things, but nothing serious. This was a complete surprise. After roll call, I approached the lieutenant to see if I could get more information.

"Sir," I said, "it may be none of my business, but could you tell me what happened to Corporal Thomas?"

"All I know is that he pulled some stunt before he joined up and it has finally caught up to him," the lieutenant said. "Orders for his arrest came down late last night."

"Do you know when he might be back? I'm looking after his things…"

"I don't know if he'll be back at all."

"Is there anything that can be done, sir?"

"I've come to value Thomas as much as anyone in this unit," he said, scratching his hairless chin. "I'll see what we can do. In the mean time, just sit tight and enjoy your rest as best you can."

It was three mornings later that Frank returned, wearing a spotless uniform and sporting a new haircut, a close shave and shiny boots. Pick spotted him coming up the road from headquarters.

"So where the 'ell have you been, Thomas?" he bellowed out the door. "You look no worse for the wear, to be sure."

"Well, that's one of the great things about jail," he said as he stepped through the door. "You get three hot meals a day, a warm bunk and a clean place to crap."

"So what was it all about?" I asked. "Give us the low-down, old man."

"It wasn't much," he said, lighting a cigarette. "Like I told them, they had the wrong bloke."

"That's it?" Pick prodded.

"Well, it seems that there was a theft committed at the last performing engagement I had before we shipped over here. It was one of those big affairs at a country estate. After three days of

113

getting nowhere, they decided the thief must have been someone else at the party. They let me go and I caught the next transport up. That's about it."

"We're glad to have you back," Simon said, showing a surprising amount of sentiment. "Did you learn any new tricks while you were sitting in your cell?"

"I think I might have something for you," he said, pulling a deck of cards out of his pocket. A crowd soon gathered, and in an instant he had them scratching their heads and laughing. Frank glanced over at me sitting on my bunk and gave me a wink. He had a certain glimmer in his eyes and I knew something was going on. I decided I would wait for an opportunity to talk to him alone, and I got ready for roll call.

Our moment alone came right after breakfast, when we were assigned to work in the officer's mess. There was a mound of potatoes that needed peeling, and Frank and I were lucky enough to get the job. It didn't involve any lifting, it was inside where it couldn't rain, and no one thought you were important enough to the war effort to shoot. It was a good job.

We sat on stools with rubbish cans between our knees and got to work. There were guns firing in the distance. It sounded like a battery of 18-pounders giving the Germans a much-needed iron ration. I waited for Frank to open up, but he didn't.

"It's almost a shame that you got sent back up here," I said, finally breaking the silence.

"Maybe so," he said. "Maybe so. Jail was pretty good by comparison. Got myself cleaned up. The food wasn't bad, either."

There was an uncomfortable silence as we went about our work. There was something to know and I wanted to know it.

"What really happened?" I finally blurted.

Frank stopped peeling and stared at the potato in his hand, then put down his knife. He looked around, and seeing no one, leaned over and put his hand on my shoulder.

"In the short time we've known each other, I've grown to trust you," he said, still fidgeting with the spud. "I must ask you, on your honor, to pledge not to tell anyone what has taken place. Not Simon or Pick or anyone."

"I pledge."

"What I told the boys was true in one respect, in that I was entertaining at the estate of this Sir Hanrahan when a theft took place, and it is true that they let me go after some questioning."

He paused and thought for a moment, looked around, and continued slowly.

"Hanrahan is a very rich man, very powerful, with friends in the House of Lords and in the military; I think he used to be a general or something in the South African campaigns. Anyway, he holds great galas at his thousand-acre country estate in the south of England, lasting three or four days at a time, with hundreds of guests, sometimes even royalty among them. This was a big one, and I was hired to entertain. I was having a grand time, strolling around doing card tricks and my coin routines, drinking free champagne, smoking big cigars.

"I had finished up for the night, probably about 12 or so, and I went looking for the loo before heading out. I looked around everywhere, but couldn't find it. And I really had to take a piss, from all the champagne. Finally, I decided to go upstairs and look, and sure enough, I found one right off.

"As I was coming out, I noticed this vase on a pedestal in a niche across from the door of the bog. It was small but really an eye-catcher, though I usually don't pay much attention to those kinds of things. This was so unusual, painted in an Oriental fashion, and I got to thinking about Lizzy back in London, and how much she would like a vase like that. She loves flowers, you see.

"So I looked down, and I had my bag in my hand there, and I thought, why don't I just slip that vase inside and take it home for here as a surprise gift? I figured that a man as rich as Hanrahan wouldn't miss that little vase, and if he did, he could buy a new one. I wasn't about to feel guilty about stealing from a rich man.

"I put the vase in my bag and buckled it tight, then went looking for a back way out, as to leave unnoticed. I found a stairway the servants used, and headed down. I thought I was away and clear, but I bumped into Lady Hanrahan in the parlor where the stairway ended. She asked me what I was doing there, and I told her that I was looking for the loo and got lost. That was true, and easy to believe, considering that their humble home has all of about 400 rooms. I apologized for startling her, and she pointed me to the door.

"It was a clear night, albeit cold, and I took a footpath back to the village. I had a few drinks of whiskey along the way to warm me up; I had stolen a bottle of that, too. When I got back to my room, I laid down, drunk as a monkey on payday. Fell asleep in my clothes, and that was a good thing. A real good thing."

"Why was that?"

"Well, I woke up the next morning with a serious headache, and some men banging on my door. As soon as I realized they were constables, I jumped up, grabbed my bag with the vase inside, and climbed out the window. I was on the second floor and had to jump. I was amazed that I didn't break the vase, or my legs, on the way down.

"I kept low and tried to make it to the nearest train station, but when I got there, I saw a group of constables looking about, poking in and out of the cars. I wasn't sure they were looking for me, but I didn't want to take any chances. I headed out across the countryside, sticking to the footpaths until I got to Salisbury. Then I took a train for London that evening. I figured that would be the end of it."

"But it wasn't, I take it," I said, hanging on his every word.

"You're right," he said. "Those buggers were already ahead of me, waiting for me to run to ground. I showed up and Lizzy was in hysterics. She said some men from Scotland Yard had been by looking for me, and they tossed the flat looking for the vase."

"No joking? Scotland Yard?"

"Yes! And it was about that time that I realized that I had stolen something more than a pretty pot for some daffodils. I showed it to Lizzy. She thought it was gorgeous, but told me to get rid of it. I changed into a new suit and shaved my moustache for a bit of disguise. Then I ran down the stairs to the cellar and out the back door in the alley. I was pleasantly surprised that they weren't watching that exit.

"I went across town and looked up this fellow I knew, an antique dealer who sometimes found old magic gadgets for me. I strolled into his shop just like I always did, and we chatted for a bit. I told him I had something I wanted him to take a look at, something my father had brought back from one of his voyages to Hong Kong. When I pulled out the vase, it was like he'd seen a specter.

"So he says to me, 'You don't have any idea what this is, do you?' and I said it had been collecting dust for a while and I wanted to get rid of it. Not my style, I said. Then he told me some guy named Ming or Mang or something like that made it, and it was worth quite a few quid. He didn't know exactly how much, but guessed at a couple of hundred pounds. At that point, I didn't know whether to piss pins or needles. So I told him I was going on a trip and asked him to hold it for safekeeping until I came back to London. I told him I was afraid it would get broken at my flat or something. He agreed to keep it in his safe in the basement until I returned for it. I gave him a couple of quid for his trouble.

"I needed somewhere to lay low for a while. First I thought I'd head up to Liverpool, and then over to Ireland until things cooled off. Then I thought, why not go to Hull instead? My father had a flat there that he used when he wasn't at sea, and my aunt and uncle lived up the street from there. I also knew a lot of the ship captains that sailed out of there, and if need be, I could make a quick getaway to just about anywhere. I left London walking north.

"I hitched rides on lorries until I made it to Sheffield. When I got there, I got a room, then sent a telegram to my uncle to let him know I'd be arriving the next day and needed a place to stay. I told them to cable me back the next day to let me know if that would be all right. I stretched out on my bed and finished the bottle in my bag.

"I slept in my clothes in case I needed to make a hasty exit. By morning, I was beginning to feel sure of myself, thinking I'd given the police the slip. That was, until the telegram arrived from Hull. Scotland Yard had been there already, and they were waiting for me to make an appearance."

"Those blokes must be part bloodhound, I say!"

"That's what I thought, too. It was beginning to look like there wasn't any way out anywhere. I didn't know what to do, but I couldn't sit still and wait to be caught. I went down to the train station and looked at the schedules. I wanted to get somewhere safe. Nothing looked good. I sat down on a bench and weighed my options.

"Then I saw the sign for the recruiting depot at the other end of the station. I talked to a kind young lady sitting at a table there, who asked me if I wanted to serve my country in France. Then I realized that France was, at least, out of the country, and the police would never think to look for me in the army.

"I asked the girl when the next train was leaving for the training camps, and she said one was scheduled for next morning. I signed up right there. I spent the day boozing it up, then slept the night on a bench in the station. I wrote a note to Lizzy to let her know where I was going, and that I would explain more later. I posted it right before we left."

"And that was when we met?"

"Yes, it was."

"And they finally tracked you down over here?"

"Yes. It turns out that Hanrahan not only has chums at Scotland Yard, he also knows some men on the General Staff. So when the police figured out where I had gone – and it took them long enough – Hanrahan started raising Cain and they came to get me. It became a matter of military justice, somehow. I'm still not sure how that worked. But I thought they were going to put me up against a wall when I got to Etaples."

"So how'd you end up back here?"

"Well, that was where things took a rather odd turn. You won't believe what happened."

117

"Get on with it, old man!"

"You've got to swear," he whispered, "you've got to swear you won't let anyone in this outfit, company, division, corps, country…I mean no one can know about this, or I'm back in a real heap of trouble."

"I can keep my mouth shut with the best of them."

"All right," he said, pausing. "I was on my third day in the hole and the guard came and got me. He said I had a visitor. I hadn't the faintest idea who it could have been. Turned out it was the lieutenant."

"Lt. Rampkin? I hadn't noticed he was gone."

"Well, there he was, waiting for me in this little room with a table and chairs, two cups and a pot of tea. He filled my cup and told me to sit down."

"'We don't have any cream,'" he said. "'War is so barbaric.'"

"'Don't mind a bit sir,'" I said. "'It'll do just fine.'"

"We sat there silent for a moment and sipped our tea, then he started giving me a lecture about honesty and integrity and the importance of being a good soldier. And that went on for a while. Then he asked if I could follow his advice for a while, and I agreed. Finally, he asked me if I knew where a certain Chinese vase might be found, and I said no, I didn't know about anything like that.

"He got that frustrated look of his: you know the one I'm talking about. He just sat there quiet for a minute, rubbed his eyes and finished his tea. Then he pushed out his chair and said it was time to go now, and I could pick up my things on the way out."

"Just like that?"

"Just like that, old man. Can you believe it? The next thing I knew, he called the guards, and they led us to the gate. We got on a train and headed back up here. Just like that."

"There's got to be more to it," I said. "What's the rest of the story?"

"For the first 20 miles or so, the lieutenant wouldn't say a thing, just staring out the window. But I wore him down after a while and he unbuttoned his lip."

"What did he say?"

"He said his father bailed me out."

"His father?"

"It turns out that his old man used to be on the General Staff, and an old school chum of none other than Lord Hanrahan."

"Well if I haven't heard it all by now…"

"Well, you haven't. The lieutenant got his father to wire Hanrahan, pleading that I was more valuable at the front than I was in jail, and that if I were released, I would assist him in finding the vase when the war was over."

"So he made a deal for you?"

"At first, Hanrahan wouldn't budge. Then the general pointed out that they hadn't found the vase in my possession, nor had they any proof that I'd taken it at all. The general told Hanrahan that if he wanted me to suffer nonetheless, he should send me back to Ypres, where the conditions are far worse than prison. Reluctantly, I assume, he agreed."

"That's amazing!"

"Yes," he said, "and I don't know whether to laugh or cry." We chose to laugh.

CHAPTER 17

Fall turned to winter and still there was no end in sight. The snow on the ground covered the dead, rotting bodies, the shell holes, and the whole mess. The battlefield looked almost peaceful in a surreal sort of way. The fighting ground to a halt all along the Western Front. I remember Christmas Day of 1915 very well. We were in the line, and my spirits were lifted upon receiving a package of homemade candy and a letter from my sister. The boys and me dug into the candy and I read her note. There was big news.

"Hey fellows," I said. "My sister is getting married."

"Who's the lucky man?" Frank asked.

"His name is Walter Healey. Second Lt. Walter Healey. He's got a college education and used to work in a bank in Manchester. He's in field artillery now."

"Sounds like a good man," Frank said. "Maybe you'll meet up with him over here."

"If he's your brother-in-law, would you still have to salute him?" Simon pondered. "That would be a bit odd, wouldn't it?"

"Send our best wishes, Richard," Pick said. "Even if he is an officer."

Later that day, they gave us a tremendous meal of roast beef, potatoes, bread, cheese and a double ration of rum. After sundown, we could hear the Germans singing carols across the field. We obliged them with a few of our own. The next day, we were shooting at each other again.

The cold weather made life in the trenches an absolute hell. Between frostbite and influenza, we were losing hundreds of men a day. It's surprising that we were able to maintain a defense at all. Trying to stay warm was an endless pursuit. We donned sheep's wool vests over our greatcoats, which made us look a lot like soldiers from medieval times. I vowed that if I made it out alive, I'd never be cold again.

While we were up on the line freezing, generals on both sides began making plans for the inevitable spring offensives. There were grand schemes devised and tremendous results expected. Surely, the generals believed, the war would be won in 1916. We hoped it would be, too, but we weren't optimistic.

As I said, the lines were static along our front that winter. But the Germans still found it necessary to harass us whenever possible, just as a reminder that they were still watching. Like at Neuve Chapelle, shelling became predictable at Wipers. They would sight their guns by day, and then give us a big dose right after sundown. So following tea and evening stand-to, we knew to get under cover for a bit, to reemerge only after the guns fell silent. I, for one, found it easy to handle, simply because it was so routine. Most of the other men felt the same way that I did; it was better knowing when a barrage was coming as opposed to not knowing.

Pick, however, never did get accustomed to it. He would start getting edgy in the late afternoon, dreading what was coming. Often times, he could not eat because of his nerves, and he started losing weight. When we went into the dugout, he would roll under one of the bottom bunks, and wouldn't come out until it was over. By then, he was a total wreck. His hands shook all of the time. He began to stammer. He cried a lot.

On one particular night in early 1916, the Germans hit us harder than usual. I don't know what came over them, but they really let us have it. We were down in the dugout for hours, and Pick stayed under a bottom bunk the whole time. When it came to an end, just after 10 p.m., we all went out to survey the damage. Except for Pick. He refused to come out of his hiding place. When I went back in to lie down for the night, he was still there, trembling all over. I left him alone.

I awoke in the morning before the others, so I climbed out of my bunk and put some wood in the stove. I put on a pot of tea and took out a box of matches to light a cigarette, but dropped them on the floor. In bending over to get them, I noticed Pick wasn't under the bunk anymore. Then I looked around at the other bunks, and realized he was not in the dugout at all. I went out into the trench, but he wasn't there, either. I woke up Simon and Frank.

"Do you blokes know where Pick is?" I asked.

"Did you look under the bunk?" Simon suggested. "He's probably still under there."

"No, he's not," I said. "And he's not outside."

They went outside to have a look for themselves, but came back a few minutes later shrugging their shoulders.

"Now I'm starting to worry," I said. "He'd better turn up before roll call, or he's going to be in some serious trouble."

He didn't turn up. The lieutenant asked us when we saw him last. We all said we saw him when we went to bed, but not since.

"You don't think he's deserted, do you corporal?" the lieutenant asked me.

"I should hope not, sir," I said.

"Did he say anything to you last night?"

"Nothing at all sir. He was hiding under the bunk the last time I saw him, and he wasn't talking to anyone then."

"You know I'll have to report him absent without leave."

"Yes sir."

"The military police will be looking for him then."

"Yes sir, I would imagine so."

"If you can find him before they do, I'll take care of him myself. But if not, it will be a matter of military justice. Understood, corporal?"

"Yes sir."

"I want you, Thomas and Keaffe to canvas the area. Go up and down all of the trenches within 500 yards. See if he turns up."

I went down the fire trench to the left of the dugout, and Frank went to the right. Simon went down the adjoining communications trench and checked along the second line. We all came up empty-handed. We reported to the lieutenant.

"Can't find him, sir," I said. "He doesn't seem to be here."

"Damn it," the lieutenant swore. "Where in hell could he be? Well, thanks for looking anyway, lads. I'm going to have to get on the telephone and report him missing."

We never did get an explanation from Pick, because we never saw him again. About a week or so after his disappearance, the lieutenant got word that he'd been picked up in Calais, trying to get on a troop transport back to Blighty. He was brought up on desertion charges and found guilty. On a cold February morning, he was executed by a firing squad and buried in a nearby field. We all took it hard, especially Simon. He became morose and distant, and didn't talk much to anyone. He was clearly depressed. It was a rare glimpse at his more sensitive side. I hadn't realized he was capable of feeling such deep emotions. For the most part, though, we didn't mention Pick or what happened to him again. It was too disturbing to contemplate.

That same month, we started hearing rumors of a great slaughter down the line near the French town of Verdun. It didn't take long for news like that to spread through the trenches simply by word of mouth. When we got out of the line, we read about the battle in the newspapers. The reality, it turned out, was a lot worse than the tales we'd heard.

Apparently, the Huns decided not to wait until spring to begin their assault against the French. They threw everything they could muster against the defenses surrounding Verdun, and the bloodbath commenced. The French were losing two or three thousand men a day. The harder the Germans fought, the more determined the French became, refusing to concede even an inch. The French army started pulling troops out of other sectors and sending them down to Verdun to fight. At one time or another, just about every Frenchman ended up there. March came, and the fighting raged on with no signs of stopping. It almost became a war unto itself. It made me glad to be at Wipers, where things were pretty much holding steady.

Spring, however, had to be the worst time on our front. The frozen earth thawed and turned into mud. Then came the rain. It was a mess. We couldn't bale out the water fast enough. Trenches eroded and collapsed. Being clean and dry became an impossibility.

We got our steel helmets around that time, replacing the caps we'd worn thus far. There was a high incidence of head wounds, mostly from snipers and shrapnel, and the helmets were supposed to reduce that. The French and the Belgians had been wearing helmets since the beginning, but it took a little time for the British commanders to catch on to their value. Tommy's were ostensibly based on the French design, but they were in no way similar. Ours looked like pregnant dinner plates, and there was a lot of debate as to whether they were good for anything other than keeping the rain off of your head. A lot of the fellows in our unit complained that they were too heavy and didn't wear them until the lieutenant started wearing his. We all had a lot of respect for him, and if he thought the helmets were a good idea, then we did, too.

At the end of March, we rotated back to rest billets. There was hearsay among the men that a big operation was being planned for us, but no one seemed to know exactly what or when. There was much speculation and a lot of opinions on the subject. The tension heightened when the lieutenant told us to assemble for a briefing after lunch one day.

"I guess this is it," Frank said. "Things are about to get really ugly."

"Don't jump to any conclusions, Frank," I said. "This could be about anything."

"Anything bad, you mean."

Simon agreed with Frank. I knew better than to argue with them.

It was about one o'clock when we gathered at a position west of Ypres, beyond the view of the Huns. There was a scale model of Hill 60 and the ridges to the south, created behind a large farmhouse. There were 21 flags posted along the simulated line. We stood in a box formation around it, and the lieutenant explained the plan.

"Gentlemen," he said, "this is a representation of the lines running from north of Ypres down the Messines Ridge. As you can see, they make something like an inverted S, with us holding the top bulge, protruding east, roughly in a semicircle, beyond Ypres. The Germans hold a corresponding westward bulge to the south. In essence, we hold adjacent salients. We find ourselves surrounded on three sides up north, and they find themselves in the same situation to the south. The bloody unfortunate aspect is that they have the high ground, and it is heavily fortified.

"Now General Haig's ultimate goal is to break out of the Ypres salient, drive north, and eventually hook up with an amphibious assault wave that will land behind enemy lines. The objective will be to capture the U-boat bases located along the North Sea coast, and shut them down. This operation, if everything goes as planned, could be a war-winner, and we will play a vital role in it.

"However, we must first improve our position to the south of Ypres, or we stand no chance of success. It is essential that we take the high ground from Hill 60 down the Messines Ridge, flatten the German bulge and consolidate the line. Only then will we be able to break out of our salient and drive to the sea.

"You are probably wondering how we are going to do this, because so far, we haven't been able to break the deadlock here. The truth is that traditional attacks have failed to wrest the high ground from the Germans, and there is little chance they will do so in the future. That being the case, General Plumer, with Haig's approval, has devised a new plan for victory; we will attack the enemy from below.

"Plumer's plan calls for laying a series of 21 enormous mines along a ten-mile front, from Hill 60 down to Ploegsteert Wood, roughly where these flags are placed. The tunnels will total about five miles in length, and will be charged with about one million pounds of explosives. A mining campaign on this level has not yet been attempted, although smaller efforts have produced favorable results here and elsewhere. For example, our boys managed to take Hill 60 for a brief period in the spring of last year by exploding a mine there, but with the Germans on the flanks, it had to be conceded once again.

"As for this campaign, tunneling companies comprised mostly of miners will lead the effort, and we will provide assistance. The work will be tedious; no doubt Fritz will pick up on what we are doing. He'll be digging counter-mines in an attempt to shut us down, but we must persevere.

"Once all of the mines are in place, they will be detonated simultaneously, cracking open the German strong points along the ridge. We will then advance and secure the high ground. Future operations in Flanders depend on it. I expect everyone's best effort. Are there any questions?"

"Sir," Frank said, "how long is this going to take to prepare? It sounds like a lot of digging, sir."

"Five of the 11 planned shafts are already underway," he said. "We will progress as quickly as possible, but General Plumer is hoping to have everything in place by June of next year."

You could almost hear the men gasping. More than a year to prepare for one battle! I got a terrible feeling in my stomach just thinking about it. We were dismissed, and Frank walked off cursing.

"What happened to winning the war this year?" Frank asked me. "I guess that's off of the table, then. We're never going to get home."

"This may change things," I said. "We could have a breakthrough, like the lieutenant said."

"And if not, what then? Another battle? When will it stop? When all of us are napoo except one German and one Englishman, and they'll have the final fight to determine the winner. That's when."

"Now you're just exaggerating," I said. "It won't come down to that."

"You don't know. The men in charge are a bunch of idiots who don't give a damn about us. This is the most fouled-up mess I've ever seen. Anything could happen. You just don't know, Richard."

While I outwardly tried to be the voice of reason, I must admit that I was more than a little apprehensive on the inside. It was ironic that I had joined the army to get out of the mines, and now I was going back underground; and while coal mining was dangerous, there was no one intentionally trying to blow you up while you did your job. Things seemed like they were going from bad to worse, and rapidly.

We were in rest billets for one more night. Frank and some of the others went out in pursuit of wine, but I stayed in and wrote a letter to Rose. I curbed my pessimism and told her that everything was going well, even though I felt differently. I figured I'd tell her the truth about the war once I got home, and not until then. I fell asleep, but Frank and the others woke me up when they came in, drunk and singing:

> *"If you want to find the old battalion,*
> *I know where they are,*
> *I know where they are.*
> *If you want to find the old battalion,*
> *I know where they are.*
> *They're hanging on the old barbed wire.*
> *I've seen 'em, I've seen 'em,*
> *hanging on the old barbed wire!*

125

I managed to get a little sleep before Hendershot came in to wake us, around four. We ate breakfast and headed for the front under the cover of darkness. About an hour before dawn, we went out the Menin Gate, then south following the ridge. We began work on a mine that very afternoon, starting a shaft about 200 yards behind the front trench. Frank and I made it down about six feet, while Simon and a fellow named Walker bagged the dirt. Frank's tender hands were soon covered with blisters. There was blood on the handle of his shovel.

"I don't know if I can do this, old man," Frank said, catching his breath.

"It doesn't look like we have much choice in the matter," I said.

"And these tunnels they're talking about. They don't look like they'll be very roomy. Did I ever tell you I was claustrophobic?"

"What the devil does that mean?"

"It means I can't stand confined places. Makes me nervous. I can barely handle being in a dugout. I'd rather be up in the open getting sniped at by Huns."

I leaned my shovel up against the side of the hole and put my hand on his shoulder.

"You know," I said, "when I first started working in the mines, I was just a boy. And when you dig coal, you don't want to mess with the slate between the seams. So a lot of times you end up digging on your knees, or maybe even on your belly. I was nervous at first, but I got used to it. You're going to be fine."

"I don't know," he said. "You must be a lot tougher than me. I don't know if I can handle it."

We went back to digging and made it a couple more feet, and then Frank stopped and leaned on his shovel.

"Hell," he said, "this is enough to wear a bugger out."

We stopped digging there and shored up the sides with wooden posts and planks, then nailed a ladder to the side. After lunch, we switched jobs with Simon and Walker and let them dig while we bagged the dirt. It was essential that the dirt be bagged; not far below the surface was a layer of blue clay, and an aerial observer might notice the odd-colored soil if it were left piled near the shaft. It would have been a sure tip-off that mining was underway. We used the bags of clay to shore up our defenses, adding to the breastwork and putting extra layers on top of the dugouts. Eventually, they set up a light rail line for transporting bags to other areas that needed them.

After a few days of working on the shaft, we got a lucky break and went back to our old routine. We helped carry up planks and posts for shoring the shaft, but other than that, it was business as

126

usual. It took the tunneling company 10 more days to reach 100 feet, whereupon they excavated a short gallery, from which several different tunnels would be started. Some of them would be used as listening posts for detecting enemy mining, and one would lead all the way to the ridge, where a large chamber would be hollowed out and a charge placed.

Soon I began to understand what Frank meant by claustrophobic. The tunnels we started were just big enough for a man to sit up in. You put your back against a cross-like brace and kicked the shovel out in front of you; we called it "working at the cross" or "clay-kicking." The dirt was put on a cart on wooden rails, and pulled with a rope back to the gallery, where it was bagged and hauled to the surface. It was tiring labor.

When we had driven the tunnel 30 yards or so, a ventilation system had to be put in place to get fresh air to the man at the face. There was some fear that methane would build up to dangerous levels in the tunnels. The pumps were accordion-like affairs operated by hand. Mechanical pumps would have been too noisy and a tip-off to the Huns.

The only advantage to working in the tunnels was that it remained a constant 52 degrees, which was cooler than the outside temperature in the summer, and warmer in the winter. It never rained on you in there, either, but they would fill with water. I nearly got trapped inside once during a heavy deluge. We installed electric pumps that ran around the clock, and kept inching forward.

After about a month of tunneling, we became aware that the Germans, at least to some extent, knew what we were doing. South of Hill 60, a tunneling company had made it about halfway to the German lines. Frank and I were working deep in a tunnel just up the line, with me at the face and him loading carts, when we felt a tremendous boom reverberate through the earth, shaking down loose dirt on top of us. We crawled out of the tunnel to the gallery, and then scurried up the ladder to see what was going on.

As it turned out, the Germans were tunneling, too, and had come close enough to the mine to our south to hear our boys digging. They laid a small charge called a camouflet atop our tunnel, and exploded it on our men. It collapsed the end of the tunnel, burying them alive. We dug through the earth with haste, hoping to rescue them. But it took us five days to reach them, by which time they had died of asphyxiation.

Now this made all of us very nervous. If the Huns knew about that mine, what did they know about the other dozen or so mines that were currently underway? We had to find some answers, and the only way to obtain information was to get some German bugger to talk. Later that night, the lieutenant assembled a "Black Hand Gang," or trench-raiding party, and we went out in search of just such an informant.

The artillery batteries obliged us with a sudden box barrage just after sundown, which cut off a section of the German line from both sides and the rear to stop reinforcements from coming up. With shells screaming overhead, we headed up International Trench, the railway cut that bisected the battlefield. It earned its name because it changed hands so often. We edged up to the German line and the lieutenant drew his revolver. Privates Radcliffe and Kemenah were right behind him, carrying a bag of bombs. Kemenah loved bombs. I think he just liked blowing things up. Radcliffe was this red-haired kid, odd sense of humor, who pretty much did whatever Kemenah did. Me, Frank, and Simon filed in behind them. To our rear were privates Sprouse and Taylor, carrying "come-alongs," which were poles with barbed-wire nooses on the end, designed to encourage a prisoner to "come along." There were another dozen or so riflemen in line behind them.

We made it all the way across No Man's Land without being noticed, which surprised the living daylights out of me. There was a glow coming from the end of a sap leading to the right of International Trench. We turned the corner and stumbled upon a half-dozen Germans warming their hands over a brazier, confident, apparently, that the shelling was just general harassment. Naturally, they were a bit surprised. One of them yelled something in German and pointed his rifle at the lieutenant. The lieutenant popped him in the chest with his revolver like an American cowboy at a gunfight. The rest fled up the trench, and we pursued.

We were close behind them until we came to a traverse. The lieutenant held up his hand, motioning for us to stop. Something was rattling on the other side, and there was definite cursing. A bomb came hurtling over the top of the traverse. It sailed harmlessly above us and landed on the parapet, giving us all a good dusting.

"Sprouse," the lieutenant whispered, "you and Taylor come up here. The idea is to take them alive, so be ready with those contraptions."

He waved Frank and I up to the front.

"Go 'round and check it out," he said.

"Oh, lovely," Frank said under his breath. The lieutenant either didn't hear him or didn't pay him any attention.

We slowly moved around the traverse until we could see up the trench. There were four Germans trying to get through a gate laced with wire. It apparently wasn't working like it was supposed to, because they couldn't get it to open to save their lives. They were shaking it with all of their might and trying to tear through it with their bare hands.

"Surrender or die!" Frank shouted, like some kind of Barbary pirate. Two of them turned and raised their rifles, but we cut them down before they could pull off a shot. The other two were still trying to get the gate open.

"Surrender or die, I say!" Frank shouted again.

The Germans turned, and, seeing that they had no way out, dropped their rifles and raised their hands.

"So you must be the smart ones in the bunch," Frank said, kicking the rifles aside. The rest of the group moved in. Taylor and Sprouse lassoed them, and we tied their hands in back with leather thongs. We quickly headed back out the way we came, moving as fast as we could with the prisoners. We got to our end of International Trench without being followed and without losing a man. I felt we were pretty lucky.

There were two officers from Intelligence waiting for us upon our arrival. They were eager to find out what the prisoners might know. They needed someone to escort them back through the maze of trenches to regimental headquarters. That was a couple of miles away, which was fine with me, since anywhere was safer than the fire trench. So me, Frank, Sprouse and Taylor volunteered to go. The lieutenant came along as well, wanting to safeguard our catch personally. I suspected that he, too, was interested in finding out what they knew about our mining.

It was tough going through the trenches at night. It was muddy and there were tremendous shell holes all the way. At one point we were knee deep in muck and I was beginning to regret coming along. But we soon reached a line of duckboards that led to the Menin Road, and things got easier. The Intelligence boys took the lead and we followed them toward town. One of the Huns muttered something to the other one, and Taylor poked him with his bayonet.

"I'd be all too happy to run you through," Taylor said, "so shut your mouth."

"It's all right," the lieutenant said. "He was just complaining that his boots are too tight and he's tired."

"I didn't know you spoke German, sir," Taylor said.

"There's a lot you don't know about me," the lieutenant said. "I also speak Italian and a bit of French."

We arrived at regimental headquarters near Hellfire Corner, the same place we'd taken the American, Schumman. The Intelligence officers told us to wait at the top of the stairs while

129

they escorted one of the Germans down into the cellar. The lieutenant tried to follow, but they told him to stay put and keep an eye on the other German.

We sat down on the remains of the foundation of the house and waited. I got out my cigarettes and Frank and I lit up.

"Mind if I have one of those Woodbines?" the lieutenant asked.

"Feeling in the mood for one tonight, lieutenant?" I asked as I passed them over to him.

"Well," he said, "you've got to do something while you're waiting. I wonder what they're talking about down there."

He walked over and sat at the top of the stairs, his ear cocked. Taylor and me were laughing about something and he hushed us down. He was listening in on the conversation below.

"Anything interesting, lieutenant?" Sprouse asked.

"This one is spilling everything," he said. "Sounds like they know a lot about the mining around Hill 60. They've got several tunnels around there, too."

"Oh really?"

"Yes. And he knows there is mining going on elsewhere down the ridge. Doesn't seem like he knows exactly where, though."

"Lovely," Sprouse mumbled. "Just bloody lovely."

The interrogation of the first prisoner lasted about an hour, and then they brought him out and got the other. He didn't say much, according to the lieutenant; as best he could tell, the second lad hadn't been up at the front for more than a few days. But the revelations of the talkative one surely put the lieutenant on edge.

"We're in a pretty tough spot," he said. "We've still got a long way to go. And they'll be on top of us. That's a sorry state of affairs."

The sun was coming up when they finished with the second prisoner. We were told to take them to the other side of Ypres to the old prison, where they would be processed and sent to an internment camp.

"I don't want to walk back up in the daylight," the lieutenant said. "We'll head back after dark to avoid the snipers. Go find yourselves something to eat, get a few hours of sleep if you can, and meet me back at the Menin Gate at dusk."

I thought it was quite decent of the lieutenant to give us the day off. We decided to go to a bathhouse, wash up and get some clean underwear. We didn't bother washing our uniforms; they would be dirty by the time we got back up to the firing line, anyway.

I was drying my hair when I caught the smell of breakfast. We followed the scent until we came to a field kitchen set up on the

130

east side of town. There wasn't much of a line, and soon we were feasting on eggs, bacon and bread and butter with plum and apple jam. We found a place to sit and devoured the meal without a word. Then we all got seconds.

Frank unbuttoned his tunic, leaned back against a broken brick wall and let out a belch that could have slammed a door shut.

"Is it too early to drink?" he asked.

"It's never too early to drink," Taylor said, wiping his mouth on his sleeve. "Besides, for us, it's actually late, seeing how we haven't been to bed yet."

"What do you have in mind?" I asked.

"There's an *estaminet* about a mile west of town, if I recall correctly," Frank said.

"I don't know," I said. "I'm kind of tired. Maybe we should get some sleep."

"To hell with that," Taylor said. "I'm with the magician."

I protested some more, but it was no use. We headed down the road and walked about a half-mile until Sprouse flagged down a lorry that took us to our destination, a rather depressed looking farm house with a hand-painted sign out front that simply said "*Vin*" in big red letters. It was all the invitation we needed.

There were four tables inside and a badly-crafted bar with racks of wine behind it. There was one other person in the place, and he was asleep at one of the tables, his head resting on his folded arms. A plump woman in an apron asked us if we wanted some chips and eggs.

"No, just *vin rouge, si vous plaît*," Frank said.

The woman brought us two unlabelled bottles and four glasses. We sat down and Taylor pulled out a deck of cards.

"How about some nap?" he said.

"That's not the kind of nap I had in mind," I said.

"Quit your moaning and drink up," Sprouse said, filling my glass. "Cheers."

We raised our glasses and took a drink. It was the worst excuse for wine that I had ever tasted, but I drank it anyway. Taylor and Sprouse started a game of cards.

After two or three glasses and a dozen Woodbines, I got interminably drowsy. I figured out in my head that I hadn't slept in about 30 hours, and that realization only made my condition worse. I started to fall asleep in my chair.

"You look like you're about ready to die," Frank said. "Maybe the *mademoiselle* will let you lay down in the back somewhere."

I walked over to the bar where the woman was sitting. She reached for another bottle of wine.

131

"No, thank you," I said, motioning for her to put the bottle back. "*Dormir, si vous plait.*"

She smiled broadly and led me to a room in the back of the house. There were four beds there, and two of them were occupied. She held out her hand and I gave her a few pence.

"*Merci, beaucoup,*" I said, and staggered over to one of the empty racks. I pulled my boots off and collapsed. I was asleep in minutes.

I awoke with a start hours later to the sound of shellfire coming from the direction of Ypres. Through the window, I could see the sun was getting low. We were supposed to meet the lieutenant at dusk. I looked around the room. The two lads that had been sleeping there were gone, but now the beds were occupied by Frank, Sprouse and Taylor. I swung my legs over the side of the bed and pulled on my boots.

"Wake up," I said, shaking Frank. "We've got to get going."

Frank rolled over and rubbed his eyes. He reeked of alcohol.

"How much sleep did you get?" I asked.

"Maybe two hours, maybe less," he said, slurring his words a bit.

"Sounds like you had plenty of *vin rouge.*"

"Not as much as those two sods," he said, motioning toward Sprouse and Taylor. "That Taylor is a real drinker. And Sprouse spent the better part of the afternoon throwing up out back."

"Well, get them up," I said. "We have to be at the Menin Gate at dusk. And it sure doesn't look like we're going to make it in this condition. The lieutenant is going to blow up when he gets a whiff of the lot of you."

"Sprouse! Taylor! Get up! Time to hit the road!" Frank shouted. Neither of them budged. "Wake up! Time to go!"

"Go away," Sprouse said, not raising his head from the pillow. "Can't you see I'm dead?"

"That goes for both of us," Taylor grumbled.

"Well, if we're late, the lieutenant is going to nail our hides to the wall," I said. "Now I suggest you get yourselves together. That's an order."

Within five minutes we were ready to go, despite the grousing. We walked back through the front room. The drunken man was still asleep at his table, his head still resting on his crossed arms.

"*Merci beaucoup,*" I said to the *mademoiselle* as we walked out into the fading sun. We headed down the road to Ypres. Traffic was light, but we eventually flagged down an empty ambulance going our way. It was almost dark by then. The lieutenant was probably already waiting for us.

He was, in fact, there when we arrived, looking at his watch and shaking his head. We waved to him as we walked toward the Menin Gate. Sprouse and Taylor were still staggering a bit.

"You boys have been drinking, I see," the lieutenant said.

"Just a little, sir," Frank said with a slur. "Got some sleep, too."

"Good," the lieutenant said. "Because I'm putting you all on patrol tonight. That's what you get for drunkenness. It says in Proverbs, Chapter 20, verse one: 'Wine is a mocker, strong drink is raging: and whosoever is deceived thereby is not wise.' You four are definitely not wise. And you will pay the price."

"Now he's a bleeding Bible scholar," Frank mumbled to me.

We headed out through the gate and past Hellfire Corner, then entered the trenches. It was pitch black, the moon and stars hidden behind heavy cloud cover. That made the going a bit tougher. But we made it nonetheless, and soon we were back with the unit.

"Anything to report?" the lieutenant asked Hendershot.

"Newcomer got clipped by a sniper," he said. "That's about it."

"Is he going to make it?"

"Don't know, sir. He had a pretty bad head wound, but he was conscious when they took him back."

"Well, that's always a good sign. Thanks for keeping everything under control while I was gone. So how about a game of chess tonight?"

"I'd like to, sir, but I've got to take a patrol out in a little while."

"No, I think you'll stay in. Gardener and Thomas will be leading the patrol tonight."

"I don't know, sir. I should probably take them out myself. Gardener and Thomas don't have much experience in these things."

"Well, they're about to get some."

"He's serious," Frank whispered in my ear, a little too loudly.

"What was that, Thomas?" the lieutenant asked.

"Nothing, sir," he said. "Glad to be of service."

"That's what I thought you said," the lieutenant shot back, and then turned again to Hendershot. "Who else is supposed to go on patrol tonight?"

"It looks like Valentine, McKinley, Turner and Havens are up."

"Add Sprouse and Taylor to the list. They need some experience, too. And I'll expect you in my dugout at 2200 hours for that game, sergeant."

"Absolutely, sir. Wouldn't miss it."

133

The fog came rolling in, and combined with heavy cloud cover, I knew it was going to be a bad night for a patrol. Around midnight, we went down a sap and emerged into No Man's Land.

"Stay close to the wire," I said. "We don't want anyone getting lost out here tonight."

The men filed in behind me, and we headed out. A cold bead of sweat ran down my temple. I was trying to dodge all of the shell holes I could see, but I wasn't doing a very good job of it. In the process, I led us deeper and deeper into the killing field without knowing it.

Suddenly I heard some voices up ahead, though I could see no one. The voices were definitely not English. I took my rifle off of my shoulder and the others did the same. It was apparent that we were going to encounter some Huns.

Then the strangest thing happened. We were walking along, single file, dodging shell holes, when I spotted a German patrol not fifty feet away, heading in the opposite direction. They saw us at about the same time. They stopped, as did we. We stood there looking at one another for about a minute, though it seemed like an eternity. Taylor raised his rifle, but for some reason, I put my hand on it and pushed it down. Then the Germans simply walked off in the direction they were heading. No shots were fired, no bombs thrown.

"I'll be buggered," Frank said as the Germans disappeared into the darkness behind us.

The rest of the patrol passed without incident. Why that German patrol didn't engage us, or even yet, why we didn't engage them, has puzzled me for years. I guess one gets to a point where enough is enough; there was no need for any of us to die that night.

When we got back in behind our wire, I met with the lieutenant and briefed him on the patrol. I didn't mention the encounter with the Germans; somehow, I doubt he would have approved. But he commended me for bringing back every man alive.

"I know now that I can count on you, Gardener," he said.

"Definitely, sir," I said. "One hundred percent."

"Splendid. I need more men like you. You've got a good head on your shoulders."

"Thank you, sir."

"You're dismissed. Go on, and get some sleep."

"Yes, sir. By the way, sir, who won the chess game?"

"Hendershot, of course. I don't know if I'll ever beat him before the war is over. I'll see you in the morning."

I went off to my dugout and stretched out. The brush with the enemy kept playing through my head. What if we had fired on them? What good would have come of it? I didn't know. I still don't know.

But what I do know is that I slept soundly that night, and for the first time, I saw the plight of the man across the field. He wanted to go home just as badly as I did. I didn't think that anyone of us wanted to be there. Maybe, just maybe, there was some hope for peace.

CHAPTER 18

The next morning the lieutenant called me aside after stand-to.

"I talked to the others that were in your patrol last night," he said. "That was fine leadership, I understand."

I wasn't sure what to say, not knowing whether or not he heard about our brush with the Germans.

"I try my best, sir," I finally said.

"You do quite well, Gardener, so I'm giving you another stripe. You've been promoted to sergeant. You've proven yourself. You've earned it."

I was a bit taken aback.

"Thank you sir," I said.

"Keep up the good work."

After breakfast, I got out my sewing kit and put the new stripe on my uniform. Frank laughed.

"The next thing you know, you'll be a general," he said with a grin.

"I don't think I want that job," I said. "I'm not even sure I want this one."

"You'll do fine. You're a natural leader. And you've got a lot of common sense."

"I'm glad at least one of us is confident about my abilities."

I wrote a long letter to my sister that night, telling her about my promotion. I had been writing frequently, and I started getting more letters from her, sometimes two or three a week. She wrote that she was very proud of my promotion to sergeant, and sent me a photograph of her with her husband that I carried in my breast pocket for the remainder of my time in uniform. He looked like a fine chap. She was quite worried about him; he was in France by then and had experienced some close calls with the Germans. I wrote back to her at least once or twice a week, trying to reassure her that he was going to be all right. That was hard, because I wasn't sure any of us would be all right. I hoped my letters would keep her spirits up.

Despite the promotion, little changed for me. We continued with our efforts to undermine the German lines. The tunnels were constantly collapsing or filling with water, making conditions most precarious. The danger of countermines loomed heavy. We developed a variety of listening devices to be used at the face of the mine to determine as to whether the Germans were tunneling anywhere near our position. Most of the time, the engineers sent to investigate these suspicions attributed the noises to copulating rats. So we tunneled on.

One serious problem that emerged was poisonous gasses accumulating in the tunnels. These came from two sources. If the Germans blew a camouflet near our tunnel, the gas from the explosion would fill the tunnel immediately, and everyone that could do so had to evacuate. The second source was from the gas shelling up at the surface. Being heavier than air, the gas tended to sink to the lowest possible point. The air in the tunnels became saturated with chlorine and phosgene. You didn't know this was the case until you actually got down into the tunnel and breathed. Then it became apparent that gas was present. Despite our best efforts at ventilation, the air in the tunnels remained poisonous for the most part.

To combat this problem, the army devised a contraption called a proto set, which weighed about thirty pounds and strapped around the waist, with air tanks and a mask that went over the face. Though cumbersome, you could go back to work digging in a gas-filled tunnel with one of these sets. You didn't want to wear one of these things unless it was absolutely necessary, as the tunnels were cramped enough. And there was no effective means of determining whether the gas in the tunnels was at lethal levels.

A Welsh sapper suggested using the same method for detecting gas that worked in the coal mines back home; we started using canaries. The caged birds would be taken down the shaft, and if they fell over dead, you knew it was time to get out and get your proto set on. It was a very simple solution to a vexing problem.

Now canaries are vivid birds, and quite noisy for their size. Large cages of them were kept in the rear, and great care had to be taken to ensure that none of these birds escaped, especially not in a front position. As they were unlike any bird native to Flanders, the sight or sound of a canary would be an obvious tip to the Germans that there was mining underway somewhere nearby.

I once heard a tale of some fellows down the line in Arras who were carrying three of the birds up to a mine entrance when they were hit with a mortar shell. One of the birds was killed, and another was quickly captured. But the last one had tenacity. It flew and landed on a string of wire way out front, and just sat there singing like there was no tomorrow. A sergeant ordered the lads to shoot it dead before it got any further. It took a few shots, but someone finally popped it.

You would think that would be the end of the story of the Arras canary. It should have been, but it wasn't. About an hour after the sergeant reported the incident to his lieutenant, an order came up that the canary was to be recovered before nightfall. The reasoning was that some unusually lucky German sod might somehow find the bird in the darkness. That seemed pretty unlikely, but the order stood nonetheless. The unfortunate circumstance was that the lines were very close together at that particular place; there probably wasn't more than 50 feet between our wire and theirs. And the machine gunners and snipers knew every square inch of the field. Six men died before that bird was recovered, or so I heard.

I never had to go out and chase a bird myself. But there was one time that I came pretty close to it. Frank and I were working at the cross one night in May, and we had this canary with us. We had worked up a good sweat, so I decided to go back and get a canteen of water. I crawled to the shaft, climbed out, filled my jug and went back down below.

I had good timing. I shined my torch down the tunnel, and I was stupefied to find it blocked. The boards on one side had sprung a leak, and sand was pouring in. Frank was trapped and yelling for help.

"Hold on," I said. "I'll get you out."

I took a drink out of my canteen and left it lying in the tunnel. I crawled back out and got a shovel, and several volunteers. The plan was for me to dig out the sand and pass it back to the men behind me. A few more men came down into the gallery to hoist the sand to the surface.

I dug like mad. My chest was tight and my clothes were soaked with sweat. Eventually, I cleared a small airway to the other side and I could hear Frank yelling again.

"I'm all right!" he shouted. "Make sure you fix the boards! They burst like a cracked dam!"

I sighed in relief. He wasn't buried under the sand. I wiped my brow and caught my breath. Then I went back to digging.

I was almost startled when I felt a hand on my shoulder. I turned around and saw it was the lieutenant. It was the first time I'd seen him that deep in the mine.

"What happened here?" he asked.

"Boards sprung a leak, sir."

"What about Thomas?"

"He's all right, sir, and we should have him out in no time."

"Let me switch places with you. I need to talk to him."

We crawled around each other and the lieutenant got in front. He leaned up to the air passage that I had dug.

"Thomas, can you hear me in there?"

"Yes sir."

"Are you injured?"

"No sir."

"Tell me something, Thomas. Do you have a canary down there?"

"Yes sir, I do."

"Is he breathing properly?"

"To the best of my knowledge he's doing splendidly, sir."

"Just jolly. Make sure you bring him out with you."

"I've got him right here, sir."

Then I heard a thump and a crash, followed by, "Oh, no."

"What's the matter, Thomas?" the lieutenant asked.

"I hit my head," he replied, "and then I dropped the damned cage."

"Did you hurt the bird?"

"No, he's just lovely. But the cage broke open and now he's loose in the tunnel. He's flying around trying to escape."

"Well, then, you should probably catch it before we dig you out. We don't want that thing flying out of here. Can you do that for me?"

There was a silent pause.

"I say, can you catch that bird?"

There was another silent pause.

"Is something wrong, Thomas?"

"Yes sir, there is," he said. "I'm afraid of birds. I hate them with a passion."

"Surely you are joking!"

"No, sir, I am not. The one thing I'm afraid of and I'm stuck alone with it in a dark tunnel."

"Thomas, you've got to pull it together now. I'm not going to let these fellows dig any further until you secure that bird. Do you understand?"

He meekly agreed. I listened through the airway and I could hear him swearing. Then I heard what was forever after referred to as "the encounter."

"Bastard! You bastard bird! Come here, you bugger. Come to old Frank. Whoa! Whoa! The damn thing is trying to kill me! It's in my hair!"

The canary kept flying and thrashing around, and Frank was swearing a streak that would have made a Liverpool dockworker blush. It gave us a tremendous laugh. Even the lieutenant was fighting to keep a straight face.

"You all right in there Thomas?" the lieutenant asked. "I say, are you all right in there?"

"Yes sir. I've just about got him."

There was more swearing.

"All right," Frank said. "I've got the bloody thing in my hat. Now let me pass it through. Get this winged rat away from me!"

"No, Thomas," the lieutenant said. "Hold on to it securely or else you'll have to catch it again. Can you get it back in its cage?"

139

"Well, I sort of fell on the cage when I was chasing the bird. It's flat, sir."

"Keep it secure, and we'll dig you out. Just hold on for a few more minutes."

I went back to digging away at the sand and I could see Frank's light on the other side. I widened the hole and I could see him sitting in the dirt, holding his cap out in front of him like it was full of dynamite.

"Come on up and try to crawl through," I said.

"I don't have anywhere to carry the bird," Frank said, his voice cracking a bit. "I can't dig. Or crawl. It might get loose."

"Stuff the hat and all down your shirt," the lieutenant called out.

After some foul, muffled grumbling, Frank unbuttoned his shirt and put the hat and bird inside. The bird started flapping. I thought, for sure, that it was going to kill him.

"Damn it, I'm getting out of here!" he shouted.

Frank started digging with his hands to make the hole bigger, and as soon as he got it to shoulder width he crawled through. We all crawled rapidly back to the gallery. Frank stood up straight and saluted the lieutenant.

"One bird for you," he said as he pulled out his rustling cap. The canary was missing a few feathers, but was none worse for the wear. He held it out to the lieutenant. Everyone started applauding.

"Good show, Thomas," the lieutenant said. "Good show."

"Thank you sir," he said, and then turned to the rest of us.

"What?" he asked, just as cool as could be. "Haven't you ever seen a magician pull a bird out of a hat before?"

I guess maybe his sense of humor is what I miss about him the most.

CHAPTER 19

Summer came, and the days were sunny and mostly dry. Our mining efforts were proceeding well. We became more efficient with time, and even Frank was getting used to working underground. All of the mines from Hill 60 down the Messines Ridge had been started, and a few were nearing the enemy lines. The best thing about that summer, though, was that the Germans hadn't felt it necessary to attack in Flanders. They were too busy down at Verdun, trying to break the French lines. By that time, there had been hundreds of thousands of Frenchmen and Germans killed or wounded in that battle alone, and neither side was ready to capitulate.

Then word came up the line in July of a massive offensive against the Germans in the vicinity of the River Somme, a small stream of no real importance in military terms. The battlefield was chosen simply because that was where the French and British sectors met, and the offensive was supposed to be a joint effort, shared equally by both armies. But because of the Verdun entanglement, the French could not supply as many troops as they had pledged, so the lion's share of the fight was left up to our boys. The stories we were hearing weren't good.

It started with a bombardment by more than 1,500 guns that lasted more than a week, with thousands of tons of shells dumped on an 18-mile stretch of front. The generals envisioned complete destruction of the enemy's defenses, and officers told their men that all they would have to do was walk across the battlefield and occupy the German trenches. Some units made a game of it by trying to see who could kick a football across the German wire first. But as you can imagine, things didn't go according to plan.

When our boys climbed out of their trenches and ran forward, they found that the wire hadn't been cut in many places. Not only that, but the manual cutters they'd been given weren't strong enough to sever the heavier German wire. They also found that the Germans were dug in much deeper than they had imagined. Fritz hadn't been dislodged or demoralized, and his machine guns were very much in working order. One attack wave after another fell in the face of heavy resistance. There were more than 30 battalions – normally comprised of 700 or 800 men each – in which 500 or more were killed or wounded. By the end of that first day, the British Army had suffered nearly 60,000 casualties, and in most places, the first objectives had not even been taken.

One would think that such a disaster would be the end of the offensive, but it was not. The generals believed they were winning, despite the number of men killed and wounded. In a London newspaper I read, one commander was quoted as saying the losses were "acceptable," and that victory was at hand. It would be several months before the men at the top would decide to call off the party. At the front we called the Somme offensive "the great foul-up," but we didn't use the word "foul."

When we went back into the salient in August, they were still fighting on the Somme and at Verdun, lifting some of the pressure on our front. With autumn just around the corner, I began to feel relieved; it looked like 1916 would pass without an offensive in Flanders. That was something to be thankful for.

The mining, however, was going at a hurried pace, and that meant a lot more time underground. We finally completed the main Hill 60 tunnel -- all 1100 feet of it -- as well as a number of shorter branches that were used as listening posts. More than 53,000 pounds of ammonal and guncotton were laid at the end, right below the hill. The charge was wired and the tunnel backfilled. We then dug another branch to the south that went below the Caterpillar, a heavily fortified, man-made hill across the railway cut from Hill 60. Some 70,000 pounds of ammonal would be placed at the end.

One cool evening, around the first of September, we were pulled out of the Caterpillar mine and sent to work on another tunnel to our south. Simon and I were working at the face of this tunnel late into the night and we stopped to have a rest and a drink of water. In the silence, we could clearly hear digging above us.

"What the devil?" Simon said under his breath. He put his ear to the face.

"What do you hear?" I asked.

"They can't be more than three or four feet away," he said.

Now this didn't make any sense to either one of us. Intelligence reports had said that the Germans knew nothing of this particular mine, and that they had no mining operations going on nearby. Apparently, they were wrong.

Simon still had his ear to the face.

"That isn't fornicating rats," he said. "They're right on top of us. I don't think they know we're here."

"What should we do?"

"Go back and tell the lieutenant. Then get some explosives. We'll lay a charge and blow them in."

"Do you think we have time for that?"

"Just go get the bleeding explosives," he said, putting his ear back against the face. "Now I think they've stopped. Get those explosives now, or they're going to blow us in first. Go!"

"Come on," I said. "Let's get out of here."

"No. We'll lay a charge and beat them to it."

Simon stayed at the face and I crawled back through the tunnel. I reached the gallery, which was being expanded perpendicular to the tunnel to facilitate listening posts, and Frank was standing there, helping the men who were lowering tools down the shaft.

"The Germans are getting ready to blow this mine," I said.

"But they're not anywhere near here," he said.

"I'm telling you they are. We need to get some explosives back up to Simon so we can take them out first."

I started to climb the ladder to the surface. That was when the Germans blew their charge, and it was a big one. I remember feeling the concussion, but I can't remember hearing it. It knocked me off the ladder and I fell backwards down the shaft. The men lowering the shovels dropped their load, and the tools went crashing down around me.

I know I landed pretty hard, because I was out for a few seconds. I sat up, and saw Frank holding a gash across his head.

"What happened?" I asked.

"Shovel hit me in the head," he said. "Split me right open."

My head was pounding and I had a terrible pain in my back, as well as a gash across my left hand, though I never did figure out how I got it. I shook my head and slowly stood up. It made my back hurt worse. Then I remembered Simon. I grabbed a torch and shined the light down the tunnel. All I could see was smoke and a big wad of clay blown up toward the gallery.

"Do you think he made it?" Frank said.

"I wouldn't bet on it," I said. "I told him he should get out of there. I'd say he's napoo."

"That's Simon," Frank said. "Never one to listen to reason."

The gallery was beginning to fill with gas, and several men with proto sets came down the ladder to attempt to rescue Simon. They found him in pieces in the clay.

Frank and I made our way up the ladder and into the open. By the dim light of the moon, I could see Frank's face covered with blood. I was bleeding pretty badly from my left hand, but my head felt like it was going to explode. My back felt like someone had smacked me with a cricket bat. We slumped down on the fire step. I pulled out a tin of cigarettes and we lit up.

"What a gorgeous day," Frank said. I paid him no mind.

"Simon and I were seven when we met," I said. "He talked me into joining up. I figured when this was over, we'd be back working in the mines together. Like in the old days."

"The old days? You make it sound like it was a hundred years ago."

"Don't you feel about a hundred years older now?"

Some stretcher men and medics came running up the trench.

"Are there any more wounded?" they asked

"Just us," I said.

"That's a nasty head wound you've got there," one of them said to Frank. "That's going to require a few stitches. Put this pad on it and keep pressure on. We've got to get the bleeding stopped."

He turned to me.

"What's wrong with you?"

"My head is killing me, and I think I hurt my back," I said. "And I've got this cut on my hand."

He looked at my hand and wiped away the blood.

"Looks like you're in for some stitches, too," he said. "Do you feel dizzy or nauseous?"

"A little bit of both."

"You've probably got a concussion. We're going to send you back to the casualty clearing station. They'll be able to treat you there. Can you walk, or do you need a stretcher?"

"No, I think we can walk," Frank said. "Just point us in the general direction."

He told us the way and we wandered down the line, leaning on each other for support. The station was right where he said it would be, and we walked down into the dugout and woke up the medics. It must have been a pretty quiet night elsewhere, because the place was empty. There was an older, plump fellow with a tall lanky one helping out. The tall one helped me get off my tunic and cleaned my wound. It looked worse in the light of the kerosene lantern hanging on the wall. It was more of a rip than a cut really.

"We're going to have to sew that up," he said, handing me a fresh cotton pad. "Looks like you got caught on a nail. Put some pressure on it. We'll get the bleeding stopped. Do either of you fellows care for a tot of rum?"

We both raised our hands. The fat one poured us two tin cups of rum and passed them over. He was generous with it. It took me two swallows to get it down.

They finished with their exams and gave us each a couple of tins of fags. The fat one said I would have some nasty bruises on my back, but it didn't look like I'd broken anything. He said I definitely had a concussion. Then he turned to Frank.

"What hit you on the head? Shell fragment?"

"No," he said. "A shovel."

"That must hurt a bit."

"You're quite right it does."

144

"Let me give you both something for the pain."

He handed us painkiller tablets and cups of water.

"That'll knock it. Just give it a few minutes."

The bleeding from my hand was stopping, but there was still a gusher coming down Frank's face. I was starting to calm down a bit. The tall one was using scissors to cut the hair around Frank's wound. There was a cut across his scalp running from the crown of his head to his left temple. It was a straight cut and they finally got the bleeding stopped. They shaved a patch around it and applied a dressing.

"We're going to send you down to the regimental aid station," the fat one said. "They'll finish you up down there."

"Fabulous," Frank said sleepily. "Just fabulous."

I was feeling the medication by that time, too. I got warm in my chest and it spread to my arms and legs. Everything seemed really slow and deliberate, and I felt happy in a strange way. My friend was napoo, and I was numb to it. I wanted to cry; I truly wanted to, but it wasn't in me. Then I felt guilty about not feeling sad. The fat one, who seemed to be right up in my face, talking in long, drawn-out words, interrupted my concentration.

"You'll need some time to recover," he said. "You won't be going back up to the line for a while."

We happened to be in luck as far as our location was concerned. Not fifty yards from the clearing station was a light-gauge rail spur, with flat cars for carrying wounded and supplies and so forth. I heard it rolling up the line after a few minutes. I was so wiped out that the medics had to help me get onto the car. Frank was staggering, but made it on his own. I pulled out my cigarettes. I offered one to Frank, but he had passed out. I put my arm around him for support.

"Good for you, old man," I said. "Good for you."

The train pulled out and went almost all the way back to Ypres. I was impressed that the engineers could keep any length of track in operation with the Germans watching. The sun was starting to come up, and I could see the outline of the Menin Gate and the Cloth Hall. I remember feeling so calm when we stopped, like I hadn't felt in a long time. We were going to leave the jaws of Wipers, having narrowly escaped the beast. We had met the challenge of death, and we had prevailed.

We made it to the railhead just south of town, and there were a few other fellows there who were being evacuated. One fellow had both his eyes bandaged, and his hand shook as he put a cigarette to his mouth. Another fellow was lying on a stretcher, badly burned. The medics came by and shot him full of morphine to keep him from waking up. Looking at those two, I felt pretty lucky.

We had to wait a while for an ambulance, so they passed around a jug of rum for those of us who were fit to drink. I had a good swallow for me, and a second swallow for Frank, who was still asleep. Then they dispensed more pain medicine, for which I did wake Frank. I didn't tell him about the rum. We had two cigarettes apiece before the ambulances arrived.

The ride in the Ford ambulance alone was enough to kill us.

"They must be going out of their way to hit every hole in the road," I groaned.

"Particularly the bloody huge ones," said the man with the bandaged eyes, who was in the bunk below me.

The hospital was on the west side of Ypres along the road to Pop. In its previous life, it must have been a convent or a school of some sort, constructed of limestone and marble. They led us up the stone steps that had been worn down from the thousands of times they had been tread upon. They took us to a small room, except for the burn victim. He went elsewhere, but I never saw him again. I guess he was napoo. A young doctor came in, had a look at my hand and put in about a dozen stitches. You can still see the scar there. See? I swear, the stitches hurt worse than the wound did to begin with, but I didn't dare let on, mostly because there was a willowy, red-haired English nurse there, very pretty, and I didn't want to embarrass myself. She leaned over me, and her hair smelled unbelievable, like it had just been washed. She was the first English-speaking girl I had set eyes on in a while. I was enamored.

Now Frank, he was in much worse shape. He must have gotten 30 stitches in his scalp, and he cursed at every one, paying no mind to the lady present. The nurse giggled a little at Frank's ranting. I guess she'd probably heard it all by then. I don't think she blushed, but I think I did a bit.

When they got done with him, Frank had this oblong bald spot off on one side of his head. He looked pretty funny, but once it was dressed and he gingerly placed his cap on, you could hardly notice.

"Good as new, mate," Frank said.

They gave us more pain medicine and assigned us to different wards. Frank protested, and insisted that we be placed in the same room. They didn't seem to have any objections, so Frank and I ended up assigned to beds next to each other. Two rather attractive nurses came in, wearing long capes and blouses starched so heavily that the creases could have cut metal. They put us in wheelchairs and rolled us down the hall to our ward. I don't know

146

why they didn't let us walk. Thank god, we both still could. The man with the bandaged eyes was taken somewhere else. I never saw him again, either.

Upon arrival at our ward, they gave us baths, which I found embarrassing but enjoyable in a perverted sort of way. Then they got us a set of bedclothes each, and helped us into beds at the end of a long, dark room. The sheets were clean and they felt good against my skin. And there were no lice crawling around in there. I stared at the ceiling and got to thinking about Simon.

"I can't believe Simon is dead," I said. "He shouldn't have died like that."

"I don't know," Frank said. "Maybe that's exactly how he was supposed to die."

"What the devil do you mean by that? That's awful."

"Well, you know how some people talk about some German out there having a bullet with their name on it? Like they are predestined to die with that bullet? Or that they can spot a man who's not going to make it by the look in his eyes?"

"Did Simon have that look?"

"To be honest with you, yes. I had a feeling for a while that he wasn't going to make it. I'm not sure why, but I knew it. I knew he was going to get clicked."

"I never saw it."

"Maybe you were too close to him to see it."

"What about me?" I said, rolling over on my side.

Frank stared into my eyes.

"I don't see anything," he said. "Neither good nor bad. I can't tell."

"You wouldn't be saying that just to make me feel better?"

"No, honestly. I see nothing."

We talked late into the evening. The nurses kept coming by to tell us to be quiet and get some sleep, but we didn't listen. There were men at the far end of the ward, no one close enough for us to disturb. So we smoked cigarettes and talked about the meaning of life and Simon and all kinds of things. Mostly we talked about how we wanted the war to end. We pondered what it would be like when we got home.

"We'll get back to Blighty and go on with our lives when it's over," Frank said, "or at least I will. Except I won't ever worry again. Not a care in the world. If I can make it through this, I can survive anything."

"But you can't help but wonder whether we'll see Blighty again."

"We will. I know it. And when we do, we're going to drink until there isn't a drop left in all of England. Then we'll go to

147

Ireland, and drink them dry, too. That will be a bit more of a challenge, don't you think?"

He went on for a while, but around four in the morning or so, Frank started snoring like a buzz saw. My thoughts wandered along aimlessly until I fell asleep also. I had vivid dreams of pretty English girls, and pints of stout and music, where there were no more shells or rats. Just utter happiness and freedom and safety. I awoke periodically, and remembering where I was, wished my dream would be reality. The dream resumed each time I fell back asleep.

We were awakened at eight o'clock, which was a lot later than normal for us. The nurses were going their rounds, checking and changing bandages and seeing how we were feeling. The nurse that changed my bandage was an old warhorse who lectured me about infection and the importance of keeping my hand clean. Then she tortured me for ten minutes with a cotton pad and alcohol before reapplying a dressing. Frank got similar treatment, and he objected vehemently, to put it politely.

Just as they were finishing up, the charge nurse came in with the doctor, who gave us the once-over.

"How are you two feeling today?" he asked us.

"My hand hurts a bit and my back is sore, but I can't complain," I said.

"I've got a serious headache," Frank said. "Can I get some more of that pain medicine?"

"Are you sure you need it?" the doctor asked.

"Yes, I'm sure I need it!" Frank blurted. "I got hit in the bloody head with a bleeding shovel!"

"You've got quite a colorful vocabulary, corporal," the doctor said, looking offended. "But we'll set you up with another round."

"All right then," Frank said, laying his head back down on his pillow. The nurse went off to get the pills and came back shortly. They gave it to both of us, even though I hadn't asked for any.

"Can you both walk?" the doctor asked.

"Sure we can," Frank said. "We can dance a little jig if you like."

"No problems standing, no dizziness, nothing like that?"

"No sir."

"Well, then, I've got some good news for you both. We're giving you three weeks of recuperative leave, which you can either spend here in this hospital or go back to your homes in England."

Frank and I looked at each other dumbfounded.

"England," we both said in unison. It was like my dream the night before had become reality.

148

"You'll need to check at a hospital every other day to get your bandages changed," the doctor said. "But since you both seem to be getting on rather well, I don't see any reason why you can't have a little bit of leave."

I sort of stammered, not really sure what to say except "thanks." Then I thanked the nurse with the alcohol.

"Keep that clean," she said sternly. "You don't want to lose a flipper."

The nurse and the doctor left. Frank had this big grin on his face.

"Well I don't know about you," he said, "but I can't wait to get home."

"Sounds good, doesn't it?"

"You bet it does. Got any fags?"

We smoked a couple of cigarettes and discussed what we would do.

"I don't know," I said. "Maybe I'll go up to Sheffield and over to the home. I'd like to see Simon's parents."

"No disrespect for Simon here, but that's not a plan," he said. "I think you should come with me and stay in London. Now that's a plan, old man. Lizzy is keeping my flat for me while I'm away, so we'll have a place to stay. We'll have champagne for breakfast every morning and brandy and cigars after tea. And the women! They'll be dripping off you, seeing how you are a decorated war hero. I promise you, we'll get you a woman."

"You think so?"

"Certainly! We're going to tear up the town. You'll probably have to fight the girls off with a stick, since most of their men are over here."

Frank always had a way of talking people into doing things, and it was only moments before I decided that going to London would be more fun than going back home by myself. And I had never really been to London, except for the train station.

"Are you sure it wouldn't be a bother to have a geezer like me hanging around your flat?"

"It would be my pleasure."

"Well then, I guess it's settled!"

We clinked our teacups together and drank a toast. We got clean uniforms and underwear and some Red Cross sundries, packed up our duffels and started looking for the quickest way to Blighty.

CHAPTER 20

We got some breakfast, probably the best one I'd had since I left home. I ate five fried eggs, a dozen or so sausages, several helpings of stewed tomatoes and a half-loaf of bread with butter and plum jam. It was fabulous.

The nurse on the ward told us that there would be a lorry coming soon to pick us up and take us to the train station. Frank talked me into pinning my medal on my tunic. I felt kind of silly, but like I said, Frank had a way of talking people into doing things.

The waiting seemed like it took forever. We must have smoked a tin of Woodbines between us before our transport arrived. We rode in the back and got bounced and beaten senseless all the way to the train station.

After about a half-hour we arrived and were loaded on nice passenger cars, like the ones we'd ridden when we went to training. A vendor came through the car selling cigars, and I bought one for me and one for Frank. Frank tried to teach me to blow smoke rings. He was a champion blower, but it seemed that I would never be.

"You'll catch on, old man," he said, trying to assuage my frustration. "Keep trying."

I stood to crack the window next to our seats, but with my sore back and my damaged hand, I couldn't budge it. Frank stood and gave it a good heave, and the fresh morning air poured in. I stared out the window as the train yard disappeared. Frank stuck his head out of the window and looked back.

"You hear that click-clack on the tracks?" Frank asked. "With each one of those, we are farther from Wipers and closer to Blighty. It's a fine sound, I must say."

He sat back down and puffed on his cigar. The rolling countryside gave few hints that war was in the land. After a bit, you couldn't really tell at all.

We left many things behind us: mud, barbed wire, rotting bodies, lice, rats, machine guns, sewage, snipers, Hill 60 and the mines. Right then and there, I didn't have to contend with any of those things. I was overcome by a strange sense of peace.

We got to Calais in the afternoon, only to find out at the docks that we had just missed the last troop transport across the channel for the day. The next one wasn't scheduled to leave until eight the next morning.

"I don't want to be stuck in this hole for the night," Frank said, and went on a rant, cursing steadily -- and quite creatively -- for a good five minutes before he ran out of steam. There was a Red Cross canteen across the road from the station, so I suggested we get some tea and scones. Frank agreed, and across the road we went.

We sat at a table, the only souls in the place. A waitress came and took our order, but when I tried to pay, Frank pushed my hand aside.

"That's all right," he said. "I've got this one."

"Well it's free anyway," the waitress said with a smile. "You boys get as much as you want. We've also got some post cards to send, and a recreation room with a snooker table. Do you like snooker?"

"I've never played it," I said. "But thanks for the food, and the tea is excellent."

I took one of the post cards and wrote a note to Rose. I told her that I'd been injured, but not too badly, and that I was getting a few weeks' rest from the line. The waitress came back with two more scones and tea. She took my post card and said she'd send it out that afternoon.

"Now remember," Frank said, "when you are in London, you are my guest. Anything you want or need, I'll take care of it for you."

"I can't let you do that."

"Worry not, my friend. You name it, you've got it."

"No, Frank, I'm serious. I can take care of myself."

Frank looked indignant.

"You are my guest, and that is final," he said.

We didn't talk about that issue much the rest of the afternoon. I didn't want to rely on Frank's generosity. I still had a few coins in my pocket, and I was going to make them last.

We walked out of the canteen and sat on a bench. It was a fairly warm day, I remember. Frank chain-smoked about half of his cigarettes. He was thinking. I could tell.

"The way I see it," he said, with smoke rolling out of his mouth, "we have two choices. We could either wait here on this bench until the troop ship arrives in the morning, or we could find transport of our own."

"But there is no other way back. We're only allowed to travel on certain ships, and I'm sure some career officer would shit three shades of green if we broke any of the rules. And the channel is full of Hun submarines, no less. I say we wait until we can go in a convoy."

"Well, that might be all right with you, but I'm going down to the waterfront to poke around. Wait for me here. If you need to

151

go to the crapper or something, go ahead, but come back. I won't be gone very long. An hour or two at the most."

He was back much sooner. Frank came striding up the street from the docks, with one hand in his pocket and the other one holding a bottle. He walked up and plopped down on the bench beside me.

"We leave late at nine, land at Dover around midnight," he said in a secretive tone. "I got us on a freighter."

"How did you manage that?"

He held up the bottle. It was good Irish whiskey.

"Let's go somewhere and have some liquid dinner, then we'll hash out the details. All right?"

"Sounds better than sitting here. You certainly have a way with words."

"Thank you. I consider it to be one of my finer qualities."

We stood and walked down toward the cargo area near the docks, slipped by some guards and found ourselves in the middle of a maze of crates and totes of all variety, filled with God-only-knows-what. We had about three hours to kill, which we did, along with most of the whiskey. Frank seemed sober, but I was drunk as piss. I couldn't feel the pain in my back, and I couldn't feel my hand at all.

"So you never answered my question," I said with a slur. "How'd we get on a boat?"

"Easy as one, two, three my friend," he said with a broad gesture. "That is if you know the right people."

"What do you mean?"

"I was walking along the docks, trying to look official, when I saw a boat there that I knew from Hull. The *Sea Wraith.* I remembered the captain was a bloke named Murphy who knew my dad."

"I'm starting to see where you're going," I said, taking another swallow from the bottle.

"Well, I walked up to the boys from the ship and asked if I could see Captain Dan Murphy on some urgent and official business. Naturally, they led me right to him. And you know what the best part is?"

"What's that?"

"He remembered me better than I remembered him! It was like a family reunion. He started talking about my dad and some of their adventures together when they were younger, and how much he'd like to see him again."

"I knew you were going to pull something out of your arse," I said.

"So I asked him if he had room for a couple of stowaways tonight, and after I convinced him that we weren't deserters, he naturally said he'd take us on board."

"So I guess he gave you this bottle?"

"Yeah. And he said to come back at nine and we'd go."

We sat there amongst the crates and finished what was left of the whiskey.

"I don't suppose you'd have any more of that on you."

"No, I don't."

"That's a shame."

"Be cheerful, now Richard. We're going to Blighty! Tonight!"

"Old man, if it weren't for you, I'd be sitting back at the hospital for the whole three weeks. Or up home by myself."

"What do you miss the most? About Blighty?"

"Everything."

"No, no. You have to be more specific than that. What are some of the things you want to do when we hit London? It's a big town."

"I'd like a pint of good stout and some fish and chips," I said. "That's for starters."

"Well, whatever you want to do, we'll do," Frank said. "And the ones you like, we'll do over again!"

I started laughing like the drunkard I was, and he was laughing at me. He picked up the empty bottle and smashed it against a crate. I laughed so hard my side hurt.

It was starting to get dark, so Frank said we should get on over to the *Sea Wraith.*

"We'll be a little early, but it won't be a problem," Frank said.

"Can we get some more whiskey there?" I asked, as if I needed more. "I'll buy us another bottle."

"It sure tastes better than rum, doesn't it?"

"You got that right."

I stood and teetered a bit with my duffel bag on my shoulder. I was definitely drunk. I followed Frank down to the docks and along a line of ships moored there. There was a cold breeze from the ocean, and I could smell the salt.

Now in my mind, the name *Sea Wraith* evoked images of a swift, sleek blockade-runner that slipped through the night unnoticed like a ghost. Of course, I was wrong. She was the worst-looking ship I'd yet seen there along the docks: a hulking, barnacle-encrusted rust bucket that looked like she'd seen her better days, and way far back they were. It wouldn't be much of a challenge for a U-boat, I thought to myself.

"This is it?" I asked aloud.

153

"Yes, indeed."

"It looks like a heap of junk."

"Well, that junk heap is going to get you back to England."

I couldn't argue with that. We scurried up the gangplank hooked on her side and hustled up the stairs. I was dizzy from the whiskey, and I was leaning against a wall when a ruddy-faced crewman walked over to us.

"Permission to come aboard?" Frank asked.

"Who are you, and what the bloody hell do you want?"

"We're guests of Captain Murphy on your trip back across the channel."

"Well then," he said, not looking too impressed, "let me show you to the pilot house. And don't muck around with anything."

I don't blame him for being skeptical, as we both reeked of whiskey. But he took us up to the bridge and announced our presence to Captain Murphy.

"Hey, Francis!" the captain said, giving Frank a bear hug. "I see you enjoyed my little gift. And this must be your mate."

"Sergeant Richard Gardener, sir," I said, extending my hand.

"A sergeant, you say?" the captain said. He was quite animated and personable. "Glad to have you on board, Sergeant Gardener."

"You can call me Richard, sir," I said. "I don't go in for the titles much."

"Well what's that medal on your chest for?" the captain said, touching it with his finger.

"It's a Distinguished Conduct Medal," Frank piped in. "Richard here won it by taking a whole French village by himself."

"Is that right?" the captain said.

"Well…" I said, but the captain cut me off before I could finish.

"We must all have a drink."

He reached in a cupboard and pulled out a bottle and three glasses.

"I hope you like scotch," he said.

"I love it," I said.

"Then here's to winning the war," the captain said as we touched glasses.

"We'll be leaving in about 20 minutes or so," he said. "We'll make Dover at about midnight. You can catch a train from there to London. It's a pretty quick trip. Probably the busiest stretch of rail in Blighty."

"In the mean time, make yourselves comfortable. The galley is down one deck, and I think they've got tea on. Help yourselves to whatever you want."

We went down to the galley and sat at a table. We got some dinner and waited for the ship to leave port. Soon I could feel the engines revving up. The deck plates vibrated as the ship heaved.

"Let's go up top," Frank said. I thought that was a good suggestion, as I was beginning to feel a bit sick, either from drinking or the motion of the ship. The fresh air would do me good, I thought. We watched as France disappeared behind us.

"Maybe they'll get all the fighting over before we have to go back," Frank said.

"We'd never be that lucky," I said. The ship was rocking a little and the deck was vibrating again. I lit up a cigarette to try and calm my stomach, but it was no use. I dropped my fag and threw up over the side. It was mostly whiskey and it tasted awful. The ruddy-faced deck hand came walking up.

"Feeding the kippers, are we?" he said with a grin. "Just breathe deep. You'll be all right."

"Nothing wrong with being a little seasick," Frank said. "Now if it was the whiskey that made you vomit, I'd be disappointed."

I got the last of it up and sat down on the deck next to the rail.

"What do you say we go get some more tea?" Frank asked.

"No way. I'm not going to go below deck. I know I'll vomit again. I'm just sure of it. I need the air."

"I'll get some for both of us and come back up. If we get torpedoed, it would be best to be on deck anyway."

Now I sure wished that he hadn't said that, because it left me terrified. I walked around the deck twice, peering into the night, looking for what might be a periscope, although I didn't even know what one would have looked like anyway.

One of the crew must have seen me looking for submarines. He came out a nearby portal, walked over and put a hand on my shoulder.

"No need to worry tonight, Tommy," he said. "We're running empty back to England. Fritz is only interested in sinking the ships carrying supplies or troops. He couldn't care less about us."

I wasn't totally convinced, but it made me feel less edgy. Frank came back with the tea, and we found a place on some coiled rope that was comfortable for sitting and where I could still see the water. I began to feel less nauseous. After about an hour, I could see one faint light at Dover. For the most part, the town had been blacked out. I stood and stared at the light. About 90 minutes passed and I could see the distinct white cliffs of the English coastline.

We watched England grow closer and closer. I felt relieved, knowing that I would soon be off of the ship and on English soil. A tugboat came out and met the *Sea Wraith* and led her to her berth. Deck hands came up and prepared to tie us in at the dock. Frank and I took our teacups and went back up to the pilothouse.

"I owe you for this one," Frank said to the captain. "You've done a great deal for the war effort, I assure you."

"I'm glad I could do my bit," the captain said, grinning. "But the girls in London are now in danger! There are so few men, and so many beautiful, lonely girls there. You'll have some tough choices to make in the days to come!"

"We'll take our chances," Frank said, smiling. "Truly, thank you for the passage and the whiskey."

"Anything for one of Chester Thomas' boys," the captain said. "I'll see you off."

We shook hands and he walked us out to the gangplank, which was just being put into place. We hoisted our bags and walked down to the dock.

"Be careful out there," Frank hollered to the captain. "The Huns are hungry."

"You take care of yourselves and we'll whip them altogether!" he said.

It was the middle of the night and I was starting to feel sober, probably from throwing up so much. As our luck had it, we missed the last train to London for two hours, so we sat inside the train station and drank the free tea that the Red Cross girls were giving out.

"Back in Blighty," Frank said. "I can't believe it. What's Lizzy going to say when I show up at her doorstep in the morning? It will be the shock of her life."

Some time around four o'clock or so, a train full of soldiers pulled into the station. They were green and bound for France, or maybe even Wipers. Their uniforms were clean and yet to be bleached by the sun, nor stained by the blood and mud. Their boots were polished to a sheen and their rifles were clean and oiled. They were pale and thin, mostly school boys.

"Do you believe we looked that foolish when we arrived here?" I pondered.

"My guess is that we may have looked even more silly," he said. "After all, we're grown men. These are boys, and they have an excuse because they aren't old enough to know any better. A grown man, it would seem, would have more sense than to get involved in this mess."

"Every time we get replacements, I feel like I've aged another ten years," I said. "I've seen everything. Done everything.

We've been through enough punishment for a hundred years, yet it was less than two years since we were standing about like this lot."

"I guess there will be a lot more headed their way now, what with the Somme and so forth."

"How many of those boys do you think will make it back? Half of them? Maybe? I bet half of them are napoo before we return. Poor sods."

We sat there gawking for a few more minutes before we realized we could catch their train on its way back to London. We found some comfortable seats and stowed our gear. There were only a couple of other people on the train when it pulled out of the station around dawn. I was asleep in a few minutes. Frank covered me with my coat and let me doze until we were within sight of Victoria Station.

"Come on, sergeant," he said, poking me with his finger. "Time to reenter the real world again."

I was somewhat surprised that I had slept, but it did seem like I got more and more relaxed the farther I got from Wipers. I felt good, considering the night I'd had, and I was ready to go. I slipped on my coat and grabbed my duffle.

"All right, Frank," I said, poking him with my good hand. "I want to see it all."

"And you shall, good fellow. And you shall."

Frank hailed a taxi for us, and the driver helped us with our bags. We found that to be a bit amusing. Frank told him a West End address, and we were off in a shot. My hand and back hurt, but not so much that I couldn't enjoy the ride through the city. London was just waking up, and there weren't many people on the street. Frank and I concurred that the ride was much smoother than those Fords back in Wipers.

It was the first time that I had really seen London. I noticed how beautiful the gardens were, even though the flowers were dying off. The streets were clean, and there was glass in all of the windows. I thought about that, at the time, how odd it was that a thing as common as an unbroken windowpane could be pleasing to the eye. Here there were no shells to blast away the windows. There was no mud, no rotting bodies, no dead horses, no Fokkers and no Huns. I felt so uplifted as I noticed these things. I wanted to drink in the life that was around me. I had three weeks: three weeks that I wouldn't be shelled, or shot at, or buried in a tunnel or picking up pieces of what used to be a friend.

We turned down a narrow street and stopped in front of a theater that didn't look open. The driver again insisted on helping us with our bags, and Frank tipped him well. The taxi pulled away and left us standing on an otherwise very quiet street.

157

"Do you perform here?" I asked.

"Nah. They used to do plays and such here. Shakespeare, that kind of thing. But this is where we'll be staying."

"In a theater?"

"I've got a loft up in the back. Lizzy is staying there, taking care of things for me."

We walked around to the side of the building and went down an alley. There were two flights of stairs that led up to his flat. We got about halfway up and Frank stopped.

"You know," he said quite seriously, "This is certainly going to be a surprise for her at, uh, what time is it?"

"I think this is what they call the break of dawn."

"Then it's over the top with the best of luck," he said and bounded up the second flight of stairs. We got to the top and he fished around in his pockets for a key, but he couldn't find one and couldn't remember the last time he had one. So he rapped on the blue-painted wooden door with his knuckles. There was no reply, so he resorted to giving the door a good pounding with both fists.

"She's a deep sleeper," he said with a smile, then banged on the door some more. Soon I heard footsteps inside and a woman started shouting.

"It's six o'clock on Sunday morning, for heaven's sake!" she shouted. "I'm coming!"

Frank looked at me and winked.

"Just wait until she sees us," he said, just as the locks slid and the doorknob turned.

"What the devil do you want?" she said as the door swung open. "I was…"

Shock passed across her face as if she'd seen a specter. She was pretty, tall and trim with messy, light brown hair down to her shoulders, wearing an old house coat but still looking lovely.

"Frank!" she cried. "Frank! What are you doing here? And what's that bandage on your head? Are you all right? Why didn't you let me know you were coming?"

"We had a run-in with the Germans yesterday," Frank said. "We're on medical leave. Surprise!"

"Frank, I love you, you terrible man!"

They embraced and kissed each other, long and hard. When she caught her breath, she looked me over.

"And who might this be?" she asked.

"Elizabeth Case, this is Sergeant Richard Gardener," he said, pointing his thumb at me. "He's a decorated war hero."

"Oh my, yes," she said. "You've written about him many times."

She took my good hand between hers and shook it gently. Then she leaned in and kissed me on the cheek. I was surprised and must have looked like it. She stepped back.

"It's just that I've heard so much about you, I feel I already know you," she said. "I'm sorry if I'm too forward."

"No offense taken, ma'am," I said. "I've heard a lot of good things about you, too. But he never told me how pretty you were."

"Thank you," she said shyly. "Now let's get inside and get some tea on."

We stepped into the flat, which was basically the theater's attic converted and partitioned into living quarters. The ceilings were high with open rafters. Posters of magicians – including several of Frank – decorated the walls, along with a few modern-style paintings. The rest of the furnishings were a mismatched collection that somehow seemed to work together.

"I got most of this stuff from the theater," Frank said. "Props and such that would otherwise be wasted. Make yourself comfortable."

They went into the kitchen and I followed. It was spacious, with a tile floor and yellow-striped wallpaper. There was an enamel table and four unmatched chairs around it. We sat down, and I caught the scent of Elizabeth's perfume from across the table. There was no smell of death mingling in. It all felt a little odd, and it made me a bit out of sorts. I sensed that Frank felt the same way. He smiled nervously and winked at me.

Elizabeth poured the tea and sat back down. I noticed her hands were tinted yellow.

"You're wondering why they're colored," she said, looking at me. "It's the latest fashion in London. Me and all the other girls in the shell factories have yellow hands from the explosives."

"So when did you start working in the shell business?" Frank asked disapprovingly.

"They needed girls to work there and it pays better than working at the pub," she said. "I didn't tell you because I didn't want you to worry."

Frank started to object when we heard another woman's voice in the next room. It caught us both by surprise.

"I've taken a flat mate, Frank," Elizabeth said. "A girl from the factory, Rebecca. I was so lonely and this place is so quiet without you. It helps with the rent, too."

"It's all right," Frank said. "I don't mind a bit. Sounds splendid."

Rebecca came walking into the kitchen in slippers and a pink housecoat, rubbing her eyes and brushing her long curly hair back from her face. She was a good bit shorter than Elizabeth,

159

pleasantly curvy with big brown eyes. Her mouth was small with full lips. I was immediately intrigued. I'll even go farther than that; if there is such a thing as love at first sight, that was it.

"Elizabeth," she said, yawning, "who are these strange men in our kitchen?"

"Rebecca MacAuley, this is Frank and his friend, Sergeant Gardener," Elizabeth said.

"That's Richard to you, ma'am," I said.

"Pleased to meet you, Frank and Richard. Frank, I'm surprised I didn't recognize you from the posters around the flat."

"Well, I've taken off a little weight since then," he said. "And the uniform probably threw you off a bit."

"What happened?" she asked. "Why are you here? Did they call the war off?"

"No," Frank said, "we had a bit of trouble from the Germans a couple of nights ago. They sent us back to rest up."

"You still haven't told us what happened," Elizabeth said.

"I got a whack on the head, and the sergeant ripped his hand and took a pretty bad tumble."

"I fell off of a ladder," I said. Rebecca giggled.

"Only because the Germans were trying to blow us out of our hole," Frank interjected.

"So did you fall off a ladder, too?" Elizabeth said.

"No, I got hit in the head."

"Were you shot? Did you get hit with a shell?"

"He got hit with a shovel," I said. Rebecca giggled some more.

"Hey, that's enough," Frank said. "Besides, I have it on good authority that the shovel was an enemy collaborator."

"Does it hurt much?" Rebecca asked me, brushing the dressing on my hand.

"No, ma'am. Frank's the one that really took a beating."

"Don't call me ma'am. It makes me feel old."

We all laughed and then we sat there for a minute just looking at each other. I don't think anyone knew exactly what to say. Elizabeth put her hand on Frank's head and a tear rolled down her cheek. Then she started sobbing.

"I can't believe you're home, Frank," she said. She stood and held his head to her bosom. "Oh, Frank, I love you, and I miss you so terribly."

"It's all right," he said, putting his arm around her waist. "We'll be here for a good three weeks. That will give us plenty of time to catch up."

Rebecca stood up and got the teapot and poured us some more. I was staring at her, because by the light of the window, I could

160

see through her housecoat a little. She caught me looking, and I turned away embarrassed.

"Do you have any family or friends here in London?" she asked as she sat down next to me.

"No, I don't."

"Where are you from?"

"Sheffield. Well, near Sheffield, anyway."

"Are you going on to Sheffield then?"

"No, I don't have any family there, either. There's my sister in Manchester, but Frank's invited me to stay on here."

"Good," she said. "It's going to be nice getting to know you."

Elizabeth was sitting on Frank's lap, and he was whispering something in her ear. She laughed and smacked him on the chest. Then they got up and disappeared into her room. I didn't figure they'd be out for a while, and neither did Rebecca, so she cooked us up some eggs and toast.

"So tell me more about what happened," she said. "That is, if you don't mind telling me."

"No, that's all right. Basically, there was a mine explosion…"

"A mine?"

"It's when you tunnel under the enemy and try to blow him up from below."

"It sounds terrible."

"You never know if you are standing on top of one of them; that's the worst part."

"Those Germans," she said. "They are such barbarians to do something like that."

"Oh, no. We do it, too. We were in the middle of digging this great one when my mate Simon heard the Huns digging toward us. I went out with Frank to get some explosives so we could blow in their tunnel, but before we could get back, they blew a charge in on Simon. I was halfway up the ladder to the surface when it went off, and it knocked me down the shaft. Some tools came crashing in about us, and that's how Frank got hit on his napper."

"What about this Simon fellow?"

"He didn't make it."

"Was he a close friend?"

"I'd known him since we were boys. We lived next door to each other. Worked in the same mine together. He talked me into joining up."

"I'm sorry. I hope I didn't upset you. I won't ask about it anymore."

"No, it's all right," I said, looking into her deep dark eyes. "I'm…I'm fine."

"You'll miss him."

161

"Yes, I will. He was a good soldier and had a cool head. As a matter of fact, I don't think I ever saw him really scared, not even in the worst of it. And he went through some pretty tough spots with me and Frank."

Rebecca and I talked all morning. We didn't discuss much more about the war. She had all kinds of questions about mining and the work I did back home, what I liked to do on my time off, about my parents and my sister. We drank three pots of tea and smoked a tin of cigarettes between us. She had a beautiful smile and a lovely laugh. Her voice was like a symphony to me. I felt like I could have sat there and talked to her forever. And she seemed interested in me, too.

Eventually, my exhaustion caught up to me. I looked at the clock on the kitchen wall and it was almost noon. I figured I hadn't had any sleep in thirty-odd hours, during which time I was wounded, drank half of a bottle of whiskey and sobered up again. My eyelids grew heavy and I think I dozed off at the table.

"Why don't you get some rest and I'll clean up the kitchen?" she said.

"Where can I lay down?"

"Well, since I'm up, why don't you sleep in my bed?"

I think I blushed a little, because she giggled at me.

"No, really, it's all right. Just go in and make yourself comfortable. We'll make arrangements later. Go on now."

I lifted my duffle with my good hand and followed her across the living room and down a short hall. She opened the door to a spacious room with a skylight in the ceiling and a large window looking out over the street below. She pulled the door closed behind her when she left. I got out of my uniform and boots and stretched out on the bed in my long underwear and stockings. I pulled a blanket up around my shoulders and closed my eyes. Her pillow smelled heavenly. I was asleep in minutes.

CHAPTER 21

I woke up with a start and looked out the window. The sky was a cold, dark gray. I figured I must have slept through the afternoon, though it seemed I had been asleep only seconds. I was a bit groggy and my hand was throbbing a little. My back didn't hurt until I started putting my uniform back on. I didn't try for the boots and walked out into the living room in my stocking feet. I found the girls there, dressed in work clothes and boots, just like a man would wear.

"Well hello," Rebecca said. "Did you sleep well?"

"What time is it?" I said, rubbing my eyes.

"Half past seven. Time to go to work."

"In the evening?"

"No," Rebecca said, handing me a cup of tea. "It's Monday morning."

I had slept nearly 18 hours without a twitch.

"Where's Frank?"

"He's still asleep," Elizabeth said. "He didn't make it much longer than you did yesterday. He barely got his boots off. How long has it been since you boys had a decent night's sleep?"

"I don't know," I said. "What year is it?"

"Well, I hope you're all rested up now," Rebecca said. "Because tonight we are going out to celebrate your homecoming. Be ready when we get home from work."

"Sounds like a wonderful plan," I said. I fished some cigarettes out of my breast pocket and offered them to the girls, but they declined.

"It's time to go," Rebecca said.

"I promise I won't chase you out of your room tonight," I said as she walked to the door.

"You didn't chase me out," she said. "You were so sound asleep that you wouldn't budge, not even when I punched you in the arm. So I gave up and let you stay."

"You were there all night?"

"Until about an hour ago."

I know for sure that I blushed that time because I could feel my cheeks and ears getting hot.

"It wasn't a problem," she said with a giggle. "You were a perfect gentleman."

"Come on," Elizabeth said. "We'll be late for our shift."

They walked out the door and I could hear their boots going down the steps. I walked into the kitchen, sat down at the table and unbuttoned my tunic. Rebecca was very pretty, even in her work clothes. She had a smooth, pure complexion, cheeks tinted just slightly pink, and eyes that reminded me of a woman I saw in an Italian painting in one of my school books. Elizabeth was quite fetching as well. I wondered if they were attractive to me because I'd been away from English girls for so long, or whether they were genuinely gorgeous. I opted for the latter.

Then I wondered if a woman as lovely as Rebecca could possibly be interested in a simple coal miner like me. It was the first time I'd considered such a possibility. I got butterflies in my stomach, but not like the ones I got before an attack. I wondered how I might win her heart.

Frank came staggering into the kitchen wearing some kind of oriental robe. His hair, or what was left of it, was standing straight up, and his eyes were narrow slits.

"What time is it?" he asked.

"It's going on eight."

"In the morning or night?"

"Morning."

"Oh, no," he said, opening the cupboard. "We've got a lot to do today."

"There's tea already made," I said.

"I'm not looking for tea. Ah, there it is."

He pulled out a bottle of scotch and two glasses. He poured us generous portions. We clinked our glasses together and knocked it back.

"Ah, yes," Frank said. "She always buys the good stuff."

"Good indeed," I said. "How about a nip more?"

Frank obliged, and we drank them down.

"So you like her, don't you?" Frank asked.

"Elizabeth is quite lovely," I said.

"No, you know what I'm talking about. You've got, shall we say, more than a casual interest in Rebecca?"

"No I don't."

"You're lying! You're a damned liar!"

I tried to stare him down and defeat him in silence, but naturally he won.

"I think she's a very nice girl whom I'd like to get to know better," I said.

"That can be done."

"But I'm not the same class of people as you and the girls. I'm just a coal miner."

"The last time I looked, you were a sergeant with a medal who had the respect of both his subordinates and superior officers. That's nothing to discount so quickly."

164

"I'm just afraid I don't have much in common with Rebecca. I would run out of things to talk about, except things about the war, which I don't want to spend a minute thinking about while I'm in Blighty."

"Well I heard that you two talked for about five hours yesterday morning and didn't run out of things to say. And I also heard from an inside source that Rebecca thinks you are quite dashing."

"Dashing? She really said that?"

"I'm just telling you what I heard."

"But I don't know anything about being with a woman."

"What do you mean?"

"I've never been, shall we say, romantic with a girl. Ever."

"Never?"

"Not once."

"Well, no wonder you look so lovesick, old man!"

"Please don't tell any of the boys about this, Frank."

"Never. But I think your inexperience may be a thing of the past before we go back up to the line."

"You think so?"

"Definitely."

"I've worried about that. About getting killed before having ever been with a woman."

We sat quietly for a while, drinking our tea. Then Frank got up and cooked a monstrous breakfast and we ate until we were ready to pop. We got cleaned up and put on our uniforms.

"We need to do a couple of things this morning," Frank said. "First, we'll stop at the army hospital and get our bandages changed. Then I need to stop and see a friend of mine, and after that, we'll get us some civilian clothes. How does that sound?"

"You lead the way."

We walked down the stairs, through the alley and out onto the street. It was starting to rain.

"I wonder where the nearest hospital is," Frank said. A taxi came along and Frank waved him down.

"Could you take us to the nearest army hospital?" he asked

"Sure, soldier," the driver said. "Climb in. There's one not far from here."

We hopped in the back and we were off. It took us about five minutes to get to the hospital. Frank paid the driver and gave him an ample tip.

"Do you want me to wait for you?" the driver asked.

"No, you can go," Frank said. "We might be a few minutes."

The driver pulled away and we walked up the steps to the front doors of the hospital. We checked in at the front desk, and they

165

led us to a ward down the hall. We sat and waited about a half-hour before a portly nurse came to look at our dressings.

"You've been doing a good job keeping this clean," she said to me. She pulled the bandage back. "That is a nasty cut."

"It's not that bad," I said. "His is worse."

After she finished putting a new dressing on my hand, she had a look at Frank's wound.

"That's the strangest cut I've ever seen," the nurse said. "It looks like you were hit with a sword."

"A shovel, ma'am," he said.

"I bet that hurt."

"Still does. Got any pain killers?"

"I don't think you need any of that."

"Oh no? When was the last time you got hit on the head with a shovel? Let me tell you, it isn't pleasant."

"All right, all right, I'll get you something for the pain."

She walked out of the room and came back in a few minute with a bottle of pills.

"Don't take these unless you need them," she said. "Some of the boys get addicted to them."

"I'll be careful," Frank said, popping a pill into his mouth. He put the bottle in his pocket. "Thanks for your help."

"Come back and see me on Wednesday to get new dressings," she said.

"We'll be back," Frank said, and we headed out of the ward. We got down to the street and the rain had stopped.

"I need to pay a visit to a friend of mine before we go any further," he said. "His shop is just a few blocks from here. What do you say we walk a bit?"

"That's fine with me."

We rounded a corner and came down a street lined with shops of all sorts. Frank stopped in front of a café.

"Go in here and order some tea and toast," he said. "I'm going over to that antique shop. I'll be back in a few minutes. Just sit tight."

He dashed across the street and I turned and walked into the café. It smelled good inside. I sat at a window table and watched the girls and the pigeons on the street. I ordered some tea and picked up a newspaper that someone had left at the next table. I read a while and ordered more tea. I was almost done with the second cup when Frank walked in and sat down across from me. He was carrying a fat brown envelope in his left hand.

"You ready?" he asked.

"Sure. Where to?"

"To the tailor's. We're going to get us some suits to go to

166

dinner tonight."

"But I can't buy a suit. I can barely pay for this tea."

He slid the envelope across the table to me.

"Look inside."

I opened it a bit and saw a stack of pound notes, at least a hundred, probably more. I had never seen so much money in my life, nor have I since.

"How the hell…"

"You know how the hell."

"You sold it," I whispered.

"Why are you whispering? Nobody here cares about that certain piece of Asian pottery that shall remain nameless."

"What if the police find out? You could go to jail."

"Well, being in the worst jail in Blighty would be better than sitting in the best dugout in Wipers. The queen mother of all dugouts, even."

"You told the lieutenant you'd help get it back after the war. What then?"

"You know my theory. This war is never going to end. Ever. So we might as well have a good time now. Besides, they still can't prove I took it in the first place."

"What about the girls?"

"What about them?"

"They'll wonder how a soldier could have money for suits and such."

"We'll tell them I won it playing cards. Lots of cards. Cheating. For months."

"You're right," I said. "They'd probably believe that."

"I bet that fellow in the store was surprised to see you."

"Yes, but it didn't take long for us to decide on a fair price. He'll sell it for a lot more than he paid me for it, probably in Amsterdam."

"You think?"

"Sure. Amsterdam is a great place to get rid of anything and everything you can imagine. Now let's get going!"

We paid our tab and Frank left a huge tip. He hailed a taxi outside.

"No more walking for us, Richard," he said, and gave the driver an address. I stared out the window at the people on the streets, the tall buildings and gardens. The sun was poking through the clouds to the east. We drove what seemed like halfway across London and the driver didn't even need directions. We stopped at the curb in front of a small shop with an Italian name. Frank paid the fare and we went in.

"Francis!" a man shouted from behind a counter.

"Vincent!" Frank shouted in a mocking voice.

"Francis, it is good to see you again," Vincent said with a thick accent. "How are you doing with the Germans? Are they giving you trouble?"

Frank pulled his cap off.

"We got a little too close to the action a few nights ago," he said. "Me and Sergeant Gardener here are on medical leave for three weeks."

"Sergeant, it is a pleasure to make your acquaintance," Vincent said, extending his hand. "It looks like you got a little too close to the action as well."

"Just a scratch, really," I said.

"Francis," he said, "you've lost some weight. I'll take in your uniform a bit if you want."

"What I'm really interested in is a couple of nice suits," Frank said.

"Vincent will take good care of you, Francis. How long has it been?"

"About a year and a half since I was in here last."

"Tell me more about the war."

"I'm tired of talking about the war. Let's talk about London. We're going out on the town tonight with a couple of lovely ladies, and we want to look good. Can you get us a couple of suits ready by this afternoon?"

"For you Francis, anything. I'll fix you up with the best. And I'll tailor your uniforms for free. How does that sound?"

"Wonderful. Let's see what you've got."

Vincent rolled out several racks of suits with quite a variety of styles. Different colors and materials like I'd never worn. Frank picked out a black suit with a gray vest, a wide-collared white shirt and a black tie with white stripes. I didn't know what to do. They didn't even have prices marked on them.

"Take your pick, Richard," Frank said. "Cost is no object."

Vincent's eyes widened with the delight of an impending sale. He guided me first to a dark gray suit, but I decided I liked a brown wool number better. The jacket was deep brown, with lighter brown trousers and a tan vest. I got a shirt like Frank's, and a brown wool tie.

"That will look good on you," Vincent said, patting me on the shoulder. Then we put on the suits, and Vincent marked here and there with chalk, pinned up a few places and measured where necessary. It took about an hour for both of us.

We got back into our uniforms and Vincent said he'd put everything else on hold so he could get our suits done by five.

Frank pulled out the envelope and handed several notes to Vincent.

"When you get those done, would you mind sending them over to my flat? We'll be there," he said, and pressed another pound into Vincent's palm.

"Most definitely, Francis! Now you fellows have a splendid day. Come back and I'll tailor those uniforms! No charge!"

We went to about five or six shops after that, and in each of them, they greeted Frank the same way. Everyone was overjoyed to see him, and they waited on us like we were princes. They fetched us tea and showed off their wares. We had brandy at one shop and sherry at another. Frank bought us shoes to go with the suits, as well as bowlers to match. I had never had a pair of shoes or a hat that wasn't the working kind. The shoes were lighter and more comfortable than my boots. Later in the afternoon we got shaves and haircuts. The barber worked around Frank's bandage the best he could and we both looked good when we were finished.

We caught a taxi back to the flat and arrived around three. Frank and I were having another nip from the bottle when the suits arrived. We decided to put on our new clothes, to surprise the ladies when they came in from work. The suits fit perfectly, and when I checked myself in the mirror I was surprised at how different I looked. I was polished to the highest degree, wearing the best suit in London and a new haircut. I also noticed that I was looking thinner, especially in the face. I was getting lines at the corners of my eyes and on the sides of my mouth, and there was a touch of gray in my hair. But I looked handsome.

Elizabeth and Rebecca came walking up the stairs just before five. We jumped up from the table and stood in front of the door to greet them. The girls were laughing on the other side of the door. When they opened it, they were struck silent. Frank waved his hands in a flourish.

"Good heavens, Frank, what have you done?" Elizabeth said. "I mean you look smashing. Just smashing!"

She ran into his arms.

"Thank you, thank you," he said. "And may I introduce Sir Richard of Wipers?"

"You look smashing too, Richard," she said, not looking away from Frank's eyes.

"Yes, Richard," Rebecca said, walking over to me. "You look like a barrister or banker or something. I am definitely impressed."

She took my hands from my sides and I got that fluttering feeling in my stomach again.

"I'll be very proud to be seen with you tonight," she said. "You look very handsome this evening."

"You look good as well," I said. Then I realized that I had told her she was pretty in her work clothes, but again, I thought she was. I stammered a bit and couldn't find the right words to say.

"Look, Sir Richard," she said, "you're going to have to relax if you want to have any fun at all in London."

I was speechless. She let my hands drop back to my side, then winked and walked off to her room.

"You can quit blushing now, Richard," Frank said. Elizabeth smacked him on the shoulder.

"Be quiet, you geezer," she said.

"This is still my flat, and I can say whatever I want."

"Well I say it's my flat now, and I'll make all the rules."

"And what are your rules?"

"You have to kiss me anytime I ask."

"That's pretty rough…"

She nuzzled up to him, then looked over at me, still standing there looking awkward. They stopped.

"Why don't we discuss this over dinner?" Elizabeth asked.

"We'll go to Chez Antoine," Frank said.

"Chez Antoine? Since when do we go to restaurants like Chez Antoine?"

"Me and Richard made some money playing cards. We saved up."

"Is that so, Richard?"

"Yes, ma'am, it is."

"You weren't cheating, were you?" she asked.

"Well, maybe a little," Frank said. "But not much. And Richard didn't cheat at all."

"Well then, Rebecca and I will have to get presentable to match you two handsome devils," she said, and walked off to her room. Her door closed.

Rebecca was in the bath and I could hear her singing. Even her voice was beautiful.

170

Frank disappeared into Elizabeth's room after her turn in the bath. Rebecca was in her room getting ready. That left me sitting in the kitchen, smoking nervously. I had high hopes of a romantic night, and it had become obvious that the others were thinking the same way. My stomach rumbled.

I got the half-empty bottle of whiskey out of the cabinet, pulled the cork, took a big swallow and put it back. I was wiping my lips on the back of my hand when it occurred to me that I could have at least used a glass. The war had made me uncivilized. So I got the bottle back out, poured a good gulp into a glass and drank it. To civilization.

Rebecca came into the kitchen wearing a deep green velvet dress with a scooped neck and a pearl necklace, and her hair was curly and flowing. The dress accented her curvaceous form. I had never in my life seen a woman so beautiful, nor have I since. I stood and sat my glass on the table.

"You look truly lovely," I said. "I really mean that."

I pulled out a chair for her and she walked across the room.

"Just stand there for a minute," she said to me. "I want to get another look at you."

I pushed the chair aside; I don't know why. She walked over to me, and I could smell her hair and her perfume and her eyes were sparkling. She stopped about two feet in front of me and clasped her hands behind her back.

"It's going to be a terrific evening," she said, looking up into my eyes. "I can sense these things."

My knees were weak. I looked into her big dark eyes and it was like I could see into her soul. I think she was waiting for me to kiss her, but I didn't have the nerve.

"It will be a terrific evening," I said. "If I were back in Wipers, I'd probably be eating cold bully beef with a biscuit if I were lucky."

"The food is that bad?"

"I've eaten enough corned beef to last me a lifetime."

"I don't think that's on the menu at Chez Antoine."

We were still looking into each other's eyes. I had the urge but I just couldn't do it.

"Want another whiskey?" she asked. I nodded yes. My mouth was too dry to say anything. I could stand up to a drumfire barrage, but this romance business was scary. I guess you could say I had the wind up.

She refilled my glass, then filled her own. She raised hers.

"To peace. And a good dinner."

"Yes. And no more bully beef."

I knocked back my whiskey, and I was impressed when she did the same, in one swallow. She wiped the corner of her mouth and we both started laughing.

"That's pretty good for a girl," I said.

"I'm no girl. I'm all woman."

We laughed again and Frank and Elizabeth emerged from their room. They looked tremendous. She was wearing a long red silk dress that properly accentuated her delicate figure. She was quite pretty.

"Aren't we all aglow, now," Rebecca said. "We'll be the best looking ladies and gentlemen in the place!"

"You two look great," Frank said to me with a wink. "What do you think about the ladies?"

"I don't think I've seen two prettier girls anywhere," I said.

"Not even in France?" Elizabeth asked. "I heard that all of the French girls are beautiful."

Frank and I looked at each other, and I know he was thinking the same thing as me: When did we ever see a pretty girl in France, or Belgium for that matter? The ones near the front were tired and old.

"No," Frank said. "French girls aren't this pretty. Do you agree, Sergeant Gardener?"

"Certainly."

We continued praising our own good looks for a while, and then went out and down the stairs to the street. It was a brisk evening, but not too cold. Rebecca took my arm.

"It's not that far to Chez Antoine from here," she said. "Why don't we just walk?"

Frank and Elizabeth agreed and we started off. We walked past at least a dozen restaurants on the way there, and some pretty fancy ones at that. I remember thinking that Chez Antoine must be one posh *estaminet* if we were passing these by to get there; I thought about holding Rebecca's hand but my palms were sweaty.

We arrived at the restaurant in about twenty minutes, just as I was starting to get cold. It was in a dark, red brick building with a black and white canopy over the walk. A doorman dressed in a tuxedo motioned us in. An authentic Frenchman wearing a white jacket greeted us.

"Good evening," he said with an accent. "What is the name on the reservation?"

"Frank Thomas."

The Frenchman looked down the list and naturally didn't find his name.

172

"I'm sorry, *monsieur*," he said. "There is no reservation here."

"Then it must be under Richard Gardener. That's what it must be."

He looked again and came up blank.

"That's odd. I wonder how that happened? Well, we'll take whatever table you have left."

"There are no tables, *monsieur*. I am sorry."

"But we are only in London tonight, and then we have to get back to the front. Surely you have room for a couple of soldiers, now don't you?"

Now I knew that Frank was going to get us a table in the end, so I anticipated a good show. I just kept smiling and nodding.

"Now see," Frank said, "Sergeant Gardener here retook a whole French village with nothing but a bayonet. Now isn't there anything for us?"

The Frenchman looked annoyed and said nothing. I decided to jump in.

"*Monsieur*," I said, "Corporal Thomas here was given the *Croix de Guerre* by General Foch himself. Show him your medal, Frank."

Frank played along and frisked his pockets. The Frenchman was getting impatient.

"I thought it was here somewhere," Frank said. "Oh, here it is."

He held his hand out to the Frenchman and slipped him a pound folded in a tight square. The Frenchman gave me the eye.

"*Vive la France*," I said, slowly and deliberately.

He looked down his list again and miraculously found my name. He showed us to a corner table in the gas-lit dining room.

"*Merci beaucoup*," I said. He pulled out chairs for the ladies and we all sat down. Frank ordered some expensive champagne and the porter came with a bottle in a great silver bucket, along with a plate of sliced strawberries. He popped the cork and poured a sample for Frank. He took a sip and nodded, and the porter filled the rest of our glasses. Frank tipped him well.

I took a sip and found it to be the driest thing I had ever tasted. I wondered what the cheap kind tasted like.

"Let's have a toast," Elizabeth said. "What shall we drink to?"

"To Blighty," I said.

"To Blighty," Frank concurred. We clinked our glasses and drank. A waiter arrived with menus, but when I looked inside, it was all written in French. There weren't any prices on anything, either. I was lost, and sat in silence for a moment, staring at the list of fancy food like I had never eaten.

"I can't read this," Rebecca said, placing her hand on mine. "Could you help me?"

I looked at Frank. He was suppressing a laugh.

"Uh, I think that, uh, Frank's French is much prettier, I'd say. Best let him read it to you."

"Yes, Frank," Elizabeth said. "Why don't you order for the four of us this evening?"

"Splendid plan," Frank said, holding the menu close at first, then farther away, like he couldn't see it clearly. "No problem."

Frank pulled it off somehow, but I didn't pay much attention to what he ordered. I just took it all in. It was probably the classiest place I ever did see. Small chandeliers hung through the parlor, and there were full-length windows, some with stained glass. The walls were paneled with mahogany and adorned with beautiful paintings of Paris. I don't think I've ever been more proud in my life as I was that night, to have such wonderful company in a place so far from the front.

The waiter came to our table and asked me what wine we would be having with the meal. I deferred to Frank, naturally.

"More champagne," he said. "Is that all right with everyone?"

We all nodded and finished the glasses in front of us.

"How can a soldier afford this?" Elizabeth asked, as I knew she would eventually.

"We play a lot of cards," Frank said to her. "Right Richard?"

"Yes, but I'm not as good as Frank. He cleaned out a bunch of Frenchmen just before we left. Took everything they had."

"Those Frenchies couldn't play cards real well, but they had a lot of money," he said, building the lie. "I think they were officers or something. I figure I'm over there fighting for their country, so they owe me a little in return."

"You weren't cheating them, were you?" she said. "You're pretty slick with the cards."

"Not that particular time, no, I wasn't cheating," Frank said. "I do have a little honor."

The porter showed up with another bottle and popped the cork.

"We must have another toast," Frank said as the glasses were filled. "We must come up with a good one."

"Why don't you give us a toast, Richard?" Rebecca said, brushing my arm. I looked into her dreamy eyes and my mind went blank. I couldn't think of anything befitting the situation. I looked over at Frank and raised my glass.

"Over the top with the best of luck," I said.

"Over the top," Frank said, and we all clinked glasses.

The appetizers arrived. There were two kinds of caviar, one black and one pink, served on little triangles of toast with lemon. I

174

tried both kinds, but to me, it just tasted like dead fish. Frank and Elizabeth were inhaling it by the mouthful and discussed ordering more.

The first course of the dinner was consommé; basically clear soup with nothing in it. A platter of prawns and something black that I couldn't identify followed it.

"What on earth is that?" I said, being a bit drunk by then.

"Just try it," Frank said. "You'll like it."

The girls giggled as I speared one of the black things with my fork. I held it up.

"Come on," I said. "What is it?"

"Just try it."

I put it in my mouth. It was smoky but rubbery as could be. I didn't like it much at all. I swallowed it nearly whole and washed it back with a gulp of champagne.

"Now tell me what that was," I demanded.

"It was *escargot*," Frank said. "Smoked snail."

"You bastard," I blurted, like I was in some shady *estaminet* in Pop.

"Oh my," Elizabeth said, fanning her face. "You soldiers have such a vivid vocabulary."

"My deepest apologies," I said, feeling incredibly embarrassed. "But why didn't you tell me what that was?"

"Because I knew you wouldn't try it if I did," Frank said.

"You're right about that," I said. I tried some of the prawns and they were quite good.

"You know, Richard, you might have liked those snails," Frank said. "It's got to be better than bully and biscuits."

"You're right about that, too," I said. I turned to Elizabeth. "Did you ever notice he always has a way of being right?"

"That's just Frank," Elizabeth said. "He's as smooth as silk."

Frank hailed the porter and ordered a third bottle of champagne. It arrived with the next course, which was mixed greens with dressing and some kind of cheese that was stinky but good.

The main course was magnificent. It was chicken cooked in white wine with garlic, mushrooms and onions. I didn't know chicken could be so flavorful. I devoured mine, finishing way ahead of everyone else.

"You like that chicken, there, Richard?" Frank said with a smart look on his face. It got a good laugh and made me a bit self-conscious, so I reached for the champagne and poured myself another glass.

"Do you want some of mine?" Rebecca asked. "I don't think I can finish all of this."

175

"No, thank you. I'm fine."

"Are you sure? Because it would be a shame to see such good food go to waste."

I paused for a moment and looked at her plate.

"Are you sure you can't finish it?" I asked.

"I'm sure. Here you go." She forked about half of her chicken onto my plate. Frank grinned and I ate a little slower.

"I'm certain you've been craving a meal like this for a while," she said to me. "They must do something about getting you boys some better food."

There was a pause in the conversation, and then Frank launched into some embellished tale about our ventures. Soon we were all laughing again and Frank decided we definitely needed a fourth bottle of champagne.

For dessert we had a platter of peeled fruit, strawberries and pastries. By that time, we were all pissed and we ate every last scrap of it, laughing the whole time. I think we annoyed the couple seated next to us. They kept glaring at us. I didn't care. I was feeling good. We told more stories about our better times and had some more chuckles.

The waiter brought the check and Frank pulled out a fat roll of cash. The girls actually gasped when they saw it. Once the waiter left, the interrogation began.

"How did you get all of that money again?" Elizabeth said.

"Playing cards," Frank said.

"That's right, playing cards with Frenchmen," I blurted.

"Plus there's not much to spend money on up at the front," Frank said. "A bottle of wine here and there on leave, and that's about it."

"Really?" she said, sounding unconvinced. "Does this have anything to do with a missing vase?"

Frank looked at me and back at Elizabeth.

"What are you talking about?"

"Well, the police did come by to ask me a few questions after you suddenly joined the army," she said. "Do you think I've forgotten? They tore the place apart!"

"Oh, yes," Frank said, his eyes darting between Elizabeth and I. "That vase. Well, I didn't steal anything, but I was accused. The vase came up missing after I left some rich man's party, and for some reason, they thought I might have it. I don't. Isn't that right, Richard? I don't have any vase."

"Right," I said soberly, because he did not, in fact, have the vase. There was a pause.

"And you didn't cheat at cards," she said again. "You seem awfully lucky."

176

"I do have you, don't I?" he said.

"To luck," I said, raising my glass. We drank down the last of the champagne and Frank left a most generous tip for the waiter.

We went out into the cool night air and started walking back to the flat. This time, I held Rebecca's hand confidently. We passed a spirit store that was still open, so I suggested to Frank that we stop in. We picked up a bottle of scotch, a bottle of gin and some cigarettes and continued on our way. Rebecca put her arm around my waist, and I put my arm across her shoulders and held her closely. I was getting brave. It must have been the champagne.

Once we got home, Frank and Elizabeth, predictably by now, disappeared into Elizabeth's room and closed the door. That left Rebecca and I alone. I started getting nervous again. I lit a cigarette and offered one to her. She took it and we sat down on the sofa.

"Would you like a whiskey?" she asked. "I think I'd like a good strong drink right now."

"That would be fine," I said, and she went into the kitchen. She came back with two glasses and the bottle of scotch we'd bought. I had never met a woman before who actually liked to drink. She sat down beside me, put her hand on my shoulder and ran it down to my hand. Now I was terrified. I fumbled with the cork and I was visibly shaking when I poured the two glasses half full.

"What should we drink to this time?" Rebecca asked.

"Why don't we drink to the war?" I said, somewhat surprising myself.

"Why would we want to drink to the war?" she said. "It's horrible."

"Yes, it is horrible," I said. "I know exactly how horrible. But if it weren't for the war, you and I would never have met."

She paused and sank back on the sofa, her glass in hand.

"Would that make it all worth while? Just to have met me?"

"It makes it much less horrible."

She sat up and raised her glass.

"To the war," she said, and we knocked back our drinks. She coughed.

"My god, that's rough stuff," she said. "Maybe we should have gotten something better."

"No, it's fine," I said. "A lot better than rum in a tin cup."

"That doesn't sound very tasty."

"Indeed, it isn't. But after a night on patrol or digging or whatever, it is comforting."

She leaned forward and put her hand on my knee.

177

"Tell me what it's like. What it's really like. Not all the funny things."

"You don't want to know what it's really like," I said. "I assure you, you don't."

"Yes I do," she said. "I want to know how it is."

"Imagine the worst possible situation one could be in, then triple the misery," I said. "It's worse than anything anyone who hasn't been there can fathom."

"I can take it. Tell me."

"Every day I see death. It stalks us, on both sides of the line. Shells and bullets, clubs and bayonets. I've seen men die in every imaginable way. Every day. My mate from home that died the night Frank and I were wounded? They dug him out of the mine in pieces. Some of him they didn't even find. Mines are the worst thing, followed closely by flamethrowers and gas. It's all so awful. It's amazing I'm still sane."

"How do you do it? Stay sane, that is?"

"After a while it gets to be one big horrible routine that you go through out of habit. We shoot at them, they shoot back. We shell them, they shell us. You spend most of your time hiding like a rat in some hole or crevice, waiting for it all to stop. You don't dare stick your head up to look around, or else a sniper will nail you. The landscape never changes. Just the muddy trench below and the sky above."

"Tell me more," she said, looking into my eyes.

"There are other things that make it worse," I said. "Everything is infested with lice. Then there are the rats. There are millions of them and they're enormous from feeding on all of the dead bodies lying about. There are bodies everywhere, in pieces, bloating in the sun until the rats pick the bones clean. The smell is vile. Then you throw in the sewage and gas and smoke."

"You never read about all of that in the papers."

"What you read in the papers isn't real at all. Some of the stories that come back from the front are unbelievable, full of patriotism and other such nonsense."

"Weren't you feeling a bit patriotic when you signed up?"

"Yes, I was. I was caught up in the fever to beat the Kaiser. And I didn't want to die in a coal mine. The army seemed like the right choice at the time."

"But you have second thoughts?"

"Yes, I do. But there's not much I can do about it now. I signed up for the duration of the war. And the way it's going, I'll be an old man before I get out."

"You really think so?"

"I know so. We pay thousands of lives for little strips of land

178

that bring us only a few yards closer to Berlin. It's nothing for us to lose a thousand men in a glorified trench raid. The generals come up with brilliant plans from the comfort of their desk chairs without any idea as to what we face every day. You'd never see one of them up on the line, dodging shellfire. We just keep digging in deeper, waiting for the next attack. They don't know what it's like to charge a machine gun position, or choke and gag while trying to get on a gas helmet. They don't know what it's like to go for days without getting a few uninterrupted hours of sleep somewhere. You get so tired you fall asleep standing up."

I'd gone on enough, so I stopped. I finished my whiskey. Rebecca got up from the sofa and went into the kitchen for a moment. On her way back she turned out the lamp next to the sofa and sat down, leaning back against me.

"Do I make you nervous?" she asked.

"Why would you make me nervous?" I said unconvincingly. "Shells don't even make me nervous anymore."

"Then why don't you put your arm around me and hold me?"

"Would you like that?"

"It would be nice."

She put her head on my shoulder and I put my arm around her. She kicked off her shoes and pulled her feet up on the sofa. I turned and put my nose in her hair and smelled it. I nearly melted into the furniture.

"Are you comfortable?" she asked.

"Yes, this is nice," I said. Even if I had been uncomfortable, I wouldn't have said so. It was as close to a woman as I'd ever been.

179

I awoke on the sofa, an empty glass in my hand and Rebecca asleep, still cuddled on my shoulder. I rubbed my eyes with my free hand and looked at the clock on the mantle. It was after two.

I caught the scent of Rebecca's beautiful hair once more, and since she was sleeping, I leaned forward, buried my nose in her curls and took a deep breath. I could not get over how that sweet scent made me weak in the knees and made my heart pound. Rebecca stirred and clasped the hand I had over her shoulder.

"This has been a truly wonderful night," she said in a sleepy, dreamy voice. "I don't want it to end."

"Neither do I," I said

"I've never had such a time before. I'm so happy that you are here with me tonight. I feel so safe with you next to me."

"It is rather marvelous," I said, clearing my throat. It didn't make the lump go away. She turned on the sofa, took my hands and looked into my eyes.

"I need to know something," she said.

"Anything at all."

"I need to know…I want to know…is there anyone waiting for you back home?"

"No, there isn't. I think I would have told you by now if I were married."

"I don't mean married. Just a girl waiting for you to come back from the war. A girl from your town. Or is there anyone waiting for you to come back to the front? A pretty little Belgian girl, perhaps? You can tell me."

"No, honestly, there is no one."

"But you are so handsome, so kind, so gentle."

"That's awfully nice of you to say…"

"No, I mean it. Girls dream of meeting a man like you. Someone who is warm, caring, polite. So tall and so strong. I know I've never…" Her voice trailed off.

"Never what?"

"I've never met a man like you. Maybe I've been looking in the wrong places. So many of them, all they want…"

"I guess that makes me different."

Then there was that moment. I stared into those perfect, deep brown eyes, adorned with long lashes, and she was so close to me. My heart was pounding.

"I know I've never met a woman like you before," I said, my voice cracking.

She leaned forward, as did I, and our lips met. Hers were so soft. My stomach fluttered. We embraced and held the kiss for a moment, then parted.

"I've got something to confess," I said.

"What's that?"

"I've never kissed a girl before."

"Never?"

"Not as a man, I mean."

She leaned forward and we kissed again, this time much more passionately.

"You certainly do a good job of it for someone whose never kissed before," she said, her lips barely moving against mine.

Now she was inclined in my arms, her ample breasts against me. I felt as though my heart would leap from my chest. I was falling in love. It was a feeling I'd never experienced.

After a few more minutes of passion, she pulled away.

"It's getting so late," she said. "I'm sure I won't be up for work in the morning."

"I'm sorry."

"The last thing you should be is sorry. They won't miss me. I'll tell them I was sick. It's not like you can lose a job in a shell factory when a war is on."

She kissed me quickly and stood up.

"I guess this is good night," I said, standing up as well. I was about to ask her where I might find a blanket and pillow for the sofa when she took my hand in hers and pulled me close.

"I don't think I'm ready to go to sleep yet," she said. It was going on three. I didn't know what she meant.

"Come with me, and hold me some more," she said, and led me to her bedroom. I must admit that I was scared to death, but it felt good.

We walked inside and she shut the door behind us. She did not turn on the light, but the moon cast a pale glow through the skylight. She sat down on the bed and patted a spot beside her. I sat down with my hands clasped on my lap. She started unbuttoning her dress.

"Are you going to sit there, or are you going to get ready for bed?"

"I'm sorry."

"How many times do I have to tell you not to be sorry, you silly man?"

She stood and stepped out of her dress, then out of her slip. I was still sitting there like a schoolboy. She sat beside me again and slipped my jacket off, then unbuttoned my vest and shirt. I slid them off my shoulders and she threw them into a pile next to the dresser.

"You don't want to sleep in your shoes and trousers now do you?"

I kind of shook my head, kicked my shoes over into the pile and took off my trousers. I sat there in my underwear, not knowing what to do next. She leaned over and kissed me.

"You're going to have to learn to relax a bit," she said. "I'm not going to hurt you, you know."

"I know."

"Then why are you so nervous?"

"Well, I've never, uh…"

"Never what?"

"I never, you know…"

"Never?"

"Well, I told you I'd never kissed a girl before, so I thought you'd understand."

"It's all right, Richard. It's all right. Just do what comes naturally."

We kissed some more, and then she took my good hand from my side and moved it to her breast. It was soft and warm. It suddenly hit me that I was in for a wonderful experience, and I got a knot in my stomach.

"Come on," she said. "Let's get under the covers. It's chilly in here."

We stood and she pulled back the blankets. I took off my socks and climbed in. She stood in the light of the window and took off what remained of her undergarments, showing me the silhouette of her curvy figure.

"You are so beautiful," I said as she got into bed and snuggled against me. "I don't know what you could see in a man like me."

"You sell yourself short. It's a bad habit, you know."

She rolled over, facing me, put her head on my shoulder and her leg across mine. Then she touched me. I'll leave out the details, as a gentleman should. We fell asleep in each other's arms just as the sun was coming up.

CHAPTER 24

The sun came shining through the skylight at about ten, drawing me out of my deep slumber. Rebecca was still cuddled close against me, her arm across my chest. I just stayed there for a while, reflecting on the previous night. I felt wonderful and alive and invigorated, like I hadn't felt since I left for the army. In fact, I don't think I'd ever experienced anything like it. My whole world had changed overnight. I liked it.

I finally had to get up, my craving for a cigarette and a cup of tea outweighing the bliss I was feeling. I rolled out from under her arm and sat on the side of the bed. I pulled on my trousers and shirt and socks and went out to the kitchen. She looked so peaceful sleeping there that I didn't want to disturb her. I also didn't quite know what I was going to say to her in the morning light. I had to get my thoughts together.

I stumbled into the kitchen, rubbing my eyes and feeling a bit of a headache. Frank was sitting there alone, stamping out a cigarette. There were about 20 butts in the ashtray, and an empty glass sat in front of him. He turned and looked at me with a grin.

"You're looking a little worn out there, Richard," he said. "Didn't get much sleep?"

"I got a few hours," I said. I poured myself a cup of tea, lit a cigarette and sat across the table. "How about you?"

"What can I say?" he said. "I've been away a long time. A lot of time to make up for."

I smiled meekly. He laughed.

"Well, I think this calls for a drink." he said. "I finished the whiskey, what was left of it. How about some gin? Gin is better in the morning anyway."

"Gin is better in the morning if you don't have any whiskey," I said.

He got up and got a second glass and took the bottle of gin out of the cupboard. He poured us each a good gulp.

"Here's to making love to a beautiful woman," he said, lifting his glass. I smiled and lifted mine. We kicked back our drinks. I shuddered. I never did like gin that much. Tastes too much like you're drinking a pine tree. But we each had another, and I was feeling good by the time Rebecca got up and came walking into the kitchen, barefoot and wearing an old robe, her cleavage clearly visible. She walked up behind me, put her arms around my shoulders and kissed me on the cheek.

"Good morning, soldier," she said softly, her lips touching my ear. "Did you sleep well?"

"Like a rock," I said. "How about you?"

"I feel wonderful," she said, and kissed me again. She poured herself a cup of tea and sat down at the table with us.

"Where's Liz?" she asked.

"Still sleeping," Frank said.

"So she decided to stay home today as well. I'm sure they'll get along just fine without us."

She lit a cigarette and took a deep drag.

"So, Richard," she said, "seeing how I have the day off, what would you like to do?"

"I don't know," I said.

"He wants to go back to bed," Frank said with a smirk.

"Frank, shut up," I said, turning a bit red. "I don't know, Rebecca. I haven't been to London before."

"Maybe we could go see some sights," she said. "There are lots of things to see."

"That sounds good," I said. "I'd like to see where the king lives."

"We can do that," she said. "Maybe we could go to the wax museum. That's fun."

"Excellent," I said. "I'll let you be my guide."

She put out her cigarette.

"I'll get ready and we'll go," she said. "I'll just be a few minutes. You get dressed."

She walked out of the room, my eyes following her all the way.

"Looks like you two are in love," Frank said, smirking again.

"I don't know what it is," I said. "But it feels good."

Frank poured us two more glasses of gin.

"Here's to love," he said, and we drank. He fished around in his trouser pocket and pulled out his roll of money. He peeled off about a dozen pounds and handed them to me.

"Show the girl a good time," he said. "Lord knows she showed you one."

I took the cash. It would be nice to take her to lunch, or maybe buy her some flowers, I thought. And I definitely wanted to buy another bottle of whiskey. The gin wasn't getting any easier to drink. I went back to the bedroom, and Rebecca was inside getting dressed. My suit was in a pile in the floor.

"I want you to wear your uniform," she said. "With your medal. I want everyone to see me with a hero."

"You noticed that medal?" I asked.

"Yes, I did. But you never did tell me how you got it."

"I'll tell you over lunch."

"I can't wait to hear it. You are such a good storyteller. Not like Frank. He has a tendency to exaggerate, I believe."

"That he does," I said. "But it's entertaining nonetheless. I like his stories, true or not."

I got into my uniform and pulled on my boots. I put my cap on and checked myself in the mirror. The uniform did a lot for me. Maybe I actually *was* dashing. I looked over and saw her buttoning up her dress. Our eyes met.

"About last night..." I said.

"Yes?"

"It was, uh, well...it was, uh, incredible."

"I'll take that as a compliment," she said with a smile. She sat on the edge of the bed and laced up her shoes. "I thought it was incredible, too."

"So what does it mean?"

"It means we had a wonderful experience together."

"No, that's not what I'm saying. What I'm trying to say is, are you my girl now?"

She looked up and brushed the hair back from her face. She was smiling.

"Would you like that? If I were your girl?"

"Yes, I would like that very much."

"I would like that, too."

"But do you think it's odd, seeing how we just met two days ago?"

"No, not really. It's wartime, and we have to make good use of the time before you go back to Belgium. If I had any doubts about us being together, I would never have invited you into my bed last night."

"Truly?"

"Yes, truly. You're very special to me. I felt close to you since we met that first morning. I feel like I've known you forever. I wouldn't let just any man..."

"That's not what I was implying."

"I know."

"Do you feel any differently about me this morning?"

"Of course. I feel closer to you."

"I feel closer to you, too. I think you are the warmest, most loveable woman I've ever met, and I feel it is a privilege to be with you."

"Now, now, Richard. Flattery will get you everywhere."

We both laughed and I sat down on the bed beside her, taking the cap off my head. We embraced and kissed passionately. My heart skipped.

185

"If you kiss me like that again, we'll never get out of this room," she said, her lips still touching mine. She eventually pulled away and stood up.

"Let's get going," she said. "There are a lot of things for us to do today."

"I'm starving. Why don't we go get some lunch?"

"That sounds like a good idea. There's a pub down the street that has some excellent fish and chips."

"Do you know how long it's been since I had fish and chips?"

"Probably too long. And you can tell me about your medal over a pint."

"Splendid. And I'll try not to exaggerate."

I put my cap back on and we headed out into the parlor. Elizabeth had gotten up and she was sitting on Frank's lap at the kitchen table.

"Where are you off to?" she asked.

"The pub, for starters, and then to Buckingham Palace," Rebecca said.

"You two have a wonderful time. I think Frank and I are going to stay in today."

Frank wiggled his eyebrows up and down. Rebecca and I both laughed.

"You two have a wonderful day as well," I said grinning, and we turned and went out the door, down the stairs and onto the street.

"The Wheat Sheaf is just a couple of blocks away," Rebecca said. "We can walk from here."

"That sounds good. I like to walk."

She put her arm around my waist, and I put my arm around her shoulders. I must have been walking three feet off the ground I was so proud. In a few minutes we reached the Wheat Sheaf and walked inside. We got a table away from the door, then ordered fish and chips and a couple of pints of stout.

"Now tell me the story," Rebecca said as she munched on a chip. "What kind of medal is it?"

"It's the Distinguished Conduct Medal," I said. "But I don't know what I did that was so distinguished."

"Well, you must have done something to impress someone."

"That would be Lt. Rampkin. He's the officer over our platoon. He's the one that recommended me for the medal."

"Is he a good man?"

"The lieutenant is the best. He's one of the smartest people I ever met. Very proper and professional. A good leader. He's the one that convinced the police to leave Frank alone. I bet he would lay down his life for any of us."

186

"But you put your life on the line for him, I take it."

"Not exactly. I just did what I had to do; otherwise, we'd have been pinned down."

I related the story of the sniper, and the assault on the machine gun nest. Rebecca was transfixed on every word. I watched the expressions changing on her face as I told the tale.

"I would have given you a medal, too," she said. "You are so brave."

"No, I just happen to be a pretty good shot. That's all."

"Well, I think you're a hero, whether you do or not."

We finished our meal and beer, and talked for a while before going out to see the sights. We went to Buckingham Palace and watched the changing of the guard, then went to a wax museum. It was the first time I'd been to one, and I was very impressed. In one room, they had the entire royal family, and they looked so lifelike and real. I almost expected them to speak to me. They also had a room full of the leaders of the warring nations, including Herbert Asquith, Czar Nicholas and Kaiser Wilhelm.

We caught a taxi to go home, and we had the driver stop at a spirit store on the way back to the flat for a bottle of whiskey. I hadn't spent that much of Frank's money yet, so I bought a bottle of expensive, single-malt scotch. I believe it was Grand McEntyre, or Grand McGinty, or something like that. We got home at about three, and Frank and Elizabeth were nowhere to be seen. We sat on the sofa and tried the scotch. I had never tasted anything smoother. It went down easy, and it gave me a warm, glowing feeling. It didn't burn my mouth like the stuff we'd had the night before. Rebecca slumped back on the couch and kicked her feet up on the table.

"I think I could take a nap," she said, yawning.

"Yes, I know what you mean," I said. "We were up pretty late last night."

"We've got a few hours before tea," she said, "so why don't we retire to my room?"

"That sounds good," I said, and followed her back to her quarters. Then she started getting undressed right in front of me. I stood there, ogling her curves, blatantly staring.

"Are you coming to bed?" she asked.

"Yes."

"Then take off that uniform and get in."

It was chilly in the room, and the sheets were cold. We snuggled up together to get warm. The next thing I knew, we were kissing and caressing each other. Needless to say, we didn't get any sleep, although I was thoroughly exhausted.

187

At about five I heard the front door open, and Frank and Elizabeth laughing. They sounded like they were a bit drunk. We lay there for a few more minutes, then got up and got dressed. We went out into the parlor. Elizabeth started giggling.

"What's so funny?" Rebecca asked her.

"You two," she said. "Have you been in bed all afternoon?"

"No, just the last two hours. We needed a nap."

"I bet there wasn't much napping going on," Frank said, laughing at me.

"What do you want to do about tea?" Elizabeth asked. "I don't thing there's a thing in the kitchen to cook. Maybe some eggs."

We decided to go out for Italian food, which I'd never had before. The girls went into their rooms to get ready. Frank said we'd be fine dressed in our uniforms, seeing that the Italians were on our side. He sat down next to me and leaned in.

"So, what's the news?" he asked in a low voice.

"News about what?"

"You know bloody well what!"

"I don't know what you're talking about."

"What I'm talking about is you and Rebecca. You've hit it off well, shall we say."

"Yes, we have."

"How do you feel about that?"

"If I tell you, do you promise not to make a joke out of it? Or repeat it?"

"You have my word. Tell all."

"I think I'm in love. I've never been in love before, but I'm reasonably sure that's what I'm feeling. I love her big, brown eyes, her curly hair, her curves…"

"What are you going to do about it?"

"What am I supposed to do about it?"

"That's for you to figure out."

"To be honest, Frank, I don't know what in the world I'm supposed to do. But I do know that I can't stand the idea of having to leave and go back to Wipers, where I can't be with her."

"Maybe she'll wait for you until the war is over."

"You said it yourself; this war could last forever. That's a long time to wait."

"Yes it is. But you could take out a little insurance."

"What do you mean?"

"I mean that if you two got married, she'd definitely wait for you."

"Married? Are you insane? I've known her for three days. Not even three days."

188

"So? What does your gut tell you?

"My gut tells me that I want to be with Rebecca forever."

"Then it sounds like you've got to have a talk with that girl."

He reached in his pocket and pulled out his roll of cash. He gave me another dozen pounds or so.

"What's this for?" I asked.

"So you can buy her a ring."

When he said that, a lot of things went through my head. What if she said no? How could I provide for her on a soldier's salary? When would I ask her? Where would I ask her? Where would we get married, anyway? I seemed to be standing at a crossroads, not knowing which way to go. I decided I'd take my chances.

"All right," I said. "I'll ask her to marry me. As unbelievable as it is. Things are happening so fast. What if she doesn't want me for a husband?"

"I don't think you have anything to worry about, old man. I see how she looks at you. She's definitely in love also."

"Are you sure?"

"Absolutely."

"So when do you think I should ask her?"

"Tonight after we eat. Lizzy and I will go out the pub and leave you two alone here. Have a few drinks, then tell her how you feel."

"I don't know if I can do it. The thought alone makes me shake in my boots."

"You can do it. And I know a vicar who will perform the ceremony. Lizzy and I can be your witnesses."

That was about the time that the girls came out, looking gorgeous. I was afraid they'd overheard us, but they didn't say anything. We walked out the door and found it had turned rather cold after sundown, so we took a taxi to the restaurant.

All through the meal, we joked and laughed rather loudly, but it didn't seem to bother anyone there, not like at Chez Antoine. I must say, however, that while I appeared to be at ease on the outside, my insides were in knots, knowing that in a couple of hours, I would be proposing to Rebecca. I thought I was going to jump out of my skin I was so afraid. But I didn't let on at all.

I paid the bill with some of the money Frank had given me. I estimated that I had plenty left over to buy wedding rings, but I wasn't sure, because I'd never shopped for one. If things went well, I would take her out in the morning and buy a set. My mouth was dry, just like before an attack. Would I be victorious? I prayed that I would be.

We caught a taxi, and Frank directed it to take us to the Wheat Sheaf. He looked at me and winked.

"Richard, you're looking a little tired," he said. "Are you up for the pub?"

He winked at me again.

"No, I think I'd rather go back to the flat and relax a bit. But you go ahead."

"I'll go home with you, Richard," Rebecca said. "I don't want you to get lonely."

Frank and Elizabeth got out at the Wheat Sheaf, and Rebecca and I took the taxi the rest of the way home. My knees were weak as I climbed the stairs. My chest got tight. We went inside and sat on the sofa. I looked at the clock on the mantle; it was getting close to nine. It was now or never, I thought. The time had come.

"I've got a confession to make," I said.

"What's that?"

"Well, uh, I think I've fallen in love with you."

She leaned over and put her arms around me and gave me a kiss. I took it as a good sign.

"And I've got another confession," I said.

"Go on, Richard," she said, pulling back.

"I was wondering, sort of thinking, you know, that we should...that we could get married."

"Richard Gardener, are you proposing to me?"

"Yes, I think...no, definitely yes, I am. Will you marry me?"

She put her arms around me again and kissed me.

"I've fallen in love with you, too, Richard," she said, with tears of joy running down her rosy cheeks. "So the answer is yes. I would love to be your wife. Yes."

What a relief it was. It was probably the most wonderful moment I'd ever experienced.

"So tomorrow, we should go buy rings," I said. "Frank says he knows a priest who can marry us. It will be the proudest day of my life. I love you madly."

We had a toast, and then went back to the bedroom. I didn't get much sleep that night, either. We held each other tightly, and talked into the wee hours of the morning, about all sorts of things. I couldn't wait to tell Frank and Elizabeth the news.

Then it occurred to me that if I hadn't joined the army, if I hadn't ran into Frank that morning by accident, if we hadn't been injured in the mine shaft that night, none of this would have happened. All those things, by some miracle, had led me to that moment. Was it God working in my life, leading me to fulfill some sort of destiny?

I believed it was.

190

I got out of bed at about nine a.m. and got dressed. Frank and Elizabeth were in the kitchen drinking tea. I went in and poured myself a cup and sat down.

"How are you this morning, Richard?" Frank asked.

"Wonderful," I said. "Absolutely wonderful."

"Did you…"

"I did. Rebecca said yes. She and I are getting married."

"Congratulations!" Frank said. Elizabeth's jaw nearly hit the floor.

"Talk about your whirlwind romances," she said. "When is this going to take place?"

"As soon as possible," I said. "We're going out today to buy rings. Then I thought we'd stop in and see that vicar you told me about, Frank. What's his name?"

"Father Samuels. He's at St. Ignatius, down past the Wheat Sheaf."

"I thought we'd make arrangements for tomorrow, if he can fit us in."

"He's probably not too busy, today being Wednesday."

Rebecca came walking into the kitchen in her robe. She was smiling.

"I guess Richard already told you the news."

"Yes, he did," Elizabeth said. She stood up and hugged my bride-to-be. "Congratulations. I hope you have a happy life together."

"So where is the nearest jeweler?" I asked.

"Steinman's," Frank said. "Go up the street, take the first right, go about a half-block and his shop will be on the left."

"I think I can find that," I said.

"Don't worry Richard," Rebecca said. "I know where it is. Have you two eaten already?"

"No," Frank said. "We just got up a few minutes before you did."

"Good. I'll cook us some fried eggs and toast. Does that sound good?"

"It sounds good to me," I said.

We ate, then got dressed properly and went to a jewelry shop. We bought matching gold bands. Afterward, we went to the church Frank had suggested. We went in the front door and ran into a nun.

"Can you tell us where to find Father Samuels?" I asked her.

"He's in his study," she said. "It's down the side hallway, all the way at the end. Knock loud. He's a bit hard of hearing."

We walked down and pounded a few times on the wooden door. A soft, frail-sounding voice beckoned us inside. I pushed the door open and went in. Father Samuels was sitting behind a large, messy desk. He was small and thin, nearly bald, and looked like he was somewhere between 80 and 200 years old.

"What can I help you with?" he asked. "I wager you are here to get married. We get a lot of soldiers who get married before they get shipped off to the war. Am I correct in my assumption?"

"Yes, you are, father," I said. He told us to sit down in two chairs across from himself. He gave us a lecture on the sanctity of marriage and so forth that lasted a good hour.

"Now, when do you want the ceremony performed?" he asked.

"As soon as possible," I said.

He looked around his cluttered desk for a calendar, but couldn't find one.

"I don't think I have anything scheduled in the morning. Why don't you come by at about nine, and we'll perform the ceremony."

"That sounds good," I said.

"Will you have many guests?"

"No, we won't," Rebecca said. "Just my flat mate and her gentleman."

"What about parents?"

"Mine are both dead," I said.

"Mine live in Inverness, so there wouldn't be time for them to travel this far," she said.

"So it will be just the four of you then."

"That's right," I said.

"Well then, I'll expect you at nine."

We left the church and headed down the street.

"Funny," I said, "I didn't know your parents lived in Inverness."

"When you get back from the war, I'll take you to there," she said. "Hopefully in the summertime. It gets terribly cold there in the wintertime."

I remembered then that I had to go to the army hospital and get my bandage on my hand changed. I couldn't recall where it was exactly, so we hailed a taxi and asked the driver to take us to the nearest facility. We ended up in the same place as Frank and I did two days prior.

"This should only take a few minutes," I said to the driver. "Can you wait for us?"

"No problem, mate," he said, and we went up the stairs and into the hospital. We stopped at the front desk and I told the nurse that I needed my bandage changed. She told me to go down the hall to the fourth door on the right.

"I'll wait here," Rebecca said as I walked down the hall. I saw the same nurse as before.

"Still no signs of infection," she said as she cleaned the wound with alcohol. It burned like fire, but I didn't complain. Then she put a new dressing on it and told me to come back in another two days. I thanked her and headed out and down the hallway.

There was a man on crutches in front of me, making his way toward the lobby where Rebecca was waiting. One of his legs was amputated just above the knee, and he had a bandage around his head. I thanked God that my injuries were so slight compared to his. I pondered what it would be like to lose a leg. Or an arm. Or both. My hikes in the country would be over. Even fishing would be difficult. Hunting would be out of the question. I couldn't take my eyes off of him as he crossed the lobby and headed down an adjacent hall. Rebecca noticed I was staring. She stood up and walked over to me, and put her arm around my waist.

"That poor man," she said. "I guess you probably see a lot of that at the front."

"Yes, I do. But it doesn't make it any easier."

"I'm sure it doesn't."

"What if that was me? What if I lost a leg? Would you still love me?"

"I would love you no matter what."

"Do you mean that?"

"Absolutely," she said, and kissed me on the cheek. The man on the crutches disappeared into one of the rooms at the end of the hall. We turned, walked out the door and got into the waiting taxi. Rebecca gave him the address of the flat and we were off.

It was still fairly early in the afternoon when we arrived home. Rebecca showed the rings to Frank and Elizabeth.

"Now all you need is a dress to wear," Elizabeth said. "When is the ceremony to be held?"

"Tomorrow," I said. "At nine."

"Well that doesn't give us much time," Elizabeth said. "Rebecca, we're going to have to go out and get a dress before the shops close this afternoon."

"We can go to Smithfield's," Rebecca said. "I'm sure we can find something there."

I reached into my pocket and handed her the four or five pounds I had left.

"That should cover it," I said. "Don't you think?"

"It's plenty, Richard," she said. "More than enough. I'll bring you back what's left."

"Spend it all," I said. "I want you to get whatever you want."

"You are so thoughtful," she said, walking over and putting her arms around my neck. She gave me a kiss and a hug. Frank winked at me.

"Are you ready to go, Rebecca?" Elizabeth asked.

"Let me get my coat," she said.

The ladies headed out the door and down to the street. I still couldn't get the man with one leg off of my mind. I told Frank what I was thinking about.

"Don't worry, Richard," he said. "We've made it this far. We've been through some bad things, and we've come out all right. There have been plenty of opportunities to get killed, and we've survived them all. I don't think it is our destiny to be maimed or die in this war. I truly don't."

"I wish I shared your confidence," I said. "We could have died in the tunnel that night."

"But we didn't."

"Yes, but Simon did. It could have been either one of us."

"But it wasn't."

I decided not to argue with him about it. He obviously had the conviction that we were impervious. And I knew Frank was usually right about these things. We sat in uncomfortable silence for a few minutes.

"So," Frank finally said, "what would you like to do as far as a honeymoon is concerned?"

"I don't know," I said. "I hadn't thought that far ahead."

"Well, it's time to think about it. You've got about 18 hours to figure it out."

"What do you suggest?"

"You should go somewhere romantic for a few days. Like Bath. That's not too far away. I've been there before. It's a nice town. And I know of a few good restaurants there."

"Sounds good. But I am out of money. I gave the last of it to Rebecca."

"Don't worry about the money," he said, reaching into his pocket. "I've still got plenty."

He pulled out his roll of pound notes, counted it out and gave me half of it. It was about 40 pounds.

"I can't take that, Frank," I said. "That's a lot of money."

"Consider it a wedding gift," he said. "Besides, we won't need it when we get back to the front."

"I can't."

"Just take the money, Richard. I insist on it."

194

"Aren't you going to need it? We've still got a couple of weeks before we have to report back."

"Look, I've still got a fat roll," he said, holding up his half. "Now just take the money."

I finally capitulated and put the money in my pocket.

"So Bath you say?" I asked.

"Definitely. Go there, get yourself a nice hotel room, and live it up."

"On your money."

"You know it's not my money. It's Lord Hanrahan's money. And he'll never miss it. There should be a train leaving in the morning out of Victoria Station. What do you say we go down there and check the schedule?"

We took a taxi to the station and found that a train was leaving for Bath the next morning at 11:15. I bought two tickets and we decided to stop at the Wheat Sheaf on the way home for a couple of pints to celebrate. A couple turned into quite a few, and we got crawling drunk. I looked at the clock on the wall. It was after six.

"It's getting late," I said. "We should head home, don't you say?"

"Let's just have one more. Then we'll go."

I agreed. At about half past six we stumbled out of the pub and staggered up the street toward the flat, leaning on each other for support. Frank ran into a lamppost and fell down. We both burst out laughing.

"Why didn't you tell me to look out for that?" Frank said with a slur. "Dangerous, those things."

"I'll keep lookout for the rest of the way," I said, still laughing.

We weaved down the sidewalk until we got to the theater. We started up the stairs to the flat and Frank stopped.

"All right now," he said, "just…act straight. They'll never know."

I held onto the handrail all the way to the top. Frank fumbled with his keys and dropped them twice. The door came open and Elizabeth was standing there.

"We were starting to wonder where you two went," she said. "I should have known. You've been at the pub."

"We only had a pint or two," Frank said. "Right Richard?"

"That's right," I said. "A pint or two. That was it."

"Somehow, I think you're both lying," she said. "Come on in. We'll make some coffee."

We walked inside. I could smell something good cooking in the kitchen. I didn't see Rebecca anywhere.

"Where's my bride?" I asked.

"She's in trying on the dress she bought," she said. "I think you'll like it, if you can actually focus your eyes enough to see it."

"Oh, I can see it," I said. "I can see just fine. I'm sober. How about you, Frank?"

"I can't see crap," he confessed. "Actually, I can see crap, but I can't see anything else."

Frank and I both laughed. Elizabeth looked annoyed.

"You two booze hounds sit on the sofa where you can't hurt anything," she said. "I'll get your coffee as soon as it's ready."

Frank and I slumped on the sofa and put our feet up on the table. The room was spinning slightly. I put one foot on the floor to make it stop. It didn't. I was obliterated. I laid my head on the back of the couch.

I heard Rebecca's door open, and her footsteps in the hall. I sat up, rubbed my eyes and tried to focus. At first there were two of her, but I soon got it narrowed down to one by closing my left eye slightly. She was dressed in a long, white linen dress with lace around the neck and cuffs. She looked stunning.

"What do you think?" she asked.

"You look marvelous," I said, trying hard to enunciate properly. "What do you think, Frank?"

I looked over. Frank was passed out with his head slumped down. I shook him and woke him up.

"Look at Rebecca's beautiful dress," I said, struggling with my words.

Frank raised his head up and shook it back and forth a few times. He looked at her, squinting.

"Yes…it is…beautiful," he said, stumbling over every word.

"Have you two been drinking?" she asked.

"Just…a little," Frank said. "We were celebrating…and Richard's got a surprise for you. Tell her, Richard."

"What are you talking about?" I asked.

"The tickets."

"Oh yes, the tickets," I said. "How would you like to go to Bath for a few days?"

"That would be wonderful," she said. "You bought us tickets to go?"

"Yes, I did. The train leaves at a quarter past eleven tomorrow. It was Frank's idea, really."

"Well, it sounds lovely to me. I've never been there before."

"Neither have I. But Frank says it's really nice. Right Frank?"

He was passed out again. I shook him and he raised his head.

"Yes," he slurred, "you…look…fantastic."

He laid his head back on the sofa and closed his eyes.

"Is he going to be all right?" Rebecca asked.

196

"Sure," I said. "Frank can really hold his liquor. He'll be fine."

About that time, Elizabeth came out carrying two cups of coffee. She handed one to me and sat the other one on the table in front of us. She stood over Frank and lightly slapped his cheeks with her hands.

"Come on, Frank," she said. "I've got some coffee here for you."

Frank sat up again and rubbed his eyes.

"Coffee," he said. "Good. Coffee for old Frank."

Rebecca went back to change clothes. Frank sat on the couch, rocking back and forth, holding his coffee with both hands. Elizabeth went into the kitchen, and I followed her. I wanted to find out what smelled so good.

"What are we having for tea?" I asked.

"Steak and kidney pie," she said. "Do you like that?"

"I love it. It's been so long since I had any, I can't wait to dive into it. I bet you're a good cook."

"I'm fair at it. Rebecca is a great cook, though. She really knows her way around the kitchen."

"That's good to know."

"She'll have you fattened up in no time. You look like you could use a few more pounds."

"Well, I've lost a lot since I joined the army. My uniform is getting a bit baggy."

"I think you and Frank look great in your uniforms. I never thought I'd see the day that Frank Thomas would wear one. Is he a good soldier?"

"Frank is excellent, although he doesn't care for authority much."

"That's Frank, to be certain."

"And he has this sixth sense about things. Like he can see things before they happen. It's uncanny, really. He also has a knack for finding things that are difficult to come by, like cigarettes and rum and so forth. I don't know what I'd do without him."

She opened up the oven and looked inside.

"It should be ready in about 15 minutes," she said. "Go on back to the sofa and enjoy your coffee."

Frank was still sitting there rocking, sipping out of his cup. Rebecca had changed dresses and was sitting across from him.

"So how much did you two really have to drink?" she asked.

"A bit too much, it seems," I said.

"Frank isn't looking so good. How are you feeling, Frank?"

He mumbled something unintelligible and drank some more of his coffee. He actually looked a little green.

"I've never seen him like this before," I said. "We drink together all of the time, but I don't ever recall him being so pissed."

Elizabeth came out of the kitchen and announced that tea was ready. She pulled the steak and kidney pies out of the oven and put them on plates on the table. I got up to go into the kitchen, but Frank didn't budge. He just rocked back and forth.

"Come on, Frank," I said. "Let's get some food in you. You'll feel better."

"I need to go to the bog," he mumbled, and then stumbled over to the bathroom. He shut the door.

"Let's go ahead and eat while it's still hot," Elizabeth said. Rebecca and I sat down at the table and dug into our pies. They were delicious. I practically inhaled mine.

"Come on Frank, it's going to get cold," Elizabeth called out. There was no response from the loo.

"Maybe I should go and check on him," I said, wiping my mouth with my napkin. I got up, walked over to the bathroom door and knocked. There was no answer, so I pushed the door open. Frank was lying in the floor face down, with his pants down around his knees. He wasn't moving, so I nudged him with my foot.

"Hey Frank," I said. "Tea is ready. Get it while it's hot."

He rolled over and sat up. His eyes were narrow slits.

"I've got to use the toilet," he said. "Help me up."

He extended his hand and I heaved him up on his feet. He walked over to the toilet, pushed his pants down to his ankles and sat down.

"Just give me a minute," he said, then took a couple of deep breaths and vomited right into his pants. It ran down the inside of his trouser legs. It was funny and tragic at the same time. He sat up when he finally emptied his stomach. Elizabeth came walking in.

"Frank Thomas, I am ashamed of you," she said in disgust. "Let's get you cleaned up."

"No, I'm fine," said Frank. "Just give me a minute or two in here, all right?"

We both walked out of the bathroom and pulled the door shut behind us. We went back into the kitchen and sat down. Rebecca was about finished with her pie.

"I doubt Frank is going to eat his," Elizabeth said to me. "Why don't you go ahead and eat it?"

"I don't mind if I do," I said, and slid the pie onto my plate. I devoured it as fast as the first one. She had also made custard, and I ate mine as well as Frank's. There was still no sign of him.

"Do you think he's all right in there?" Elizabeth asked.

"I don't know," I said. "I'll go check on him again."

I knocked on the door. No answer. I pushed it open again, and there was Frank, stark naked, lying on the floor with his clothes in the bathtub. The room reeked of regurgitated alcohol.

"Elizabeth!" I hollered. "Get Frank's bathrobe. His clothes are a mess."

"It serves him right for drinking that much," she said, and went into her room. She brought out his robe and helped me get it wrapped around him. We got him on his feet, one of us under each arm. We halfway dragged him into Elizabeth's room and dumped him on the bed.

"My, what a gorgeous day," he mumbled, and then passed out again.

"He'd best be ready in the morning," Elizabeth said. "We're going to have to get up early."

"He'll be all right," I said. "Just let him sleep it off. He may, however, have a bit of a headache tomorrow."

"He deserves it," she said. "The fool."

I went back into the kitchen with her and helped her clean up. Rebecca went to her room to pack for our trip to Bath.

"Leave enough space in your suitcase for my uniform and so forth," I told her.

I dried the last of the dishes and put them in the cupboard. I had another cup of coffee, and then went into Rebecca's room. I took off my uniform and put it in her suitcase.

"I thought you'd wear that tomorrow," she said.

"No, I think I'll wear my suit. It's a special occasion."

I got out an iron and ironing board and pressed my shirt and pants, which had been lying in a pile for two days and were wrinkled. I hung them up in Rebecca's wardrobe.

"I guess we're all set to go," I said.

"It's going to be wonderful. I doubt I'll be able to get much sleep tonight, I'm so excited."

"So am I."

"We should at least try, though," she said as she got undressed. "Come on. Let's get under the covers."

I climbed into bed and lay on my back. I could see the moon shining through the skylight. She snuggled up close to me. Her skin was warm against mine. It was peaceful and quiet.

CHAPTER 26

I awoke before dawn and couldn't go back to sleep. After tossing and turning for a while I decided just to go ahead and get up. I was careful not to wake Rebecca as I got dressed.

The clock on the mantle in the living room said it was five a.m. Four more hours and I would be getting married. I was nervous as hell and shaky, yet surprised that I didn't have a headache from all of the drinking the night before.

Frank wasn't so lucky. As the smell of coffee filled the kitchen, he came stumbling in wearing his robe, a cigarette dangling from his mouth. His eyes were barely open and there was a big bruise on his forehead. He ran his fingers through his hair and sat down at the table.

"Why is my uniform in the bathtub?" he asked. "And how did I get this knot on my napper?"

It was obvious that he didn't remember anything that had happened after we left the Wheat Sheaf the night before.

"You sort of had a close brush with a lamppost up the street," I said. "Then you didn't feel so good. You threw up on your clothes."

"Bloody hell," he said, shaking his head. "I feel like I've been ran over by a train. A long train going very fast."

"You were so pissed," I said as I poured our coffee. "I've never seen you like that before. What happened?"

"What happened was I drank too much," he said. "That and the fact that I took some pain pills before we went to the pub."

"How many pills did you take?"

"Well, the doctor told me to take one. So naturally, I took about four or five."

"Four or five? Which one was it?"

"Five."

"And beer on top of that? You're lucky I didn't have to drag you home by the ankles."

"What did Lizzy say?"

"She said you were a damned fool."

"That's all? Then it must not have been as bad as I thought. Or was it?"

"It was pretty bad. Drink your coffee. You'll feel better."

"What I need is a different kind of drink. That will fix me up. Where's that scotch?"

I got up and looked in the cabinet. There was about two-thirds of a bottle left.

"Will this do?" I asked, holding it up.

"That will do just fine. And get a glass for yourself."

"It's five thirty in the morning."

"Yes, but it's five thirty in the evening somewhere. Give me the bottle."

I handed it over to Frank, and he pulled the cork. Then he tipped it up and took a mighty gulp.

"Ahhh," he said. "That's the stuff. Here."

He handed me the bottle. I didn't really want a drink, but I felt I needed one. Just for my nerves. I took a big swallow and shuddered.

"That's like being kicked by a mule," I said. "You want another drink?"

"Yeah. Hand it over."

This time he took two gulps before giving it back. I took another drink myself. I could sense the alcohol coursing through my veins almost immediately. I always loved that feeling. You don't get it with beer or wine, only whiskey and so forth.

"Feel good?" Frank asked as I put the bottle back on the shelf.

"Sure. How about you?"

"Never better. Never better."

We drank our coffee and smoked fags until about half past six. Frank went to the bathroom to get cleaned up just as the ladies were getting out of bed. Rebecca walked in and sat down next to me.

"Are you excited?" she asked.

"I feel like I'm about ready to blow a gasket," I said. "Did you sleep well last night?"

"No, but you did. You snored the night away. How's Frank doing this morning?"

"A little rough around the edges, but he's fair, considering the circumstances."

"Are you hungry? I can cook some sausages and eggs."

"I'm so nervous, I'm not sure I could eat anything right now."

"I know how you feel, but you've got to eat something. It's going to be a busy day. At least try to eat. Will you try if I cook it?"

I nodded and lit another fag. In a few minutes, the smell of breakfast cooking on the stove aroused my appetite. I ate four eggs, a half-pound of bacon, and four slices of toast. She left the kitchen and had a look at the mantle clock.

"Oh my goodness," she said. "It's after seven and Elizabeth's not even up yet. We must leave in an hour or so. I've got to wake her."

I cleaned up and went back to her room to finish getting dressed. I pushed the door open and she was standing there naked.

201

"I'm terribly sorry," I said, closing the door in embarrassment.

"Come on in," she said. "We're getting married. It doesn't matter."

"I guess not," I said, and went in. I put on my tie and vest and jacket while she got into her wedding dress. I could hear the others moving around the flat. I sat on the bed and stared out the window while she brushed her hair. It was raining buckets.

"Looks like we didn't pick such a good day," I said.

"Don't worry. It will be fine."

I checked myself in the mirror and went out to the living room. Frank was sitting on the sofa wearing a blue suit, drinking a cup of coffee. Elizabeth came out of her room at about 8:30, wearing a long black dress that looked expensive. She walked over and knocked on Rebecca's door.

"Come on," Elizabeth said. "We've got to get to the church."

"I'll be ready shortly," Rebecca said.

The seconds seemed like hours. I could hear the clock ticking. My heart was beating hard and my mouth was dry. I started pacing the floor. I truly had the wind up. At about 15 minutes before nine, Rebecca came out wearing the white dress she had modeled the night before.

It was still raining hard, so we took a taxi to the church. Father Samuels was waiting when we arrived. He greeted us and we followed him down the center aisle of the church to the altar.

"I must apologize," he said. "My memory isn't what it used to be. What are your names again?"

"I'm Richard Gardener, and this is Rebecca MacAuley," I said.

"You're the two getting married?"

"Yes, we are."

"And who are you?" he asked, looking at Frank and Elizabeth.

"I'm Frank Thomas, and this is Elizabeth Case."

"You two aren't married?"

"No, we're not," Frank said.

"We can take care of that this morning, if you want," Father Samuels said with a smile. "I've got nothing else on my schedule."

"No, father, one wedding today will be enough," Frank said.

"He likes his freedom," Elizabeth said, poking Frank in the ribs. "But I'll keep trying."

"Well then, we'll get started, with, uh…"

"Richard and Rebecca," I said.

"Right. Richard and Rebecca. Let us proceed."

Father Samuels started reciting the ceremony, but I don't remember much of what he said. I felt like my knees were going to buckle any second. The next thing I knew, we were exchanging rings, and he told me to kiss the bride. The whole thing only lasted about ten minutes.

"Congratulations," Father Samuels said, giving a handshake that felt like a wet dishrag. "I'll pray for your safe return from the front, which hopefully will be soon."

We took a taxi back to the theater and I told the driver to wait for us. We ran inside and got the suitcases Rebecca had packed. They weighed a ton.

"What did you put in here, Mrs. Gardener?" Frank said as he carried one of the cases to the door. "It feels like a load of bricks."

"Mrs. Gardener," Rebecca said. "Mrs. Gardener. I like the sound of that."

"I like the sound of that, too," I said.

"When do you think you'll be back from Bath?" Frank asked.

"We hadn't really discussed it," I said. "Monday, I guess. What do you think, Rebecca?"

"That gives us four nights, including tonight," she said. "It will be wonderful. Now let's not make that driver wait any longer."

Frank and Elizabeth waved from the top of the stairs as we left.

CHAPTER 27

We had tea in the dining car, and arrived in Bath in the late afternoon. I fetched our bags and we got off the train. Outside it was misty and raining. The air was chilly. We climbed into a taxi and I told the driver to take us to a nice hotel.

"Do you want to be near the baths?" he asked. "That's what most people come here for."

"That will do," I said. "Is there one that has a restaurant?"

"Certainly. I know just the place. It will take just a few minutes to get there."

Even under the gray sky, with the sunlight waning, Bath was a beautiful town. The Romans built the city around the hot springs that rose from beneath the ground, and people from all over Great Britain and Europe had been visiting the baths for centuries. As we drove through the streets, I noticed the exquisite architecture of the buildings, some new and some ancient. There weren't many people out, and traffic was very light. We pulled up to the curb in front of a hotel – the name escapes me now – and the driver helped us with our bags. I paid the fare and tipped him well.

Rebecca and I went inside and registered at the front desk. The dining room was at the other end of the lobby. A bellboy came and took our suitcases for us, then led us to our room.

"I hope you enjoy your stay," he said. "If you need anything, let us know. Tea will be served downstairs for another two hours, if you are interested."

"Possibly," I said. "Thank you."

We went inside. The room was large, with mahogany furniture and silk wallpaper. There was a large bed, and at the far end of the room next to the window, there was a table and two chairs. There was a room service menu on the table, and a telephone that connected with the front desk. I sat down at the table, lit a cigarette and had a look at the fare. Rebecca unpacked and hung our clothes in the closet, then took off her shoes and reclined on the bed.

"There's a lot of good stuff on this menu," I said, slipping out of my jacket and loosening my tie. "Instead of going downstairs, why don't we have tea brought to us?"

"I've never had room service before," she said. "And I am tired. It sounds like a good plan."

"What would you like?"

"Why don't you order for both of us? I'm not choosy."

I selected Cornish game hens and all of the trimmings to go with them. I called and placed our order, and asked if they could also bring us a bottle of scotch. They said they'd sent it up with the meal in about a half-hour.

The meal was excellent. We discussed possibly going to the pub across the street for a while, but we decided to stay in. We went to bed early, and did what normal people do on their wedding night. Rebecca fell asleep with her back against my chest.

I tried to sleep, but I could not. I started thinking about going back to Wipers in two weeks. I wondered what fate awaited me there; I wondered if I would make it back to England again. I got an uneasy feeling, and it got worse as the night wore on. The minutes turned into hours. My mind was racing. Everything seemed uncertain and surreal.

I broke a sweat and threw the covers off of myself. Rebecca was still sound asleep. I gently rolled her over and slipped out of bed. I went over to the table, sat down and lit a cigarette. My hands were shaking. I felt miserable. Maybe a drink would help, I thought.

I uncorked the bottle and took a big slug of whiskey. I finished my cigarette and lit another one. I didn't feel any better, so I took a second drink. That was the last thing I remember doing.

I woke up in the dark, sitting with my knees pulled up and my back against the wall. I didn't know where the hell I was. The bottle was between my legs, and it was empty. I felt around and realized I was in the bottom of the closet with the door pulled shut, but why I did not know. I had apparently drunk myself into a blackout. I opened the door and crawled out. The clothes that had been in the closet were strewn about the floor. Through the window, I could see the pale light of dawn. Rebecca was still. Maybe she didn't know anything happened, I thought. I picked up the clothes, hung them back in the closet and climbed into bed beside her. I fell asleep quickly.

The next thing I remember was Rebecca waking me up. She had ordered a pot of coffee from the kitchen, and was trying to get me to drink a cup. I sat up and took it from her. I had a vicious headache.

"You'll feel better if you drink that," she said. Apparently, she knew what had happened.

"I see you picked up the clothes," she said. "You must have been really drunk."

"What do you mean?"

"You don't remember, do you?"

She had me nailed. I decided I couldn't fake my way out of it.

"I'm afraid I don't know. I couldn't sleep, so I decided to have a drink. Then I woke up in there."

"I know. You woke me up after midnight, tearing everything out of the closet and cursing. You were using words I hadn't even heard before. I asked you what was going on, and you said, 'We have to get down in the dugout before Fritz shells us.' Then you took the bottle and went into the closet. I couldn't get you to come out, so I left you there."

"Oh, no."

"Oh, yes. Now drink your coffee."

I was humiliated. Maybe I drank too much, and too often. Maybe I was losing my mind. The thought startled me to the core. I felt sick.

"I'm so sorry," I said. "I truly am. I hope I didn't frighten you. I feel like a fool. You must be quite angry."

"A little. But I'm not going to chastise you for what you did. I know you weren't thinking clearly."

"I was getting nervous, knowing that I'd be going back to the front soon. I guess my fear just took over. You have my deepest apologies. I won't let it happen again."

"Promise?"

"Yes, I promise."

"Then we won't mention it again."

"Thank you."

I had a second cup of coffee and a cigarette, then got a bath and shaved. I put on my uniform while Rebecca brushed her hair and dressed. We had a late breakfast, and then went by taxi to an army hospital to get my bandage changed. Afterward, I suggested we find a photographer's studio and get our pictures taken. I wanted one of Rebecca to take back to the front with me, and one of us together to send to Rose. We flagged down a taxi, and the driver said he knew of a studio not too far away. We each had an individual photo made, as well as one of us together. The photographer said the prints would be ready by the following Monday.

The day was a bit warmer and it wasn't raining, so we decided to take a stroll through the town. I took her into a jewelry shop and bought a silver locket in which she could keep my photo.

"You are so thoughtful," she said. "I'll wear it every day until you come home."

"Hopefully, that will be soon," I said.

We didn't get out of the hotel much during the rest of our stay in Bath. We ate from the room service menu and spent hours under the covers. I didn't drink much after the closet incident; I didn't want my asinine behavior to be foremost in her memory when I left for the front. The days passed quickly, and soon it was

206

time to return to London. We caught a train after we picked up our photographs, and made it into Victoria Station that evening.

I tried to enjoy myself as much as possible for the rest of my leave, but I started getting this edgy feeling of intangible doom, realizing that I would be back in the line soon. It hung heavy over my head, but I didn't say anything to anyone about it. I imagined that Frank was feeling the same way. There was no point dwelling on it; nothing could be done to change our situation. We still managed to have some more laughs, nonetheless, and I will always remember those days in London fondly.

We went to the hospital to get our stitches removed the day before we were to ship out. Both of us were healing well, but Frank complained to the doctor that he was still having a lot of pain. Although he was hesitant, Frank eventually convinced the doctor to give him another bottle of pills to take with him. He swallowed two in the hallway outside the stitching room and offered me some. I declined and he put the bottle in his pocket.

I took time out that afternoon to write a long letter to my sister telling her about everything that had happened since my last correspondence. I told her about my injuries, but downplayed them as minor. Then I told her about my leave in London, and my marriage to Rebecca. I enclosed the photograph of me with my bride, and told her that we'd come to see her when I made it back next time, although I didn't know when that would be. I asked her to pray for my safe return, and that it would be soon.

We went out for one last evening of fine dining with the ladies, but I can't remember where or what we ate. In my mind I was miles away; all I could think about was the fact that the next night, I'd be in France or maybe Belgium, far from my wife and the safety of her arms. Everything else seemed trite by comparison.

Rebecca and I cuddled in bed and talked all night about what we would do when I got back, where we might live and raise a family, and all sorts of other things. Neither of us slept at all. When the sun rose, I kissed her and got out of bed. I donned my uniform and put the last of my personal items in my duffle. The four of us took a taxi to the train station around eight o'clock. Rebecca and Elizabeth cried terribly. They were inconsolable.

"Write to me often, Richard," Rebecca pleaded. "I want to hear from you every day if you can. And I'll write to you. Every day. I promise."

We hugged and kissed and said goodbye. The train whistle blew.

"Be careful, please," she said as I climbed on board. Frank and I waved to them as we pulled out of the station. Then I started crying. Frank tried to boost my spirits with a few card tricks, but it didn't do any good.

"It will be over soon, Richard," Frank said, putting his hand on my shoulder. "We'll be back this way again, I know."

"Are you certain?"

"Absolutely certain. We'll come back and pick up where we left off, and forget all about the war. We'll never think about it again. And every day will be like a holiday from then on, because we'll know the worst is over. Forever."

"I'm afraid it will never be over. We're never going to be the same. Not after all that we've been through, all the horrible things we've seen. We've got scars that will never heal, Frank. You can't see them, but they're there, deep inside. Damn it all, anyway."

I stared out the window and wiped the tears from my cheeks. We didn't say much the rest of the trip. It was still morning when we boarded a troop transport that was going back across the channel. We must have been the oldest ones on the boat. Those around us didn't even look grown enough to wear a uniform. They were just boys. I stood at the rail and watched England disappear behind us.

I felt lost and hopeless, demoralized and spiritually bankrupt, like the day my father died. That same uncertainty had me in its grips; there was no way of knowing what the future held for any of us on the ship, but I was convinced that it would be rife with pain, misery and suffering. Indeed, that much *was* certain.

CHAPTER 28

We arrived in Calais in the afternoon and boarded a train going to the front. It took us as far as Pop, and then we had to walk the rest of the way. The boys we came with were laughing and joking the whole time. It reminded me of the day I marched to Neuve Chapelle with Frank, Simon, Jack and Pick. Now it was just Frank and myself. As we neared Ypres, the boy beside me curled his nose.

"What in the world is that smell, sergeant?" he asked.

"That's the battlefield," I said.

"Does it always smell like that?" he asked.

"No," Frank said, "only on days that end in 'y.'"

"Why is it so foul?" he asked.

"Dead bodies, gas, sewage, smoke," I said. "After a few weeks, you won't even notice anymore."

"I hope so," he said. I thought to myself that he may not even be around in a few weeks. Then he definitely wouldn't notice.

We found our unit in rest billets outside of town. There were a lot of new faces. Some of the old ones were gone. This disturbed me; it was as if somehow, I'd been under the impression the fighting would be put on hold until I got back. I came to the realization that it would continue with or without me, and I couldn't do anything to change that.

I caught up to the lieutenant before tea. He said he was glad to have me back, and hoped that I enjoyed myself on leave. I told him that I had gotten married and proudly showed him my photograph of Rebecca.

"Congratulations, sergeant," he said, shaking my hand. "She's a lovely girl. I hope you have a long and happy life together. I plan on getting married and settling down one day, maybe when this is over. I must say I'm a bit envious."

"How have things been up on the line, sir?"

"The same as always, only more of it."

"That's what I expected, sir. Bad."

"Yes, very bad. We've made some progress with our mining, but Fritz has stepped up his efforts as well."

"I noticed there are a few men missing, sir."

"We lost about a dozen five nights ago when the Germans staged a raid. It was a bloody mess. There must have been a hundred of them. We think they were trying to find tunnel entrances. Either that, or they wanted to get soil samples. We fought them off and managed to capture a few. They didn't say much, but they were carrying satchel charges, probably for collapsing mines. Fortunately, we stopped them."

"When are we supposed to go back up, sir?"

"In about ten days. You picked a good time to return, if there is any such thing. Get plenty of rest in the mean time. We've got a lot of work ahead of us."

Later that day, I got my hands on some old newspapers and read until the sun went down. I hadn't really kept up on the news while I was on leave, mostly because I didn't want to think about the war at all. So I was surprised, if not horrified, to learn that we were still attacking on the Somme. It hadn't even slowed down. In fact, it had escalated in mid-September. The generals didn't want to abandon something that had cost so much already, and the French begged them to keep the pressure on so that the Germans couldn't shift all of their strength to Verdun, which was still very hot as well. So new plans for the offensive were devised.

One of these plans relied on a new weapon called a landship, better known now as the tank. The first of these were basically armored, motorized machine gun platforms that carried a crew of eight. The army didn't think they would be of much use and rejected the plans, but the Admiralty, under the leadership of Winston Churchill, felt it could be an effective tool. About 50 of them were built and sent up to the Somme for a renewed push.

It looked promising initially, but like everything else in the war, there were problems. The tanks were underpowered and only capable of moving at about three miles per hour, which was slower than the infantry could advance on foot. And most of them broke down on the approach to the front. Only one-fourth of them actually made it to the battlefield, and they all broke down by the end of the first day. I personally thought the tanks sounded like a good idea, but it was clear that their design needed some fine-tuning.

The failure of the landships and even more casualties still didn't deter the offensive spirit of the generals. Another drive had been made along the Somme on September 25, with French support on the flanks. Once again, thousands of men fell, and there was little, if anything, gained. It was tremendously depressing; I decided not to read any more, and passed the newspapers on to someone else.

On a positive note, I started getting letters from Rebecca nearly every day. Some days I wouldn't get one, and then the next day I'd get two. Getting my mail was always a bright spot in an otherwise dreary routine. I wrote back to her four or five times a week, telling about everything that was happening and my dreams of seeing her again. As with my letters to Rose, I tried to be optimistic, so she wouldn't worry as much.

I began to worry myself, however, because I hadn't heard from Rose since I'd gone on leave. I wrote to her several times during the first week of October, asking if everything was all right. I was getting very concerned. Then one day I received five letters from her all at once, as well as a package of butter cookies. Frank received some letters as well. We sat beneath a tree after tea, ate cookies and read. I soon found out why she had been out of touch.

"My brother-in-law was wounded on the Somme," I told Frank.

"How?"

"Fritz dropped some howitzer shells on his battery. Everyone was killed except him."

"Is he going to make it?"

"She says he's still in one piece and resting in a hospital down near Amiens, but he's probably out of the fight for good."

"Then it's not that bad, really. Not if he's going to pull through."

"Not bad? What do you mean?"

"He's fortunate to be in artillery. If he were in the infantry, he'd probably be napoo by now. It's a real mess down there."

It was unusual for Frank to find the positive aspect of anything, and I appreciated his words of comfort. I knew it didn't come easily for him. I stayed up late writing a letter back to her, about fifteen pages worth. I told her that I'd say a prayer for her husband, that he would recover quickly and fully. Then I wrote a letter to Rebecca, telling her what had happened. I mailed them both the next morning.

The second week of October we went back into the salient. Most of the time we stayed near Hill 60, but on several occasions we moved down the ridge to work on tunnels. And under the cover of darkness, we started bringing up tons and tons of ammonal. That was the kind of thing you didn't want to do in the day, because you were napoo if a sniper hit the load you were carrying. Probably everyone around you would be napoo as well.

One morning we were eating breakfast, sitting on the fire step in the front line opposite Hill 60, when five German Fokkers made a pass at us, flying in low to the ground. They circled above and then made a second pass.

"What do you think that's all about, sergeant?" one of the replacements asked me.

"They're taking a good look," I said, "probably hoping to get some pictures that might give an indication of where we are mining. Don't worry about it. Eat your food before it gets cold."

211

The Fokkers turned to head home. Then I heard planes coming up from our rear. They were British Sopwiths – seven of them -- and they were going after the Germans. An all-out dogfight commenced in the sky overhead.

At first, it looked like the British had the upper hand. Two of the Fokkers were sent running for the horizon with smoke pouring out of their engines. Some of the new boys started cheering. Two of the Sopwiths pursued the damaged German planes, leaving five to handle the three remaining Fokkers. The odds looked good, but soon the tables were turned. One after another, the Sopwiths were forced from the sky. They fled to our rear in flames. Finally, there was only one of our boys left, and he was facing three Huns who seemed to know a good bit about flying.

He fought valiantly, and shot down another Fokker before he was hit himself. The Sopwith, blowing black, oily smoke, came tumbling down from the sky directly above us. The Fokkers came down behind him, peppering him with machine gun fire all the way. The pilot of the Sopwith tried to pull out of the dive, but his recovery was a little too late. He came in low and crashed between our position and Hill 60, hitting the ground nose first and flipping over. His plane caught fire, and the Fokkers scurried away.

I looked out at the wreckage through a sniping loupe. I was sure the pilot must have been killed on impact, but then I saw him dragging himself out from under the crumpled fuselage, trying to get away from the flames. He was on fire, and screaming in agony.

"Help me!" he yelled. "I'm burning! Please help me!"

It curdled my blood. I turned to Frank.

"Go get the lieutenant," I said. "The pilot is going to die."

"What do you think we can do about that?" Frank asked sarcastically. "I'm not going out there. No, sir."

"Just go get the lieutenant," I said. The pilot was still screaming. I looked back out at the flaming wreckage. He was clear of it, but his clothes were smoldering. There wasn't much cover offered in the hundred yards or so between our wire and the plane. There were just a few shell holes, and they were far apart. His cries made my heart pound and my knees weak. I could not avert my eyes.

"What's going on, sergeant?" the lieutenant asked from behind me. I turned around.

"Pilot's burnt, sir," I said. "We've got to do something. Now."

"What do you have in mind?"

"We have to go out there and bring him in."

The lieutenant took a look out the loupe.

"That's a long way to run," he said. "Even longer if you're carrying a wounded man. The odds of getting there and back safely are slim, at best."

"I'm willing to take the risk," I said. "I'll go get him."

"I don't want you to go out there. I need you. Find some volunteers for the job."

"Sir, I can't ask another man to do something I would not do myself. It's not right."

"You really don't want to go out there, sergeant."

"But I must, sir. I insist on it."

He took another look and turned around.

"You know, Gardener, you must be the most stubborn bastard I've ever met. All right. If you must go, take five men with you, and have two of them carry a stretcher. I'll call the artillery and get you some protective fire. Maybe they can lay down some smoke between here and there."

"Thank you, sir."

"Over the top with the best of luck, Gardener."

The pilot's cries of agony had agitated the new boys, and I got more volunteers than I needed. I picked the five that looked like they could run the fastest. The lieutenant got on the telephone and almost immediately, a battery of 18-pounders opened fire on the German front line across the field. They shot some smoke shells, too, but the wind was blowing in the wrong direction for them to be effective cover. I prayed as we climbed out of the trench and ran through our wire.

We only made it about 15 yards before two of the boys were shot by a sniper, who no doubt had anticipated our rescue attempt. The remaining four of us went diving into a shell hole. I could still hear the pilot wailing. I rose up and looked over the lip of the crater. A bullet ricocheted off of my helmet, knocking my head back and leaving a good dent. I recoiled and swore.

"What are we going to do now, sergeant?" one of the boys asked.

"We'll have to run for it," I said.

"No disrespect intended, sergeant, but that doesn't sound like much of a strategy."

"Well, if anyone has any better ideas, speak now."

No one said anything.

"There's a couple more holes between here and there," I said. "They'll offer some protection. We'll have to move fast."

"What about those two?" one of the boys said, his thumb pointing back at his fallen comrades.

"They're probably napoo. Don't think about them right now. We'll get them on the return trip. Now keep your heads tucked in and your tails low. Ready?"

They nodded. I yelled, "go!" and we ran forward. The two carrying the stretcher were picked off. Me and the other lad dove into another shell hole. I looked over the lip, very cautiously this time, and estimated that we were still about 50 yards from the plane.

"That's a long way to go," I said, "but I think we can make it."

"What about the stretcher, sergeant?"

"Damn it. I hadn't even thought about that. I don't know. I guess we can either go back for it, or try to carry the pilot without one."

"What do you think?"

"Let's keep going. We can put him on the stretcher on the way back if we have to."

"Whatever you say, sergeant."

The shells were still tearing through the sky. We took off running for the plane and made it there, probably because the smoke and smoldering wreckage obscured the Germans' view. I crawled over to the pilot, who was now unconscious. His trousers were almost completely burned off. The skin on his legs was charred black and still smoking. His clenched hands were also badly burned, and he was bleeding from about a dozen places. The stench was nauseating.

"My word," the boy said, "I think I'm going to be sick."

He vomited so violently that I expected him to bring up a vital organ. I'd never seen anyone get sick to that degree. He coughed and spat, then wiped his nose and mouth on his sleeve.

"Are you going to make it, private?" I asked.

"Sorry sergeant," he said, then wretched again.

"Get it together now. We can't stay out here all day."

"I think I'm done. I'll be all right. Let's go."

We each took an arm and hoisted the pilot.

"This is going to be the tricky part," I said. "Try not to drop him."

We moved as fast as we could, racing to get to safety. We made it most of the way before the boy caught a bullet in his back. He fell to the ground. Napoo. I held onto the pilot and drug him along, and by some miracle, I reached our trench without being hit. I slid the pilot over the parapet, and then jumped in myself.

"Get a medic up here!" the lieutenant shouted. "Now!"

We stretched the pilot out on the fire step.

"That was amazing, Gardener," the lieutenant said. "At least they didn't get you."

A medic and two stretcher-bearers came in a couple of minutes. They lifted the pilot onto the stretcher and the medic put his hand on the side of his neck.

"I hate to tell you this, but it's too late," he said. "He's dead."

"Are you sure?" I asked.

"Unfortunately, yes," he said. "Damn the luck."

I cursed in anger. It had all been in vain, and I felt responsible for leading those boys to their graves. For nothing. I had an overwhelming sense of guilt and remorse. I sat down on the fire step to catch my breath, and I watched them through teary eyes as they carried off the dead pilot. The lieutenant knew what was going through my mind.

"You didn't kill those boys, Gardener," he said. "A bloody Hun killed them. That's what happens in war. Men get killed, and there's nothing you or I can do about that. It's over. Don't let it fester in your mind. It will drive you insane."

It's strange, but I never did find out the names of those five boys. I did not know where they were from, whether they left families behind, or what they did in civilian life. I did not know their dreams and aspirations. In fact, I did not know anything about them. They were just anonymous faces. But I vowed that as long as I was living and breathing, I would not forget them or what they did that morning. And to this day, I have not.

CHAPTER 29

As October waned, the days got noticeably shorter and cooler. By the first of November, it was just plain cold. I dreaded spending another winter in the trenches, and I really didn't know how I was going to cope with it. Like the previous winter, there would surely be plenty of influenza and pneumonia to go around. They were enemies you couldn't see, much less drive away or kill. Mere survival, even for the most fit among us, would be a challenge in itself.

I received some news, however, that greatly boosted my spirits and helped me rise above the agony. We had rotated out of the line and were settling into our billets when the mail came. I got a box wrapped in brown paper and tore it open like a child on Christmas morning. Inside was a letter from Rebecca and a couple of pounds of shortbread. Frank came over to my bunk and helped himself. I opened the letter and read it. I was stunned, to say the least. Maybe even startled. A bit scared, too.

"Hey Frank," I said. "It seems that I'm going to be a father."

"What? Really?"

"Yes, really. She went to the doctor to make sure, and he confirmed it. She's about six weeks along. The baby should arrive in June."

"That's great, Richard! I'm going to have to get us some cigars, for sure. How's Rebecca doing?"

"She says she gets sick in the mornings a lot, but the doctor told her that would go away soon. She quit working so she could stay home and rest. Frank, old man, I can't believe this is happening. I can't believe it!"

"You're going to be an excellent father. I know it."

"I sure hope you're right. I don't know a thing about babies."

"You'll learn, and quickly. So do you want a boy or a girl?"

"A son would be nice. I could teach him to fish and hunt, like my father taught me. And I'd keep him out of the coal mines. And the army."

"What if it's a girl?"

"A girl would be nice, too. She'd be beautiful and classy, like her mother."

"And smart, like her father."

"You know, I could teach a girl to fish and hunt as well. It is 1916, after all. Girls do all kinds of things these days."

"Now what if you got both?"

"Twins? I don't even want to think about that. One is enough to worry about, thank you."

"What about a name? Does anything strike your fancy?"

"Rebecca says she likes Peter for a boy. That's her brother's name. I rather like it myself."

"And for a girl?"

"She says Rachel, because then all of our names would start with 'R.' But I'm not sure about that one. If she wants one that starts with 'R,' then I think Ruth would be a better choice. Or maybe Rose, after my sister."

"Well, you've got a few months to get it all sorted out. Right now, we need to celebrate. What do you say we go into Pop and tear the town up?"

"It's ten o'clock in the morning."

"So? That's never stopped us before. Come on. Let's go."

"How about later, say after tea? I first need to write back to her and tell her how happy I am. Then I need to write to my sister and let her in on the good news. I'll take a nap after lunch, and when evening comes, I'll be ready to go. All right?"

"All right. A nap sounds good to me as well. I think I'll go over to the bathhouse first, though. I want to wash Belgium off my skin and kick a few passengers out of my hair. Are you coming?"

"I'll go later. I want to get these letters done."

I got out my paper and pencil and started writing. I didn't know where to start. There was so much I wanted to say. My mind was racing. I finally gave up trying to put my thoughts in order; I figured Rebecca could sort it all out on the other end.

Frank came back looking much better.

"I'm going to lay down for a while," he said as he climbed into his bunk. Within a few minutes, I could hear him snoring.

The lieutenant came strolling into the billet.

"Where's your pal?" he asked.

"He's sleeping."

"Wake him for tea. I heard we're getting steaks today, enlisted men and officers both. That's the best news I've heard in a while. How about you?"

"Actually, sir, I got some incredible news today. My wife wrote that she's pregnant."

"That *is* incredible, Gardener. Congratulations!"

"Thank you, sir."

"When will the baby arrive?"

"In June, sir."

"Smashing. Who knows? Maybe we'll be home by then."

"You think so, sir?"

"Miracles do happen, sergeant. It's certainly not out of the question."

"I pray you're right, sir."

217

"I pray I am as well."

Later, a fellow came by and gave me a copy of the *Wipers Times*, a trench newspaper printed on a press that some soldiers had salvaged. It was usually good for a few laughs, but I didn't feel much like laughing. I felt like I should be home with my wife. Especially then. My earlier joy was quickly turning into melancholy.

I got a bath and cleaned up my uniform, then decided to go back to our billet and catch a little sleep. Perhaps that would make me feel better. When I got there, Frank was still snoozing away, a trickle of spit coming out of the corner of his mouth. I pulled a blanket up over him before I climbed into my bunk. It took a while, but I finally drifted off.

The sound of cannon fire awoke me with a start. I jumped up, put my helmet on and ran outside. The sunlight was fading, and I could see the flash of shells exploding among the shattered remnants of Ypres, about a half-mile away. I didn't know why the Germans even bothered anymore. You can only destroy something once, after all. To hell with them, I thought; I was hungry and it was time for tea. I roused Frank and we had the best meal we'd had since London.

Then we got drunk as planned.

CHAPTER 30

We had a few days of good weather in the middle of November. The skies were clear and the air was unseasonably warm, and I knew I should enjoy it while it lasted. I found a lot of excuses to stay out of the tunnels, at least until the winter weather really kicked in. Then the tunnels would be a good alternative to standing outside in the cold.

General Haig took advantage of the fair days and staged what would be his final assault along the Somme. We heard that it was a relative success; our boys had pushed a bulge a couple of miles into German territory and took the town of Beaumont-Hamel. Fritz was left holding a flimsy, improvised line. That was the good news.

It was, as always, greatly outweighed by the bad news; thousands more had been killed or wounded in those last days. The whole Somme affair seemed atrocious --questionable at best -- especially to those of us at the front. Victory, if you could even call it that, came at an exceedingly high price. British casualties were more than 420,000, while the supporting French suffered 195,000. The costly, ill-conceived German counter-attacks had left about 650,000 of their boys killed or wounded. It made me sick just to think about it.

To make matters worse, my fear of a tough winter became a reality. The days got short and the temperature dropped. The mud froze, and so did we. It turned out to be the coldest winter of the war. In fact, it was the coldest winter Europe had seen in 30 years. Sickness started spreading through the trenches like a wildfire. Thousands fell ill every day. Even the hardiest men succumbed.

Staff Sgt. Hendershot, whom I never knew to be sick, came down with a terrible fever the first week of December. He developed a horrible cough and became weak. I remember seeing him break a sweat one day when it was way below freezing. He looked wan and pale, but he stoically denied there was anything wrong and refused to see a doctor. The lieutenant finally had to give him a direct order to either go to a hospital and rest up or face a court martial. He begrudgingly capitulated, and groused under his breath as he walked off.

That was the last we saw of him. He died from pneumonia about a week later. The lieutenant, who had relied on him from the beginning of the whole mess, was devastated. He vacillated between tempestuous anger and unfathomable grief. It was like someone had cut off his right arm, the poor fellow. He became distant. Sometimes, he'd just sit and stare at the ground between his feet, a blank expression on his face and nothing to say to anyone. We just left him alone.

I became Hendershot's replacement. My promotion to staff sergeant came a few days after we heard of his death. I was given a little insignia of a crown to go over the three stripes I had on my shoulders. I wasn't too happy about it. It was a rotten way to move up the ranks, and it was going to be tough to fill Hendershot's shoes. I didn't know whether the lieutenant would ever see me as a reasonable substitute for him, regardless of how hard I tried to be.

That winter was hard on everyone, even those who weren't doing the fighting. With all of the men off fighting, agricultural production was at a minimum, and ships carrying food from overseas were being sunk by German U-boats. What food was available went to the military first. The result was massive food shortages just about everywhere, and civilians had to wait in long lines just to get the most basic necessities. Rebecca said in one of her letters that she had to wait in line for an hour to get a loaf of bread and a dozen eggs.

That was a hardship, to be certain, but at least she could actually get bread and eggs. Across most of Europe, you couldn't. The only food available to most people that winter was turnips, which, until then, had been used exclusively to feed livestock. Pretty soon, people were waiting in lines to get those, too. When we would rotate back to the rear, Belgian women with hollow eyes would stand along the road, crying and begging for cans of bully beef and biscuits to feed their families. It made me grateful for what I had, and I thought sharing my bounty with the less fortunate was the right thing to do. I always set aside a can or two for the women along the road, even if it meant I had to skip meals. Giving them money would have been pointless. There was nothing to buy with it.

To make matters worse, there soon developed a severe shortage of coal all across Europe. Production was down, as many miners were now serving in the armies. The navies of the warring nations got theirs first, and then whatever was left went to the civilians. Most homes used it for heat, and demand grew as the temperatures dropped well below what they normally were. By the end of the year, many people were trying to survive without any. Fortunately for Rebecca and Elizabeth, their flat was heated with natural gas. Rebecca said they started having a lot of visitors in December, most of whom were just looking for a little respite from the cold. It was sad.

The fighting in Verdun came to an end about a week before Christmas, after ten months of horrific bloodshed. By and large, the battle had been fought on Germany's terms, but the French turned that around in the last weeks. They had taken their time, and amassed hundreds of guns and 30 million pounds of shells, all for one final drive. They started pushing in October, and in two months, reclaimed much of the land and many of the forts they had previously lost. It was a victory of sorts, I guess, but like the gains on the Somme, it was very costly, maybe even more so. When it was all added up, the French reported more than a half-million casualties, while the Germans, who started the fight, suffered more than 400,000. The German general in charge – a fellow named Von Falkenhayn – lost his job over the fiasco, even though he came close to bleeding France to death that year.

The holidays came, but there didn't seem to be much to celebrate. While there had been no major offensives at Wipers during 1916, casualties in our sector continued to mount by the thousands every day; it had remained at that level since the end of 1914, only changing during offensives, at which time it went up. With this endless carnage in Flanders, the unprecedented slaughter on the Somme and around Verdun, the massive naval clash at Jutland, the grim fighting on the Eastern Front and the Italian quagmire of the Isonzo, just about every family in Europe had lost at least one son or father or brother that year. Many families had lost several members.

All in all, the death toll on the Western Front alone stood at two and a half million by the end of 1916. An additional seven million had been wounded. A like number had been killed or wounded on the Eastern Front, in Africa and in the Middle East. Millions of people were living as refugees, driven out of their homes and off of their land by the war. The civilians and soldiers alike were cold, tired, hungry and demoralized, and frankly, 1917 didn't seem to hold much promise. It looked like it was only going to bring more of the same.

We went up to the front line three days before Christmas. It had been between ten and 20 degrees for more than two weeks. The wind was incessant, and we were miserable. Then it started snowing. We got more than I'd ever seen before. A lot of the boys came down with "trench foot," which was a kind of frostbite that sometimes led to amputations. As I did the previous winter, I vowed that if I made it home alive, I'd never be cold again. Ever.

On Christmas Eve, we were treated to rather good dinner of roast beef, potatoes, gravy and Yorkshire pudding, and an extra ration of rum. I remember thinking at the time that we were probably the best-fed people in Europe. Later we were brought hot tea and the mail was delivered. I received a box from my sister and another one from Rebecca, and Frank got a parcel from Elizabeth. We eagerly opened them up.

I was very pleased. Rose had sent me cigarettes, a dozen chocolate bars, three pairs of wool socks, a pocket-sized copy of the New Testament and a tin of homemade anise cookies, along with a letter. Rebecca's package contained a letter as well, plus a couple of pounds of hard candy and a beautiful, navy blue scarf that she had knitted herself. I thought it looked rather good with my uniform.

Frank's package from Elizabeth contained a letter, a box of chocolates, and a box of cigars. She's also made a scarf, but apparently wasn't as good at knitting as Rebecca. His scarf was four clashing colors, and one end was much wider than the other. It was barely long enough for him to wrap around his neck, and it looked absolutely awful with his uniform. We had a pretty good laugh, and the lieutenant even made a joke about it. But nonetheless, he wore that scarf for the rest of the winter. He said it made him feel closer to home.

By the time we were done opening our presents, it was too dark to read the letters. We had to wait until our shift was over, then went down into the dugout and read by the light of a kerosene lantern. I was glad to learn that Rebecca's morning sickness had passed, and that she had been resting a lot. She said her pregnancy was showing by then, and she had to buy some maternity clothes. I decided to send her a little extra money to help her with those kinds of expenses. I was also glad to hear that Rose's husband was being sent to a hospital in London for rest and recuperation. He'd probably be there for a couple of months and then discharged, she said. His wounds were bad enough, it seemed, that active duty was out of the question, but he would be able to return to his job at the bank in a few months. She said she missed him tremendously, and that she hoped to go to London in January to visit him in the hospital. A thought crossed my mind.

"Frank, do you think Elizabeth and Rebecca would mind having some company for a while?" I asked.

"I don't know," he said. "Probably not."

"My sister wants to go to London to spend some time with her husband while he's recovering. It's a long way from Manchester, and she probably can't afford to stay in a hotel. I thought maybe she could stay with the girls."

"I'm sure that would be fine, since it's your sister. Rebecca would probably welcome the opportunity to get to know her baby's aunt. And I know Elizabeth would make her feel at home. I think it would be a smashing arrangement."

Frank and I ate some of the candy and chocolates, then made tea and smoked a couple of his cigars. He tried to teach me once again to blow rings, but to no avail. I stayed up late into the night and wrote long letters to Rebecca and Rose, thanking them for their gifts and suggesting my plan. I hoped they would think it was a good idea.

Christmas Day seemed like any other winter day at the front: bleak and pointless and grim. We didn't sing any carols, and neither did the Germans. I guess they were tired, too. I wanted to do something befitting the occasion, however, so I got out the testament my sister had sent and read the story of Christ's birth in the gospels. It made me feel a good bit better about things, so I decided to read some more. By the end of the day, I'd finished all four gospels in their entirety. Some of the language was hard to decipher, but I got the general idea. I went back to look at a few things again.

"What a gorgeous day," Frank said, his teeth chattering. "It is bloody cold out here today, don't you think? It is December, I guess. What have you got there, Richard?"

"My sister sent me this," I said, and handed it over to him. He took a seat next to me on the fire step.

"Have you ever read it?" I asked.

"No, I can't say that I have," he said. "What's your take on it?"

"It starts a fellow to thinking. There's a lot to ponder. I would imagine that's why people are still reading it after all these years. All kinds of people, in all kinds of places. What about you? Do you believe in God?"

"I'm afraid that I don't."

"Why is that?"

"Look around you. Look at where you are, and where you've been the past year and a half. Think about all of the death and destruction. If there is a god, how can he let this war go on? How can he let so many young men die? It doesn't make any sense. God is supposed to be all-powerful and all-good. Why then doesn't he wave his hand and make this all go away?"

"That's a tough question."

"You're damn right it is."

"I'm not sure how to answer it, but there must be a reason. Maybe he allows it because there has to be evil for us to see good."

"That's a pretty harsh way to teach mankind a lesson. If we are his children, why does he let us suffer? I wouldn't make my child go through this hell. Would you?"

223

"No, I guess not. But the way I understand it, God's love is unconditional; he places no terms on his love for us. That means he loves all men regardless of whether they uphold his law. Take Jesus for example. In the books I read today, it said that he went out and associated with the unclean, the sinners, and the harlots, because he loved them."

"That still doesn't answer my question. Why does he allow this destruction?"

"Because he loves us no matter what, he lets us make his own decisions. Certain men – believing they have God on their side – decided to start this war. It's not his will, but it happens, because man has the freedom to choose his own path."

"I don't know, Richard. It all sounds pretty far-fetched to me."

"Perhaps. But I choose to believe in him anyway…"

"And I guess you're going to tell me why."

"…because believing in God is the smart thing to do. It said several different times in here that if you believe in God and Jesus, you will have eternal life."

"Those are just words. Written by a man, no less."

"You may be right. But then again, you may be wrong. I don't want to take that risk. Can you imagine dying without faith, then suddenly finding yourself face to face with God? I don't think he'd be very happy with you."

"So what you are saying is that because there is a remote possibility that there is a god and an afterlife, you are a believer."

"I have nothing to lose and everything to gain. Think about it, Frank. If you believe, and then it turns out that there is no God or Jesus or Heaven, what have you lost? Nothing. But if you don't believe, and it turns out you were wrong, you don't get to go in. Then you suffer in hell."

"You know, I'm probably going to hell, anyway."

"That's being pretty pessimistic there, Frank. Why have you resigned yourself to that?"

"Well, like I said, I haven't read that book, but I'm sure it says in there somewhere that killing a man is wrong. I have no idea how many I've killed."

"There's a difference between murder and killing in war."

"Why? Killing is killing, in my opinion. The motivation doesn't matter."

"I think you're wrong on that, Frank, but I'm not going to argue with you about it. No matter which of us is right, one thing holds true; Jesus said if you believe he was the Son of God, and that he died for our sins, then you are forgiven of all sins. Including killing."

224

"What about the Germans? Do you think God will forgive them for killing Simon and Jack and all the other boys we've left behind? They caused all of this."

"It says all men can be forgiven. There is no nationality requirement."

We sat and talked all afternoon, and I made a little progress. Frank went from being an avowed atheist to a moderate agnostic by evening, and even asked if he could read my Bible a little that night. I hoped he would find something in there that would comfort him.

I felt better knowing that I helped sow the seeds of faith in Frank's heart. Even though we were cold and tired and in the firing line, that is one of the best Christmas memories I have. I prayed for Frank that night, that God might reveal himself to him; I prayed that if something happened to Frank, the gates of heaven would open upon his arrival.

And I prayed that I would meet him there some day.

CHAPTER 31

New Year's Eve of 1916 was unbelievably cold, well below zero with a strong wind coming in from the sea. I was sitting next to the stove in our dugout, trying to stop shivering, when the year came to an end. A gun to our rear marked the arrival of 1917 appropriately, firing 17 shells at the Germans. To the tune of "Auld Lang Syne," we sang our own song:

> *"We're here, because we're here, because we're here,*
> *because we're here, because we're here, because*
> *we're here, because we're here..."*

That, unfortunately, was the extent of our celebration. Would it be the same when 1918 arrived? Would I still be in the trenches? Somehow, I felt that I wouldn't. Surely, the war would be over by then. I hoped I was right.

We went back to our billets at the end of the second week of January. There were six letters from Rebecca and three from Rose waiting for me. They had been in contact with each other, and Rose was going to London on January 20. Rebecca told her she was excited about meeting her, and she could stay at the flat as long as she wanted. I was very pleased.

Frank, of course, got a few letters from Elizabeth, but what was unusual was the large, heavy crate he got from his father. He'd never before received as much as a letter from his father, who spent most of his time at sea, piloting a freighter; in fact, he didn't hear from his mother much, either. You can imagine his excitement as he opened the letter attached to the box. It was a short note, not even a page long.

"Hey Richard," he said. "You're going to like this. You're going to like this a lot."

"What's that?"

"Help me get the lid off of this crate and I'll show you."

I took my bayonet and pried at the lid, the nails squeaking as they were pulled out. Inside, there were twelve pint bottles of liquor packed in straw. I pulled one out.

"Old Forester," I said. "I've never heard of it. What is it?"

Frank pulled out another bottle and had a look.

"It says it's Kentucky bourbon whiskey, from America," he said. "Wasn't that where that Yank came from? The fellow who wanted the chewing tobacco?"

"You mean Mullins. Yes, I believe he was from Kentucky. So how did your father come across this stuff?"

"He says he made a run from New York City to Liverpool a couple of weeks ago, and when the ship was unloaded, they had four boxes like this, and none of them were on the manifest. He says he's not sure how they got there, or where they were supposed to go, so he gave three boxes to the crew and sent one to me."

"It sounds like your dad has a gift for 'finding things,' too."

"It's a family tradition. What do you say we take a nip?"

"You don't have to ask me twice."

I broke the seal, pulled the cork out and held it up to my nose. It smelled powerful. I tipped up the bottle and took a big slug. It burned all the way down. I thought I was going to bleed through the eyes.

"Damn," I coughed. "That is some rough whiskey."

"Yeah?"

"Yeah. And it doesn't taste anything like scotch or Irish whiskey. It's richer."

"Let me try. Hand it over here."

Frank took a swallow, gasped, and wiped his mouth on his sleeve.

"You're right," he said. "That is rough. But I bet you won't even notice after a few drinks."

"Well, there's only one way to find out. We don't have anywhere we have to be, so I say we experiment a little."

"Certainly," Frank said, and handed me my own pint. We made a toast to his father, and headed for the bottom of the bottles. An hour later, we were completely drunk.

"I wish Mullins was here now to share this with," Frank said.

"I wish a lot of people were here to share it with," I said.

"So what do you think we should do with the rest?"

"I don't know. Drink it, perhaps?"

"We really should give a bottle to the lieutenant. Then we'll have to find somewhere to stash the rest so it won't get pinched. There are a lot of thieves in the army."

"And you're one of them."

"I suppose you're right. And I certainly wouldn't trust me with…how many bottles?"

"Nine more, if we give one to the lieutenant."

"Nine more bottles. They'll be good for a few days of entertainment, I'd say."

My head was spinning and my mouth was dry. I hadn't been that drunk since I spent the night in the closet. I had to lie down for a while. Frank put the crate under a bunk in the back of the billet where it was well concealed, then laid down himself.

227

Late in the afternoon, we got up and went to tea. We each got a tin of Woodbines after the meal. On the way out, we saw the lieutenant leaving the officer's mess. Frank pulled a bottle out from under his coat and handed it to him. The lieutenant was clearly puzzled.

"Bourbon?" he said. "Where did you get it?"

"Dad sent a few bottles to me, sir," Frank said. "He picked it up in America."

"It smells like you already had some. Is it good?"

"It'll light you up in short order, sir," I said. "Be careful, though. I would imagine it has a bit of a boomerang effect."

"I appreciate the warning, sergeant. Thank you very much, Thomas. I'll enjoy this later."

"My pleasure, sir," Frank said.

We casually strolled back down the road to our billet, smoking a couple of cigarettes on the way.

"I don't know about you, Richard, but I think I'm ready for a little more," Frank said.

"You read my mind."

We went inside, and as there was no one around, or at least no one awake, we dug out the crate and got a bottle each. Frank and I stayed up until nearly dawn, smoking one cigarette after another and drinking bourbon. At some point, we got a third bottle to split, and by the time we got to the bottom of that one…well, you can imagine what shape we were in. We actually debated as to whether or not we should get a fourth bottle, but after a bit of drunken discussion, Frank fell over in mid-sentence, rolled off the bunk and hit the floor. He didn't move. He was passed out cold. I lifted him into a bottom bunk, covered him with a blanket and went to bed myself.

We got maybe two hours of sleep before it was time for roll call. I was still drunk, and I imagine Frank was, too. We staggered outside and stood in formation, trying not to weave or fall down. The sun was shining and it hurt my eyes. All I wanted to do was go back to bed.

"What a gorgeous day," Frank said. "I feel like my head is going to explode."

"That makes two of us," I said.

After roll call, the lieutenant stopped us as we left for breakfast. His eyes were bloodshot, and he looked a little pale. Sort of gray, really.

"How are you boys this morning?" he asked.

"Excellent, sir," I said. "And you?"

"I'm not sure, sergeant, but you were certainly right about that bourbon. It made me sicker than a damned dog. If I didn't know better, I'd say someone hit me over the head with a lead pipe."

"Come back to our billet and I'll give you another bottle," Frank said. "That will take care of your headache."

"No, definitely not, Thomas. I don't think I'm going to drink anything for a while. And I'm never drinking that stuff again. Not that I don't appreciate your generosity, but I don't think I could hold it down. I don't even know if I'll be able to eat breakfast."

"I'm sorry it didn't agree with you, sir," Frank said.

"No need to be sorry. Like I said, I appreciate the gift. I blame only myself. It was my decision to drink the whole bottle, not yours. I think I just need a little more sleep, that's all."

He walked off, and then turned back around.

"By the way, do either of you fellows play chess?" he asked. We shook our heads. He looked disappointed.

"Do you know any men in our platoon that do?"

Again, we answered no.

"Well, I thought it was worth asking. I'd really like to play a game later. Thanks anyway. Cheers."

"Poor bastard," Frank said once the lieutenant was out of earshot. "He hasn't been the same since Hendershot died."

"It will take some time for him to recover," I said.

"I'm not so sure about that. He may never recover. I feel sorry for him."

"We've all lost someone, Frank. Three of my closest friends are gone. It's not easy, but I can't dwell on it. I've got to move on."

"We all do, I know. But sometimes the lieutenant seems so incredibly lost. He gets this vacant look in his eyes, and just stares off into space like he's seeing something the rest of us cannot. His pain is almost contagious. I'm worried about him."

"I'm sure he would appreciate your sympathies, but worrying about him won't do any good. Besides, the lieutenant is a smart man, strong in character. He has a better chance of recovering than most of us. Give him time."

Drinking was pretty much what we did for the next two days, stopping our debauchery only to eat or sleep if it were absolutely necessary. Then late one night, we discovered that we only had one pint left.

"How the hell did we drink all of that?" Frank wondered.

"One bottle after another," I said. "And the lieutenant helped."

"Damn that lieutenant. He couldn't even keep it down."

"Now, come on, Frank. You're being a little hard on the old lieutenant, wouldn't you say?"

229

"I guess you're right, Richard. He's a good fellow, especially for an officer."

"He is, indeed. And he's covered your tail a few times. He deserved that bottle."

"I suppose he did. So we've got this one bottle left. Do you want to polish it off now?"

"I think we should save it. You know, for a special occasion."

"Like what? The end of the war? We'll never get to drink it."

"I don't know. I just think that we could hang on to it and drink it when we really have something to celebrate."

"Again, I don't know what would be worth celebrating at Wipers. I don't really give a damn if the sun comes up or not, much less anything else."

"How about when we take Hill 60?"

"Hill 60? You're assuming we will, in fact, take it. What if we don't?"

"We will. You remember how much ammonal and gun cotton we buried beneath it? That entire hill is going to be blown off the map. We won't actually be taking a hill. We'll be taking a hole in the ground."

"I still think we should drink it now. Who cares about that stupid hill?"

"A lot of boys have died trying to take it, or have been shot by snipers perched atop it. We'll want to mark the occasion once it is captured. We should save that bottle until then."

We argued back and forth for about fifteen minutes before Frank came up with a solution; we'd cut cards, and the holder of the high card would decide the fate of the bottle. Frank promised not to cheat, and I'm pretty sure he didn't, because he drew a five of clubs and I pulled a queen of diamonds.

"So we will drink it on top of Hill 60," I said. "Can you keep it safe until then?"

"Yeah, I can keep it," he said, "even though I still think we should drink it now. But, you got the high card, and that was the agreement, even if it technically is my whiskey. Are you sure you don't want to go two out of three?"

"I have a feeling you'd win the next two cuts, somehow."

"Ah, you know me well, Richard. A little too well. I can't get by with anything around you. I don't stand a chance."

Late in the evening, as I tried to fall asleep, I silently debated Frank's opinion on the conquest of Hill 60. He was right; even with the mine, it would still be difficult. Maybe even impossible. And once we got there, what would we do? I wondered about what kind of defenses the Germans had on the other side. Would there be wire and another trench to take? Knowing how thorough the

230

Huns were, I reasoned that there would be. And how long would it take us to break that line? I tried to convince myself that our generals had probably taken these things into consideration. But the more I thought about it, the more doubtful I became.

I stayed awake in bed most of the night, a vision of hell playing out in my mind. I was overcome by dread, hopelessness and uncertainty. Maybe it was because I'd been drunk for several days, coupled with the fact that I hadn't gotten much sleep in that time. Maybe it was because I was starting to view things realistically. I actually thought about getting up and drinking that pint of bourbon alone to ease my mind, but I did not. It would have to wait until we took the hill or died trying.

I must admit, neither of those options provided much comfort.

CHAPTER 32

We returned to the front line in February. It was still bitter cold, and I was beginning to think that winter was going to last forever. My joints started to ache, and my lips and hands were cracked and dry. I had actually forgotten what it felt like to be warm. The only respite was to go below ground, where it was at least above freezing and there was no wind. For the rest of the winter, I found a lot of reasons to descend into the tunnels. Even during my rest time, I would often go down to a gallery, sometimes reading my Bible by candlelight and sometimes just sitting there. Now and then I'd stretch out and take a nap.

One morning in particular, after I had been on patrol all night, I decided I would get some sleep in the gallery at the head of the Hill 60 works. A new tunnel was underway there for use as a listening post, and the clay-kickers had made it about 200 feet out. There were three fellows working at the face that morning, but they were virtually silent, as was necessary to avoid detection. I couldn't hear them at all where I was. In the peace and quiet, I soon drifted off.

I was asleep probably an hour or so when I awoke with a start. Private Turner was shaking me.

"Staff Sgt. Gardener," he said. "Sergeant, I think there's something you should come and take a look at."

"What's going on, Turner?"

"I'm not sure, but I don't think it's good, sergeant."

"Is everyone all right?"

"Yes. But I think we've stumbled on to something."

"What are you getting at?"

"We were digging along, and I think we ran into a German tunnel."

"Well, you either did or you didn't, Turner. Which is it?"

"You see, I was kicking my shovel, and it went into the clay and made sort of a thump. Like a hollow sound, sergeant. What should we do?"

"Let me go and have a look."

I followed him back up the tunnel. Valentine and Havens were sitting with their ears to the face.

"Do you fellows hear anything?" I whispered.

"No, sergeant," Valentine said.

"How far are we from this supposed tunnel?" I asked.

"Eight inches, maybe ten," he said. Then he took a bayonet, stuck it into the clay and pushed until it stopped.

"Right about there," he said.

I took the bayonet and poked into the clay in several other spots. It definitely wasn't a rock they had hit.

"All right," I said. "We're going to have to find out what's in there. Dig away the clay with your hands, and for heaven's sake, be quiet. I need to get the lieutenant and tell him what's going on."

I went back to the surface and found the lieutenant in his dugout making tea. I told him what had happened, and asked him what we should do about it.

"I didn't know they had any tunnels that deep, especially not so close to ours," he said. "Are you sure that's what you ran into?"

"Reasonably sure, sir."

"Did you figure out which way the tunnel was running?"

"Not yet, sir. We might be able to tell once we get some of the clay cleared away."

"Maybe I should go down and have a look."

"I think that would be a good idea, sir."

By the time we got back to the face, Valentine and Turner had exposed timbers, confirming that they had definitely hit a German tunnel. It seemed to be running more or less perpendicular to ours.

"This isn't good," the lieutenant mumbled. "This isn't good at all."

"What's the matter, sir?" Havens whispered.

"Depending on how long it is, it could be nearing our main tunnel. In fact, it might even run far enough to reach our Hill 60 charge. Maybe even the Caterpillar charge as well. For all we know, they've reached both and defused them. And if that has happened, we'll have to rewire them, or take Hill 60 and the Caterpillar without mines. I don't know about you, lads, but I don't care for that notion."

"What should we do, sir?" I asked.

"There's only one thing we can do: break through to their tunnel, follow it, find out where it goes, then collapse it with charges on the way back out."

"That sounds a bit dangerous, sir," Valentine said.

"Not as dangerous as taking those ridges without mines," the lieutenant replied. "Sergeant Gardener, I want you to lead the effort. Valentine, Havens and Turner will go with you, but you should have at least one more fellow with you who has some experience."

"Who would you suggest, sir?" I asked.

"Corporal Thomas. He's fairly sharp."

"I doubt he'll want to volunteer, lieutenant."

"That doesn't matter. I volunteer him myself. I'll get him and the supplies you need to do the job. In the mean time, clear away

233

enough clay so that you can pry some of the boards loose and slip through. I'll be back in a few minutes."

We had to dig quite a bit to expose the timbers from end to end. The tunnel apparently had height sufficient for a man to walk upright inside. I put my ear up to the wood and listened, but I still didn't hear anything.

"Do you think they know what we're doing?" Valentine asked.

"I would imagine not," I said. "Otherwise, they'd have blown a camouflet on top of us by now."

"Maybe we can keep it that way," he said.

"I doubt it. Once we start prying these boards loose, we'll probably make enough noise for every Hun in Hunland to hear."

"What will we do then?"

"Get in, lay the charges, and get the hell out. Very quickly."

Frank came up the tunnel carrying a detonator, pry bar, a club made out of a pick handle and three knuckle knives, which were like brass knuckles with a blade attached. He gave a knife to each of the boys, and kept the club himself. The lieutenant, close behind him, had two torches, four satchel charges and two spools of wire. He was also carrying a second revolver stuffed behind his belt.

"The first thing I want you to do is follow the tunnel in the direction of Hill 60 and the Caterpillar," he said. "Find out how far it goes, and if they've reached our charges. Then find the entrance, lay a charge there, and work your way back here, placing the other charges at different points along the way. The more damage we can do, the longer it will take them to recover. Do you know how to wire these charges?"

"Absolutely, sir," I said. "I've been using explosives for a long time."

"That's right, you have been," he said, stroking his hairless chin. "That's reassuring. Reassuring indeed."

He took his Webley out of its holster, checked the cylinder to make sure it was fully loaded, and gave it to me. He handed the other one to Frank.

"Those will work a lot better than trying to fire a rifle in there," he said, "but don't get into a fight unless there is no other way. Remember, the objective is to shut down this tunnel, not to kill Huns or take prisoners or anything else. Any questions?"

"No sir," I said.

"Very well, then. I'll debrief you when you get back. Best of luck, lads."

The lieutenant went back toward our gallery. I gave Frank two charges, a spool of wire, and a quick lesson in how to connect

234

them. He recited my instructions back to me verbatim. It gave me a lot of confidence.

"I want you to take Havens and Valentine to the left," I said, handing him a torch. "I'll take Turner up the other way. Go until you get to the end or the entrance, whichever may be there. If you find the entrance, lay a charge and connect the wire. Then lay another one about halfway back. If we find the entrance, we'll do the same thing. Either way, I want all four charges wired. Regroup in our tunnel, and when it's all set, we'll blow the whole damn thing."

"How much time have we got?" Frank asked.

"Three minutes, I'd say. Five on the outside, but no more."

"That's just splendid," he said sarcastically. It made me angry. Maybe it was the tension. I lashed out at him.

"I don't need your bloody smart commentary right now, Frank," I said. "I don't want to hear it, so keep your mouth shut. Just do exactly what I've told you to do. That, my friend, is a direct order. Understand?"

I guess I stunned him a little; I had stunned myself a little, in fact. He just nodded and said nothing more.

"All right, then," I said. "Let's start this party."

I tried to get the pry bar in between two timbers as quietly as possible. After a few attempts, I got some leverage and pushed on the bar. The boards creaked loudly, then snapped in the middle. It sounded like someone had fired a rifle. I kicked in the broken boards and pried two more away. That gave us enough space to squeeze through. There was no light on the other side, which was definitely a good sign. I stuck my head through and looked to the left and right. The tunnel went farther in both directions than our lights could shine. With all of the noise, I was very surprised I didn't see any Germans there. Maybe we were going to be lucky, I thought.

We crawled through the hole and into the darkness. Frank headed to the left with a torch in one hand and a revolver in the other. Havens and Valentine followed him carrying their knives, the charges and the wire. I led Turner in the direction of Hill 60.

Turner and I went about 100 yards and I thought I saw the end up ahead, but then realized the tunnel continued on, making a sharp turn to the right. The lieutenant had been correct; they would, in fact, run directly into our main tunnel if they kept digging in that direction. I switched off my torch, felt my way down the wall to the corner, and peeked around it. There was a light up ahead. I pulled back.

"Damn it," I said. "There's someone up there."

"Oh, crap," Turner muttered. "What should we do?"

235

"Move very quietly. We'll try to get as close as we can before they see us. I doubt they'll surrender, and I'm not in the mood to take prisoners."

"Neither am I."

"Ready?"

"I suppose so, sergeant."

We rounded the corner. I counted three Germans working by candlelight about 100 feet away. They were much closer to our main tunnel than I had expected, probably just a few yards from where they were working. We moved stealthily down the tunnel, hugging the wall all the way. I didn't want to fire my pistol unless I had to, in case Frank and the others were also trying to sneak up on the enemy at their end. I said a prayer and held my breath.

Then, at this most inopportune time, I heard a gunshot reverberate up through the tunnel; apparently, Frank and the others had found trouble. The three Germans ahead of us turned around, startled. We charged them. One picked up a pistol, but I shot him down. The other two came at us with bayonets. I fired twice more, but I wasn't as lucky with them. The next thing I knew, they were on top of us.

One of the Germans lunged at me, but I was able to dodge his thrust. I caught him off balance and smacked him over the head with my revolver, taking off a big chunk of his scalp. He hit the ground and I shot him at nearly point-blank range through the head. Turner didn't fare so well. His opponent managed to stab him in the gut, and he was on his knees. As the German tried to pull out the bayonet, I tackled him and got him on the ground. I put the pistol to his neck and pulled the trigger. Blood spattered in my eyes. I wiped it away and looked over at Turner. He was on his back and the whole front of his tunic was crimson.

"Turner, are you still with me?" I asked, slapping him on the cheeks.

"Yes…sergeant," he moaned. Blood came out of the corner of his mouth. I heard the distinct sound of a grenade exploding at the other end of the tunnel, followed by five more shots from Frank's revolver.

"We've got to get you out of here," I said. "Can you stand up?"

"Just…get the charge…wired," he said.

"I'm not going to leave you. Put your arm over my shoulder and hang on."

I went back toward home and stopped at the corner. I put Turner down and wired a charge there, then moved on. When I got closer to our entry point, I laid the second one and wired it.

236

Turner was beginning to lose consciousness. I had to drag him the rest of the way.

Frank came running up from the other direction, rolling off wire as he went. He had a pair of binoculars hanging around his neck. Valentine was behind him. Havens was nowhere to be seen.

"They are coming down the shaft!" Frank shouted. "I don't think we can hold them any longer!"

"Where's your other man?" I asked.

"He's napoo!" Frank said. "Fritz dropped a grenade down on him."

"You found the entrance?"

"I'll tell you about it later. Right now we've got to get out of here!"

I pushed Turner through the hole. Frank and Valentine crawled through, and I could see that Valentine had taken some shrapnel in the back. They picked up Turner and headed for our gallery. I went through last, pulling the wires from both directions behind me. I hastily hooked them up to the detonator, crossed my fingers, and pushed the plunger.

It sounded like the end of the world. There was a thunderous, deafening roar, and I felt the blast to my marrow. It knocked me off balance, and for a moment or two, I actually saw stars. Smoke and gas came pouring through the hole. I knew I had to get out quickly, but I wanted to survey our work. I stuck my head through and looked both ways. There was extensive damage. I started to have difficulty breathing and my eyes were burning. Coughing violently, I ran back to our gallery. Frank was already up top, and Valentine was climbing the ladder. Frank lowered down a harness on a rope, and I buckled Turner in. They hoisted his limp body to the surface. I brought up the rear.

The lieutenant was waiting for me at the entrance, and I could see his mouth moving, but I couldn't hear a damn thing he was saying. In fact, I couldn't hear anything except my own heartbeat. I sat down on the fire step next to Frank and lit a cigarette. Stretcher-bearers came and took Turner and Valentine away. My hearing finally returned after a few minutes.

"What did you find?" the lieutenant asked.

"Corporal Thomas found the entrance and I found the other end," I said, handing him his revolver. "We blew it in four different places. Lots of damage."

"Had they reached our charges, or could you tell?"

"I don't think so, sir. But they were headed in that direction. I think we were lucky to have discovered their operation."

"What happened to Turner?"

"We tangled with some Huns and he got stabbed. I shot all three of the bastards."

"What about Valentine? And where is Havens?"

"I don't know the details, sir. Thomas was with them."

The lieutenant turned to Frank.

"What happened, corporal?" he asked.

"We found the main gallery and the shaft to the surface, sir," Frank said. "I shot a few Huns in the process, and I thought we were home free, but then a bomb came down the shaft and landed next to Havens. He took most of the shrapnel. Valentine caught some, too. I was the lucky one."

"What are you doing with those field glasses?"

"Oh, these," he said, handing them to the lieutenant. "I got these for you. I thought you might be able to use them."

The lieutenant looked them over.

"These are made by Zeiss," he said. "They're supposed to be the best in the world. How did you get them?"

"I found them in a dugout at the top of the German shaft, sir."

"What? Why the bloody hell did you go up there?"

"I wanted to see if there were any more tunnel entrances coming off of that shaft. I popped in and found one German, so I shot him. I took a look around and grabbed the binoculars. Then I went back down."

"I don't remember that being part of my instructions, Thomas. You didn't compromise Valentine and Havens in the process, did you?"

At that moment, I was having the same thought; he hadn't been told to go up the shaft. The orders were to avoid a confrontation if at all possible.

"No, sir," Frank said, emphatically denying the allegation. "I didn't do anything to jeopardize their safety."

"Are you certain? Because I'm going to talk to Valentine later to see what he has to say. I don't want to find out that you got one man killed and another wounded so you could take a souvenir."

"You won't, sir. I promise you that."

The lieutenant just stared at him for a minute and shook his head. He clearly wasn't convinced. Neither was I, to be honest.

"I appreciate the gift, Thomas, but from now on, you'll follow orders to the letter," the lieutenant said. "Don't go about making up the rules yourself."

"Absolutely not, sir."

"Now you two should find somewhere to get some sleep. I'm going to need you to lead another patrol tonight."

"Again, sir?" I asked.

238

"We're short on experienced men right now, sergeant, and you and Thomas are the most capable soldiers I have. I'm sorry, but I need you out there, at least until these replacements get acclimated. I have no other choice. So take my advice and get some rest. You'll be going out at 2200 hours."

"Yes, sir," I said.

As we went off to our dugout, I expected Frank to start complaining, but he didn't. I guess I'd been pretty hard on him, and I thought about apologizing, but decided not to. He put some wood in the stove and we silently got into our bunks.

Lying there, I prayed that the evening wouldn't be as costly as the morning had been. I tried to convince myself that Frank wasn't to blame for that misfortune; I prayed that Turner and Valentine would recover from their wounds. It had been one hell of a day so far, and I was exhausted. So despite my anxiety, the confusion and doubt in my mind, the charge of adrenalin and the tremendous ringing in my ears, I was able to get to sleep fairly quickly.

The patrol that night passed without incident, and without me saying more than three words to Frank. Then in the morning, we got word that Valentine had gone through surgery and was going to make it. He'd probably be able to return to regular duty in about six weeks, the doctor said. That was the good news.

Turner wasn't as fortunate. The lieutenant told me that he bled to death before he even got to the aid station. He was only 18. I went off by myself, to the bottom of a shaft, and cried like a baby. I didn't understand why something so horrible had to happen.

As much as I didn't want to admit it to myself, I finally decided that Frank was, in fact, to blame. If he hadn't gone up the shaft, he wouldn't have encountered the enemy. If he hadn't encountered the enemy, he wouldn't have fired his pistol. If he hadn't fired his pistol, Turner and I could have slipped up behind the German miners and taken them down before they knew what was going on. And no one would have dropped the bomb that wounded Valentine and killed Havens.

The blood of those three boys was on Frank's hands, for certain, and I built a strong resentment against him because of it. I'd thought of him as infallible up until then. I had almost worshipped him. Now I saw him in a different light. He had a selfish, grandiose side that I'd previously ignored, but now it was glaringly obvious. I could see right through him.

For the rest of our days together, I could not forgive him for what he did. And to be honest, I don't think I ever have.

CHAPTER 33

Winter held us in a tight grip until March. Even then, there wasn't much of an improvement. The temperatures did rise slowly, which was good, but instead of snow, we were getting rain. Buckets of it. And with the ground thawing out, that literally meant mud up to our knees. The constant shelling churned the ground and made it even worse. The entire landscape was brown. Bringing up supplies, or simply going from one place to another, was virtually impossible. It was terribly depressing. Once again, I was beginning to believe that things couldn't get worse; and once again, I simply hadn't considered all of the possibilities.

There really wasn't much going on yet, at least not near our sector. But there were events unfolding hundreds of miles away that didn't bode well; after two and a half years of fighting – and for the most part, losing -- the Russian Army was plummeting into the abyss of complete disorder. The Germans had pushed them most of the way there. Yet in the end, the army simply imploded, eaten away from the inside as if by a cancer.

Frankly, it was amazing that they held on as long as they did. Front-line conditions for the Russians were brutal. One disaster followed another. There were 800,000 dead, and millions more wounded, captured or missing. Disillusioned and demoralized, cold and hungry, soldiers had started refusing orders to go back to the line. Many simply deserted and went home.

But they arrived to find that conditions at home weren't much better. There was extreme poverty, and shortages of just about everything. Inflation was running rampant; that winter, with temperatures 30 or 40 degrees below zero, most families couldn't afford firewood to heat their homes. Food was either expensive or non-existent. Russians lined up at three in the morning and stood for hours in the cold, snow and wind just to get a loaf of bread. Even then, there was no assurance they would actually get any. While the Russians waited in these lines, they started whispering to each other about taking matters into their own hands. Hunger and a hatred of the war had unified the masses, particularly against the czar.

It all came to a head in the first week of March. Workers in St. Petersburg took to the streets demanding food. More and more people joined in, and soon it became an all-out riot, complete with arson, looting and gunfire. The much-dreaded Cossacks were called in to stop it, but they sided with the rioters. Uncooperative officers were shot. The result was utter chaos.

The parliament tried to establish some kind of order, while soldiers and workers in the capital formed a rival group called a "soviet." The soviet wanted control, but feared that army officers might try to stop them. So the soviet issued an order abolishing the privileges of rank; in other words, no one had to take orders from anyone whatsoever. Soldiers at the front didn't spend much time debating the soviet's authority. Units went where they wanted, but most simply disintegrated. They shot all officers who dared to block their route home.

The czars had ruled Russia for nearly 400 years, but that soon came to an end. Czar Nicholas abdicated and turned the throne over to his brother, who in turn, stepped down himself. That left no one in charge at home or in the front lines. What would happen next was anyone's guess. Russia was like a freight train going down a steep grade without any brakes; at the first turn, there would surely be disaster. Russian history, in my opinion, seemed to be one tragedy after another, and this would be no different.

Rebecca kept me abreast of the situation with clippings from newspapers. Dramatic events seemed to be happening every day. Around the middle of March, I received a letter with several stories inside that she had clipped for me, and I was relieved to read that the provisional government promised to keep Russia in the war until Germany was defeated. I thought that was positive, but after reading the articles, Frank pointed out the worst possible scenario. The bad part was that he made a lot of sense.

"This provisional government says the army will stay and fight," he said, "but who's going to give the order to do so? There's no chain of command left."

"They must think the army will be loyal to the cause," I said. "They can't just quit now. Not after losing so much."

"Why not? They can't bring back the dead, but they can decide that no more will die fighting this war."

"Well, the provisional government…"

"…is mistaken, plain and simple. I doubt they have any real authority over anything."

"Do you think they'll just allow the Germans to march into St. Petersburg?"

"No, but they could call the whole thing off and make an armistice with the Germans. And if that happens, we are going to be up to our chins in shit. Think about it. If the Germans don't have to fight the Russians, then they can send all of their men to fight us. Hundreds of thousands of them, all battle-hardened veterans. We'll have less men and less experience. That's not a good way to fight."

"We'll just have to get more men to the front, that's all."

"After the Somme, Richard? After Verdun? Where are we going to get more men? There aren't that many left. They're sending us boys already. Have you taken a look around lately? We're old men compared to most of these lads. Just about everyone in our unit came in after we did. I think the lieutenant is the only one who's been here longer."

"But the Germans have lost as many as we have. They're stretched pretty thin, too."

"Yes, but all they have to do to win is to hold the line they have right now. For us to win, we'll have to push them all the way back to Germany. I'm not too optimistic about that. Not optimistic at all."

I couldn't argue with him. I was beginning to hate it when he was right, which he was in this case.

"So do you think we're going to lose this war?" I asked.

"I don't know," he said. "I hope not. Not after all this time and all of the boys we've lost. But there's probably some German fool sitting up there on the ridge saying the same thing to his *kamerad*. I guarantee it."

"But we are morally right. God won't let us lose."

"And as I just said, the Germans probably tell each other the same thing. They think God is on their side just as much as you do."

"Well, one of us must be wrong, Frank."

"Not so. We may both be wrong. I don't think God is taking sides in this. I'm sure he doesn't like to see us slaughtering each other, and Fritz killing Tommy isn't any different than Tommy killing Fritz."

I didn't know what to say to that. Frank cursed and spat on the ground.

"Somewhere," he said, "there will be hell to pay. Somehow for all of us. And that, my friend, is that."

As much as I hated the notion, I figured he was probably right.

CHAPTER 34

Malaise was infecting the ranks that spring, myself included. It came down to morale; the hope of victory, the will to fight, and the willingness to take orders was degenerating. Soldiers, especially those that had been around a while, were by and large apathetic. Only the new boys seemed to have any enthusiasm about our mission, and they didn't have it for long. There was constant complaining, even acts of insubordination here and there. It was worse among the French troops, and from what I heard, the Germans were having the same problem.

There was much doubt among the men I knew as to whether the war could be won at all; the Russian situation hadn't helped any. There was also the certainty of yet another round of spring offensives, and we didn't see how they would be any different than those in past years. The blood would flow in rivers; there was no reason to expect anything else. The stakes were higher than ever. No one wanted to lose after having paid so dearly already. And as they had done in 1914, 1915 and 1916, the generals and politicians and so forth pledged to win the war "this year." They said we'd all be home by Christmas at the latest. Even if they were right, Christmas was a hell of a long way off.

Around the same time that Russia was falling apart at the seams, we started hearing talk of a big French operation coming up soon. Rumor had it that they would attack the German line south of our position, along the River Aisne. There was a lot of discussion as to what might happen, but I decided not to jump to any conclusions until these rumors were confirmed. I didn't have to wait long, and it came from the top.

The French general in charge of the whole affair – a fellow named Nivelle – apparently didn't think secrecy was of much importance, and even went so far as to tell his plans to the newspaper boys. More than a million men would attack along a 40-mile front from Reims to Soissons, he said; then he gave away every target, every objective, and basically every last detail of his plans. I guess it didn't occur to him that the Germans probably read the papers, too.

For some time, the Huns had sensed that an attack was coming there, and now they knew for sure. They also knew that they could pull back and still hold a pretty big chunk of France. So they took their time building three lines of defenses, carefully picking the most advantageous positions, some as far as 50 miles behind the front. It shortened their line, which meant it could be held with fewer men. In mid-March, they began to withdraw.

They burned every building, killed every farm animal, poisoned every well and ripped up every rail line on the way out. By the time the French discovered this little maneuver, the line had collapsed and they were out of contact with the enemy.

Nivelle could have called the whole thing off. He could have occupied the abandoned land without losing anyone. But he refused to change his plans, and continued to discuss them within earshot of practically everyone. He seemed determined his battle would win the war for France, despite what other people told him. Nothing, it seemed, could stop him.

And people across the channel knew as much about Nivelle's designs as those of us at the front. The letters I was getting from Rebecca were stuffed with newspaper clippings about him and his plans. Her letters had turned very pessimistic in the preceding weeks, and she seemed to be as war-weary as I was. She thought all of the generals were idiots, especially Haig and Nivelle. She wanted them to pack it in and let us all go back home. Our baby would be coming soon, and although she still had Elizabeth and Rose to offer support, she truly wanted me to be there when she gave birth. I knew I wouldn't be, even if the war ended right then. Still, I wrote back to her that maybe Nivelle would, in fact, defeat Germany, or that a breakthrough at Wipers would lead to victory. I don't know if she believed any of it. Hell, I didn't even believe it.

I was becoming a "never-ender," just like Frank. That disturbed me.

CHAPTER 35

Around that time we got more replacements. I don't think a single one was more than eighteen or nineteen. To say they were nervous would be an understatement; "terrified" would be more accurate. A lot of their fears were well founded, but it was clear that they had picked up some misinformation on their way to the front. Tales of German atrocities in our sector were circulating in the rear areas and training camps, fueling anxiety and cementing hatred.

"Did you see the Canadian?" a boy named Gibbs asked me.

"What Canadian? There's a lot of Canadians around here."

"You know," he said, "the one the Huns crucified. Did you see him?"

"A crucified Canadian?"

"Yes, sergeant. Some fellows we met on the way up were talking about it. They said Fritz had captured a Canadian, pinned him to a cross with bayonets, and put him up so our boys could watch him die slowly."

"And where did that supposedly happen, Gibbs?"

"Somewhere around here, I think."

"And these fellows told you they had seen this first-hand?"

"Well, not exactly…"

"That's what I thought. The first thing you have to learn up here, private, is not to believe anything unless you witness it yourself. Most of what you hear isn't even remotely true, and I'm fairly certain that no one got crucified."

"I don't know, sergeant. The Germans are barbarians, and it sounds like something they'd do."

"Gibbs, there was no crucified Canadian, plain and simple. These kinds of stories take on a life of their own after a while. The more they circulate, the worse they get. Like a few months ago, a story came around that the Germans were collecting our dead from No Man's Land at night, then sending them back to Germany to be used for making soap and candles and so forth. That wasn't true, and neither is this. Next month, it will be something else, and it won't be true, either."

There were more questions from other boys, basically the same ones I'd answered each time we got replacements. I tried to give them straight answers as much as possible, but I had to sugarcoat some of them. I didn't want them to get the wind up any worse than they already had.

But my reassurances didn't seem to put them at ease; maybe I wasn't very convincing, because in my heart, I knew a lot of them wouldn't make it six months. In reality, some of them wouldn't even survive six weeks -- or even six days -- in the line. I couldn't recall how many I'd seen die by then. Their names and faces had long since been purged from my memory. If I had held onto them all, I would have gone insane. Forgetting was the only way I could keep from becoming a complete lunatic.

CHAPTER 36

It was time for tea, and I told the replacements to enjoy their sausages and potatoes because it was probably going to be bully beef and biscuits for the next week or so. I was really dreading it, and I daydreamed of sitting in Rebecca's kitchen again, eating her steak and kidney pies. They were the best I'd ever had, and I imagined that she knew many more delicious recipes that I had not yet savored. The thought made my mouth water and my stomach rumble. Maybe it won't be long, I thought; maybe I'll get some leave after we take the ridge, and then I'll sit in her kitchen and eat until the buttons pop off of my shirt. That sounded good. But for the time being, I had to settle for army food. Damn it, anyway.

We did, however, get some good news just before sundown. We had our packs on, ready to head out, when the lieutenant walked through the door of the billet. He motioned for me to come outside.

"Our rest time has been extended another six days," he said. "Tell these new lads to take advantage of it. Get plenty to eat and plenty of sleep."

"Why the extension?" I asked. "I'm sure they didn't do this out of the goodness of their hearts."

"Well...I'll tell you, but the boys can't know. Can you keep it confidential?"

"Absolutely, sir."

"It seems, Gardener, that chronic hysteria is spreading through the line along the ridge. The men know that the Germans are tunneling at full tilt to counter our mining, and now every man believes he is standing on top of a ton of explosives. The engineers are getting so many reports of suspicious noises from below ground that they don't have enough time or manpower to investigate them all."

"That's not good."

"No, it's not. It's so bad, in fact, that there is some fear that men will start refusing orders to go into the front line. We could have a mutiny."

"I don't think that will happen, sir."

"Don't be so sure of it. The French are starting to have a lot of insubordination in the ranks. Then there's the Russian situation. And we've even received reports that the Huns are struggling to maintain discipline. We could be next."

"That's never happened in the British Army, sir."

"We've never been worn this thin, either, Gardener. The general staff sees the danger. I hope these shorter stays in the line will help."

"How long will that be in effect, sir?"

"Probably until we take the ridge. Another six or eight weeks, maybe. Most of the mines are charged and wired already. The others are nearing completion. We're looking at the first week of June for the jump-off. Is Thomas in there?"

"Yes, sir."

"Could you go in and bring him out here? I want to talk to him. I need him to do me a favor."

"What's that, sir?"

"Well, as you know, there's a bit of resentment growing between us and the French. They think we aren't doing enough and that we don't consider them when making plans. It's not true, but that's what they think."

"I'm not sure how Frank could help, sir."

"There's going to be a gathering of staff officers from both armies in a few days down toward Amiens. The idea is to meet and coordinate plans for our summer operations. It's more of a show than anything else, but it is important nonetheless. It will be a demonstration of unity."

"And you want Frank to go to this meeting? A corporal?"

"Actually, it has been requested that he come and entertain after tea the last night of the conference."

"Really, sir? That seems a bit odd, don't you think?"

"They've arranged for several front-line soldiers with different talents to perform there. They've got a boy from York that plays the piano and sings, an Australian violinist and a fellow from Buxton that recites Shakespeare. So apparently, someone up the chain of command remembered we had a magician in the unit, probably from the time he was arrested. I was asked to make arrangements for him to appear there as well."

"Are you sure you want him to go, sir? Corporal Thomas isn't very 'military,' if you know what I mean."

"He owes me, sergeant. I expect him to comply. Now quit asking questions and bring him out here. Now."

I found Frank snoring loudly in his bunk opposite the door. It took me a minute, but I finally brought him around. He went out and listened to what the lieutenant had to say with great interest. I could see the wheels turning in his head.

"I'd be glad to do it for you, sir," he said. "I don't have a lot of gear, though."

"I've seen you do countless card tricks," the lieutenant said. "That in itself would be sufficient, I'd say."

248

"But I've got a few days to prepare, don't I sir?"

"Absolutely. I'll take you off the duty roster to give you more time."

"That would be excellent. I might even be able to build a few props between now and then. I'd really like to do more than card tricks. Maybe something, let's say, more dramatic."

"I'm sure whatever you do will be fine, Thomas. If you need anything, let me know."

"Sir, would you mind if the sergeant here came along as my assistant? I'm sure he could use a good meal, too."

"Is that all right with you, Gardener?"

I nodded.

"Then it's settled," the lieutenant said. "Both of you be ready to leave after lunch on Monday."

I watched the lieutenant walk off into the night. I turned to Frank to thank him, but he didn't hear me. There was a far-away look in his eyes, the kind he usually had before we got into some kind of trouble. It made the hair on my neck stand up.

"You'd better play this one straight, Frank," I said.

He didn't respond.

"Frank! Did you hear what I said?"

He snapped out of his trance.

"What's that?"

"I said you have to play this straight. No funny business."

"Who, me?"

"Yes, you."

"Now Richard, you've got to give me more credit than that. I'm not stupid, you know."

"Stupid, no. Cocky, for certain."

"Don't worry about a thing. I'll be a good boy. I promise."

He told me he was going to build some small props and scrounge a few things he could use for an act. He was so enthusiastic about it. It seemed to give him a sense of purpose. I wasn't surprised that I didn't see much of him over the next couple of days.

I was lying in my bunk the night before the performance, reading and re-reading a letter from Rebecca, when Frank came walking in. His clothes were muddy up to his waist. He looked like he'd just come out of the line.

"What the devil happened to you?" I asked.

"What do you mean?"

"You're covered in muck."

"Oh, that. Yes. I fell in a ditch along the road."

I knew Frank well enough -- and had seen him lie enough that

I could spot one of his tales a mile off. He always looked up and to the left when he was fabricating off the cuff, and that was what he was doing. He didn't fall in a ditch; that much I knew. But I couldn't figure out why he'd lie about something like that. He didn't seem to have anything to gain. I was puzzled, not sure what to say.

"I've got to go get cleaned up," he said. "If I wash these pants, they should be dry by morning, don't you think?"

I said nothing. He went off, and I read my letter again. Rebecca said she was so big by then that she often wondered if she'd fit through the front door of the flat. Rose had left London when her husband got out of the hospital, and Elizabeth was working a lot of overtime at the shell plant. That left Rebecca alone at home most of the day, because she was too uncomfortable to get out. She was very lonely. And the baby would be coming, making her anxiety worse. She was afraid. I wrote her a long reply, telling her truthfully that I was praying dozens of times each day, pleading for God to get me home soon.

Maybe I should have been more specific as to how he might do that.

CHAPTER 37

Morning came with its regular routine. Breakfast was particularly bad that day, as was lunch. I picked at my food more than anything else, and reminded myself that I was going to get a fine meal at teatime. Frank, however, ate like a horse.

"You don't seem to be nervous about tonight," I said.

"Why should I be nervous? I've been performing for years. I quit getting nervous when I was fifteen."

"I just know I'd be on edge, with all of those officers and such watching me. Hell, I'm on edge right now myself."

"Don't worry. It's all going to come off well. You'll see."

Our ride was coming soon, and Frank asked me to help him carry two crates of props from the billet out to the road. The one I carried had a hinged lid with little holes drilled in it. I almost dropped it when I heard something scratching inside.

"What in the world is in here?" I asked him.

"Homing pigeons," he said.

"I thought you hated birds."

"Yes, but I like to do tricks with animals, and I couldn't catch any rabbits or anything. So I had to settle for pigeons."

"What's the trick?"

"I don't want to give anything away. But I'm sure it will be a hit."

"I'll be looking forward to it."

While we were waiting, the lieutenant showed up and said he'd be going with us.

"I had to pull a couple of strings, but I really wanted to see you perform, corporal," he said.

Frank looked a little surprised by this. I sensed some apprehension, regardless of his claim that he never got nervous before a show. Why it bothered him, I did not know.

"Have you got anything exciting planned?" the lieutenant asked.

Frank stammered a little before answering.

"Exciting?" he pondered, scratching his chin. "Yes, I guess you could call it that, sir. It's going to be a good show. I'm glad you're coming along. Absolutely."

The car arrived about half past twelve, and we put the crates in the back. The lieutenant got in the seat next to the driver, and Frank and I sat in the rear. The driver turned the car around and headed down the road toward Amiens. He said it would take us about three hours to get to our destination.

"That's all the time it will take?" the lieutenant asked. "That seems optimistic to me."

"Not really, sir," the driver said. "The roads are in fairly decent shape once you get away from Wipers. And there aren't any operations underway, so we shouldn't run into traffic. We'll make good time."

Within a few minutes, we were farther away from the front than Frank and I had been since we were in Blighty. There was green grass, flowers and budding trees. There were farms with livestock and freshly plowed fields. We saw a group of children flying kites. It was all so beautiful, so simple, and so alive. I felt free and serene, so much so that I soon dozed off. The next thing I knew, the car had stopped in front of a large chateau. Frank was nudging me.

"We're here, Richard," he said. "Come on, now."

We got out of the car, unloaded the crates and followed the lieutenant to the front door, where two military policemen were on sentry duty. Once we convinced them that we were supposed to be there, they let us inside. We walked through an entry parlor that was, in itself, bigger than my entire house back in England. Through a doorway at the other side was a huge banquet hall, finely decorated for the event. There were about twenty tables set with candles, floral centerpieces and linen tablecloths. A baby grand piano sat on a small stage at the near end of the room. Three crystal chandeliers hung from the ceiling, and big logs burned in an enormous fieldstone fireplace at the far end. It was the most fancy place I'd ever seen, fancier than Chez Antoine, even.

"Are you nervous now, Frank?" I asked. "There's going to be a lot of people here."

"The more, the better," he said. "It's harder to perform for five people than for five hundred. Besides, I've got you and the lieutenant here; that's two familiar faces, anyway."

We put the crates next to the piano.

"What other assistance do you need, Frank?" I asked. "What am I supposed to do?"

"Nothing more," he said. "Just enjoy dinner and the show."

There was more scratching from the one crate, and it caught the lieutenant's attention. He stooped down and tried to look through one of the tiny holes, but he could see nothing. The scratching got louder.

"What's in here?" he asked.

"I can't tell you, sir," Frank said. "It's a surprise."

"Maybe you should tell me anyway, Thomas. I've found that I'm not usually happy with your surprises."

"Sorry, sir. I can't tell you. Magician's code, you see."

The lieutenant got this kind of pained look on his face, clearly revealing that he did not trust Frank as far as he could throw him.

Nonetheless, he didn't ask any more questions about the "surprise."

We had about an hour or so to relax before the festivities began, so we got some coffee from the kitchen and sat on a bench in the flower garden in front of the chateau. It was a gorgeous evening. The air was warm and still, and it didn't stink like a battlefield; rather, it smelled almost sweet.

Around five, the other performers came in. The guests started to arrive in cars about 20 minutes later. There was a steady stream of them until about six, and I remember thinking that I'd never seen so many officers gathered in one place before. All of the Brits had the rank of major or higher, including a couple of brigadier generals. I didn't know enough about the French insignias to distinguish ranks, but I assumed they were comparable to the ones we had in attendance.

The lieutenant came outside looking for us. He waved us over.

"The fellows in the kitchen say tea is ready," he said. "They've got a table set up for us in the back. Let's eat."

"I thought we'd be eating in the banquet hall," Frank whined.

"Don't complain, corporal," the lieutenant said. "We'll get the same food as everyone else. You should be thankful."

"I bet we won't get wine, though," Frank mumbled under his breath as we walked inside. The lieutenant either didn't hear him or chose to ignore him. Probably the latter. That's what I was doing.

The other performers were sitting at the table already. They stood to attention when the lieutenant came over. He told them to sit back down and dispense with the usual courtesies. They looked a bit uncomfortable; officers and enlisted men didn't normally fraternize over a meal. They began to relax somewhat after the food arrived.

Tea consisted of Cornish game hens in some kind of orange glaze, roasted potatoes, cooked celery and pickled beets. And Frank was wrong; they brought us a bottle of white wine, and when it was empty, they brought another. Desert was crème brulee, and it came with glasses of brandy. We were all feeling a little loose by that time. Frank was especially animated. He had us all laughing.

When the guests had finished their meal, one of the military policemen came into the kitchen and told us to go sit in a row of chairs in the back of the banquet hall. It was time for the entertainment.

The first fellow to perform played the piano and sang in Italian. I think it was from an opera. I know I'd never heard it before. But he must have done a splendid rendition of the piece,

253

because he got a huge round of applause. Then he sang "God Save The King" and "The Marseilles." That got him a standing ovation. He bowed and walked off the stage.

The next lad played the violin, and quite well. Again, I didn't recognize the tune, but it sounded exquisite, overflowing with emotion. He got a rousing round of applause, and one of the generals asked him to play another one. The violinist thought for a moment, then played a piece that was even more beautiful than the first. It was amazing.

The third fellow recited Shakespeare. He recited four pieces, and while I didn't understand a word of what he was saying, everyone else must have. The hall echoed with enthusiastic clapping after each one.

Then it was Frank's turn. I was very excited, because I'd never actually seen him perform on stage. He opened up one of the crates and dug out a deck of cards. Some of his tricks I knew well, but there were a few I hadn't seen before. He followed with the coin routine that I'd first seen the day we met. The whole room was captivated.

Frank continued with some rope tricks that were new to me. I remember he put one piece in a coil, and then made it rise as if he were charming a cobra. It was spellbinding. He followed with a puzzling cup-and-ball routine, utilizing sawed-off ends of 18-pounder shell casings for the cups. Next, he did some tricks with five solid metal rings that could magically be linked together and separated again. He made some jokes and got a lot of laughs. His stage patter was dead on. The lieutenant nudged me, winked and gave me the thumbs-up sign. I nodded my approval. He was definitely the most talented performer there. I could tell the lieutenant was proud.

But suddenly his act took a dark turn, like storm clouds rolling in on an otherwise sunny day. Frank took out a handful of razorblades and a piece of string and put them in his mouth. The audience gasped again as Frank seemingly swallowed, then opened his mouth to reveal that there was nothing in there. He shook his head and craned his neck, then reached in his mouth and slowly pulled out the string with the razorblades dangling from it. Some applauded, but most of the officers sat silently, wide-eyed and bewildered.

Frank's next trick was just plain disturbing. He took a bayonet out of his box, and handed it to an officer in the front of the room for inspection.

"Is there anything different about that bayonet, major?" he asked.

"No, corporal," the major said, handing it back.

254

"Observe, if you will," Frank said. He put his left hand on the piano lid, and then stabbed it with the bayonet in his right. The point hit the piano with a thud. There was a collective gasp as Frank picked up his hand and shoved the bayonet all the way through and out the other side. I saw one Frenchman turn white as a ghost as Frank held up his impaled hand for all to see. There was some guarded clapping when he pulled it out and held his hand up again, showing no wound.

The lieutenant started fidgeting in his chair, clearly uncomfortable and uneasy, worried about what was coming next. My gut started to tighten. The only person who didn't look ill at ease was Frank himself. It was as if he got a thrill from making the men squirm.

"If you liked that last one, you'll love my finale," Frank said manically. "Prepare to be stunned."

He picked up the crate with the holes in the lid and sat it on its side on top of the piano. He opened it and showed that it was empty. He even turned it upside down and shook it. Nothing came out. He put the lid back on, draped a cloth over the crate, and said some kind of incantation as he put on a pair of leather gloves. He pulled the cloth away, opened the lid and reached inside. Neither I nor anyone else in the room could have predicted what would come next.

Out of the crate he pulled an enormous rat: a fat, black, greasy trench dweller that looked like it had been born in hell. It was the most hideous, evil-looking bastard I'd ever seen, and I swear, it must have weighed ten pounds. Of course, it was very agitated, kicking and scratching and squealing, trying to get away. Jaws dropped. Some of the officers even flinched at the sight.

"Oh no, Thomas," the lieutenant said through clenched teeth. "Oh, please, no."

Frank got a twisted smile on his face and laughed, then dropped the beast to the floor. Squealing even louder, it ran among the tables, creating a great deal of panic. Officers were climbing over chairs, tables and each other to get away from the rodent-demon. It was complete pandemonium. The lieutenant jumped to his feet and shook his fist in the air.

"Thomas!" he shouted over the chaos. "What the bloody hell do you think you are doing?"

"Showing these men what trench life is all about, sir!" he shouted back.

Some French officers managed to get the thing cornered in the back of the room. One of them drew a revolver and shot it. He had to shoot it a second time to finish it off. Then with the rat out

255

of the way, all eyes turned to Frank. The only sound was his maniacal laughter.

The lieutenant tore through the crowd and up to the stage. He yanked Frank down to the floor by his collar and cursed him violently. I had never seen him that angry before. Not even close to that angry. He was red in the face, his brow furrowed and his eyes gleaming.

"You stupid ass!" the lieutenant yelled, slapping Frank across the back of the head and knocking him down on all fours. "You just can't do anything without causing trouble, now can you? I should have known better!"

Frank tried to get up, but the lieutenant – completely out of character – kicked him in the ribs as hard as he could. Frank rolled over, gasping for air.

"You should be shot!" the lieutenant screamed. "That's what you deserve!"

The room was silent. The lieutenant spat at Frank.

"In fact, I think I'll take care of you right now!" he shouted, and pulled his Webley out of its holster. He cocked back the hammer and pointed it at Frank's head.

Nobody moved. There was complete silence, everyone being in a state of shock by the surreal events unfolding before their eyes. I ran to the front and put myself between Frank and the lieutenant, hoping that he wouldn't pull the trigger.

"Get out of the way, Gardener," the lieutenant said coldly, "or I'll shoot you, too."

"Please, sir!" I said. "Please don't! I beg of you!"

The lieutenant didn't respond. It was like he was looking right through me. His hand started to shake. I could feel sweat rolling down my temple. It seemed like time was standing still. Seconds passed like hours until one of the British generals intervened.

"Stand down, lieutenant!" he barked. "That's an order!"

The lieutenant hesitated for a moment, swore some more, and finally lowered the pistol. He carefully released the hammer and put it back on his hip. By that time, the military policemen had been called in, and the general gave them the order to arrest Frank and take him away. He got up off the floor and straightened his tunic.

"For heaven's sake, lieutenant," Frank said, "it was just a little joke. That's all."

"A joke?" the lieutenant blurted. "This is your idea of a bloody joke? Have you noticed that no one is laughing? This is, by far, the most idiotic thing you've ever done. Don't expect me to pull your tail out of the fire this time. To hell with you. You are going to rot in the brig."

256

"On what grounds?" Frank argued. "I've committed no crime. What can they charge me with? Kidnapping a rat?"

"How about insubordination, to begin with?" the general interjected. "And I'm sure we can come up with a few other violations."

"What they ought to charge you with is being a bloody moron," the lieutenant said. "You'll be lucky if you live past sunrise tomorrow."

Military policemen escorted Frank out the door. The lieutenant was right; a firing squad didn't seem beyond the realm of possibility. He turned and poked me in the chest with his finger.

"Did you know about this, Gardener?" he asked accusingly. "Did he tell you what he was going to do?"

"No, sir," I said. "I didn't know anything of his plans. He didn't tell me."

"You'd better be telling me the truth, sergeant. Because if you're not, I'm going to find out, and then I'll have you locked up as well. Now go out to the car and wait for me. I've got to straighten out this bleeding mess."

I waited for a long time. It seemed like hours. Most of the guests had left by the time the lieutenant came out and got in the car.

"What's going on, sir?" I asked as the car pulled away. He didn't answer. In fact, he didn't say a single word all the way back to Wipers. He didn't look at me, either. He just stared out the window into the darkness.

We got back sometime after midnight. I sat outside my billet, smoked cigarettes and stared at the half-moon in the sky. I was fairly certain I wasn't going to be able to sleep, at least not for a while. What I really wanted to do was to get drunk, but I didn't feel like walking anywhere.

Then I remembered the pint of bourbon stashed in Frank's haversack. I dug it out and looked at the label in the dim light. I had insisted that we save it until we took Hill 60; I didn't know if Frank would even see that day. The temptation was strong, but nonetheless, my final decision was to save it as planned. If I had to drink it alone atop the ridge, then that was what I'd do. I put it in my pack for safekeeping, in case Frank's gear was confiscated.

I crawled into my bunk around three, but I was wide-awake. I tossed and turned until daybreak. It was like I was too tired to even sleep. About a million things were going through my mind and I couldn't shut it off. My thoughts went to distant places and different times, and even into the future. I was so restless I felt sick. I didn't think that night was ever going to end.

CHAPTER 38

The next morning, I found out that Frank wasn't the only one being punished for the rat debacle. When I saw the lieutenant, he was wearing the rank of *second* lieutenant; he'd been demoted.

"How can they do that, sir?" I asked. "It makes no sense. You didn't foul up."

"Oh, yes I did, Gardener. In a truly monumental way."

"Sir?"

"Brandishing my sidearm against Thomas...that was just wrong. More than that, even. Sheer, mind-boggling stupidity is a more apt description. And now I'm paying the price."

"But you were under duress, sir."

"It still isn't acceptable. I was lucky I didn't lose my commission altogether. Now I'll probably be stuck at second lieutenant for the duration."

"It shouldn't be that way, sir."

"But that's the way it is nonetheless. And I refuse to dwell on the way it should be. We need to move on. I don't want to discuss it any further."

As always, the lieutenant proved to be a man of his word; I never heard him mention it again. If he harbored any kind of a grudge against Frank, he never let it be known to anyone, not even to Frank himself. It spoke volumes about his character, and although I wondered where Frank was or if he might be back, I fought the urge to ask. I just didn't want to draw the lieutenant down into it again. I decided that, for the time being, I'd simply hope for the best, and let it go at that.

Mail arrived around nine that morning, and I got a pound of licorice from Rose and three letters from Rebecca. The doctor had told her that the baby had a strong heartbeat, and that it was going to be a big one. Maybe eight pounds or more, he said. And for some reason unknown to her, she believed it was going to be a boy. She said she'd been thinking about names again, but Peter Richard was her favorite. She didn't say anything about a girl's name. I guess she was that certain we were going to have a son.

Her certainty was contagious, and re-reading the letter, I also became convinced that a son was on the way. I was so incredibly excited – or nervous, rather – and despite the fact that I hadn't slept at all in two days, I penned the longest letter I've ever written. The idea of having a boy captured my imagination and warmed my heart in a way I'd never known. It also gave me a strange, new confidence that somehow I would survive the war and he would not grow up without a father. I went on, page after page, listing everything he and I would do together, like hunting and fishing and hiking and so forth. I realized it had been a very long time since I'd even thought about those simple pleasures and the days I'd cherished with my own father before he died.

As for his name, I made the suggestion that instead of Richard, his middle name should be Francis, because if it hadn't been for Frank, she and I would never have met. Then I realized that she and Elizabeth might not know what had happened to Frank, so I gave a brief, toned-down account of the rat incident and told them truthfully that I did not know much more than that. I promised to write as soon as I got any news.

I would have written more, but I found myself on my last sheet of paper. I reviewed my words, and realized that I needed to tell Rebecca that I'd be equally happy if we had a daughter. It wasn't really an honest statement, but it was a necessary one. Then as I struggled to seal the overstuffed envelope, I said a prayer asking God to make Rebecca's prediction come true. Maybe that was selfish, but that was what I prayed nonetheless.

Just before lunch, the lieutenant told me that we would rotate back into the line that night. He said the brass had decided that in order to maintain a fighting spirit, shorter stays in the fire trenches would continue until we took Messines Ridge.

"We'll be there for four days, or maybe five at the most," the lieutenant said. "With the mining, it's just too stressful to stay any longer. Even so, I've heard tales that the morale up there is napoo. And if it truly is napoo, it will be replaced with dissention. Possibly even mutiny."

"I don't think that's going to happen with our boys, sir," I said. "That's not the British way. We keep our chins up."

"I know, and I try to believe that. But I honestly think it's a bit naïve. Look what happened to the Russians; no one expected them to break down like they did, and now, most of the troops left on the Russian front aren't Russian at all. I've also heard about acts of insubordination here and there among the French and Italians. Isolated acts, yes; but it is happening. And intelligence reports say that there have been incidents on the other side, too. Therefore we have to accept the possibility – however remote – that it could happen with our troops as well."

I had been in high spirits, but the bottom seemed to drop out suddenly. Something about what he said disturbed me, and I couldn't put my finger on what it was. I tried to shake off the feeling, consciously willing myself to believe in British tenacity, but it lingered anyway. After tea, as I prepared the boys to move up, I was overwhelmed with a dark, detached loneliness unlike anything I'd ever experienced. It was absolutely spooky. I could not figure out what was causing it.

We mounted the road to Ypres just before sunset, and about halfway there, I realized what was bothering me: Frank wasn't marching beside me. I'd never been at the front without him, and while he wasn't going to win any awards for soldiering, he was always dependable and resourceful. He was a good sort of fellow to have around in a pinch, and I wondered on whom I could rely now. There was Taylor and Sprouse and a couple others I'd been with for a while, but the truth was that I didn't know most of them from Adam. Not even their names. I didn't see much point in learning them, either. I reasoned they'd be gone soon, just like Jack and Pick and Simon and Hendershot and countless others that I'd met along the way. Their faces were but distant, foggy memories. Sometimes, I couldn't remember what they looked like at all. And now, with Frank gone, I felt more alone than I imagined possible. A cold chill ran down my spine when the shell-blasted tower of the Cloth Hall came into view.

"Are you all right, sergeant?" I heard the lieutenant ask. I hadn't noticed that he'd been walking beside me.

"What's that, sir?" I asked.

"What's the matter? I've been talking to you for the last quarter-mile, and you haven't heard a word I've said. Something on your mind?"

I didn't want to ask about Frank, so I deflected with something else.

"I got a letter from my wife today, sir. I guess I've got some things to think about."

"Is she well?"

"Yes, sir. Getting ready for the baby to come. A big part of me wants to be there instead of here."

"That's perfectly normal, Gardener. We'd all rather be home, and I can't imagine what it would be like with a child on the way. As you know, I'm not married. But I hope to be some day. When this is all over."

"If it's ever over, sir."

"Now sergeant, that is exactly what I've warned you about. You sound like you're giving up. I can't let my right-hand man go about with that 'never-ender' attitude because it will spread down through the ranks like a disease."

"I'm sorry, lieutenant."

"Apology accepted, Gardener. But I need your promise that you will keep your pessimism to yourself. Better yet, just get rid of it altogether. I don't need it, you don't need it, and these boys don't need it."

"I'll do my best, sir. I promise."

"Good. Now let's get these lads to pick up the pace. We've got some ground to cover before it gets dark."

CHAPTER 39

We stopped just west of town and picked up a half-ton load of ammonal for the mines. It was the only way to get it up to the front trenches, and it could only be taken in at night. Even then, it was dangerous work. One lucky shot from a sniper and it would be napoo for you and everyone nearby. And the Germans would know for certain what you were hauling, too.

We made that trip safely, though, and the lieutenant and I went looking for the subaltern of the unit we were relieving. We found him sitting in his dugout, back to the door, drinking tea and writing in a journal; I think every officer at the front kept one. He turned to greet us, and then did a double take. A broad, toothy grin came across his face and he jumped to his feet.

"Birdie!" he exclaimed. "Birdie Rampkin! How the bloody hell are you?"

The lieutenant shook his head and blinked his eyes, momentarily dumbfounded. He stepped forward and extended his hand, smiling like I'd never seen him smile before.

"Trout Lockhart!" the lieutenant said in disbelief. "I'm quite well, I must say. How about you?"

"Not bad, considering the circumstances," he said, still beaming. "Who's this big fellow?"

"I apologize to you both; I've forgotten my manners. This 'big fellow' is Staff Sgt. Gardener. He's been with me since Neuve Chapelle. The very backbone of the platoon. He could shoot a Hun between the eyes from a mile away, and that's no lie. And Gardener, this is Trout...uh, I mean Lt. Kenneth Lockhart. We went to school together."

I saluted him, and he waved his hand at me.

"No need for that," he said, giving me a chuck on the shoulder. "How do you like working with this fellow, Gardener?"

"It suits me fine, lieutenant," I said. "We're all rather fond of him, sir."

"Truly?" he asked with a sly look in his eyes. "I could tell you some stories. Yes, I could..."

"Imagine running into you here," the lieutenant interjected, apparently trying to change the course of the conversation. "This is quite serendipitous. It has been a while since the university, hasn't it?"

"A lifetime. But I'd never forget you. Remember that little affair right before commencement?"

"Oh, I definitely remember it," the lieutenant said, looking uncomfortable. "Like it was yesterday."

262

"We came so close to getting the boot. But did we ever laugh! When they found that horse…"

"Let's just keep that tale between us, old man. I need to maintain the respect of my sergeant here."

"Understood. Understood. You were always the voice of reason. Well, most of the time, anyway. You know, Sgt. Gardener, you're fortunate to have Birdie here leading the way. He was always the best."

"The best at what?" the lieutenant asked wryly.

"At football, at mathematics, at Latin," Lockhart said. "I could go on and on."

"Well, don't," the lieutenant said with a smile. "My head will get so big that I won't be able to get out of the dugout. And besides, you were better than me at the most important endeavor."

"And that would be what?"

"With the ladies, Trout; I know you haven't forgotten about the ladies. You always had a steady girl and two in reserve, while I had to spend most of my nights with books for company."

"Oh, come on now. It wasn't all that bad. Remember that red-haired girl that used to hang off your arm like a lovesick puppy? What was her name?"

"Barbara," the lieutenant said. "Barbara Lynn Mackenzie."

"Yes, Barbara…What do you think ever happened to her?"

"You should know better than I."

"How's that?"

"Well, after she broke it off with me, I heard that she started keeping company with you."

"Oh yes…I'd forgotten about that. Honestly, I had. Sorry, old man."

"That's all right. No hard feelings here."

"Where do you think she is?"

"I have no idea."

"You know, Birdie, maybe after we get back to Blighty you can find out. You may still have a chance with her."

"I probably never cross her mind. Anyway, I'm sure a girl like that would be married by now. And she was Catholic, so she's probably got a half-dozen children. Or more."

"Perhaps. But perhaps she's pining over you, alone and waiting for the day you meet again. You never know."

The teapot sitting on the stove began to whistle. Lockhart invited us to sit at the table with him and have a cup, and we obliged.

"Back to reality, Trout," the lieutenant said. "Is there anything we need to know about? How has it been along this stretch?"

263

"The same as always," he said with a pained look on his face. "Actually, it had been fairly quiet until last night. Then the Bavarians on the ridge rotated out and some Prussians moved in."

"Oh, no. I hate those bastards."

"So do I. They are the absolute worst. They haven't even the slightest modicum of decency. Not one thin shred. This morning, the buggers actually hit us with mortar fire during breakfast. During bloody breakfast! Can you believe that? And the sniping has been non-stop. I lost four men yesterday afternoon."

The lieutenant shook his head and rubbed his eyes.

"Talk about your bad timing," he said, looking up at me. "I can tell right now that this is going to be utterly splendid."

"Just tell your men to keep their heads down," Lockhart said. "You can't take any chances. Don't risk anything to capture a prisoner, either. When in doubt, kill."

Lockhart stood and put a few sticks of wood in the stove, and put another pot of tea on to boil.

"I'm not going to stick around to drink this," he said, "but I thought you might want another cup."

"Thank you, sir," I said. "By the way, how is the tunneling coming along?"

"There isn't much left to be done, from what I understand," he said. "We're just carrying in explosives and laying the charges. And pumping out water, of course. They're using electric contraptions for that now. The good news is that an Australian tunneling company is taking care of the mines along through here, so you probably won't have to go below at all."

"That's fine with me, sir," I said. "I don't think the boys will mind a bit."

"But they want patrols out at least twice each night," he said. "We've been going at around 2200 hours, and then again at 0200. We've also set up some forward listening posts, so you'll need to get some men out there. If they hear anything out of the ordinary, send out another patrol to check it out."

"Three patrols in one night?" the lieutenant asked, furrowing his brow.

"Last night we sent out four," Lockhart replied.

"That's a busy night, sir," I said.

"Yes it is," he said. "Just don't send anyone out too late. They've got to get back in before the sun comes up. You don't want them to get stranded."

"Thanks for the advice, Trout," the lieutenant said. "Gardener, I want you to get a patrol together. Yourself and 13 others. It's after nine now, so be ready to go out in about 30 minutes."

"Who should I take, sir?" I asked. "Most of these boys have never been on a patrol before."

"We've got a few that have been around, sergeant," he said. "How about Valentine? He's back from the hospital. And there's Sprouse and Taylor."

"That's only four of us…"

"And the green ones have to learn sometime. We simply must make due with what we've got. Enlist whomever else you think can handle the job. I trust your judgment."

"Tell them to shoot anything that doesn't identify itself," Lockhart warned. "You can ask questions later."

Lockhart swallowed the last of his tea and excused himself. He left to round up his men, and the lieutenant and I went out to make sure our boys were situated for the night. As we walked along the line, my curiosity over the lieutenant's nickname became overwhelming. I had to know.

"'Birdie,' sir?" I asked. "How did you get that name?"

"All of us in the old gang had animal nicknames," he said.

"Do you mind if I ask how you got that particular one, sir?"

"I don't mind if you ask, but I'm not going to tell you."

"I pledge to keep it between us. No one else will know."

"And neither will you. I hated that name, and if I tell you the origin, you'll all be calling me that behind my back."

That was hard to argue with, but I decided to keep nudging a little bit.

"Didn't you tell your friends that you didn't like it?"

"You don't exactly get to pick your own nickname, Gardener. You get whatever is given to you. I got 'Birdie,' whether I liked it or not."

I could tell he was getting rather irritated, so I backed away. I figured that in time, I'd figure it out anyway.

"I won't ask about it again, sir," I said. "But what about Lt. Lockhart? Why did you call him 'Trout'?"

"Because, Gardener, he drank like a damn fish. Any more infernal questions? While you're still a sergeant?"

"No, sir."

"Good."

In silence we walked down the line. I heard a rifle crack in the distance, and around the next traverse we discovered our first casualty: a lad shot through the face, his head in a puddle of blood and a burning cigarette still pasted to his lips. He was stone cold dead. The men were just standing there staring at him.

"He lit a cigarette and took a drag, sir, and the next thing we knew, he fell over backward," one of them said. "We didn't even hear the shot."

"And what does that tell you?" the lieutenant asked.

"What do you mean, sir?"

"What I mean is that you can see a glowing fag from nearly a mile away. Let this be a lesson. Now what is this boy's name?"

"Blankenship, I believe, sir."

"Damn it all. A little more experience and he might have made it."

He kneeled down, pulled off the boy's identity disc, and put it in his pocket.

"Sergeant, get the body out of here."

"Yes, sir," I said.

I pointed at two sturdy fellows in the group.

"You and you...take a stretcher and carry him to the aid station. They can get him buried tomorrow. And don't waste any time getting back."

I looked up at the night sky. There was just a tiny sliver of a moon, not really enough to see by. For patrolling, that was both a blessing and a curse; the darkness provided fair cover, but it could leave you terribly disoriented. And there are few things worse than stumbling along in No Man's Land, trying to find your way home, and then being uncertain whether the wire you've found is yours or theirs. We'd have to stick close together.

I gathered up Valentine, Sprouse and Taylor, and they helped me select ten other men for the mission. Basically, we picked the ones that didn't look terrified. Actually, they all looked terrified, just some less so than others. We got ten clips and two bombs each and assembled at the end of a sap out beyond the wire. Before we began our sweep, I gave them some instructions.

"Now I don't want to have to go looking for any stragglers, so stay in close order," I said. "If you see me or one of these old-timers hit the ground, then you hit the ground. If they light us up with star shells, don't move until they stop. Don't talk unless you have to, because a voice carries farther than you think. And if they hear us, we'll get peppered with machine-gun fire. Above all, don't be a bloody hero if we run into a German patrol. Jump into the nearest crater and fight from there. Stay down until I tell you otherwise. You're not going to win the war by getting clicked. Questions?"

The old boys nodded. The rest just stared blankly.

"Splendid," I said. "I'll lead the way. Valentine and Taylor, take the rear. Let's get this party going."

We came out of the sap and crawled over the parapet. We were getting lined up when one of the new lads flicked on a torch. Horrified, I knocked it out of his hand and crushed the bulb with my boot heel. I smacked the boy in the side of the head a little harder than I'd intended, knocking his helmet off.

"You simple-minded twit," I said. "You're going to get us all killed."

"But..."

I raised my hand to strike him again, but Sprouse grabbed me by the arm and stopped me.

"He's new, sergeant," Sprouse whispered. "He just didn't know."

"Sorry, sir," the boy said, bending over to pick up his helmet.

Sprouse let go and patted my shoulder. I took a deep breath and rubbed my eyes.

"'Sorry' isn't going to do us any good now," I said. "And don't address me as 'sir,' either. Address me as 'sergeant.' What's your name?"

"Henry Wells."

"Where are you from?"

"Castleton."

"Did they have to hire a new village idiot in your absence, Wells?"

He didn't respond. I turned to the rest of the group.

"I had hoped we'd get through this without trouble, but thanks to Wells, every Prussian bastard up on that ridge spotted us. They're going to come out looking for us because of him. They're probably on their way now, so be prepared. And if any more of you want to do something insane, ask one of us veterans first. Understand?"

No one said anything.

"Wells, because of your demonstrated military genius, I think I'm going to let you take the lead this time."

"But sergeant..."

"I don't want to hear it. Think of it as a learning opportunity. Move out."

"But..."

"Now!"

Off we went into the night. While Wells was in front, I didn't let him get more than six feet away. For all I knew, he was both stupid *and* blind. We made our way along the wire very slowly, stopping several times to listen to suspicious sounds. After about a half-mile, we stopped, turned and headed back home. I was truly surprised that we hadn't yet run into any Huns. Just maybe my prediction had been wrong.

But it wasn't. Somehow we had drifted out into the middle of No Man's Land, and while it would be convenient to blame Wells, I must admit that I myself did not notice our erroneous course.

267

Without warning, we stumbled upon an enemy patrol that, most likely, had also become lost in the night. There was some yelling on both sides and the shooting started. I saw two of my boys fall almost immediately.

"Get down!" I yelled. "Get down now!"

We dove into the mud. Bullets were flying in both directions, but I couldn't tell how many we were up against. Valentine was cursing amid the chaos and someone was tugging on my arm.

"Should we fall back, sergeant?" the boy asked.

"To where?" I shot back.

The situation was deteriorating rapidly. I could see enough muzzle flashes ahead of us to draw the conclusion that we were outnumbered, more so with each passing second. Then I saw more on our left flank, and a couple of bombs came hurtling through the darkness. We were clearly on the losing end of the deal, and while I knew we had to do something, I didn't know precisely what. I rolled over on my back and looked both ways. I could barely see anything. But then a star shell came up to my left; I assumed it was German, and reasoned that if we were going to head to a more defensible position, it would have to be to the right. Apparently, Valentine had the same epiphany. He was calling to me.

"Sgt. Gardener!" he shouted. "Over here! Get them in over here!"

I looked in the direction of his voice and by the light of another star shell I could see what looked like either the lip of a crater or a parapet in front of an old trench. It was about 20 yards away. Whatever the case, it had to be better than where we were.

"Back to the right!" I called. "Crawl if you have to!"

I slithered through the mud on my belly, and went over the edge with the hopes of finding a nice, deep trench in which to hide. It turned out to be more of a ditch, probably three feet deep at the most, including the lip. And naturally, the bottom was thick, gluey mud. I figured the French probably dug it under fire when they got pushed off the ridges in 1914. But it was our defense now, and we had to make the best of it.

Wells, Taylor and Valentine were there already. We crouched on our knees with our rifles aimed forward over the lip, but we couldn't see much of anything, aside from muzzle flashes here and there. Valentine pulled off a shot into the darkness. Wells followed with another.

"Boys," I said, "I don't know what you are shooting at, but remember that some of our mates might be out in front of us. Hold your fire until we know otherwise."

The next couple of minutes passed like centuries. I really had no idea what was going on. Amid the sporadic rifle fire, Sprouse and three more boys made it to our hole. After a few more minutes, I conceded that probably no more would join us. That meant I'd lost six men. Six men! I was angry, and I felt like ranting at Wells, but I decided that was not what the lieutenant would do. It would have been a waste of time anyway, and in the present situation, I didn't have that luxury.

A few bombs came our way, but whoever threw them wasn't very good. We obliged by throwing a few back at them, even though we didn't know where they were hiding exactly. A few more shots were fired, and then the night became silent. By some miracle, we'd held them off.

"Is everyone all right?" I asked.

"This lad here took one in his flipper," Taylor said. "Looks like it hit the bone."

"Lovely," I said, crawling over to see for myself. It was a very nasty wound, and his arm was hanging at a strange angle. His eyes were the size of saucers, and a tear ran down his cheek. Yet he didn't make a sound.

"What's your name, old boy?" I asked.

"Hopkins," he said through clenched teeth. "Lawrence Hopkins."

"Where are you from, Hopkins?"

"Nottingham."

"Well, Hopkins, you're going to go back there soon. That's a Blighty wound if I ever saw one. Don't you think so, Taylor?"

"Oh, absolutely, sergeant. Definitely a Blighty one, that. Home in no time at all."

I dug through my haversack looking for cotton gauze. I pressed the wound with the pad. He groaned just a bit.

"We've got to get that bleeding stopped," I said. "And we've got to tie that arm in place. Anyone got a handkerchief?"

One of the other boys handed me a rag that was only a bit dirty.

"Thanks," I said. "What's your name?"

"Donaldson. From Blackpool."

"Well, Donaldson from Blackpool, keep pressure on the wound here while I rig up a sling."

Hopkins didn't flinch a bit while I worked on him. I was impressed.

"Are all Nottingham boys as tough as you are, Hopkins?" I asked.

"Most…are…tougher," he said, clenching his teeth.

"Then give me a whole platoon of them. We'd win the war in a week. Two weeks at the most."

269

He grinned slightly, but I could see he was having trouble with the pain. I was worried that he might go into shock before we made it home. I turned to Donaldson and whispered in his ear.

"I want you to keep an eye on Hopkins," I said. "He's a bit shocky. Try to keep him alert; keep him talking if possible. Can you do that?"

"Absolutely, sergeant. I'll take care of him."

"Is anyone else hurt?" I asked.

"I don't think so," Valentine said.

"I guess that's one piece of good luck," I said. "Let's try to keep it that way."

I noticed then that the battlefield had fallen silent, aside from an occasional voice in the darkness. They were still shooting star shells every few minutes, but I thought maybe, somehow, we'd be able to get out of the fix we were in.

"What do you think, Valentine?" I asked. "Have they given up on us?"

"I don't know, sergeant," he said. "They wouldn't be shooting those flares if they weren't watching something. And that something is probably this ditch. Maybe we'd better wait them out a bit more."

"How long do we have until sunrise?"

"Four, or maybe five hours at the most, I'd say."

"Damn it. We've got to move soon or we'll be stuck here. And that wouldn't be smart."

"We need to get a good look around. I don't know about you, but I still can't figure out exactly where we are. I don't even know how far we are from our own line."

"Do you want to be the one to do the looking?"

"I suppose I'll have to be. These boys…even if they did look, they wouldn't know."

He inched up to look over the lip.

"I can't see anything," he said.

"I hate to say this, Valentine, but you'll probably have to wait for the next star shell."

"Oh, wonderful. Just wonderful. I should have kept my bloody suggestion to myself…"

A shell popped in the sky above and started floating down. Valentine slowly raised his head above the lip again. Not a half-second passed when a rifle cracked. I heard a loud "ping" and Valentine fell backward, landing in the mud on his butt; I won't repeat what he said. He was all right, but there was a big dent in the front of his helmet.

"I guess that answers our question," I said. "They're just going to wait us out, the bloody Prussian buggers that they are."

"Prussians?" Sprouse asked. "Oh, holy mother of…we're doomed."

"The next time, someone else gets to look," Valentine said. "I've done my bit tonight."

My next idea was to send Sprouse to our left to see where our ditch led, or if it got deeper or wider down that way. He was back in a few minutes.

"Find anything?" I asked, even though I knew his answer.

"This seems to be the deep and wide part, sergeant. Doesn't go anywhere, I'm afraid. It stops entirely about 20 yards from here. Maybe I should try the other way."

"That's heading in the wrong direction."

"But maybe it's better than this. I'll be back."

He was back even sooner than the first time. He just shook his head in disgust. I didn't even ask for details. I pulled a cigarette out of my breast pocket and lit it.

"Isn't that dangerous, sergeant?" Wells asked.

"No more so than our situation already is," I said. "You want one?"

"No thank you, sergeant. I don't smoke."

"You will before the night's over," Taylor said.

Everyone else lit up, being careful to stay hidden behind the lip. Hopkins just stared at the sky.

"Hopkins," Donaldson said, "how about a fag?"

"I…don't want to smoke…your cigarettes," he said.

"You'll feel better."

"My right pocket…I can't…reach it."

Donaldson unbuttoned Hopkins' pocket and pulled out a little pouch.

"What's that?" Donaldson asked.

"Tobacco…and papers. Like to…roll my own."

"How are you going to do that? Your right hand is out of commission."

"I'm not…right-handed."

"All right. But if you can't, you'll be welcome to mine or anyone else's."

"I'll be fine…"

Hopkins opened a paper on his chest, and then put a few pinches of tobacco in the middle. He rubbed it back and forth, packing the tobacco together, and proceeded to roll a perfect cigarette with just his left hand.

"That has to be the most amazing demonstration of dexterity that I've ever seen," I said. "How'd you get so agile?"

"I'm a…watchmaker," he said, licking the edge of the paper. "Comes in handy."

271

"I bet it does," Donaldson said.

About an hour passed, but the star shells were still falling at regular intervals. Sprouse volunteered to take a peek, but it resulted in a shower of machine gun bullets. They must have dumped a thousand rounds on us before they stopped, and we still didn't know our position. It looked like we were going to be there for a while yet.

"Let's examine the situation," I said. "How much ammo do we have?"

The total inventory came up to 23 clips, or about three per man. That was bad, but I told myself it could be worse.

"What about bombs? How many?"

Among the eight of us, we only came up with 11. That was bad, too. There was even less in the way of medical supplies, and no one had an entrenching tool. You just don't think to take much like that on a patrol. I tried to inject a bit of humor to lighten the situation.

"Now let's get to the important stuff," I said. "What's our situation with cigarettes? We absolutely can't run out of those. That would really ruin the party."

Valentine laughed. At least he thought I was funny.

"We'll be fine as long as Hopkins doesn't get shot in the left arm," he said. With that one, most of the men chuckled. He even got Hopkins himself to crack a smile.

But there was one boy, down at the end of the ditch past where Hopkins reclined, who did not laugh. In fact, he hadn't said anything other than giving a count of his clips and bombs. Now he sat with an unchanging blank stare, his fingers tightly wrapped around his rifle. The look was familiar; it reminded me of Pick when we came under fire the first time. It made me uneasy. I smoked my cigarette down to a tiny butt, and then flicked it over the top. I leaned over to Donaldson, and whispering in his ear, asked him if he knew who the boy was.

"I think his name is Hastings," he said. "Always stays to himself. Doesn't talk much, even under normal circumstances."

"How are his nerves?"

"Don't know, sergeant. As good as anyone else's, I guess. Why?"

"When you've been up here as long as I have, you start to spot things that other people miss. When they're isolated like that...it's usually not good."

"Do you think he'll crack?"

"I hope I'm wrong, but I'm kind of leaning in that direction."

"What should we do?"

"The best thing would be to get the hell out of here as soon as possible, but I don't know if that's going to happen. The next best thing would be to get him out of his thoughts a bit. How's Hopkins doing?"

"I think I've got the bleeding stopped."

"Good. But find a way to get Hastings to help take care of him. And give him some reassurance."

"What should I say?"

"Tell him I'm working on a way out of here as we speak. It's a lie, but I think it might be a helpful one."

About that time, I noticed that the Germans had finally stopped shooting star shells. Exactly how long it had been since the last one, I didn't know, but it made me very uneasy. I assumed the worst.

"You know," I said to Sprouse, "they might be sending out a patrol to get us."

"How do you figure that?" he asked.

"No more star shells. They need the cover of darkness. They could be on their way right now."

"But if we can't see them, what are we supposed to do?"

"Just pass the word down to get into firing positions. We'll do what we can."

It must have been a moment of divine inspiration; it's the only way I can explain it. Just a few seconds later, I heard rustling wire out front and other little noises that sounded like an approaching patrol. They *were* coming for us.

Now I don't know how or why, but somewhere in the line to our rear, someone detected this movement also. A volley of star shells came up from behind us and lit up the battlefield like high noon. And right out in front of us – not 50 yards away -- was the approaching patrol, plain as day.

"Open fire!" I shouted. "Make it count!"

We caught them by surprise; that was certain. And as each of us understood the gravity of the situation, they didn't even have time to hit the ground. We absolutely cut them to shreds. In a last act of defiance, one of them tried to throw a bomb, but in an impressive display of marksmanship, Wells shot him in mid-recoil. The bomb fell where he fell, and exploded among the remaining Huns. That was pretty much the end of the assault. It had lasted but seconds, and I don't think any of them lived to retreat. I was proud of all of the boys with me, but Wells in particular. And while the expression on his face did not change, Hastings didn't crack.

The star shells kept coming up behind us for another hour, and we didn't see any more approaching Germans. I also got a good

273

idea of where we were in relation to our own lines. It was about 80 yards to the wire, and if we made it that far, we'd have to cross another 30 or 40 yards of serious entanglements. And, I realized that if we tried to make a run for it despite those odds, chances were that we would be perceived as an enemy trench-raiding party and shot by our own troops. With dawn closing in, there just didn't seem to be any way out.

"I wish I knew the time," I said to Sprouse. "We've got to get something going before the sun comes up."

"Does anyone happen to have a watch?" Sprouse asked.

"I do," Hastings said, looking at his wrist. "It's about 0330."

Sprouse and I looked each other with raised brows. We couldn't believe he'd spoken.

"Where'd you get that?" Sprouse asked.

"My brother was a lieutenant. I got it when he was killed last year."

"Where?" I asked.

"At the Somme, the first day. With his entire platoon. Not one made it past the wire."

"How many boys in the family?" I asked.

"Just us two."

"Sisters?"

He shook his head. I wasn't sure what to say given the situation, but I awkwardly tried to comfort him.

"Hastings, I'm going to make you a promise: your parents won't lose their only son tonight. I've been in some tight spots up here, but you can bank on my word that I'm going to get you back alive. Even if I have to die doing it."

"That goes for me, too," Sprouse said. "And remember, we are your brothers now. We're all going to take care of you."

The star shells from our trenches stopped, and the only light was the moon above. Sprouse suggested that we make a break for it, but I insisted we wait a bit to see what the Germans were going to do. Sure enough, they started with the star shells again just a few minutes later. So there we were, still stuck, and I felt like an idiot for not taking Sprouse's advice. Then Donaldson came crawling over through the mud.

"Sergeant," he said, "I don't know how much longer Hopkins is going to hang on. He's lost a lot of blood and his pain is getting worse. Now he's slipping in and out of consciousness. I don't think I can do anything more for him."

"Just keep an eye on him for the time being," I said. "We'll get moving as soon as we can."

I rubbed my eyes and lit another cigarette. Some Hun bugger must have seen it, because they showered us with the machine gun again. The only thing I could think at that point was that they'd probably hit us with mortar fire next. I was unbelievably frustrated, as I'm sure the others were also. I couldn't come up with a reasonable solution to the predicament, but I hoped maybe someone else could. I called Taylor and Valentine to come over to where Sprouse and I were crouched.

"Lads," I said, "the sun will be up in about two hours. That means we have about an hour before we have to start on our way. We've got to come up with a strategy. And rapidly. Any suggestions?"

"Not unless they quit lighting the place up," Valentine said, "and I seriously doubt that's going to happen."

"Maybe we ought to just run for it, lit up or not," Taylor said. "Every man for himself."

"Come on, now," I said, shaking my head. "That's not a plan; that's a last resort."

"And that's what we're down to here, sergeant," Sprouse said. "If we run, we've at least got a chance. Some of us just might make it."

"And what about Hopkins?" Valentine asked. "Someone would have to drag him along. We can't just leave him here."

"Damn it, Valentine," Taylor snapped. "Why don't you come up with a better idea? And remember, the sun's coming up, plan or no plan. So think fast."

"Maybe we could get a signal to our boys," Valentine said. "Let them know we're here and that we need to get out."

"All right, Valentine," I said, "you work on that. But we need a backup plan in case it doesn't succeed. Any more thoughts?"

"I'm still for running," Sprouse said.

"So noted," I said. "And while I don't agree with you, we'll do it your way if Valentine doesn't get the message out. In the mean time, I'm going to give it some more thought. But in any case, be ready to go in no more than an hour. God help us all."

Valentine went about looking for something with which to signal. I closed my eyes and put my head in my hands. It seemed like it had been a long time since I had last prayed, but I decided it was appropriate for the situation. And I was certain it couldn't hurt.

"Dear God," I said, "it's me, Richard. I know I haven't done much to deserve your favor lately, and I know that I have no right to ask for it. But you can see the spot we're in here tonight, and you are the only one that can help us. If I die out here, maybe it's not such a big loss. These other boys are good lads, though, and they should be spared. And I've promised Hastings that he'd get home. Show me the way, and I'll follow. Whatever you can do, I am grateful for. Please keep us safe. Amen."

Apparently, I wasn't the only one thinking along spiritual lines. There in the mud, softly and slowly, Hastings began singing a hymn. I remember it word for word, even after all of these years:

> *"The strife is o'er, the battle done; the victory of life is won; the song of triumph has begun. Alleluia...*
> *The powers of death have done their worst; but Christ their legions hath dispersed;*
> *Let shouts of holy joy out burst. Alleluia..."*

The sound of his voice and the words he sang gave me cold chills. I didn't know about anyone else there, but it gave me a strange sense of security.

"Does anyone else know one?" I asked, and after a few moments of silence, Wells obliged, singing:

> *"Jesus, Savior, pilot me, over life's tempestuous sea; unknown waves before me roll, hiding rock and treacherous shoal. Chart and compass came from thee; Jesus, Savior, pilot me..."*

When Wells finished, Donaldson chimed in:

> *"Out of the depths I cry to you; now hear me calling. Incline your ear to my distress in spite of my rebelling. Do not regard my sinful deeds. Send me the grace my spirit needs; without it I am nothing..."*

By that time, I actually had tears running down my face. I didn't want the others to see, so I rubbed them off and looked up at the sky. I watched a star shell burst in front of us, but suddenly I noticed something wonderfully odd: the light of the shell was obscured by fog. And it wasn't just wispy little bits of fog either; this was high-grade London-type fog. It was getting thicker by the minute, too. This was our way out, and it was God-given. I wasn't going to wait to see if it dispersed, either.

"The Lord must have been listening," I whispered. "Now's the time. Let's get out of here."

"Maybe we should have thought of singing a few hours ago," Valentine said.

We actually laughed a little as we stood up, stretching our cramped frames.

276

"Donaldson, you and Hastings keep Hopkins on his feet," I said. "Move quietly and quickly, and don't lose sight of the man in front of you. We don't want to get separated in this stuff. Let's go."

"Do you want me to take the lead again, sergeant?" Wells asked.

"Let's you and I together take the lead," I said. "I could use another set of eyes."

We trudged off in the direction of home. It was still hard to tell exactly where we were, or how far we had to go. I reasoned, however, that we would spot some landmark that would indicate our position, and by that landmark we would know where to find our break in the wire.

And we did, just as the sun was coming up behind the fog. There, through the gray mist, I saw the burnt-out wreckage of the airplane that had crashed months before. I immediately knew exactly where to go. I approached our wire with caution, until we were challenged by one of our boys on watch. I identified myself and gave a password, and he directed us through a sap that ran below the belt of wire.

"I can't believe we made it back," Taylor said.

"Only by God's grace," I replied.

"I wonder if we're in time for breakfast," Valentine said. "I really need a cup of tea. And I'd kill for a tot of rum."

"I'll make sure we all get extras of both," I said. "I need to go find the lieutenant to let him know we're not missing anymore. In the mean time, make sure Hopkins gets to the aid station. The rest of you fellows need to find somewhere to rest."

Once we were in, I laid down my rifle and dumped my haversack on the fire step. It was daylight by then. I fished around in my pocket and found one last cigarette. I struck a match and took a long, long drag, then blew a perfect smoke ring, just like Frank had tried to teach me to do for two years. I grinned and laughed to myself, shaking my head.

"I wish he'd been here to see that," I said as I walked down the trench to the lieutenant's dugout. I pushed aside the canvas covering the door and stepped inside. He got a startled look, then smiled.

"Where the hell have you been, Gardener?" he asked. "That must have been one rotten patrol."

"Indeed, it was, sir," I said. "Got into a bit of a tangle. Lost six men, and one wounded, but I think he'll make it."

"Sounds like a long night."

"The longest, sir."

"Well, fill me in, sergeant. I'll need to make a report."

277

We sat and drank tea while I told him the story. He seemed riveted by my account, and he asked a lot of detailed questions.

"How did you finally manage to break away?" he asked.

I hesitated to get into it, but I decided to tell him about the prayer and the singing and the subsequent arrival of the fog. It was nothing short of miraculous, I said. He smiled and nodded, and scribbled out some notes on a sheet of paper.

Now I'm not sure that he believed my theory of divine intervention; I'm fairly certain that he didn't include it in his report. He may have thought I was just plain loony, and maybe I was. But whatever the case, he told me that he was very glad to see me back.

And I was glad to *be* back. Imagine that.

CHAPTER 40

Believe it or not, the rest of that turn in the front line actually went much better than could be expected. We had no more casualties before rotating out, and that was nothing short of miraculous; in the salient as a whole, nothing had changed and thousands of our boys were dying each day. While I personally held the belief that God was watching over our platoon for some unknown reason, the lieutenant theorized that the Prussians on the ridge must have been replaced with Huns of a more hospitable variety. Either way, it worked out well for us.

I had to take out a few more patrols, but they were all quiet. Valentine and Sprouse had been promoted to corporal upon my recommendation, and were now sharing the burden of leading them. Either they were very good leaders or the enemy was doing a good job of hiding. They had no encounters, and had very little to report in general.

I had also recommended that Taylor and Donaldson be made lance corporals; the lieutenant agreed with me on Taylor, but he didn't think Donaldson had enough experience yet. I went down to his dugout after tea to argue Donaldson's case a bit. He looked up from his paperwork and told me to come in.

"What's on your mind, sergeant?" he asked.

"Donaldson, sir," I said. "With all due respect, you should have seen him out there with me a few nights ago. The lad's a natural leader. All of the boys look up to him."

"Yes, but this is his first front-line tour," the lieutenant said. "He just isn't ready. Let him log a little more time, and then I'll reconsider."

"You know, sir, Frank and I were promoted right after our first round at Neuve Chapelle…"

"And remember how many we'd lost? No disrespect intended to you either, Gardener, but I needed live bodies. With you, it worked out well; you are, in every way, the best man I've had since Hendershot. Maybe even better than Hendershot. But look at Thomas. That didn't work out so well. Not well at all."

He told me I was dismissed and went back to writing. But I glimpsed an opportunity, and after a few seconds of uncertain hesitation in the doorway, I turned and asked him about Frank.

"Speaking of Corporal Thomas, sir," I said nervously, "do you know when he's due back?"

He looked up with raised eyebrows and put down his pen.

"I was wondering when you'd get around to that," he said. "I honestly don't know if he is going to be back at all. I don't think the brass has decided exactly what to do with him. But I do know that he's not a corporal anymore, and I do know that he's in the brig down around Etaples. But that's about it. They just aren't telling me much, probably because they're still a bit peeved with me."

"I'm sorry I brought it up, sir."

"And I'm sorry I can't tell you more. I know you were close, and I'll let you know as soon as I hear something definitive. Anything else?"

"No, sir."

"Then I'll see you at evening stand-to. Get some rest."

We moved back to the reserve lines the next night, occupying a stretch next to Lt. Lockhart's platoon. "Birdie" and "Trout" spent most of their meals together, and I could hear them in the lieutenant's dugout, laughing late into the night. I was happy the lieutenant had someone to keep him company, but it made me miss my friends even more. Not just Frank, but Pick and Simon and the others. I tried to bond a bit more with Valentine and Sprouse; they were good fellows, but it just wasn't the same. I got the distinct feeling it never would be.

On the other hand, some things seemed constant; it was my third spring at the front, and I knew that spring always brought the three things I hated the most: rain, mud and new offensives. The rain started coming about every day at the end of March, and soon the trenches were inundated. We baled and baled until we were half-silly, but it didn't make any difference. Pretty soon, we were up to our knees in muck and misery. So that meant it was time for someone to attack someone else. I did not know who would fire that first shell, or where or when, but it was coming any day, and the thought itself turned my stomach.

The season's bloodshed finally began the first week of April. I was retiring at about midnight one evening when I heard the unmistakable thump of distant artillery. It was maybe 20 or 30 miles down the line at my best estimation. It caught my attention because it wasn't the routine, general-harassment type shelling that you always heard at night; it sounded like an all-out bombardment, the intensity building steadily. I was immediately struck with fear, imagining that we would have to march all night to face a German onslaught at dawn. I jumped out of my bunk and went to the lieutenant's dugout to see if he was abreast of the situation, and whether I should get the men ready to move out.

There was a light coming from within his dugout. I knocked on the doorpost and pushed back the canvas. The lieutenant was talking on the buzzer, and he motioned for me to come inside.

Trout was there, seated across the table from the lieutenant, drinking a cup of coffee. He offered me a cup, but I declined.

"Frankly, sir, the only thing I want right now is to find out what the hell is going on," I said.

"I appreciate your honesty, sergeant, but we don't know much, either," Trout replied. "But Birdie's getting that sorted out right now."

"Whom did you say?" the lieutenant asked the person on the other end of the line. "Where? I see. And when...yes. What...good. I understand. Yes. Thank you for the information. We'll sit tight."

He hung up the telephone and ran his fingers back through his hair. He gave me a tired look through squinted eyes.

"I see you've heard it, too," he said.

"Is Fritz on the move, sir?" I asked. "Is that his artillery?"

"No, it's not. Those are our guns."

"Well, that's a bit of a relief," Trout said. "I was thinking we'd have to head down there tonight if the Huns were throwing a party."

"I was thinking the same thing," I said. "It is that time of year, after all."

"So Birdie," Trout asked, "if those *are* our guns, what exactly are *we* up to?"

"I'm supposed to keep this quiet," he said in a low voice, "but I don't think it will be a secret for much longer: that is, our boys and the Canadians are going to have a go at it down around Arras. The objective is to push the Germans back beyond Douai and Cambrai."

My gut tightened again, but Trout looked horrified.

"Oh, my," he said, slumping in his chair. "I've been down there. They'll have to take Vimy Ridge first."

"That's exactly what they've planned to do," the lieutenant said.

"It's a terrible stretch of line."

"So I've heard."

"It's probably the strongest redoubt in France."

"I've heard that, too."

"What about the military geniuses that came up with this plan? Do you think they've heard?"

"I should suppose they have."

"And they're going to do it anyway? That's just brilliant! Bloody brilliant! So who are the unfortunate bastards that got stuck with this?"

281

"We're driving out from Arras, but the ridge itself has been left up to the Canadians. They're tough soldiers, and I think their chances are fairly good."

"I'll concede that the Canadians are tough, and I'll also concede that if anyone can take Vimy, they can. But don't be surprised if they cannot. And either way, they are going to lose a lot of men. In fact, don't be surprised if it turns into the Somme all over again."

"Oh, come on now, Trout. Don't you think we've learned at least a few things in the last year?"

"Soldiers like you and I? Or Gardener here? Yes, we have learned a lot. But those rear-echelon types seem to learn much more slowly, if at all."

The argument quickly wore itself out, with neither man persuaded to change his opinion. I agreed with Trout, but I wasn't about to say anything pessimistic in front of the lieutenant. We sat in silence for a few minutes and listened to the steady roar of the guns in the night. I decided to excuse myself and went back to my bunk.

I found everyone in the dugout asleep, so I didn't have to explain anything to anyone. I said a quick prayer before retiring, thanking God that we weren't the ones attacking this time. I pulled the blanket up and closed my eyes, and listened to the guns until I fell asleep.

CHAPTER 41

When I awoke in the morning, the bombardment down the line was still going as strong as it had been the night before. From miles away, I could detect the smell of gun cotton and gas in the air, and everyone – including the new boys – had figured out something was afoot. I told Valentine and Sprouse only that we were the ones doing the shelling, and kept quiet on the more sensitive details. By the end of the day, there were all kinds of theories floating about, but I didn't correct or confirm any of them.

We left the front at sundown and took the Menin Road back to Ypres. While I didn't think it possible, the town looked even worse than it had just days before. The Germans, it would seem, weren't satisfied with reducing Ypres to piles of rubble; their thorough nature dictated that they proceed to pulverize the piles into dust. The Cloth Hall had definitely seen its better days. The tower was propped up with timbers, and there were only partial walls left. The rest of the town didn't look much better.

Exhausted, I wasted no time getting into bed. Lying on my back in the dark, staring up at nothing, I listened to the distant cannonade; it reminded me of far-away thunder on a warm summer's night. It was almost comforting in a strange sort of way, and I fell asleep quickly.

I was having a shirt hunt after breakfast the next morning when the lieutenant came walking through the door of our billet with a folded newspaper under his arm. He greeted me with a broad smile.

"Sergeant Gardener," he said, "you're just the fellow I was looking for. A lot has happened while we were up on the line."

"Good or bad, sir?" I asked.

"Good," he said, handing me the paper. "Take a look."

I unfolded it and looked at the front page. The headline said the Americans had decided to join in the fight against Germany at last. A formal declaration of war had been made. I quickly scanned the rest of the story, which took up most of the page.

"So what do you think, sergeant?" he asked. "It sounds pretty good to me. Maybe we'll win this thing after all."

I wasn't quite ready to abandon the pessimism he hated so much, so I tried to subtly wrap it in more agreeable terms.

"Maybe we will win with the Americans on our side, sir," I said, "but it might be just a bit too soon to tell."

"Why do you say that? I'd say it's reasonably certain now."

He was digging for my truthful opinion. I proceeded cautiously.

283

"Well, according to this story, they only have about five divisions in uniform," I said. "That's about 100,000 men, sir. We lost half that many on the first day of the Somme. All of these Yanks could be dead in a week."

I think that made him mad. It showed in his face and in his tone of voice.

"They have millions more who could serve, Gardener," he said sarcastically. "And again I must remind you that we've learned a lot since the Somme."

"Yes, sir, but the Americans haven't. They don't know anything about fighting."

"They've beaten us a couple of times, sergeant. And they had some brilliant generals in their civil war as well."

"Pardon me for saying so, sir, but that was a long time ago."

"But it hasn't even been 20 years since they defeated Spain. They did that in a couple of months."

"That was Spain, sir, not Germany. We've been trading blows with the Huns for more than two years now, and I don't see how America could come in fresh and do something we haven't been able to do after all this time. We haven't been able to do it, and neither has France. Or Russia."

"But their sheer number added to our side tips the scales. And if they are anything like their neighbors to the north, they are vicious fighters. I'd go into battle with confidence if they were on my flanks."

"But how long will it be before that can actually happen, sir? How long is it going to take them to raise a respectable fighting force? How long will it be before they can actually attack? Or even hold the line? Six months from now, maybe? I bet it will take longer than that. Probably a lot longer. And we have to keep holding on until then. The Germans could have the whole thing wrapped up by that point."

"I don't think so, Gardener. Maybe I'm naïve, but I have a good hunch that this is the beginning of the end for the Boche."

"I hope you're right, sir. And I hope it comes sooner rather than later."

On my way to breakfast, listening to the guns firing down at Arras, I thought to myself that no matter how soon the Americans arrived, or how many there would be, it would not make a bit of difference to the thousands of men getting ready to charge up Vimy Ridge. It would not matter because they were going to die anyway.

The guns continued firing through that night, and through the next two days. Then on the third morning, just before dawn, I heard them stop abruptly, only to start firing again about two

284

minutes later. I knew what was going on; the barrage had shifted to deeper targets to allow the infantry to advance. The time had come. Over the top.

"God be with them," I said as I pulled on my trousers. "Keep them safe."

As the morning passed, I became more anxious, and I was eager to hear how the attack was progressing. I hoped for the best, but expected the worst. When I saw the lieutenant later, I asked him if he knew anything yet.

"We probably won't get a report for the first 48 hours," he said. "By then, hopefully, we'll have an indication as to whether they were able to break through the lines. I promise you that I'll pass along any confirmed reports that I receive. In the mean time, try to relax."

"That's a bit difficult, sir," I said. "I'm worried about this one. Lt. Lockhart…"

He smirked and poked me in the chest.

"Lockhart is a cynic, Gardener! A true 'never-ender.' That's just the way he's always been, at least when he's not drunk. Now I've told you before that I don't need you going down that path. Try and be optimistic, for heaven's sake."

"Yes sir," was all that I could say.

"You never know. They just might do this one the right way."

"Yes sir."

"Now go have your tea, and get some rest. That's an order."

"Yes sir. I'll get some rest."

It was a fairly nice day for April. It wasn't raining at the moment, so I sat on the ground by a tree next to our billet and stretched out my legs. It was a big tree, maybe 40 feet tall, but I don't know what kind. It was donned with tiny green buds on every branch. I remembered thinking how odd that was; there weren't any trees on the line that hadn't been blown to pieces, leaving only splintered, dead trunks rising out of the mud: places for snipers to hide, more or less. The living green gave me hope for the future, that maybe there'd be more springs to come, with more tall, bright green trees along the lanes on which I would walk. I felt at ease there.

I pulled out a pad of paper and sharpened my pencil stub with my pocketknife. There was just enough left for me to write a letter to Rebecca. Not much had changed since my last letter, and I didn't want to tell her about me and the boys getting stuck out in No Man's Land, so I was kind of short on material. I told her that I'd heard about the Yanks coming over, and said that maybe we would win the war by summer so I could come home, which was a lie. I also reported that there hadn't been any news on Frank, and asked her to send any information she might receive.

The mail came later in the afternoon, but I didn't get any letters from her. I was terribly disappointed, then worried, because I hadn't heard from her at all in nearly a week. But I did get a package of licorice drops and a letter from Rose, and upon reading it, I felt much better about the situation at home. At first it seemed like bad news; she wrote that her husband needed to go back to London because he was having some difficulty recovering from his wounds. However, she then said that she was going with him, and that she'd made arrangements with Rebecca to move back into the flat for a month or two. It really put me at ease, because I knew that during that time, Rebecca was going to give birth, and Rose would be there to help out.

I felt good, so I went back to my spot under the tree, extended my legs in the grass, and leaned back against the trunk. I pulled my cap down in "Frank fashion," with the bill touching my nose. I drifted off in my mind to thoughts of home, how happy I would be the day my child was born, and comforted by the notion that my sister would be there to give me a full report. Again, I found myself hoping for a son; I wanted to teach him to fish and hunt birds on the moors. I wanted to tell him stories that my father told me, and stories about the things I'd done and the places I'd been, and about Frank and the other boys that had came and went. Just the happy stories, though. I knew I could never forget the dark days, but I felt no reason to dwell on them once this whole mess was over with and I left Wipers for good. I hoped, above all, that that day would come soon. I had so much to live for, and I believed that once I'd been through hell, everything after would be heaven. That was a very beautiful thought, and it actually made me tear up a bit.

I pulled my cap up to wipe my eyes and saw the lieutenant was standing there in front of me. I had been so wrapped up in my thoughts that I hadn't heard him coming. I started to get up, but he told me to stay where I was.

"Catching a bit of a nap, sergeant?" he asked.

"Just thinking, sir."

"Good thoughts, I hope. I think that was the order I gave you."

"Yes, sir. Very good thoughts. Wonderful things."

He pointed to the paper sack sitting in the grass next to me.

"What do you have there?" he asked.

"Licorice drops from my sister," I said. "Would you care for some?"

"Black licorice?"

"The real thing, sir."

286

"That's my absolute favorite candy."

"Then by all means, sir, help yourself."

He sat down under the tree next to me, the informality seeming a little out of character.

"Pass that bag over here," he said

He stretched out his legs with a look of tremendous satisfaction on his face.

"You know," he said, "I'm sorry for being a bit cross with you earlier. I would suppose some would consider me foolish."

"Optimistic, perhaps, sir. But not foolish. There's no need for an apology."

He nodded, crunching the candy between his teeth.

"Do you know how long it has been since I got some good licorice? Way too long. Tell your sister that I truly enjoyed it."

"I'll have her send you a bag next time."

"How is her husband doing? The artillery bloke?"

"He's recovering, but he's going back to London for some further treatment. They think maybe they missed a couple of bits of shrapnel, but I don't know for certain. But Rose says it seems to be rather routine, so I guess that's good."

"And your wife?"

"I haven't heard from her in a few days, but her last letter indicated that the pregnancy is going just fine. She's a bit distressed at how big she's gotten, and she wants me to come home soon, naturally. But all things considered, I'd say she's doing quite well."

"Hopefully you'll get a letter soon," he said, taking another piece of licorice. "She's probably so busy getting ready for the baby that she doesn't have much time to write. And I'm sure they'll send you a telegram when the baby comes."

"You're probably right, sir. Any word from your family?"

"I got a letter from my father yesterday. Lots of talk about how we could win this war if the fellows at the top knew what they were doing. He has an interesting perspective. A bit like mine perhaps. He's convinced that our generals could have wrapped this up a long time ago. He also believes the Yanks might just be the decisive factor in this whole situation."

"I hope you're right, sir. By the way, any details on the push down at Arras?"

"We're getting bits and pieces. More bits, unfortunately, and some of them contradictory. But most I've received have tended to be good ones."

"How about the ridge?"

"Nothing on that yet. But give it some time. The assault is still very fresh. This is truly good candy, Gardener."

"Help yourself," I said, handing him the bag again. He took a few pieces and put them in his pocket, and put one in his mouth.

We sat there silently for a while, crunching on the candy under the tree. I decided to have a cigarette, so I pulled a Woodbine out of my breast pocket and lit it. A long, deep drag made me feel a little light-headed.

"Got any more of those?" the lieutenant asked.

"Absolutely, sir," I said, handing the tin to him. "Need a match?"

He nodded no, then lit his.

"Do you know who makes the best cigarettes, Gardener?"

"Who would that be?"

"The Turks. Too bad we're fighting them. Otherwise we might stand a chance of getting some cigarettes that taste the way they're supposed to."

"I heard the Americans make good cigarettes."

"Is that so?"

"A Canadian chap told me about them. Actually, an American in the Canadian Army. 'Lucky Strikes,' he called them. Supposed to be the best."

"Maybe when they get here we can get some."

"Frank could probably get some for us right now."

The lieutenant looked me in the eyes and shook his head smiling.

"I'm sorry, sir," I said. "I shouldn't have brought it up."

"That's all right, sergeant. You're right. He probably could get enough for the whole platoon somehow."

"Somehow, yes, but I've found that it is best not to ask him too many questions about that 'somehow.'"

The lieutenant grinned and shook his head. Then he took another piece of candy and crushed it between his teeth.

"You know, Gardener," he said, "Hendershot was a good man. One hell of a fighter, I must say. But your demeanor and loyalty are unmatched."

"Well, thank you, sir. It is truly appreciated. I put a lot of stock in your opinion."

"And I in yours, Gardener."

We sat for a while in silence. The sun was getting low in the sky.

"Did I ever ask you if you play chess?" he asked.

"Yes, and unfortunately I don't."

"Would you like to learn?"

"I don't know, sir…"

"Come on, Gardener. I know how boring it is back here. I'll teach you."

288

"All right. I guess I could take a shot at it."

"Why don't you come by my billet at around eight? I got a bottle of good brandy from my father today, and I'd like to share it with someone. I think it's a bit better than that bourbon you gave me. You'll like it."

"I'm honored that you would choose me, sir. I'll be there."

"Good. Eight o'clock it is. And bring that licorice with you."

"Absolutely, sir. Eight o'clock."

He stood and walked off. I had some time, so I decided to go get a bath and shave. I spent a good hour picking lice out of my shirt, then went to the canteen and bought two tins of Woodbines. I was looking forward to a drink. The time came and I walked up the road to the lieutenant's billet, which was in the basement of a house that had, for the most part, been leveled to the ground. I found the cellar door and went inside.

The lieutenant was sitting at a small table, with a bottle and two glasses. The room was dimly lit with two spirit lamps. It was Spartan, but one of the better billets I'd seen. It even had wood paneling on the walls, and there was a door leading to who-knows-where. He stood and greeted me with a handshake, and invited me to sit down.

"Nice place you have here, sir," I said.

"Do you like it?" he said like a king showing his castle. "There must be a thousand dugouts similar to this under Ypres. Old basements and cellars and so forth, interconnected with tunnels. Some better, some worse. You can actually go all the way across town without going up top."

I sat at the table and he produced two tin cups.

"Sorry I don't have actual glasses," he said. "War is so uncivilized."

"Not a problem, sir. I'm sure these cups will do just fine."

"Have you ever had brandy before?" he asked as he poured.

"Yes, I have, but it's been too long."

We raised our glasses and I took a sip. It was the warmest, smoothest thing I'd ever tasted, and I could tell it had a kick to it. I felt it go all the way down.

"What do you think, Gardener?"

"That is some excellent stuff you've got there, I must say. I usually drink whiskey, but this is truly fantastic. Thank you for sharing it with me."

"The pleasure is mine, Gardener. You just can't drink something this good by yourself. It wouldn't be proper."

I reached into my pocket and pulled out the Woodbines I'd bought, and handed him a tin.

"What's this?"

"I thought you might be a little low on cigarettes, sir. It's the least I could do."

"That's very thoughtful. I was out of cigarettes. We'll be living high tonight."

He went across the room and dug about in his haversack, producing what looked like a small oblong box with hinges on one side. Opening it like a book, he took peg-like chess pieces out of the inside. Folded flat, the box made a chess board, with a peg hole in the center of each of the silver and gold squares. I'd never seen anything like it before, and I asked him where he got it.

"My grandfather made that," he said. "He was a navy man, and he seemed to have a lot of spare time on his hands while at sea. I think he told me that he made this on a voyage to India. It's a long way around the horn of Africa and back up, so that's how he passed the time. He made a lot of interesting things over the years, but I think this is his finest piece of craftsmanship."

"What did he make it from?"

"The squares on the board are made from flattened food tins and shell casings. He carved the black pieces out of ebony, and the white pieces from some other sort of wood. Maple, I believe. He made them like pegs so they wouldn't slide around in rough seas."

"That's some pretty good thinking."

"You know, he's probably one of the smartest men I've ever known. Why he never made admiral, I don't know."

"So how did you end up with it?"

"Well, most of my family went the navy route. My older brother got it first. He was on a dreadnought when the fighting started. He was killed at Jutland, but his ship made it back. Just barely. When they gave his personal effects to my father, he sent the board to me, knowing that I liked the game. If anything happens to me, I want to make sure it gets back to my family. It's really the only thing I've got that I care much about."

"I can understand why."

"Gardener, can you promise me that you'll take care of it? I feel I can trust you."

"Definitely, sir. I'll post it back myself. But let's just hope that it doesn't come to that."

"Yes, let's hope. Now let me show you how this game works."

Chess wasn't really as complicated as I had imagined, and I seemed to catch on fairly quickly. We had a few more glasses of brandy, played a couple of games and spent some time getting to know each other.

"So tell me, sir," I said. "What did you do before the war?"

290

"The army has really been my only career. I went to Oxford University and got a degree in philosophy, with which you can't do a hell of a lot. Then I joined the army purely out of reverence to my family's military heritage. I got a lot of jabs because I didn't go with the navy, but I'm glad I didn't. I like the army."

"You like the army? What then are you going to do when this whole thing is over?"

"I'll probably stay in the army, but I don't know for certain. I'm thinking about going back to the university to study divinity."

"Divinity, sir? What is that?"

"Religious studies. For ministers."

"Why?"

"My faith keeps me strong. Do you know the average lifespan for a lieutenant at the front? Two and a half weeks! I've been up here now since 1914. I am beating the odds, but I know I'm not doing it alone."

"I often feel the same."

I lost the first two games, but I felt I was catching on. We set up the board for a third match. I was still curious about the lieutenant's philosophy, and we continued to talk as we played.

"What about heaven?" I asked. "Do you believe in life after death? That when this is all over, we go away to paradise?"

"Absolutely. No question about it."

"How do you figure that, sir?"

"My faith is based on scientific theory. A lot of people think that science is the opposite of religion, but I disagree entirely. I think religion explains science."

"And the afterlife?"

"Gardener, one of the first things you learn when you study physics is that like matter, energy can be neither created nor destroyed. Have you ever played snooker?"

"A few times, but I'm not very good at it."

"Just think about energy like a game of snooker. You take in energy when you eat, and when you draw back that cue stick and hit a ball on the table, your energy gets transferred to the cue, then from the cue to the ball, and then either on to another ball or the rail, which absorbs energy. In short, the energy you exert is passed from one thing to the next. Do you understand what I'm saying?"

"Of course. But I'm wondering what that has to do with going to heaven."

"Well, do you concede that there is a difference between a live man and a dead one?"

"Yes, of course."

291

"And what's missing from the dead man? Life. And life is an energy force, correct?

"I suppose it would be."

"So therefore, science tells us that the energy has to come from somewhere and then go somewhere else. You received this energy when you were born, and when you are done with it, it passes on to something else, just like the snooker ball."

"So what you are saying, sir, is that our life goes on in another form when we die?"

"That's exactly what I'm saying. Rules of physics are concrete everywhere in the known universe. This law of energy passing from one place to the next is a clear indication that the energy of life which currently inhabits our worldly bodies will transcend once our bodies can no long harbor it."

"And that would be heaven?"

"Precisely. Our energy remains eternal; and for that reason we will live eternally in paradise."

"That's the most logical, profound answer I've ever gotten for that question. In fact, I think it will make a big difference in my life if I view it that way."

"Don't just 'think,' Gardener. Believe it in your heart."

"That sounds like good advice."

Somewhere in the midst of this conversation, I had apparently distracted the lieutenant to the point that I had him in checkmate. He got a surprised look on his face and lit a cigarette.

"You've got to be one of the fastest learners I've ever known," he said. "Hell, you're on your way to becoming the next Hendershot."

"He played well?"

"He was practically unbeatable. I bet that within the two years I knew him, I may have beaten him a half-dozen times…"

It was well after midnight, and we'd finished the brandy down to the last drop. So we called it a night, and I walked back down the road to the billet, staggering a little here and there. It had been the first time I'd drank in a while, and I suddenly remembered why I liked drinking so much. The thought once again crossed my mind that I should get the bottle of bourbon Frank stashed and drink to total numbness, but I surprisingly convinced myself that I couldn't drink it without him.

I went to my bunk and found someone sleeping there, with his head completely covered by a blanket. There was an empty bunk adjacent to him, so I moved my gear and took it. I was sure it couldn't have any more lice in it that the other bunk, and it was probably about as comfortable.

292

I had one last cigarette and got in my bunk. In the darkness, I could hear the man across the aisle just barely snoring.

CHAPTER 42

The next day I was a little hung over, and a bit anxious for some unknown reason, but mostly I was just dead bored. I decided to take a nap to relax, but an hour or so later, a most hideous nightmare jolted me upright in my bunk. I had dreamed that the war had reached England, and the Germans were destroying London with typical zeal. The whole city was aflame and bodies were piled in the streets. The vision left my heart racing and my clothes damp with sweat.

I wiped my face with my sleeve and looked around with wide eyes. It was actually a relief – for a moment – when I realized where I was, and that the dream was no more than a dream. At least as far as I knew at the time, anyhow.

It was still daylight. The entire billet was empty, aside from myself and the other fellow in the bunk adjacent to mine. He was wrapped in a blanket like a mummy, with only the back of his shaven head visible. I lit a cigarette, and leaning over to pull on my boots, I could see a big, nasty scar across the top of his head. My heart raced again.

"Frank?" I asked with nervous caution. "Frank, is that you? Frank?"

He didn't respond, so I put my hand on his shoulder and shook him gently. At last he rolled over, and indeed, it was my old friend! Tears of joy filled my eyes and I laughed aloud.

"I can't believe this!" I said. "Where in hell have you been?"

Frank sat up slowly and rubbed his eyes, showing a sort of half-hearted grin. I extended my hand and helped him up off the bunk. He'd dropped weight, probably a whole stone's worth. His face was taut and weathered.

"You bugger!" I said. "Why didn't you wake me?"

"I wanted to make sure you got your rest," he said sarcastically. "You got any more of those cigarettes? I'd kill a nun for a cigarette. No, I'd kill two nuns…"

"Smoke all you want," I said, handing him the tin.

He took only one, which was odd, and he nearly burned it end to end with a single voracious drag. He closed his eyes and let the smoke roll slowly out of his mouth.

"So what happened?" I asked.

"Does it matter?" he asked in return, looking down at his feet.

I didn't want to push him, and we finished our cigarettes without conversation. Then I lit another one and gave a second to Frank. He was excruciatingly distant, staring at the ground without a blink. It actually startled me when he finally spoke.

294

"They put me in the brig," he said.

"Where?" I asked.

"France, I think."

"That's as specific as you can get?"

"Nobody told me anything. And I didn't ask."

"Did you have a court martial?"

Frank shook his head.

"Not that I know of," he said. "I don't think they knew how to proceed. There isn't anything in the code of military justice about breaking up a dinner party with a rat."

I laughed. He did not.

"Well, what did they do to you?" I asked.

"Field Punishment Number One. Chained to a post, standing up, from sunrise to sunset. No shade, no shelter. Wind. Rain. Nothing to eat all day."

"Good heavens, Frank. For how long?"

"I guess about a week or so. I quit counting after five days."

"That must have been…"

"You don't have any idea how it must have been."

"No, I suppose I wouldn't…"

"I had to shit in my trousers, Richard. In my bloody trousers. And then at night they put me in the hole."

"That doesn't sound good."

"Solitary confinement in the smallest cell imaginable. I could touch the walls to the left and right at the same time. I barely had enough room to lie down. Bread and water twice a day. There was no window, no lights at all. But at least I got to crap in a bucket."

"That's barbaric."

"Look around, Richard; everything is barbaric."

"But…"

"But what? That's the way it is. That chapter in this bloody tragedy is closed, and here I am again in Wipers, getting ready for the next chapter. You got another cigarette?"

It was time for tea, so we got up and headed for the kitchen. I couldn't remember Frank having ever been excited about army food before. I had to take great strides to keep up with him. He ate ravenously; when I was about halfway done with my food, he went back for more. In minutes he was wiping up the last bit of gravy on his plate with a piece of bread.

"Have you heard anything from the girls?" he asked.

"They are both doing well," I said. "Rebecca is spending a lot of time in bed. The good news is that Rose will be staying with her through the delivery."

"They should let you go home for that."

"I agree. The lieutenant agrees. But nobody's going home right now. They need every man they can muster for the attack on the ridge. That's why I'm still here, and probably the reason you are back as well."

"I can't imagine why they'd miss just one man."

"I know. But 'how it should be' and 'how it is' are two different things."

Frank stared me in the eyes for a few seconds, then turned and cursed under his breath. I don't know what he said but it didn't sound good. He rinsed his mouth with coffee and spat on the floor.

"So should I dare inquire as to the nature of our current situation?" he asked.

"The 'situation' remains unchanged," I said. "Nothing unusual, really. Had a couple of hairy patrols and lost some new boys, but that's about it."

"New boys don't have a bleeding chance."

"We were new boys once, Frank, and we're still here..."

"Have they started the usual round of spring parties yet?"

"Something's going on down toward Vimy and Arras."

"Us or them?"

"Us. And the Canadians. Word has it that the Germans are just holding the line. They lost too many men at Verdun."

"What about the French? They lost just as many at Verdun. Are they just holding as well?"

"Not if you ask General Nivelle..."

"Is he still planning to make that big push on the Aisne?"

"You know about that?"

"Who doesn't know about it? The lad in the cell next to mine said a Frenchie told him that he'd found a copy of the plans in a Hun trench."

"Did you believe him?"

"Just as much as I believe anyone else in uniform. Except for you. I believe you. And I believe the lieutenant."

"Does he know you are back?"

"I don't know. I haven't seen him, but one would think that he'd get some kind of paperwork, or a letter or something. Honestly, Richard, I'm not in a great hurry to face him again. Is he still ready to shoot me?"

"He hasn't said anything, at least not to me. But you know he got demoted, don't you?"

"Oh, no. I didn't know that. He'll probably give me every dirty detail that comes along..."

"The lieutenant's a fair man, Frank. I've gotten to know him a lot better since you left. Personally I think that, somehow, he's above resentment."

He stamped out his cigarette on the bottom of his left boot.

"Anything else?" he asked. "Maybe something good?"

"The Americans are coming," I said

"Really? When did you hear about that?"

"Yesterday, or maybe the day before. It was in the lieutenant's newspaper."

"When are they going to get here?"

"They didn't say. But they don't have a lot of men in the army, so it might take some time to build up to fighting strength. The lieutenant thinks it's the beginning of the end."

"What do you think?"

"I think a lot could happen between now and then. So who knows? Maybe he's right. But I'm certain they won't be there to help us take Hill 60."

"Any idea when that might happen?"

"It has to be coming soon. The mining is done, or so I've been told. Now we're just laying charges and listening closely. We still don't know how much the Germans have learned."

"How long before we go back up?"

"A few days. But they're still keeping the rotations short; we'll probably be in the fire trench less than a week."

"The thought makes me sick to my stomach. I think I need a drink. Do you need a drink, sergeant?"

"I'm not averse to the notion."

"You probably drank that pint of bourbon, didn't you?"

"No, I saved it. For the ridge."

"To hell with that. Let's go back and pull the cork tonight."

"That's not what we planned, Frank. Let's keep the bourbon for its intended purpose. We can go to Pop instead. I think we can get most of the way there before dark."

It didn't take too much prodding to get Frank to see things my way. We started down the road to Pop but it was in terrible shape due to heavy traffic, spotty shelling and aerial bombing. And rain, of course. We decided to cut overland to the railroad and walked the crossties all the way into town.

I knew a decent *estaminet* for NCOs on the outskirts of town, but the owners didn't discriminate against enlisted men, provided they had money, didn't stink and didn't fight. As we approached, we could hear the sounds of a raucous party under way; we could also smell someone cooking chicken.

"That smells fantastic," Frank said. "Can I borrow a shilling until payday?"

297

"You're hungry already?" I asked jokingly. "I'm still full from tea, and I ate half of what you did."

It perturbed Frank.

"Can I borrow the money?" he asked.

I handed him some coins and we went inside. The place was crowded with thirsty soldiers who'd had plenty already. Some looked like rear-echelon types. Others looked like they'd just come off the line. There was one empty table in the back of the parlor, and it took a couple of minutes to wade through the crowd to get there. I flagged down a girl in an apron and ordered two bottles of the red stuff. Frank ordered a plate of chicken, too. He didn't even touch the wine until he'd inhaled everything on his plate.

"It was that good, Frank?" I asked.

"Absolutely," he said. "Beats the hell out of bread and water."

Frank belched loudly but no one else noticed, especially not the rowdy Canadians that occupied the next table. With the exception of Australians in general, they had to be the loudest people I'd ever encountered. By their uniforms and conversation I could tell they were pilots. One of them had a very nasty cough, and the man next to him kept pounding him on the back. I began looking around the room to see if there was another available table, because if that fellow had tuberculosis or influenza, I didn't want to catch it. Suddenly, they burst into song:

> " O Canada! Our fathers' land of old
> Thy brow is crown'd with leaves of red and gold.
> Beneath the shade of the Holy Cross
> Thy children own their birth
> No stains thy glorious annals gloss
> Since valour shield thy hearth.
> Almighty God! On thee we call
> Defend our rights, forfend this nation's thrall,
> defend our rights, forfend this nation's thrall!"

They cheered and raised their glasses.

"To our boys on Vimy Ridge," the loudest of the three proclaimed. They emptied their glasses and poured more. Their toast piqued my curiosity, and suddenly I wanted to talk to these blokes. I stood and stepped over to their table.

"I don't mean to be rude," I said, "but I heard you talking about Vimy Ridge."

"That's right," the loudest one said. "It is now a province of Canada. Right, fellows?"

They all cheered again and raised their glasses.

298

"Was it a hard fight?" I asked.

He looked at me like I was stupid.

"What do you think?" he said. "It's only the hardest, toughest redoubt in the entire line."

"Correction, Higgins," the coughing one said. "It *was* the hardest, toughest redoubt in the entire line. Subtle, yet significant difference."

"Actually, Johnson," the other said, "it *still* is the hardest and toughest, except hard and tough for the Germans."

"Were you part of the show?" I asked.

"Yes, we were," Higgins said. "We flew almost constantly for three days, supporting the tanks and the infantry and generally keeping the Huns out of the sky. Seems to have made a bit of a difference in the way things turned out."

"Here, here!" Johnson cried, and started hacking violently again. Higgins beat his fist on his back until he stopped.

"What's wrong with him?" I asked. "Tuberculosis or something?"

"Castor oil," Higgins said. "Lubricant for the plane's engine. It blows out during flight and you breathe the spray. After a while, it builds up in your lungs to the point that you can't quit coughing. Johnson's been flying since the beginning, so he's got it the worst."

"Is it permanent?"

"Nobody knows."

"It's worth it," Johnson piped in. "I've shot down three of those bastards, and two balloons. And it's getting easier. The Huns are sending up boys."

"Have a drink with us," Higgins said.

I got my glass from our table, where Frank was sitting expressionless, staring into space. Higgins filled it with *vin rouge*. We had another toast.

"Where's home for you fellows?"

"Vancouver. It's in British Columbia."

"I can't say I'm familiar with it."

"It's in the far western part of the country, just north of the American border."

"What's it like?"

"It is a beautiful place, wonderful people, right on the water. I can't wait to go back."

We had another glass of wine.

"So what's with your friend over there? Shell shock?"

"You mean Frank? No, he's just been through a tough spot. He's normally the life of the party. He's a magician."

"Really?"

299

"Yes, and quite good. Hey Frank!"

He didn't respond.

"Frank! Come over here and join us!"

He stamped out a cigarette and pulled his chair over to the table, his expression unchanging.

"The sergeant here says you're a magician," Higgins said.

"Do a trick for us!" Johnson cried.

"Sorry," Frank said. "I don't have a deck of cards with me."

"I've got a deck," Johnson said, and handed them across the table.

"Sorry, fellows," Frank said. "I didn't come here to play cards. I came here to get stinking pissed, and that's what I'm going to do."

He pushed the deck back over to Johnson. I was dumbfounded.

"*Mademoiselle!*" Frank yelled. "More *vin rouge, si vous plait.*"

I realized at that moment that Frank had finally been broken. And it was a very painful sight to see. I wondered if he'd ever be the same again.

CHAPTER 43

A few days later we were back in the line. The Germans had been pouring on indirect fire from behind the ridges all bloody day. There wasn't really anything unusual about that, but it made me wonder what they were scheming to do. Frank and I both doubted that there would be an all-out attack of any kind because we didn't have anything worth having. The lieutenant suspected that they might have been trying to disrupt the mining as much as possible, but that seemed pointless, seeing how the tunneling and charging were virtually complete.

"They're just being German bastards," Frank said. "I've got to go piss."

"It's a bit dangerous for that right now, Frank," I said.

"What do you want me to do? Go right here in the dugout? As if this hole couldn't smell any worse. Besides, I simply don't care. They haven't hit me yet."

He pushed back the canvas and went out into the trench. I heard a couple of shells burst very close to our dugout and Frank came dashing back in.

"Decided not to risk it?" I asked.

"No, it just doesn't take me all day to use the loo," he shot back.

Aside from us, there were six other men in the dugout: Donaldson, Wells, Taylor, Sprouse and two new fellows I didn't know, but they seemed to be holding up well under the shelling.

"How long does this go on?" one of them asked.

"At Wipers, you never know," Sprouse said. "Hell, this could last a week."

"Or longer," added Taylor.

"Are we going to have to sit in here the entire time?" the new boy asked.

"What's your name?" Frank asked him.

"John Marvin," he replied.

"Well, John Marvin, you ask a lot of damn questions. And no, we're not going to have to sit in here the whole time. We'll also sleep and eat in here. But still yet, you have the option of going out for a stroll any time you like."

"How about you?" I asked, pointing at the other one. "What's your name?"

"Chapman," he said. "Wilbur Chapman."

"Do you have any questions?"

"No, sergeant, I suppose I do not."

"Good. Now it's going to be getting dark soon, so we should all try and get some sleep. I know it's hard with all hell raining down around you, but you'll handle things a lot better if you manage to get a few hours in. Would anyone care for a cup of tea first?"

Everyone nodded, so I put some wood in the stove and soon had a hot pot of tea using some worn-out leaves that I'd been saving. It wasn't half bad, and it seemed to calm everyone down. After we all had a few cigarettes, I climbed into my bunk, with Frank below me. A couple of the boys made a "piss dash" as Frank had done earlier, and they came back and got in their bunks. I think everyone fell asleep quickly considering the circumstances.

I awoke, choking, around midnight or so. My eyes were burning and there was a smell of wet hay. By those indications, my best guess was that they'd hit us with some "white cross," a combination of chlorine and phosgene. They mixed the phosgene with chlorine to make the phosgene spread more effectively.

"Gas!" I yelled, coughing. "Gas! Get your helmets on! Now! Now!"

Everyone bolted upright and jumped out of their bunks. I was hacking horribly as I got my gas helmet situated. Everyone else was doing the same except Marvin. He was down on his knees, in the thick of the gas, looking under the bunk.

"Marvin!" I yelled, the mask muffling my voice. "Get on your bloody helmet!"

He was coughing violently and could barely speak.

"I...can't find...it...sergeant!" he gasped.

The gas was getting thicker by the second. We all started looking for the mask, but it was nowhere to be found. By that point, Marvin was lying in the floor holding his chest, coughing up mucous. He was dying. Rapidly.

"Somebody do something!" Chapman was screaming. "Somebody help him!"

"I'll help him," Frank said, and walked over to the door. There was a big club standing there, about as long as a cricket bat, which we had been using to beat rats. Frank picked it up and walked over to where Marvin was gagging on his own fluids.

"What are you going to do with that?" Chapman asked with alarm.

"I'm going to help him," Frank said.

As cold as could be, Frank lifted the club with both hands, then swung it down hard into the side of Marvin's neck. It audibly snapped, and the gagging stopped. I stared in disbelief, as did most of the others.

302

"You bastard!" Chapman said. "I thought you said you were going to help him!"

"Yes, I did," Frank said. "He's not suffering anymore. He would have died before the stretcher men could get here anyway."

"That's bloody barbaric!" Chapman said. "You animal! You…"

"Welcome to Wipers," Frank said coldly. "*C'est la geurre*."

Chapman leapt at Frank and tackled him to the floor. While Chapman was a bit bigger, Frank had more fighting experience and I believed that he would easily come out on top. But for the time being, Chapman was astride him, slugging him in the stomach. Frank got him by the neck, and pushing him off, reached for the club.

"Break it up!" I yelled. "Chapman, get over there! And don't touch that, Frank!"

Sprouse and Taylor grabbed Chapman by the arms to restrain him. He struggled for a moment, and then gave up.

"You're lucky the sergeant stepped in," Taylor said. "Thomas would have beaten you senseless."

"You're right," Frank said. "I would have. And a good lesson for you it would have been."

"That's enough!" I said. "It's over!"

I noticed that the shelling had all but stopped, although the gas was still thick. I told Sprouse to take Chapman outside to cool off, and told Taylor to go and get the lieutenant. Donaldson and Wells went out, too, leaving Frank and I alone.

"What are you going to tell him?" Frank asked.

"What am I supposed to tell him, Frank?" I replied.

"Marvin was dead. It was just a matter of minutes. Painful minutes."

"I know. But Chapman might have a different version."

"You don't owe me any favors, Richard. But I need you to back me up on this one."

"You know, I've never seen you that cold. As cold as Simon, even. I've seen you kill a lot of men, but that..."

"I did the boy a favor, Richard. You saw him gagging."

"Maybe a doctor…"

"A doctor couldn't fix that! Men die in war, and no one can do anything about that! He was in the grave already."

I was pondering Frank's point when the lieutenant came in with Taylor.

"What happened to him?" he asked, pointing at Marvin's body.

I made the split-second decision to go with Frank's version.

"Gas, sir," I said. "We didn't hear anyone ring the gas gong, and by the time we woke up, it was filling the dugout. Marvin couldn't find his mask in time. He choked to death, sir."

"Chapman out there told me a different story," the lieutenant said, "while Sprouse and Taylor say they were busy with their helmets and didn't see anything. Donaldson and Wells said the same thing. Yet if you've given me your official version, sergeant, that is how I will put it in my report."

He turned to Frank.

"Thomas," the lieutenant said, speaking directly to Frank for the first time since he'd returned, "I don't necessarily disagree with what you did. But wait for the medics next time, all right?"

"Yes sir," Frank said.

"Now you and Chapman get a stretcher and take him back. And Gardener, you go with them."

"Yes sir," I said.

The lieutenant turned and went to the door, then paused.

"He doesn't look a day over 18," he said with his back to us. "I love this bloody war."

The day was reasonably quiet, and that night, Frank and I were put on sentry duty. It was black as pitch. I couldn't even see past the parapet. At least we weren't out on patrol.

"Got any cigarettes?" Frank asked quietly.

I felt around in my pocket for my tin. I knew I had only four left, and I was hoping to make them last awhile. It would be several days before I could get any more. But I couldn't tell him no, and I reasoned that one less fag for me wasn't going to be the end of the world. I took one out for each of us.

"You know, Richard," he said, "I've developed a theory."

"What's that, Frank?"

"How many Germans do you think there are?"

"Quite a few."

"Are there more of them than us?"

"If there were…"

"Exactly. They'd have won by now."

"What's your theory then?"

"Given that there are about the same number on each side…"

"All right…"

"What if every boy on our side made it a point to kill at least one German tomorrow?"

"What if they did?"

"The war would be over because there wouldn't be enough Huns left to hold the line. Each man kills one; it's so bloody simple, I'm surprised Haig hasn't thought of it."

"Maybe you should write him a letter, Frank."

304

"Maybe I will. And maybe he'll appoint me to his staff, and maybe I'll go down in history as the most brilliant military mind of the entire war."

He flicked his cigarette butt over the breastwork and spat.

"Honestly, Richard, do you think we're ever going to go home?"

"The war has to end sometime, Frank."

"I don't mean that. I mean you and I. Are we going to go home?"

"They haven't managed to kill us yet. Look at some of the things we've been through."

"Yes, and how long will our luck hold out?"

"I believe that one day I will, in fact, go home to my family, Frank."

"How do you know that?"

"When I think about going home, I can see it very clearly in my mind. That day will come. I can feel it in my gut."

"You know what I see in my mind?"

"What?"

"Absolutely nothing. Nothing beyond the mud and blood and barbed wire. I can't see past that. Thinking about the future is pointless. There is no future. There is only now. And now, I am here."

"Yes, but what matters…"

"How many men do you think you've personally killed?"

"I have no idea."

"I've been trying to add it all up. So far, I can remember killing at least 37 Germans. And Marvin. And you've killed more than me, I'm certain."

"What's your point?"

"My point is that we've seen too much, and we've killed too many men for life to ever be the same again."

"I think that our experiences will make life better after we get home. Every day in England will seem like paradise."

"Well, I'm glad you feel that way, Richard, but I see nothing but pain."

"To hell with it," he said, shaking his head. "This war is never going to end anyway."

A few hours before daylight, as it began raining rather hard, the lieutenant told us that Nivelle had launched his attack on the Aisne. The French were on the move.

And despite Frank's prediction, the war was about to come very, very close to being over.

305

Before I go any further with this unfortunate episode, I feel it necessary to dispel a myth about the French. I must admit that, for one reason or another, I never liked them very much in general. But their reputation as being inferior soldiers is completely unfounded. I could go through countless historic examples where French valor on the battlefield was nearly unparalleled.

Hitler's war tarnished that tradition, and unfairly, I must say. By the time the German blitzkrieg roared across the French frontier, it had already overrun nearly all of Western Europe. The French weren't prepared -- and neither was anyone else for that matter -- when Hitler's overwhelming mechanized forces came crashing through. They did manage to hold out for about three weeks despite the odds. We, too, had to retreat. And other defeated countries like Poland and the Netherlands and so forth never received the white-flag-waving label the French were given.

People seemed to forget quickly that in our war, the French held four-fifths of the Western Front and had performed some virtual military miracles. Had they not stopped the Huns on the Marne, Paris would have been captured. It was a brilliant maneuver, a sort of combination of improvisation and desperation that, in itself, kept the Germans from winning on the Western Front in those early months. And not two years later, when the Germans threw everything they had at Verdun, the French held on one inch at a time and stubbornly refused to yield, even though they were losing thousands of men every day. Or every hour. That is the definition of what the French call *cran,* or "guts."

The French soldiers themselves had it tougher than most, too. People tend to think of the Germans as overly stern, but French discipline was even harsher. They got paid less than most of us; it was so little, in fact, that they hadn't even enough to pay for their own needs, much less send anything home. And behind the lines, when they were on leave, there was nowhere to go and nothing to do except wait for the time to go back to the front.

Yet down to the lowest infantryman, the French were convinced that the attack on the Aisne was going to be the end of the stalemate on the Western Front. In fact, some believed it would end the war in two days. Admittedly, Nivelle hadn't lost a battle yet. Nineteen divisions – well over one million men -- went into battle on a 40-mile front with the enthusiasm of the early days. These were soldiers who knew, without a doubt, that they were going to win.

What went wrong was...well, a whole lot of things went wrong. It was pissing rain in the fashion that was typical for the opening of an offensive. There was actually a belief at the front that the intense shelling before an attack actually caused it to rain. True or not, there had been a massive bombardment by 7,000 guns followed by a massive deluge. Draw whatever conclusion you care to.

After the jump-off, Nivelle had planned a "creeping barrage," which would slowly inch its way ahead of the advancing troops. That would have been splendid, but the soldiers, burdened with equipment and advancing over rough ground in slippery mud, couldn't keep up. Moreover, German airplanes soon controlled the sky above, and without air reconnaissance, the French gunners just had to fire by timetable alone. That's a bad way to advance.

Then there was the unknown, that pivotal feature of every military action. What the French didn't know in this case was that the Germans – fully aware of the plans of the attack – had withdrawn to a much more heavily defended line. That meant the soldiers had to advance across unknown territory and assail a system of equally unknown redoubts that were built using every advantage the geography could offer. The Germans had also concentrated 100 machine guns for every 1,000 yards along the front; that's one gun every thirty feet. Little wonder they repelled the French assault with ease.

For the French, it was a disaster comparable only to the opening of the Somme offensive in 1916. By the end of that first day, the French had taken 40,000 casualties, and a large portion of the 200 Char Schneider tanks deployed had been knocked out. Nivelle, however, believed that he was making progress, and pushed on. The second day didn't go any better than the first.

Nivelle had made a promise to his superiors – many of whom were skeptical to begin with – that if significant gains weren't made in those two days, that he would cancel the offensive altogether. As you might imagine, he didn't do that. Instead, he kept ordering his men to advance.

Again, I must say something about French persistence. They did eventually manage to capture two miles of the heavily-fortified Chemin des Dames Ridge, and penetrated the German line about three miles in places. But the number of casualties climbed at an alarming rate, with some divisions suffering sixty percent killed or wounded. Total casualties mounted up to 120,000. Even the best soldiers will break at some point.

And that is exactly what happened. On May 3, one of the French divisions refused orders to go back to the front. They mutinied against what they saw as senseless attacks, and their dissent spread rapidly, particularly in rear areas. Within a matter of days, as much as three-fourths of French units were refusing orders to go to the front. They had simply abandoned all hope that the war could be won the way it was being fought.

Now it was this mutiny that came close to ending the war right then. Fritz could have easily waltzed right through the line, all the way to Paris. That would have left us hanging on in our corner of the front, our entire flank turned and nowhere to go.

By some kind of miracle – and I believe it was a miracle – the Germans never found out about the French mutiny. Somehow, the whole thing was kept quiet. The French soldiers agreed to hold the line, but not attack in the manner of the Aisne offensive. In fact, French offensive operations for the rest of the year had to be called off.

So where did that leave us? If the war was going to be won in 1917, it was going to be up to British boys. And the big plan was Messines, a subsequent breakout at Wipers and a drive to the sea.

I thought there were a lot of things in there that could go wrong.

CHAPTER 45

It truly was, as Frank would say, a gorgeous day. It was the first week of June, and it was warm, with the sun shining through a clear sky, and there was a fresh breeze coming in from the east. Despite the artillery fire up front, I'd slept well, and had that rare feeling of ease. For the first time in weeks, we hadn't been sent off for training for the Messines attack. Frank and I were sitting outside the billet watching vehicles pass on the road, trying to think up a way to kill the morning. By default, we settled on flipping cigarette butts for distance and accuracy.

"What the hell is this?" Frank said, pointing up the road.

I immediately spotted the source of his curiosity. There was a man in the distance dashing down the road at full trot. He was fast.

"Look at that son of a bitch run," Frank said.

"'Son of a bitch?'" I asked.

"It's Australian. Heard it the other day. Pretty good, huh?"

"Sounds more German, though, don't you think? 'Bitchen die herren' or something such like. But you're right. That 'son of a bitch' can run."

As the man got closer, we became even more puzzled. It was the lieutenant, his cap in one hand and a piece of paper in the other.

"What in the world..." Frank mumbled as he stood up. I got on my feet as well. I didn't like the looks of it.

"Sergeant Gardener!" he shouted. "Sergeant Richard Gardener!"

"Oh, this is going to be good," Frank said.

The lieutenant slowed down as he came into the compound, but he was still running until he held out the paper for me to see.

"You..." he said, catching his breath, "got a telegram."

"Sir?"

"Just read...the paper...sergeant."

I looked down and nearly fell to my knees. It read:

PETER RICHARD GARDENER BORN 18:23 JUNE 4 STOP. 8 POUNDS 6 OUNCES STOP. MOTHER AND BABY DOING WELL STOP. HOPE YOU WILL SEE HIM SOON STOP. LOVE ROSE STOP.

"He's a big one," Lt. Rampkin said, "just like his dad!"

Frank grabbed the telegram out of my hands and immediately let out a tremendous whoop.

309

"Congratulations!" he shouted. "It's a boy!"

They were slapping me on the back and laughing and I didn't know what to say. The baby had come early. It was the biggest surprise of my life. I was emotionally overwhelmed, but it was good.

"Maybe that's why I slept so well last night," I said. "This is…I don't have the words…"

"I've got the words," Frank said. "How about, 'Let's get drunk?'"

"Well, I…"

"Or maybe the lieutenant here can send you on leave? Why don't you get him on the next lorry out of here, lieutenant?"

"Actually," the lieutenant said, "I have to talk to the sergeant about something. Alone."

"All right," Frank said. "I know when I'm not wanted. But then we're going to get drunk!"

He strolled off, ambling lazily up the road, his hands in his pockets.

"Sergeant, I can't send you on leave," the lieutenant said apologetically. "There's something you should know."

"We're going over the top," I said. "Very soon."

"Where did you hear that?"

I pointed toward the front.

"The guns," I said. "They've been dueling for weeks, but now it is systematic, at least since midnight or so. And the tanks. I heard them coming into the rear assembly areas last night as well. I've counted dozens of planes today, too."

"You're very astute, Gardener," he said.

"With all due respect, sir, any idiot that's been here a while could figure that out."

"Is there a lot of talk?"

"No more than usual."

"That much? Let's hope the Huns aren't as smart as we are."

"Exactly when is it, sir?"

"I'm not supposed to tell you that, sergeant."

"If I can't go see my son, sir, I have the right to know when we're jumping off. Just a polite request, sir. No offense intended."

"None taken. You've made a good point, so I'll break the rules."

He looked at his watch.

"It's noon now," he said, looking up, "so we go in roughly 39 hours. Plus or minus an hour. That's when they'll blow the mines."

"Sooner than I thought," I said. "When do we move up?"

"Tomorrow," he said. "At sunset. Have the men ready."

"Yes, sir. And sir, when did you learn to run like that?"

"I was a sprinter at the university."

"That's incredible."

"But I'm not as fast as I used to be, sergeant. Definitely not."

He lit a cigarette and chucked me on the shoulder.

"All the best to you and your family, Gardener. I don't know how you plan on celebrating, but how about a game of chess tonight? Around 2100 in my billet?"

"I think Thomas wants to go into Pop…"

"I've got a bottle of brandy."

"That's hard to pass up, lieutenant. Hard to pass up. I guess I'll have to compromise. I'll go to Pop with Frank, but I'll be back for the game. I don't want to miss that.'

"Jolly good, sergeant. I'll see you around 2100?"

"Yes, sir.

"Congratulations again, sergeant. I know you'll make a good father."

"Thank you, sir."

Frank hadn't gone far. I yelled out his name as I walked down the road. He caught up to me and we headed toward Pop.

"Peter Richard Gardener," Frank said. "Why not Francis?"

"Peter was Rebecca's grandfather's name."

"Well, I still think you should have gone with Francis. At least for his middle name. Anyway, did the lieutenant say when you'd be going home?"

"No, he didn't."

"That bastard."

"There's a reason, Frank. There's a reason."

"What's that?"

"I can't tell you. Swear on my mother's honor."

My mother's honor must not have been worth much, because I finally told him.

"Tomorrow night's the night," I said.

"Over the top and all?" he asked.

"Mines. Tanks. The whole party."

"All the more reason to send you home today."

"They need every old hand up there they've got."

"We're old hands?"

"I'm an old hand," I said. "I don't know what the hell you are."

"Now just a minute…"

"I'm just giving you a hard way to go, despite your rank. I'm surprised you didn't know by now."

"How's that?"

311

A squadron of planes flew low overhead.

"How's that?" he asked again.

"That proves my point. You're not an old timer. Haven't you noticed the airplanes? There must be hundreds of them. All ours."

"So?"

"And the train tracks. There's not enough room between the inbound trains to toss a potato through. Full of men and shells. And speaking of shells, haven't you noticed the drumfire outbound?"

We walked through a break in the trees and there were tanks lined up nearly track-to-track.

"I guess I've been away too long," Frank said. "We're going over the top tonight."

"Not tonight," I said. "Tomorrow night. Why do you think they gave us the day off?"

"Because you had a baby?"

"That's bloody stupid reasoning, private."

"Oh, sure," he said. "Pull rank on me here."

"It's just that anyone could figure out what's going on. We've been here two years and you can't tell when there's an attack coming?"

"I can now that you've pointed it out."

"Now you don't tell a word of this to anyone? Nobody."

"Where did you hear?"

"The lieutenant told me when you weren't around."

"Why would he tell you?"

"He trusts me."

We walked a mile along the tracks. The cars were all inscribed in chalk with "To Berlin."

"I guess they're pretty hopeful," Frank said.

"You never know. We could have a serious breakthrough tomorrow night."

"Not bloody likely."

"Frank, someone could hand you a bank note for a million pounds and you'd moan about the color of the envelope."

"Yes, you son of a bitch. But I'm not as bad as Simon, you must admit."

"Are you going to use that all of the time now? You're right again, though. No one was as bad as Simon. But I wish Simon were here to complain about it. That was one fighting man, Simon. I wonder how many men he killed."

The train heading in our direction had slowed considerably, and there was a car coming past with an open door. We decided to jump it, which we did with surprising finesse. It smelled sweet and there was yellow dust all over the floor. Frank started to light a fag and I knocked it out of his hand.

"Do I have to tell you everything?" I asked him sarcastically. "That's bleeding ammonal on the floor. We're lucky you didn't blow us to slivers, you stupid…"

"Son of a bitch?"

"Exactly."

"It looks like you picked the wrong damn car to ride, then didn't you?"

"This was by mutual agreement."

"Sure it was."

"I don't recall discussing it at all."

"Whatever you want to believe, sergeant."

"That's it. I'm not talking to you anymore."

My vow of silence lasted all of about 15 minutes, ending when we came to the edge of town. We'd picked up speed considerably by then, and this time, there was quite a bit of discussion about what to do.

"Maybe it will slow down when it goes through Pop," Frank theorized.

"Maybe it won't. Maybe it will speed up. We don't know."

"This may be as slow as it gets."

"Then we get off now?"

"I don't know. You're the sergeant."

"But I'm not a bloody train engineer, Frank."

"Fine. I'm going now. You can do what you want."

Frank squatted in the door and looked down.

"I'll just hit the ground running. If I can match the speed of the train, I'll be fine. No trouble at all. How fast do you think we're going?"

"Faster than you can run. Faster than the lieutenant can run even."

"Horse shit. I can do it."

"Want to wager on that, Frank?"

"I'll wager."

"Let's make it interesting. If you can make it without falling, I'll buy the wine."

"That's not interesting enough."

I think the train was actually speeding up at that point.

"What is interesting enough then?" I asked anxiously.

"If I make it, you have to find out why they called the lieutenant 'Birdie.' Tonight."

"How did you know about that? And that's a bit too interesting."

"Take a chance, you lily-livered bastard. And you'd better decide now."

"All right. What if you don't make it?"

"I'll buy you three tins of fags."

"Five tins and you've got a deal."

Before we could shake on it, he leaped head-on out the door. He hit the ground running just fine, except his stride was a span of about eight feet. I think he made it all of four steps before he went flying, then rolling and tumbling in the cinders along the tracks. I looked out the door and just as he came to a stop, the train started to slow down. It stopped entirely in less than a hundred yards.

Once I got back out, Frank had arrived. He didn't look too good either. His bleeding knees showed through his torn trousers.

"I've got one question, sergeant," he said, wiping blood on his tunic. "Who won that bet?"

"What do you mean, 'Who won?'"

He cursed me worse than anything I'd ever heard Hendershot say.

"You'll have your bleeding fags. I hope you enjoy smoking every last one of them, you selfish git."

He was serious.

"Let's just call off the wager and get to an aid station. What are you going to tell them?"

"I don't know. They didn't believe me when I told them I'd been hit in the head with a shovel. Don't look at me to make up a lie. Not me. No, sir."

We eyed each other and instantly burst out laughing.

CHAPTER 46

We found an aid station on the south side of town. It looked like we were the only ones to walk in ourselves. There were a lot of stretcher cases. I was speechless, but Frank, of course, came up with a line.

"We were unloading barbed wire," he said. "Yes, that's what we were doing. I slipped and fell off the car into the gravel, and..."

"That's your story?" the doctor asked.

"That's it," Frank answered definitively.

"Really? And why would you be unloading wire back here?" He wasn't taking the bait.

"Swear on the Bible, it's true," Frank said. "I'd go get the lieutenant in charge of the operation, but he went back down the line to, uh, check on something. He's not around, but he sent us over here."

The doctor went over to a basin and washed his hands. He dried them and turned back around.

"I can see I'm getting nowhere, so let's get you patched up," he said. "You're going to need a new uniform, private. Your knees and elbows are gone."

"Elbows?" he asked. "I didn't even notice the elbows. Damn."

Frank stripped down. He was rather vocal through the whole process. Especially when they had to put a few stitches in his knees.

"Stand up," the doctor said. "How does that feel?"

"It hurts," Frank said. "It burns like fire."

"You're lucky," the doctor said. "You didn't break anything."

"It still hurts, sir," Frank said.

An orderly came in with Frank's new uniform. Once he got it put on, you couldn't even tell he was hurt except for his hands. I wondered if the lieutenant would notice. He probably would, I decided.

We went on into Pop afterward. It had lost all of its charm, if it had any to begin with. We stopped in an *estaminet* and had some lunch and a couple of bottles of wine. We talked a little about fatherhood, but other than that, we didn't seem to have much to say. I was more nervous than joyous, and it didn't help that we knew we'd be going into battle in less than two days. By time for tea, we decided to make our way back to our billet. This time we walked the whole way.

"You know, this may be the last time we see that town," Frank said.

"Let's not think about that," I said. "This may be our greatest triumph yet. You never know."

"Between here and the ridge, maybe. But what's on the other side? Another redoubt? Another trench system?"

"I guess we'll find out. Sooner rather than later. Besides, the ridge is the objective. Anything after that is a bonus."

"But we've worked on this for two years now. With that much effort going into it, you'd think we were preparing for a major push. I don't know. The whole thing seems quite surreal, really."

"I wonder what will happen when the mines go off."

"If they go off, that is."

"When they go off, it will be one tremendous blast. We'll turn Hill 60 into a bloody volcano. I can't imagine much resistance afterward."

"You must remember that the Germans seem to be resilient when it comes to those sorts of things. It won't take them long to regroup."

"There won't be many of them to regroup, at least not on the line in front of us."

"I hope you're right. I hope it kills them all. However, I remain skeptical…"

"And I remain cautiously optimistic. For the most part. I know I am looking forward to leave as soon as we wrap this up."

"I wonder if I could get some leave. How long has it been since London?"

"About nine months, figuring it's been that long since Rebecca and I…"

"It seems longer. A lifetime ago."

"Talk to the lieutenant. He's a reasonable fellow, you know."

We arrived in our compound just in time to get something to eat before the dining hall closed. They had a lot of leftovers that night. Steak, potatoes, beans and so forth. So Frank and I were given two of everything.

"I can't eat all of this," Frank said.

"It's either give it to you or throw it in the rubbish," the cook said. "It's all quite good. Enjoy."

It was good, and we managed to clean our plates. I still had an hour or so to kill before the chess game with the lieutenant, so we went outside and resumed our game of flipping cigarette butts. Frank was winning the competition, but he was quiet. I think he was getting the wind up. I was glad it didn't rub off on me.

I walked up the road toward Wipers slowly. There was a lot of artillery fire, most of it outbound. The Germans must know an attack is coming by now, I thought. But would they be ready for what we had in store? Probably not.

I found the lieutenant's billet and went inside. He was sitting at his table, the chessboard ready, looking a little drunk. There was also a fancy-looking bottle with two glasses sitting off to the side. The bottle was open and about a quarter empty.

"It's good to see you sergeant," he said. "How was the trip to Pop?"

I told him the whole story about the train. He started laughing.

"Well, I'm glad you aren't angry," I said.

"Gardener, I'll let you in on a secret," the lieutenant said, leaning over the table. "Half the time, when Thomas gets into trouble, I walk off and laugh hysterically. Even though I just chewed him out. He's quite a character. Not much of a soldier, but good for a lot of chuckles. Promise you won't tell him though. It would only encourage him."

"Your secret is safe with me, sir."

"I'm pleased that we have that kind of relationship."

"Do you trust me, sir?"

"Absolutely. No question."

"Then there's something I really need to know. A question I must ask, you see."

"I see. Go on."

"Well, sir, tell me why Lockhart calls you 'Birdie.'"

"We've been over this before, Gardener."

"I know. But we're going into what may be the greatest battle we've seen yet. In case something happens to you or I…I'd just like to know."

He silently poured us each a glass of brandy and took a drink. I took a drink and found it smoother and warmer than what we'd had last time, which was hard to believe. He was still thinking, so I took another drink and lit a fag. He motioned for me to give him my tin. I slid it across the table and he took one and lit it. He exhaled very slowly.

"Sergeant, if I tell you the reason, will you keep it to yourself?" he asked.

"Absolutely."

"And you're not even going to tell Thomas?"

"No, sir," I said, but he and I both knew I was probably making a false pledge. He told me nonetheless.

"In my circle of friends at the university, we all had animal nicknames. There was Trout, whom you know. We also had Rhino, who had a big nose. And Tiger, he was always prowling for ladies. There were several others, but Trout, Rhino, Tiger and myself were the core of the group."

317

"So what trait gave you your nickname?"

"Very simple really. My first name is Robin."

"That's it?"

"That's it."

"Begging your pardon, sir, but I'm a bit disappointed. That's nothing to be ashamed of. Kind of like Robin Hood, sir."

"Yes, but I don't want it going about the platoon. Because, as I've said, the men will be calling me Birdie behind my back. I don't want that."

"I understand, sir."

"That being said, let's get on with drinking and chess."

He beat me the first game, but I got him in checkmate the second round, seemingly without much difficulty.

"Sir, you seem distracted," I observed.

"A little. I was thinking that by this time tomorrow, we'd probably be passing through Hellfire Corner on our way to the front line."

He poured us two more glasses of brandy. I was beginning to feel a little lightheaded.

"What do you think our odds are, sir?"

"Odds of taking the ridge? Better than average, I'd say. Mining has produced some favorable results in the past. And it's never been done on this scale before. Better than average, Gardener."

"But we've got to take the hill. Do you realize how many men have died trying to do that?"

"I realize that. But our boys mined Hill 60 back in 1915 and ended up holding it for some time. They did have to give it up, however, because the rest of the ridge was still in German hands. They couldn't secure their flanks, so they pulled back to the line. This time, we're taking the whole damn thing, from Hill 60 on down. And because we're anchoring the north end, we won't have to advance very far to make our objective. Only a few hundred yards. We can do that."

"It's a very long way from Berlin."

"Chances are we'll make a breakthrough. If that happens, we may be given orders to keep advancing beyond the first objective."

We talked and drank late into the night. Finally, the lieutenant told me to go home and get some sleep. I sauntered out the door and headed down the road. I doubted if I could actually sleep, though. There were probably many others who would have the same problem that evening.

CHAPTER 47

I awoke before dawn to the sound of heavy traffic. I went outside and I could hear airplanes firing up for a morning run over the lines. There were a lot of men in new uniforms standing around like they didn't know what to do. An officer walked by with a dog on a leash, and there was a large group of soldiers on horseback across the road.

Frank came out a minute or two later.

"You're up early," I said.

"Way too early for all of this," he said. "Couldn't sleep."

"Busy day ahead."

"What time do we have to go up?"

"We'll pack up our gear after tea, head up the road after dark. Normal."

"It doesn't feel normal."

"I know. Anything but normal."

"When is the lieutenant going to tell the boys?"

"Not sure. But probably at roll call, and probably no more than they need to know."

"He won't want anyone to get the wind up."

"Too late for us, wouldn't you say, Frank?"

He kind of laughed.

"Remember the morning we took Neuve Chapelle?" he asked. That was when I had the wind up."

"I think I was too stupid to have the wind up properly," I said. "Now, with all of this…"

"And our experience…."

"It just seems to have a bit more intensity this time."

"I have to agree with you, Richard. But if you're right, this might be the easiest one yet. A whole lot easier than plugging the line with the Canadians, anyway."

"I'd rather be going with Canadians. They're a good lot."

The planes flew overhead and I noticed the sun was coming up. There were going to be long lines for breakfast, so I woke the boys early.

"Better get it while it's hot," I said. "And after roll call, I want all of you to get a bath and a shave. Clean underwear and socks. You'll thank me later. Trust me."

They fed us steak and eggs that morning. We even got some stewed tomatoes to go with it. No one was complaining and I don't think anyone left hungry. We went back across the compound and assembled in front of the billet. The lieutenant was waiting, looking like he'd finished the brandy after I'd left the

319

previous night. He walked over and gave me a sort of half-cocked salute.

"Anything to report this morning, Sgt. Gardener?"

"I've told the men to get baths and clean underwear after roll call, sir."

"Good idea," he said, and leaned in a little. "Do they know?"

"Fellows like us, sir, yes," I said. "Those that have been around a while know. The new boys don't have the slightest idea, I don't think."

"Well, I'm going to tell them only what they need to know right now. Keep talk to a minimum today, all right?"

I nodded yes and he stepped back in front of the formation.

"I need everyone to be in the compound by time for tea this afternoon," he said. "Assemble here at 1800 hours and do not even dream of being late. Between now and then, do as the sergeant instructed and get cleaned up. Make sure all of your gear is in good working order. If anything needs mending, do it today. If anything needs replaced, see the supply officer. If you have questions, see Sgt. Gardener. If he's not available, get an old-timer, like Sprouse or Taylor."

He looked over at Frank in the front row.

"Or Thomas," he said. "He'll help you out."

I saw Frank turn his head in disbelief then go back to attention, a little taller.

"I would also recommend getting a nap in if possible," the lieutenant said. "And don't drink any more than your rum ration. I'll see you here at 1800. Dismissed."

I went into the billet to get my shaving kit and Frank followed.

"Maybe I'll make corporal again," he said.

"Maybe."

"And maybe hippos will fly."

"Frank, you don't know this, but the lieutenant has a pretty high opinion of you."

"How do you know that?"

"I play chess and drink brandy with the man. There's plenty of time for talking."

"What else does he say?"

"He secretly thinks you are funny. But don't say anything."

Frank laughed. He grabbed his kit and we walked to the bathhouse.

"So tell me more, Richard," he said.

"Like what?"

"Something I don't know. Like why they call him Birdie."

"I swore I wouldn't tell anyone, Frank."

"So you know?"

"Frank, I…"

"You know! It's just a matter of time before I wear you down now, Richard. You might as well tell me now. Go ahead. Tell me."

I knew immediately that he was right, so I decided that I would tell him if he swore himself to secrecy. Of course, a pledge like that from Frank wasn't really worth much unless a really good prank was involved. But he swore and I told him.

"The lieutenant's first name is Robin," I said.

"And…"

"That's it."

"That's a secret not even worth having! I am truly disappointed. Nicknames are supposed to come from a night you got in a drunken brawl with some sailors in Brighton over a couple of Spanish girls or something. Robin. Birdie. That's not even bloody creative."

"Yes, but it stays between you and I. The lieutenant can't know that I told you. He needs to be able to trust me."

We got haircuts, shaves, a bath, delousing and new underwear. We washed our uniforms and walked in our boots and underwear back to the billet to hang up our laundry to dry. I noticed my boots were looking bad, so I decided to give them a good polishing. I sat on my bunk and got to work. Frank came over and stood there staring at me.

"What are you doing?" he asked.

"What does it look like I'm doing?"

"They're just going to get muddy tonight."

"So they'll look good until then."

He stood and watched me for a minute or two, then sat down next to me and started working on his own boots.

"Nothing wrong with looking good," he said.

It took a good hour and most of a tin of polish, but I guarantee that Frank and I had the best looking boots in the whole company. I decided then to clean my rifle; I had apparently been remiss in my maintenance. I started stripping it down and Frank followed suit with his own rifle. We disassembled the entire mechanism and polished each piece with a clean oiled cloth. We polished the barrels inside and out. After putting it all back together, we wiped down the wood and metal surfaces with a second oiled cloth.

"Looks almost new," Frank said, holding up his rifle for inspection.

"Looks good, works good," I said.

"What now?"

"I think I'll write letters to Rebecca and Rose."

"Aren't they at the same address?"

"Yes, but I'd like to personalize a bit. You don't want to say the same thing to your sister and your wife, if you understand me. Are you going to write to Liz? You know, there is the possibility that you may not get another chance."

"Yes, I'm fully aware 'there's a possibility.'"

"So are you going to write?"

"Well, I guess I am now."

I wrote until it was time to eat. Frank had finished his letter much earlier. After the meal, we decided to go have a nap, but neither of us could sleep.

"Can't sleep, can't drink," Frank said from the bunk above me. "What the hell are we supposed to do now?"

"Just calm down, Frank," I said. "I know you're nervous. Try to relax."

"Don't tell me to relax, damn it. You're as nervous as I am. Nervous is natural."

I got up and got into my duffel bag. I found a virtually new deck of cards and put them in my pocket. I went over to Frank.

"Come on, let's get up," I said. "Let's find something to do."

He got down out of the bunk and pulled his boots on.

"Like what?"

"Just come outside and sit down by the tree. And bring your own fags."

I went out and sat down. It was warm and breezy, and it would have been a lovely day except for the now-constant rumble of outbound artillery. Frank plopped down beside me and lit a cigarette.

"So?" he asked.

"Well, we could count airplanes or lorries," I said, then pulled out the cards and tossed them in his direction. "Or you could show me some card tricks."

He stared for a long moment at the pack now lying on the ground.

"I don't know, Richard," he said. "I'm kind of out of practice. You've seen all of my tricks by now anyway."

"But there's some I wouldn't mind seeing again."

"Richard, I said…"

"Come on, Frank. It's time you got back to doing this. And it beats the hell out of counting various vehicles."

"Well, you've got a point there. Give me those cards."

He started into his routine and soon he was alight like I hadn't seen him in a long time. He fell back into his stage patter, and there was no indication that he was out of practice in any way.

Frank had entertained me for about 15 minutes when the lieutenant came walking over. Frank had his back to him and

322

didn't see him coming. He stood behind Frank for a moment and listened in. When the lieutenant walked around him, Frank was clearly startled and fumbled to put the cards away. It wasn't one of his more impressive slick moves.

"That's all right, Thomas," the lieutenant said. "I was just wondering if you would mind if I sat and watched for a few minutes. I find it bloody amazing."

"Sure, uh, lieutenant, that would be…marvelous," Frank stammered. He shuffled the cards back and forth a few times and started back where his routine had been interrupted. He was a little subdued at first, but he became more at ease every time the lieutenant laughed. The lieutenant and I sat and watched until Frank ran out of tricks, which was every bit of two hours later.

"Does it feel good?" I asked Frank as the lieutenant got up to leave.

"Well, I wasn't at my best," he said. "But yes, it was very nice."

"Are you relaxed a little more?"

He smiled but didn't say anything. He didn't have to.

"Very good, Thomas," the lieutenant said. "We'd better get tea. It's getting late."

I can't remember one thing about our dinner that night. What I do remember is rounding up the platoon for assembly. I must say that for the most part, they were there and ready before the appointed time. There were a few new boys, though, that were confused as to what time 1800 was, and I was lucky enough to find them in time. If we'd been late, the lieutenant would have been highly upset. He was always very punctual and expected everyone else to be so as well.

I called the platoon to attention before the lieutenant arrived. I walked up and down the rows of men, inspecting their uniforms. I was becoming a real sergeant like Hendershot.

"Put that cap on straight," I said to one lad.

"Button the bottom of your tunic," I said to another.

One lad had horrible looking boots.

"Have you ever polished those, private?" I asked.

"Yes, sergeant."

"When was that? Back in training camp?"

"No, sergeant."

"Well, you polish them again tonight, and put a little effort into it this time. Understood?"

"Yes, sergeant."

By that time I saw the lieutenant coming, so I walked back up and took my position at the end of the front row. Frank was standing beside me.

"Gentlemen," the lieutenant said, "the time has arrived. Time to take Hill 60. At dawn we will show the Germans what we've got. We will be moving up to our attack positions in three hours. You will draw rations for two days, 20 clips of ammunition, and two bombs apiece. The supply lorries should be arriving any time. Until then, get your haversacks ready and prepare to move out. We will reassemble here at 2100 hours. Sergeant, dismiss the men."

"Remember lads," I said, "2100 is nine o'clock. Dismissed."

CHAPTER 48

The sun was getting low when we got into formation. I was surprised that the lieutenant didn't have any kind of speech or wisdom to share. When the guide showed up, the lieutenant told us to move out.

"You look out for me, and I'll look out for you," Frank said.

"As always," I said.

"We've made it through a lot worse than this. We'll be all right."

"You can count on it."

"Do you really think so?"

"It's getting kind of windy around here."

It was dark when we reached Hellfire Corner, so we didn't get shelled. But past Hellfire Corner you were into the jaws of the salient. There was a half moon, just enough to paint the landscape that deep cornflower color. It was a beautiful night, but that made me nervous. It seemed that some Hun with good eyes would see us and call down some artillery.

But he did not. We made it to our trench without incident. It was actually one of the better trenches I'd occupied in the salient. It was a deep breastwork affair with steel sniping loupes and duckboards with chicken wire. And it was dry.

I put my rifle on my shoulder and took a walk down the trench to check on things, mostly the new boys. They looked like the best new batch we'd ever had. Then I came upon this one lad having a bit of a tussle with his rifle. He was trying to insert one of his clips into the magazine, but he had it crooked or jammed or something. When I got to him, he was cursing and slapping it with his hand.

"Hold on, hold on," I said and the boy turned around. He stood and set his rifle aside, ashamed of himself.

"What's your name?" I asked.

"William Butler, sergeant."

"Did they teach you how to load the rifle in training camp?"

"Certainly, sergeant."

"It's no different up here. Let me have your rifle."

I took it in my hands and popped out the jammed clip.

"Did you see how I did that, Butler?"

"Yes."

"That's how you do it when you're getting shot at, too. Now come over here. I'm going to give you a refresher course."

"But it's dark, sergeant."

"I'll show you by feel. You can do that whether it's daylight or pitch black, without even looking down."

I showed him the technique and he caught on quickly. I was impressed.

"Think you've got a handle on that now, Butler?"

"Yes, thank you, Sgt. Gardener."

"Now try and relax a little bit."

I turned to continue my walk and nearly ran over the lieutenant.

"How long have you been standing there, sir?" I asked.

"Long enough to see how you handled that situation," he said. "As soon as this operation is over, I'm putting you in for a promotion."

"Thank you, sir. I appreciate it."

"No, Gardener, I appreciate it. If I had a whole platoon of men like you…"

"Then we'd all be in serious trouble. Sir."

He laughed and went about his way. I continued my walk down the line. I came to a sap that led out to a listening post, so I decided to go have a look. I think I startled the two privates who were manning the post.

"Anything happening?" I asked.

"Nobody's doing anything, sergeant," he said, "aside from the shelling up there."

"Good. Let's hope it stays that way for a few more hours."

I went back to the trench. I soon came across Frank surrounded by a bunch of new boys. He was telling some fantastic tale about one of our exploits, really giving it a good stretch, too. One of them scoffed in disbelief.

"Sergeant Gardener!" Frank said. "That's exactly the way it happened, wasn't it? Tell them. You were there."

I knew there was no use in refuting the story, nor would it have served any purpose.

"It was precisely as Private Thomas said."

Frank nearly cracked up laughing.

"See, I'm not lying. I've got all kinds of stories like that. Let me tell you about the time…"

He had them hooked again. I smiled and headed back down the line. The sky above was remarkably clear, with a moon that didn't hide the stars behind its glow. Millions of stars. I sat on the fire step, lit a cigarette and tried to find the constellations Frank had struggled to teach me. I got the Big Dipper and Orion, but that was about it. I took a moment for prayer before I walked down the trench. I saw the lieutenant.

"Any news, lieutenant?"

"Yes, actually. They've let us know when."

"Well?"

"The plan is for detonation at 0317. All of them."

"That's less than three hours from now, sir."

"I know. Let the men know that they need to be ready to go at 0230. At that time we'll get a rum ration and cotton wool for plugging the ears. At 0300, we will all get out of the trench and lay on the ground out front."

"Why is that, sir?"

"The engineers suspect that the shock wave from the blast may be so intense that our front trenches collapse."

"That's quite a blast."

"Gardener, that's an understatement. Do you realize that if all of these mines go off together, it will be the greatest explosion in the history of mankind?"

I didn't quite believe him, although he was indeed telling the truth.

"I'll definitely get the men out of the trench, sir."

"And remember 0230. Everyone is ready in every way to jump off."

"I'll take care of it, sir."

I went back to my position where I found Frank entertaining again. He saw me and came over.

"What do you know?"

"We have to be ready for jump-off at 2:30. Help me spread the word."

"Sure. But when does this party really get started?"

"If you mean the mines, they go at 3:17. But tell the men they have to be ready to go by 2:30, all right?"

"2:30. Ready. Affirmative."

For most of the men, I think that knowing the time was a relief. The few that seemed distressed were relatively new and had never been in combat before.

"What do you do for a living?" I asked one of them.

"I'm a haberdasher. In Leeds," he said.

"What the hell is that?"

"Hats. I make them and sell them."

"Did you always know how to do that, or did someone help you along?"

"Well, my father…"

"Exactly. So don't expect to know everything when we jump off in a couple of hours. Stick to an old timer. Go where he goes. Dive when he dives. Run when he runs. And don't set out to win the Victoria Cross your first day. Understand?"

"Yes sergeant," he said. "Thank you."

Then we stood there for a half-hour with our haversacks on and our rifles ready. It was probably the longest 30 minutes of my life. I smoked five cigarettes in a row. I was wracked with anxiety, and I'm sure that Frank was feeling the same way, because he wasn't saying anything.

The shelling of the ridge had reached a new peak and I was certain it would be soon. A hefty rum ration came around, and certainly enough, the lieutenant came by moments later and told us to get out of the trench.

We climbed out and walked through a gap in the wire. There we laid down shoulder to shoulder. We put in our earplugs and waited for the fruition of our months of labor.

Suddenly, the guns fell silent. There for a moment, the only sound was a small dog barking somewhere way off.

Then I head someone yell, "Fire!"

Hill 60 exploded, a dreadful column of fire shooting into the sky. The sound was beyond deafening; I was certain that my ears would bleed. The ground didn't shake; it rippled like when you throw a stone in a pond. The caterpillar mine went at the same time, producing similar results. I looked down the line and I could see other mines that had gone. Then came the rain of dirt and rocks and body parts and everything else. We were far enough back that we didn't get too much coming in on us, just small stuff.

"Good heavens!" Frank said. "They probably heard that all the way in London!"

The lieutenant stood, drew his revolver and blew his whistle.

"To the hill!" he shouted. "Advance!"

I jumped up and got behind him. Frank was beside me. The lieutenant started walking, then went to a slow jog. We'd gone 50 yards and no resistance yet. I was expecting a machine gun or *minenwerfer* any second. But there were none.

When we got close enough to Hill 60 to see it clearly, I noticed scores of Germans coming down the side in our direction. For a moment or two, I was sure it was a counter-attack. Apparently, I wasn't the only one and I heard several rifle shots.

"Hold your fire!" the lieutenant said, looking through his binoculars. "They're surrendering! They're not carrying weapons!"

We met them midway between where we were and the hill. Most of them were heavily dazed, some of them barely able to walk. There were walking wounded of all sorts. Then there were some who looked like there wasn't a thing wrong with them. We weren't sure what to do with them all so we just told them to go back to our lines.

Within minutes, we were at the base of Hill 60. Aside from the occasional barbed wire, it had been an easy and rapid advance. And we were still moving. Hundreds of us started up the slope of the hill. I remember being very disappointed to see how small it really was. When we reached the top, we saw the damage of our mine.

The crater itself was the width of the hill and at least 100 feet deep. It was still smoking. There was an entire concrete bunker sitting upside down on the lip. There were abandoned rifles, machine guns, bombs and other equipment. And body parts. Heads, legs, arms, everything. I have no idea how many men died when that mine went off, but it was a lot.

We had made our objective in all of about 20 minutes.

CHAPTER 49

We climbed down into the crater and up the other side to have a look. There were more lines, but there were also grass and trees. The lieutenant looked through his binoculars.

"They seem to be in disarray," he said. "We could take that next line, couldn't we, Gardener?"

"I should think so, sir," I said.

"So let's go," Frank said. "No need to wait."

"Gardener, see if Butler has that telephone up here yet," the lieutenant said.

I found Butler, looking a little stunned.

"The lieutenant needs the buzzer," I said. "Is it working?"

"As far as I know, sergeant," he said, and began hauling it over to the other side of the crater.

About that time a runner came dashing up the hill and down into the crater.

"Lt. Rampkin?" he asked.

"Yes, what is it?"

"Message from headquarters, sir. You are to hold here until further notice."

He saluted and ran back the direction in which he came.

"Oh, that's bloody brilliant," Frank said. "It's wide open out there and we have to sit here and hold."

He turned and walked back up the other side of the crater.

"Richard, come here," he said.

I climbed up on the lip next to him.

"See that tangle of barbed wire over there with the three pickets, at the end of the sap?"

"Yes, I see it."

"That was where we started this morning! All of that tunneling and we get a few hundred yards! This is insane!"

"Thomas," the lieutenant said, "we've known for months that our objective was Hill 60. We've taken it. We accomplished the mission's goal."

I heard guns roar and seconds later two shells hit nearly on top of us. It was either falling short or coming from the other side. The others went for cover. We didn't even flinch.

"I don't believe this!" Frank yelled. "Now what? Dig in?"

"Just hold the hell on, Thomas!" the lieutenant retorted. "I'm going to get artillery on the buzzer and find out what's going on. For now, you will not panic. Is that clear?"

"Bugger off, Birdie," Frank snapped.

It was the most blatant display of disrespect that I'd seen out of Frank, and I'd seen plenty. The lieutenant pointed his finger at

Frank and just stared. After a moment he turned his gaze on me, knowing that I'd told Frank in the first place.

"Now is not the time to deal with this," he said. "But be certain, there will be consequences."

Another shell came whizzing in, this one a bit closer. The lieutenant and I ducked for cover, but Frank just stood there. There was a bang and something spun him around.

"Thomas!" the lieutenant yelled. "Are you all right?"

"I think I took a piece of shrapnel through...my haversack," he said.

Frank turned around and there was a big tear in the bottom of the bag. He was leaking something.

"Think it nicked your canteen, Thomas," the lieutenant said.

Frank put his hand on the wet spot and smelled it.

"It's the whiskey! It's the damned whiskey! Those Hun bastards broke our bottle. I'm glad we killed all of these men. Bloody buggers deserve it. And you, Richard, I told you we should have drank it yesterday. Now we won't get any at all! I hate this pointless war! To hell with all of it!"

Right about that time, the skies opened up and it started to rain. This was the last straw for Frank Thomas. He threw his helmet on the ground and went into another tirade. I had never heard him curse like that before.

Somewhere during all of this, we failed to hear the big gun fire. We didn't hear the shell come tearing across the sky. We didn't know it was coming in on top of us. Frank was still swearing. He raised his hands to the air.

"My, what a gorgeous day!" he shouted.

The shell exploded amongst us. I don't recall hearing it, just a searing white light and the sensation of being lifted into the air. I landed hard in the mud. I was in tremendous pain but I couldn't tell where. I tried to get up but I couldn't move. I collapsed back to the ground.

The next thing I knew, a stretcher man was leaning over me.

"Sergeant, just hold on," he said. "We're going to get you to the hospital."

"How...bad is it...sir?"

"It's a Blighty one, for sure. You'll be home before you know it!"

"See...my boy. Hold...my wife..."

As they lifted me up, I rolled over and saw Frank lying in the mud. He had a gaping head wound.

"What about...him?" I asked.

"He's napoo, sergeant. I'm sorry."

"Where's the...lieutenant?"

331

"What lieutenant?"

"Lieutenant...Rampkin."

"Who?"

"Need...his chess board..."

"No sign of him here, mate."

I never saw the lieutenant or Frank Thomas again. I guess they're probably buried around Hill 60 somewhere.

EPILOGUE

The silence was edgy and uncomfortable. Both the afternoon and the whiskey were gone. With hands slightly trembling, Richard Gardener lit a cigarette and sunk back in his chair.

"Then what happened, Dad?" Peter asked.

"You know what happened," Richard said sarcastically. "There isn't any more to tell. Nothing worth telling, anyway."

"Well, how long was it until you got back home?"

"I was in a hospital in France for about a month. Maybe six weeks. It was an awful place. Some of the things I saw there…"

"I know. I've visited friends in military hospitals before."

"But you got to leave when you wanted to. Try living in one. That's a whole different story."

Peter didn't know how to respond, so he quickly turned the conversation back to its previous course.

"So you got back to England in July?" he asked.

"Maybe August," Richard said. "I had to stay at a hospital here in London for nearly six months, but your mother brought you to see me every day. I'll never forget the first time I saw you: plump, rosy cheeks and lots of hair. And you were always hungry."

"I swear I can remember that hospital. I remember blue tile on the floor…"

"That's odd. There was, in fact, blue tile on the floor. How could you remember that?"

"I don't know, to be honest. But I also remember a tall woman with a red coat at the hospital. She held me on her lap."

"That would have been Elizabeth. I can see how you wouldn't forget her."

"Where is she now?"

"I couldn't tell you for certain. After the armistice, she packed and sailed for the United States. I thought maybe she'd fallen in love with an American soldier; there weren't very many young Englishmen left who were intact and unmarried. But she told us that there were just too many memories in London and she needed to get away from them. We got a postcard from New York City and a short letter from Philadelphia, and that was it. We never heard from her again."

"It's strange how people come and go and life keeps moving along anyway."

"Like your mother…"

Peter had hoped the conversation wouldn't lead to that subject, but just about every conversation did eventually.

"You know," Richard said, "I could have made things different."

"No, Dad…"

"Yes, I could have, Peter. Hitler himself was at Wipers. He was probably across the field from me, or maybe up on Hill 60. I was a good shot. If I could have just shot him down…"

"You had no idea who he was, Dad. Or what he looked like, or what he would become."

"Yes, but…"

"Then I'm more to blame that you are. I was in the air that morning, as I had been every morning. We stopped most of the bombers, but some of them got past us. One of them dropped his load on the shell plant…"

"I told her not to work there. I told her it wasn't safe, but she insisted. She wanted to do her bit again. And we needed money because I couldn't work…"

"It was a bloody tragedy, but we aren't the ones responsible. Blame the bloody Huns. They killed her."

"I'll never, ever forgive those worthless bastards for what they did. What they didn't take from me in the first war, they took in the second. Except for you, of course. Thank heavens they didn't take you."

"And Henry. You've been through a lot with that mutt."

There was a long pause.

"I'm going to have to go," Peter said. "My wife is probably wondering where I am. If I go now, I can catch the 5:15."

"Go ahead and go," Richard said. "Thanks for listening to my old, tired stories."

"There was nothing old or tired about them."

"Give your wife a kiss for me."

"I will. And I'll bring by another bottle tomorrow. Are you all right?"

"I'm fine. Go. Go!"

Peter put on his coat and picked up his umbrella and walked to the door. Henry followed him, wagging his tail. He was disappointed when he didn't get to go out the door.

"Do you want to go out, Henry?" Richard asked.

Henry sat at his feet whining, his tail pounding the floor.

"How about we go down to the pub?"

The whining and thumping increased.

"Let me get my coat."

He turned and wheeled his chair across the room to the coat rack. He pulled down his rain slicker and opened the door.

"Come on, Henry."

He wheeled down to the end of the hall to the door. He looked down at the stumps of what used to be his legs: one cut off above the knee, the other just below.

"You know, Henry," he said, "you'd think they could have at least made them the same length."

Richard opened the door to the garden. The rain had stopped. Henry ran outside.

"My, what a gorgeous day."

13240011R00192

Made in the USA
Lexington, KY
20 January 2012